THE PSYCHOLOGY OF
COMMUNICATION

THE PSYCHOLOGY OF
COMMUNICATION

JON EISENSON
Stanford University

J. JEFFERY AUER
Indiana University

JOHN V. IRWIN
The University of Wisconsin

New York
APPLETON - CENTURY - CROFTS
Division of Meredith Publishing Company

6.50

PREFACE

The Psychology of Communication began initially as a revision of *The Psychology of Speech*, a work authored by Jon Eisenson and first published in 1938 by F. S. Crofts and Company. It has become in fact, not only because of its expanded size and authorship but also because of its broadened scope, a completely new successor to rather than a revision of the 1938 text.

In setting to work on what promised to be only a revision, the author of the original work soon perceived the magnitude of his task. Fortunately, he was able to persuade two leaders in the field of communication to join him as co-authors and to contribute chapters on subjects in which they are recognized authorities. He was also fortunate in being able to include chapters by two other leading authorities in areas of their special competence—Chapter 10 by Dr. William Etkin of The City College of The City University of New York, and Chapter 11 by Dr. Milton Valentine of the University of Colorado.

Although the original author served as general editor of the book as a whole, each contributor, whether author of one or more chapters, holds primary responsibility for the organization and content of his own material. This responsibility is apportioned as follows:

Jon Eisenson—Chapters 1, 2, 3, 4, 5, 9, 12, 13, 19, 20, 21;
J. Jeffery Auer—Chapters 14, 15, 16, 17, 18;
John V. Irwin—Chapters 6, 7, 8;
William Etkin—Chapter 10;
Milton Valentine—Chapter 11.

Jon Eisenson
J. Jeffery Auer
John V. Irwin

CONTENTS

ILLUSTRATIONS

I.

THE NATURE, ORIGIN, AND PURPOSES OF SPEECH

1

The Nature of Speech

In a book that deals with human communication we consider it wise to define certain terms that are commonly understood—or assumed to be understood. We would like, for example, to present clear-cut definitions of a term such as *speech*. Any student interested in getting such a definition from a source other than a dictionary would soon discover that the term *speech* has many uses and is variously defined. Frequently it is used as if it were synonymous with the term *language*. *Speech* is also used to designate linguistic systems that are orally produced and aurally received. On the other hand, some authorities are careful to distinguish between speech, or speaking, *as a method of producing* oral symbols, and the symbols themselves, which constitute a language. Before presenting our own definition we will consider several representative definitions, explanations, and observations that include the terms *language* and *speech*.

SPEECH AND LANGUAGE AS VIEWED BY LINGUISTS

Hughes (1962, p. 6) in his *Science of Language* uses the term language to mean "a system of arbitrary vocal symbols by which thought is conveyed from one human being to another." Implied in this definition are the concepts (1) that language is a *system*—a code or a set of rules; (2) that language is *arbitrary*—there is no intrinsic reason for any word (symbol) to mean what it does, or for the system as a whole to have the particular structure (characteristics) it (the system) developed; (3) that language is *vocal*—it is made up of sounds that are produced by the human oral speech mechanism; (4) that oral language production is a function limited to *human beings*.

Pei (1949, p. 100) in his *Story of Language* says that "spoken language is characterized by language—sound, produced by the human voice, received by the human ear, and interpreted by the human brain." Except for the notion that speech is a product of the human voice rather than of oral behavior (articulatory actions) usually accompanied by voice, we have essential agreement between Pei's concept of spoken language and the other "definitions" of language we shall consider.

Sapir's definition seems to be the basic one from which those we presented were developed. According to Sapir (1921, p. 7), language ". . . is a purely human and non-instinctive method of communicating ideas, emotions and desires by means of a system of voluntarily produced symbols." These symbols, Sapir indicates, are auditory and produced by the organs of speech. Sapir's concept of language implies that animals may be able to communicate, but that the extent to which they engage in communication is limited by instinctual rather than by learned behavior. Voluntarily produced symbols are learned as they exist within a system of symbols.

In his text *On Human Communication*, Cherry (1957, p. 32) incorporates concepts of language and speech in his observations on the essence of communication. According to Cherry, "communication essentially involves a language, a symbolism, whether this be a spoken dialect, stone inscription, a Morse code signal, or a chain of binary-number pulses in a modern computing machine. Language has been called the 'mirror of society,' truer perhaps of speech than of writing, especially of colloquial speech." Speech, according to Cherry (1957, p. 147), is basically an articulatory process that employs ". . . both a visible and aural set of signs."

Cherry's observations include the inter-relationships between a given language and a given society that are reflected *in the way people speak.*

This notion is developed by Hockett (1958, p. 141) who views language as *a set of habits* common to a *speech community.* "Each language defines *a speech community:* the whole set of people who communicate with each other, directly and indirectly, via the common language" (1958, p. 8).

In his *Words and Things* Brown observes (1958, p. 156) that ". . . language is often equated with speech, and the most obvious attribute of speech is vocal production. . . ." Brown expands his concept of language with the statement: "For language, in the full, is nothing less than an inventory of all the ideas, interests, and occupations that take up the attention of the community." (1958, p. 260)

In his Introduction to *Linguistic Structures*, Hill (1958, p. 9) presents a lengthier definition or explanation of language which includes several of the factors the other authorities on linguistics incorporate in their definitions. Hill holds that language is:

. . . the primary and most highly elaborated form of human symbolic activity. Its symbols are made up of sounds produced by the vocal apparatus, and they are arranged in classes and patterns which make up a complex and symmetrical structure. The entities of language are symbols, that is, they have meaning, but the connection between symbol and thing is arbitrary and socially controlled. The symbols of language are simultaneously substitute stimuli and substitute responses and can call forth further stimuli and responses, so that discourse becomes independent of an immediate physical stimulus. The entities and structure of language are always so elaborated as to give the speaker the possibility of making a linguistic response to any experience.

SPEECH AS VIEWED BY AUTHORITIES ON SPEECH

The definitions we have just considered, despite individual variation, reflect the viewpoints of scholars who are identified with the *discipline of linguistics, the scientific study of the form, structure, and functions of language—the nature and the workings of language.* Most students of linguistics seem not to be concerned with the need to distinguish language from speech. We will now turn our attention to definitions from other authorities who are primarily identified as scholars in the *field of speech.* We will note that they tend to make distinctions between language as a system of symbols, and speech as a form of human behavior employing a symbol (language) system.

Black and Moore (1955, p. 2), for example, observe that: "Speech has been described as a form of human behavior in which words may serve both as substitute stimuli to evoke responses in others and as substitute responses. . . . Speech . . . is both a stimulus to behavior and a behavioral response to a stimulus."

Oliver and Cortright (1961, p. 6) say: "In using the term *speech processes,* we refer to the means by which any act of speaking is accomplished. They include knowing, thinking, believing, and analyzing speech content; using oral language; using voice and articulation; using visible symbols; and integration of attitudes and adjustments." We should note the emphasis on the term *using* and the clear implication that speech *is a means* or a form of behavior that employs a symbol system.

Weaver and Ness (1957, pp. 10-11) consider speech to be:

the psychophysical process by which one person attempts to influence another person (or other persons) through light waves and/or sound waves produced solely and directly by the action of his own muscles. It should be noted that, under this definition, a smile, a shrug of the shoulder, a lift of an eyebrow, a growl, a querulous inflection, or a spoken phrase or sentence, any one of these alone or any combination of them may be speech. . . . Speech is always a pattern of stimuli by which the communicator *stirs up* meanings (ideas and feelings) in the communicatee by inducing him to recall his past experiences.

Thus it comes about that no one ever can really tell another person a story; the best that the storyteller can hope for is that the communicatee may be stimulated into telling himself a story of the sort that the communicator wants him to hear. As speakers, the best that we can do is to use audible and/or visible symbols which may touch off in our listeners certain elements of their past experiences; this we try to do in such a manner that the listeners will produce for themselves the meaningful patterns which we want them to have.

This concept of speech, as we shall see, comes closer than any of the others to the one we shall adopt for this text.

SPEECH DEFINED FOR PURPOSES OF THIS TEXT

In a restricted sense, speech is a medium that employs an oral linguistic code that enables one human being to express feelings and to communicate thoughts to another human being. In a broader sense, speech may be characterized as the use of linguistic forms which man is able to produce without calling upon mechanisms external to his own organism. Man produces linguistic forms for speech through his oral (articulatory), vocal, and pantomimic mechanisms. When speaking, an individual may use all the mechanisms simultaneously, or use one exclusive of the others either momentarily or for a sustained period of time. Normally, all three mechanisms are used to produce linguistic forms, although we are probably most aware of the forms produced as a result of articulatory activity. We vocalize as we articulate, and we employ facial and other bodily (pantomimic) movements to accompany the actions of the organs of articulation. Deaf mutes who are untrained in oral language but trained in a visible sign code, use speech with only incidental reflexive activity of the vocal and articulatory mechanisms. Voice serves several purposes in speech. It may be used to establish phonemic differences in sounds otherwise not distinguished by manner of articulation, as in the g and k of gut and cut, and the p and b of bay and pay. Voice is also used tonally to distinguish meanings in words and groups of words, as in the inflectional changes of English, and in the tonal changes of Chinese which make their words of one syllable capable of carrying a variety of meanings. Voice, of course, is also used affectively, to lend feelings to our meanings and to reveal, when there is no intent to deceive or conceal how we feel about what we think.

In a still broader sense, speech may be considered the end product of all that takes place covertly and overtly when an individual uses sounds, word forms, or words for expressing himself, for relating to someone, or for communicating with someone. In speaking in social situations, an individual normally uses conventional linguistic units. To a large degree, he follows social conventions in their use. He speaks, however, as an individual, and so he speaks himself—for and of himself—because and despite the effects of conventions in regard to language usage. Although man conforms in large measure to the impositions of language upon him, he nevertheless usually speaks in manner and content so that a discerning listener is able to recognize individuality in speech.

WORDS AND WORD FORMS

Through speech, after the age of two, most physically and mentally normal human beings begin to make their needs and wants felt and in general to make themselves understood. Arbitrary sound groupings or word forms which are learned in rapidly increasing numbers are used to replace or to supplement reflexive vocalizations and total bodily behavior. Specific sound complexes (verbal symbols) are produced by the individual to elicit relatively specific and anticipated responses. The word forms or sound complexes with meanings which have been derived through a process of association and environmental experience are used by one speaker to share or convey meanings and feelings to another, a listener, who is also a potential speaker. It is important to appreciate that the word forms we use are not only capable of suggesting many meanings, but that we may also employ them in non-meaningful, or at least in non-intellectually meaningful ways. We may use word forms to utter acknowledged nonsense, and to express feelings or emotions that may be highly variable. Some word forms are used more often for what they do not literally mean—for their non-semantic implications—than for what they may literally and only occasionally mean. These word forms may have no more intellectual significance than a so-called inarticulate oral sputter. Words through individual association and general acceptance have taken on certain more or less specific ideas, meanings, or concepts. Word forms are similar to words orthographically and resemble words phonetically, but they are used affectively rather than ideationally. Word forms are used to express feelings rather than to convey thoughts. When we use word forms we are not concerned with matters of genetic consistency or accuracy of biological hierarchy. We mix the fauna and the flora and make references which are logically impossible and biologically inconceivable. For an American boy the utterance "hot dog" may mean something to eat not in any way related to a canine, or an expression of enthusiasm not in any way related to food. One person may swear at another he dislikes, or at someone who does something at the moment not to his liking, and in swearing attribute to the object of his feelings a posterity and an ancestry in no way genetically related to his presently alleged phylo-genetic status. So man uses word forms or sound complexes which resemble words, to express his feelings when his thinking is only incidentally involved.

Other uses made by man of sounds which resemble words will be considered in our later discussion of the purposes and functions of speech.

PROPOSITIONAL LANGUAGE

When we speak we employ selected linguistic entities and combine and organize them into units according to the structure and conventions of a given linguistic code. The ability to combine simple linguistic units (words) into more complex linguistic units (sentences) is the ability to use language propositionally. It implies an ability to use language to refer to situations not immediately present, to talk about what was, what may be, what might have been, and what should be. It permits recollection and projection. Through the use of propositional language, man can yearn for what is not and strive to bring it about. The capacity to use language that is not bound to specific and physically present situations is dependent upon the normal human being's capacity for symbolization.

A *symbol* is something that stands for something else. By "stand for" we mean that symbols derive their meaning or significance, their power to evoke responses from us, through associations that have been made between them (the words) and objects, situations, relationships, or ideas.

A child's first response to an object such as *dog* is direct and concrete. It will be determined initially by the specific properties and behavior of the dog and the reactions of the child to the animal. The child's response to the word *dog* is not related to the properties of the sounds that comprise the word. The response is related to the recollected experiences —the associations—that have been made by the child to one or more dogs. It includes responses made to real dogs with which the child may have had direct experiences, to dogs observed in picture books, or seen and heard on television screens or moving pictures. It also includes stories of dogs told him by other children and by adults. All of these experiences, direct and vicarious, become part of the symbolic significance of the word *dog*. These experiences are obviously not related to the physical properties of the word because they might well be essentially the same for a French child's *chien* or a German child's *hundt*. There is some possibility that a comparatively few words because of their auditory or articulatory characteristics do suggest meaning by their sound or the peculiar nature of the articulation needed for their production. These attributes, however, are not likely to explain how the vast majority of words acquire meanings.

SYMBOL vs. SIGNAL BEHAVIOR

Although man is distinctively man, human and unique because of his ability to deal with symbols, man varies from man in this same ability. Intellectual capacity is positively related to the ability to deal with symbols. The lack of such capacity is reflected and measured largely by a limitation in this ability. Mental illnesses, personality disorders, and impairments associated with brain damage are all related to modifications or failures in the development of the capacity for dealing with symbols.

Signal Responses

In some instances an individual may develop an ability to deal with words, or other representations of situations, as signals rather than as symbols. A signal is a response which is invariably made to a situation, if any response is made at all. It is unvariable and unconditional in regard to the situation. The dog that salivates at the sight of food, or at the sound of a bell, or at the word *food* that accompanies the presentation of food, is responding to a signal. The same response is likely to be made every time the same condition is fulfilled. The chimpanzee that learns to ride a bicycle, to stop at a red light and go at a green, *regardless of conditions*, is demonstrating signal response ability. Human beings respond to some representations in a signal fashion, but are usually able to modify their reactions according to existing conditions. If a man is driving his car on an icy road, and another driver is uncomfortably close to him, he may decide not to stop on the red light because of the accident that might occur if he did. The key terms in the last sentence that distinguish symbol behavior from signal behavior are the words *decide* and *might occur*. A signal response, because it is invariable, takes place without evaluation and decision in the light of particular situations and in anticipation of the consequences of an action based upon an evaluation. Most human beings who have at least normal intellectual capacity determine their responses to situations, including those that are representative, by *evaluations according to conditions*. Intellectually limited persons, and in some instances emotionally disturbed persons, may lack this capacity. Instead, they may respond without regard for immediate conditions in an established, pre-determined or signal fashion. This is about as far as primates are able to develop their capacity to respond to and use linguistic symbols. It is also about the extent to which human beings who are severely limited mentally are able to deal with language. On occasion, transient emotional disturbance may be associated with an apparent regression of language usage from the symbol to the signal level. Chronically emotionally disturbed and, in isolated instances, brain damaged persons who suffer linguistic impairment may also manifest signal rather than symbol capacity for language. In general, however, most human beings have correlated capacities for symbol behavior and linguistic usage. The size of an individual's productive vocabulary and the meanings he knows are positively related. Almost always, however, his ability to comprehend and respond to symbols will exceed his ability to produce the symbols. Both comprehension and production develop as the individual matures in a world calling for symbol behavior.

In the chapters that immediately follow we will consider some aspects of our oral linguistic system, theorize on its possible origin, and investigate the nature and purposes of speech. Through these considerations it should be possible to arrive at an appreciation of the multiple aspects and purposes of speech, and the role of speech in communicative as well as noncommunicative situations.

REFERENCES

Black, J. W., & Moore, W. E. Speech: code, meaning, and communication. New York: McGraw-Hill, 1955.

Brown, R. Words and things. Glencoe, Illinois: The Free Press, 1958.

Cherry, C. On human communication. New York: Wiley, 1957.

Hill, A. Introduction to linguistic structures. New York: Harcourt, Brace & World, 1958.

Hockett, C. F. A course in modern linguistics. New York: Macmillan, 1958.

Hughes, J. P. The science of language. New York: Random House, 1962.

Oliver, R. T., & Cortright, R. L. Effective speech. New York: Holt, Rinehart, and Winston, 1961.

Pei, M. The story of language. Philadelphia: Lippincott, 1949.

Sapir, E. Language. New York: Harcourt, Brace & World, 1921.

Weaver, A. T., & Ness, O. G. The fundamentals and forms of speech. New York: Odyssey Press, 1957.

2

The Oral Speech Code
And Its Origin

THE COMPONENTS OF SPEECH

MOST ORALLY PRODUCED AUDIBLE words are a combination of articulated sound, voice, and gesture. Usually, the three components of speech are simultaneously employed when we produce linguistic symbols. Together these components enhance the likelihood that what we say will serve the particular purpose and function of the content of our speech. In general, the combined efficacy of the speech components makes it possible for us to reveal how we feel about what we think or how we think about what we feel.

To a large degree, each of the components may alone serve the function of the components combined. Through articulated sound (whispered speech) alone, through voice alone, or through gesture alone we are able to convey or to express a considerable amount of what is more frequently accomplished through articulation, vocalization, and gesture. Moreover, we have linguistic systems which employ a single component of speech. Gesture language and tonal language, both of which will be considered in the discussion that follows, are examples of these predominantly single component linguistic systems.

Voice

Ordinarily, the vocal component of speech reflects the speaker's affective state in regard to his utterance. Through voice the speaker tends to reveal how he feels about what he is saying. The vocal component is the indicator of the mood, emotion, or attitude of the speaker. The relationship between affect and voice may be explained on the basis of muscular

11

tonicity. Voice production is a muscular activity, and so is tied in with the emotional state of the organism. Heightened feelings are associated with hypertonic muscle states, and so result in laryngeal tensions which are conducive to elevated pitch. In contrast, depressive states are associated with hypotonicity and thus with reduced laryngeal tension and lowered pitch. When we speak without strong affect, our vocal tones are likely to be in the intermediate parts of our pitch range.

Changes in loudness and in the rate of utterance usually accompany the modifications in pitch levels. An elated speaker is likely to talk more rapidly and more loudly than a depressed speaker. Depressed states are revealed in utterance which is slow and reduced in loudness from that which is "normal" for the speaker.

Even in those linguistic systems in which vocal tone is used to reveal how the speaker feels about what he says, voice may also be used for essentially semantic purposes. In English, tonal differences, so used, may imply a contradiction or reservation between the utterance as it is usually understood and the utterance as the speaker specifically wants it understood. Here we have mixtures of thought and feeling, of semantic value and affect, that can be better suggested through vocal change than through lengthy utterance. More generally, tonal differences may be used, as they are in English speech, to distinguish meanings of groups of words (utterances) or for an individual word when it is a complete utterance. For example, the word *him* suggests one meaning if accompanied by a rising inflection and another when accompanied by a falling inflection.

Patterns of pitch or inflectional change give rise to "melody" in a language. These "melody" changes are referred to as *intonation*. Specific inflections and intonations characterize spoken language. They also punctuate the language and help an American-English speaker to suggest that thoughts are complete or incomplete, that he is positive about what he says or entertains some doubt about his thought.

In some languages tonal differences are a regular and essential rather than incidental factor for signifying semantic differences for word forms. Chinese, which has an entirely monosyllabic word structure, employs tonal changes to distinguish word meanings. The word form *ma* has meanings as diverse as *mother, flax,* and *horse* depending upon the accompanying tone. The word form *shih* in the Mandarin dialect may signify *corpse, ten, scholar,* or *arrow,* according to whether the tone is level, rising, falling, or falling and rising.

Gesture

Most oral speakers use intentional gestures to enhance their oral symbols. Such gestures tend to emphasize meanings, to underscore oral words. Not infrequently, however, gestures are employed when oral words are not adequate for our speech purpose. The implication of this use of gesticulation is that gestures are more universal and so can convey ideas and moods when oral words fail.

Though the tendency to use gestures is a natural one, it is nevertheless subject to considerable cultural modification. Southern Europeans on the whole use gestures more frequently and more freely than do Northern Europeans. Individuals vary in habits in their use of gestures according to the cultural groups with which they become identified (Efron, 1941).

Gesture languages are found in many parts of the world. Sometimes they exist as separate systems where, for some reason, oral language is not readily possible, or where, because of special circumstances, they are more desirable than oral language. Such is the case in the gesture system used by many deaf mutes, by some orders of monks such as the Trappists,[1] by many North American Indian tribes, and by members of the international Boy Scout movements. These gesture systems bear a remarkable resemblance to one another and constitute almost a universal language.

Autistic Gesture

Many of us express our unconscious feelings, as well as express our feelings unconsciously, through gestures. Tics, grimaces, ritualistic movements, are examples of physical mannerisms which fall under the general category of autistic gestures. Even those of us who do not habitually have gesture-mannerisms display them on some occasions. The prospective employee waiting to be interviewed who adjusts a tie already well made and in precise place is employing an autistic gesture. So is the young lady who adjusts perfectly coiffured hair while waiting for her important date. Expectant fathers have been known to engage in interesting overt behavior while waiting for the news of their parenthood. Krout (1935) made a study of autistic gestures and found, as we would guess, that most persons have a few tics, mannerisms, or ritualistic movements.

Some persons demonstrate compulsivity in regard to gesture behavior. Some engage in compulsive routines in dressing, or eating, or walking. Such behavior probably has dynamics deep in the unconscious and represents symbolically a form or action or a deep-seated drive the individual prefers not to entertain consciously. Blinking of the eyes, for example, may be a symbolic way of ridding oneself of viewing the forbidden,

[1] This use of gesture should not be confused with the visible signs used by many deaf persons which spell out or stand for words or phrases employed in the oral systems of speakers in the same cultural community as the deaf.

even if the view is from within. Shrugging of the shoulders may be an unconscious way of throwing off responsibility. In general, we may conclude that gestures, whether they are produced consciously and have essentially an intellectual significance, or produced unconsciously and have an underlying affective significance, fall in line with the time-honored observation to the effect that, "Every little movement has a meaning all its own." Some gestures reveal thought, others betray feeling. Still others, by their manner of production and their specific form, suggest both feeling and thought. It is small wonder then that gesture language continues to survive despite the number of developed oral linguistic codes. It should also not be surprising that when oral words fail us, we resort to gesture to communicate our thoughts and to express our feelings.

Articulated Sound

An articulated speech sound is produced by a modification of emitted breath. The modifications occur by action of organs in the larynx, throat, mouth, or nasal cavity. Oral words consist of individual sounds or successions of sounds produced and arranged according to the conventions of a linguistic system which have acquired meaning through a process of association.

Oral words have obvious advantages over either gesture or voice alone for communicative purposes. The speaker employing a gesture system needs to be seen to be understood. The oral speaker needs only to be heard, and can speak to any person who understands his oral code providing only that he can be heard.

Gesture speech limits the freedom of activity of the speaker. Oral speakers are free to engage in other activities as they talk. These activities may include the use of supplementary gestures to enhance oral speech content. On the other hand, the activities need not be related to what the speaker is saying. A speaker may smoke, knit, sew, or otherwise keep his hands occupied while he is talking.

GESTURE AND THE ORIGIN OF ORAL SPEECH

According to some language theorists, articulated speech is directly related to gesture activity. Among these theorists are Wundt (1928), Bloomfield (1933), and Paget (1930). They argue that animal sounds are a product of movement; human speech sounds are a product of movements of the oral musculature. Paget elaborated the gesture theory along the following lines.

The earliest human language most likely consisted of gesture signs. Through bodily movements, and especially through movements of the hands and face, primitive man was probably able to express a variety of ideas and feelings, and to evoke responses from his neighbors. With the development of gestures, there was concomitant though unconscious development of laryngeal sounds. The sounds resulted physiologically from breath passing through the respiratory and oral mechanisms while in action. They were in this respect by-products of the total response patterns of the human organism reacting to specific situations. When, for example, a primitive man was engaged in an occupation requiring energetic physical effort, such as chopping a log of wood, or lifting a heavy stone, or throwing a spear, many organs of his body became associated in the act. The organs assume different positions during the execution of a given act. Each position is assumed by the body as a whole, while particular muscle groups assume related positions. The muscles of the speech mechanism are similarly involved. At some point during the performance of an energetic activity the muscles of the speech mechanism are likely to be in a state of adjustment conducive to the production of a particular speech sound. Each time the act is repeated, the same oral product or speech sound is likely to be produced. So, theoretically, articulate sound was at first a by-product of activity in which an individual was engaged. Repetition of activity became associated with repetition of articulated sound. The sound thus acquired significance. In time the articulated sounds acquired meanings and became oral words.

Oral gesture theorists are able to put their conjecture to the test in contemporary behavior. Young children learning to write can be seen screwing their lips and moving their tongues about as they concentrate on controlling their fingers to make the desired visible markings. Young uninhibited children write not with their fingers alone but with all parts of their bodies. If they breathe hard when they write, articulate sounds are produced. We may put the oral gesture theory to our own test.

Let us take a simple human activity such as looking up at a tall tree top and determine precisely how a particular sound might become associated with it. Primitive man—and civilized man when uninhibited—looks up with all parts of his organism: his toes, his legs, his torso, his head; all the organs which are included in the speech mechanism join in the act. Now, if at some time while the lips, jaws, and tongue were busy gesticulating (reaching up), air were to pass through the oral or nasal cavities, the result would be a whispered sound, an audible gesture which was produced because of oral and laryngeal activity while breath was being emitted from the mouth. If primitive man happened to be vocalizing, as he might have been were he grunting, or singing, or in some other way giving expression to his feeling, the result would have been a voiced sound rather than a breathy or whispered sound. So, quite by accident, primitive man probably produced audible speech sounds.

Having discovered audible speech, primitive man probably soon became aware of its superiority over the exclusive use of visible speech. Our ancestors realized that they could then elicit responses from their neighbors without being in their sight and could engage in speaking even when their hands were occupied. Soon our brighter ancestors began to analyze the speech process and its products. They found that some of the gestures of the tongue and the lips were better able to produce audible speech sounds than others. Up-and-down and to-and-fro tongue and lip movements were found to be superior to lateral movements. And so, because certain movements were successful and satisfactory, and because other movements were found to be generally unsatisfactory, the satisfactory movements were learned and maintained. Thus human speech evolved from a system of conventionalized gestures of the organs of speech. Says Paget:

Human speech arose out of a generalized unconscious pantomimic gesture language—made by the limbs and features as a whole (including the tongue and lips)—which became specialized in gestures of the organs of articulation, owing to the human hands (and eyes) becoming continuously occupied with the use of the tools. The gestures of the organs of articulation were recognized by the hearer because the hearer unconsciously reproduced in his mind the actual gesture which had produced the sound. (1930, p. 174.)

In support of this "oral gesture" theory, Paget (1930, p. 174) presents a series of "synthetic words" which are made by descriptive gestures of the tongue, lips, and jaw. The "synthetic words" are compared with words in primitive languages which are phonetically almost identical and semantically alike. (See table 1.)

The important elements in the oral gesture hypothesis are the pantomimes and gestures rather than the sounds. The sounds are significant only because sequences of oral activity make it possible for the listener to distinguish between the sounds heard, and so to respond to them differentially. Voice itself is significant because it serves the purpose of attracting attention to articulatory activity. Voice, per se, is merely affective expression which requires movements of the organs of articulation for appropriate explanation. The changes in the attributes of sound—pitch, loudness, quality, and rate of utterance—of the speaking voice carry the affective meanings, while the specialized pantomime of the mouth and tongue carry whatever intellectual messages accompany the affective expression.

Table 1.

Summary of Ten Gesture Words, and Dr. Whymant's Selection of Proto-Polynesian and Archaic Japanese Words of Similar Meaning.

Meaning	Pantomimic Gesture	Phonetic Result	Proto-Polynesian Archaic Japanese
Reach up	Tongue reaching up to *touch* palate	að, aθ, or ad	ada, adha-adaru, idaru, Arch. Jap.
Feel, stroke	" feeling palate backward and downward	θra, ðra, lra, dra	tura, tula, tataru, Hazlewood 246.
Feel smooth, stroke up	" feeling behind lower teeth and up behind front teeth	aɪl, ɔɪl, øɪl	-aɪla, -ɛɪla, -taira ārɪ, orɪ, olo, oloi (Nine. Futuna) (W. Churchill Pol. Wand. 391).
Draw back suddenly	" protruded and withdrawn	ærʌp, æðʌp	eðhupu, ðupi, (Indonesian), Brandstetter and Kern rap (Pol. Wand. 305) Aneityum.
Scrape	" scraped between teeth	ðʌp, ðup, ðu	ðubu, ðuu (Indonesian), Brandst. and Kern.
Wave aloft	" waved, touching palate	leðl-leðl ledl-ledl	lete-lete, vele-vele (Proto-Indones), Brandst. and Kern. lele.[1] (Hawaiian, Fijian) Pol. Wand. 421. Hazlewood 66.
Shake (like a mat)	" shaken (behind the teeth)	pla-pla	ore-ore (Japanese). ulia, urea. Fijian. Hazlewood 142. ruru-ruru, Rapanni. East. Isld. 299.
Stab or spear	" protruded between lips and teeth	peð, pʌð, or possibly pʌl	bulu, mbulu (Indonesian), Brandstetter. m b a l e (Fijian), Hazlewood 241. pili (Hawaiian) Pol. Wand. 289.
Shoot (with bow and arrow)	" reflexed, grip at back of tongue, and sudden release	ðr-ki, ðr-kui or dr-ki, dr-ku	koki, ikoki. (The initial K representing a strongly reflexed R) Author. Cf. çári (Skt.) arrow.

Meaning	Pantomimic Gesture	Phonetic Result	Proto-Polynesian Archaic Japanese
Pull down	Tongue reflexed and lowered	tra, trɔ	ndrei (Fijian), Hazlewood 30. tore, ataru (Japanese) Chamberlain and Ueda. Tr. Asiatic Soc. of Japan.

(Per Dr. Whymant) lɛlɛ in Fijian—the outer end of tree-branches in Samoan, Hawaiian, Tongan, Futuna, and Efate, either meteor or wind-driven.

OTHER VIEWS AS TO THE ORIGIN OF SPEECH

We have moved from gesture to oral articulatory behavior and presented one theoretic exposition of the origin of speech consistent with our theoretic bias. We do not, however, wish to leave an impression that other theoretic viewpoints of the origin of speech are not deserving of consideration. The student interested in conjecturing on the origin of speech may find theories and viewpoints reviewed in texts by Jespersen (1928), Vendryes (1931), Pei (1949), and Hockett (1958). These are but a few of the books that consider the origin and prehistory of man and his possible ways with words. For the purposes of this text we shall not yield to further temptation to conjecture how our remote ancestors first came upon the miracle of speech. Instead we shall study how young and available-to-be-observed children come upon this miracle. With this emphasis, conjecture can be minimized and a moderately scientific attitude maintained. There is still room for difference of opinion because most children are unable to recall their first words or the motivation for their utterance. Although most children probably learn to speak for much the same reasons, and according to the same psychological principles of learning, children are seldom aware of the reasons or the principles. When they become adults, they have forgotten precisely how they began to speak. If they are interested, they may again resort to conjecture.

REFERENCES

Bloomfield, L. *Language.* New York: Holt, Rinehart, and Winston, 1933.

Efron, D. *Gesture and environment.* New York: Columbia University Press, Kings Crown Publication, 1941.

Hockett, C. F. *A course in modern linguistics.* New York: Macmillan, 1958.

Jespersen, O. *Language, its nature, development, and origin.* New York: Holt, Rinehart, and Winston, 1928. Ch. 21.

Krout, M. H. *Autistic gestures: an experimental study in symbolic movement.* *Psychol. Monogr.*, 1935, 208.

Paget, R. *Human speech.* New York: Harcourt, Brace & World, 1930.

Pei, M. *The story of language.* Philadelphia: Lippincott, 1949.

Vendryes, J. *Language, a linguistic approach to history.* New York: Knopf, 1931.

Wundt, W. *Volkerpsychologie.* New York: Macmillan, 1928.

3

The Functions
And Levels of Speech

SPEECH FUNCTIONS

WE SHALL FALL SHORT in our understanding of speech if we fail to appreciate that only part of man's articulatory efforts and verbal habits are employed for the purpose of communication. Jespersen, some years ago, wrote: "We shall never thoroughly understand the nature of language, if we take as our starting point the sober attitude of the scientifically-trained man of today, who regards the words he uses as means for communicating, or maybe further developing thought." (1925, p. 169) We are not arguing that speech, or in Jespersen's sense language, is not used for the communication and the development of thought. Our emphasis is rather that communication and the development of thought are only part of the functions served by speech. We speak for many reasons and to accomplish many purposes. Not always are we conscious of the dynamics that underlie why we talk or what we say. Sometimes the forces or purposes may actually be in conflict with one another. For example, we may need to express aggression, and yet make a favorable impression on a listener. Or, we may need to conceal in order to be defensive, or to remain superior to a listener whom we may also wish to inform, or to seem to inform in order to create a favorable impression.

Communication

Sometimes we may wish to communicate information or a point of view to one or more listeners. (*Communication per se* involves either the passing of information or the formulation of thought by one person for the sharing or understanding of one or more other persons, or for the control of the behavior of one or more listeners or observers.) The term *listener* will hereafter be used whether speech is observed (visible sign or pantomime language employed) or is heard. This, however, is but one of the reasons and one of the purposes served by speech. The special nature of communication and the processes of codification (encoding and decoding) will be considered later. For the present, we will consider some of the non-communicative functions of speech. We should appreciate, however, that a listener may interpret a speaker's content as a communicative effort even if the speaker had some other underlying purpose for his speech. It is also possible that a speaker, despite himself, may reveal what he is consciously or unconsciously trying to conceal in his speaking. In this situation the speaker has unintentionally communicated something to the listener which, consciously at least, was not part of his speech purpose.

Non-Communicative Speech Purposes

The need to express or to reveal feeling is high among the noncommunicative functions of speech. Often this need accompanies a communicative effort. Sometimes the speaker may engage in a pseudo-communicative effort and seem to be trying to inform, direct, or persuade a listener by what he says. Actually, or perhaps better, unconsciously, the speaker may be using an alleged listener as an opportunity to "sound off," to express his feeling sweet, tender, bitter, angry, or whatever it may happen to be at the moment of the evocation.

Oral pleasure is a recognized function of the sound-making of children. Sound production for the combined pleasure of the oral activity and the resultant audible product continues as a function of speech in the adolescent and the adult. Often this function is disguised. Most of us pretend to say something to someone when we are engaged in the oral production of noises. Older persons talk to infants who are innocent of understanding; many of us talk to animal pets who are not really capable of understanding human speech sounds. We sing under the shower, or elsewhere in our homes when alone, or when so full of feeling that its expression must have an outlet. We enjoy producing nonsense sounds, or sounds that resemble words, or word forms that have no more significance than nonsense sounds. If we are fortunate and knowledgeable, our needs for oral pleasure can be met by the singing of a nonsense song. Such songs have greater respectability than nonsense words without a song.

It should be apparent that talking for the pleasure of making sounds frequently incorporates the function of talking to express pleasant affect. It is possible also that even when unpleasant affect is expressed there is an associated oral pleasure as well as pleasure derived from the very act of producing loud, angry, or hostile noises.

Verbal Contact. It is fairly well recognized that young children who have just begun to speak use word forms as substitutes for the direct physical contacts they previously had with members of their environment. Their cries as well as their words enable them to continue to be in contact with human beings who are necessary to them. Such verbal contact may incidentally allay anxiety and provide both oral pleasure and the pleasure of the potency of the word. These pleasures are of course reinforced when an oral response is returned. Child and mother may be able to fondle one another with warm words when actual physical contact is not readily possible. Speech to satisfy the need for contact and to substitute for physical contact or physical proximity does not cease with childhood. The need continues and may even grow stronger as children become adolescents and adolescents grow old enough to be adults.

Merloo (1952, p. 85), in listing the needs served by speech, includes one characterized as "the need for contact; for human companionship. The desire to conform, to be cozy. The word bridges interhuman space." Our telephone companies are mindful of the need for contact served by words. We are apprised of this in their advertising through words and through pictures. We are permitted by listening and viewing to share the happy feelings of members of families who appreciate how the telephone makes familial contacts possible. Such contacts are not, of course, limited to members of a family. Words reach out and bridge distances between persons who alternate in their apparent roles as speakers and listeners. If permissiveness and depth of understanding exist between oral interchanges, the words may give way to word forms, and these, on occasion, to avowedly nonsense sounds. Some persons who can engage in utterances that are apparent nonsense and do so with depth of feeling and mutual understanding may reach a point at which they are no longer in need of utterance and seem at ease with silence. It is significant, however, that words or word forms must first be employed to help the speakers to be comfortable as non-speakers. For most persons a relationship bound by silence is not readily possible. For most of us, words must be used to bridge gaps or voids that have occurred or might occur if silence were to prevail. Often we speak to prevent silence or to overcome its effects because a wordless relationship may not be comfortable or even bearable.

Social Gesture

Speech is frequently used as a social gesture. Sometimes the social gesture precedes or leads to actual communication. At other times the social gesture is all that a given situation requires. A telephone call or even an actual visit to a physician may begin with an interchange of "How are you?" on the part of the physician and a "Fine, thank you" on the part of the caller. This interchange may be immediately followed by listing evidence of poor health, because the caller, finished with his social gesture, is ready to reveal the state of his health and the purpose of his visit.

Many "vignettes" of conversation do not go beyond the social gesture format. A verbal gesture of "Hello" may be met by another "Hello" or by a "How are you?" If the latter gesture is used, the question mark is conventional rather than semantic. A respondent who proceeds to answer the "How are you" gesture as if a real question were asked commits a social *faux pas*. He has taken advantage of a social situation to say what is not expected of him.

Although social gesture speech has format, its content does not require specific linguistic formulation. The language used depends upon the relationship of the speakers. We greet and respond to greetings from equals in language different in form than that we use with superiors. For intimates, the word forms used may be quite different than for either equals or superiors. Terms that under some circumstances may be considered derogatory or profane may be mixed with terms of endearment. Snarl words without snarl voice and purr words may be blended with terms that defy semantic interpretation and still be considered appropriate for a particular situation. What if anything do the following mean?

"Hi, lughead."

"Gosh, you're a sight for sore eyes."

"Hi, Joe, what do you know?"

"Don't take any wooden nickels."

"Well, I'll be the son of a sea cook!"

Persons not altogether initiated in the customs of a culture, or of a sub-culture, may become embarrassingly involved in responding to social gesture. Owen Wister's hero in *The Virginian* had to remind a stranger who greeted him with terms that appeared to be biologically inconsistent that the particular utterance had to be accompanied by a smile or else. It takes a while for strangers in a society to learn when and what words need to be accompanied by visible or vocal smiles so that they will not be considered snarls. Along a different line, it takes a while to learn when a social gesture is used and when one is expected. The possibilities of error when the intent of a social gesture is not understood may be gathered from the following anecdote relating the reactions of a West African student with social gesture language used in an academic social situation. The narrator, who had been in the United States less than a year, was accompanied on his visit to a professor's home by a Chinese student. (Hartley & Hartley, 1947, pp. 76-77) [1]

At three o'clock, the Chinese and I arrived at the professor's door. Forgetting to ring the doorbell, I knocked at the door as though I were at home in Nigeria. For three minutes no one came to the door, and I had just begun to wonder whether we had the correct address when the Chinese reminded me to ring the doorbell.

The host, hearing the bell, opened the door.

"How do you do?" he said.

To this, we each replied, "I do well."

We were then introduced to the hostess who too wanted to know how we did. Of course, we "did well," at least until the doorbell incident occurred.

Half an hour later, the two girls arrived. To my bewilderment, instead of replying, "I do well," they simply repeated "How do you do?"

I thought something was wrong either with us or with the girls. After they had been introduced to us, I set to work right away:

"Why girls, did you repeat, and not answer the question?"

"It's the way we return greetings in America," answered the bolder of them.

"So we were wrong in the way we answered?"

"Not at all! It makes no difference. You could answer either way."

I accepted this explanation but still thought it was too clever to answer a question by itself.

At eight, I thanked the professor's wife for the hospitality which we had enjoyed very much. As I looked around for our coats and hats, the host asked, "You want your wraps, don't you?"

"No," I said, "we brought no wraps with us."

"He means your coats and hats," his wife instructed.

"Oh, I see! Yes," I quickly picked up, "we want our wraps." I blushed and laughed faintly.

Quickly we were escorted to the door. As the host opened the door, his wife made this little but wonderful speech.

"Oh, boys, we've very much enjoyed your company. Come back again." As she completed the word "again" we had both cleared the threshold and her husband had slammed the door.

Not realizing that we were not supposed to "come again" *now*, I asked the Chinese what we should do. He said, "When I was in China, I met an Amer-

[1] Cited by E. L. Hartley and R. E. Hartley, in *Fundamentals of Social Psychology*, New York, Knopf, 1952. The excerpt is from M. Ojike, *I Have Two Countries*, New York, John Day, 1947. Reprinted from *I Have Two Countries* by Mbonu Ojike, by permission of The John Day Company, Inc., publisher.

ican missionary who advised me that whenever in doubt what the Americans mean, I should go and ask them."

Gr-r-r-r! Gr-r-r-r-r! went the doorbell again.

The hostess opened the door, and, being surprised to see us again, she asked, "What's wrong, boys, have you forgotten something?"

"No, madam," I said, "you asked us to come back again and—here we are."

They were too human to laugh at our horrible bamboozlement. "Sorry, boys! That's the American way of saying goodbye," she courteously apologized.

"In my country," said I, "when we want to say goodbye to our guest, we say 'May you go home in peace.' The idea is to make sure your guest goes home; why say 'Come back again'?"

They obliged me with applause and said, "May you go home in peace."

Thanking them again for both the dinner and the phrases, we hastened home, quite mentally dwarfed by the intricacies of the American idiom.

Speech to Disarm Hostility

The use of speech to prevent or allay hostility is another aspect of language in social situations. Sometimes a man talks to himself when he suspects that he ought to be afraid, without knowing whether there is actual danger in the situation. We pretend to talk to someone else when entering a dark room, even though the someone else may not be in hearing distance of our words. We approach an ominous-looking stranger and talk to him to "show him that we are not afraid." He may answer us for the same reason. In reality, we are doing the only thing we can do, using words to prevent an emotional response—fear—when such a response is not adequate for meeting the situation and may result in actual harm.

Many of us talk, and according to some psychoanalysts talk too much, when confronted with threatening situations. Children may betray themselves by overtalking when their parents, unaware of their misdeeds, ask innocent questions. Thus many a cookie jar raider is discovered! Anxious and neurotic individuals of any age may engage in defensive talking. Usually the function of such talk is to cover up or defend a rationally indefensible position.

Speech to Ease Anxiety

When, in accordance with our purposes and objectives, we are confronted with new situations we attempt to adjust to them with specific behavior based upon past experiences. New situations call upon our resourcefulness and our ability to reorganize and adapt established response patterns to the present demands. Sometimes we are confronted with situations too novel or too demanding for our resources. At other times we may be frustrated or prevented from doing what we consider to be appropriate. In such situations, internal responses of anxiety and alarm may take place. When an individual is repeatedly frustrated in his goal-directed activities, when attempts at constructive action are frequently blocked, a state of chronic anxiety may be established. According to Ruesch and Bateson:

When fight, flight, playing possum, and communication are barred, the readiness of the body for action cannot be consummated. The continuous alarm becomes a permanent state, which is referred to as anxiety. . . . The individual is then psychologically and physically sick; the focusing of protracted attention upon the impending danger monopolizes the mental resources, and perpetual readiness of the body results in anxiety and fatigue. . . . The process of talking, though not an act of great physical expenditure for the individual, will absorb the overflow of readiness, and eventually a person is again enabled to find his bearings. (1951, p. 37)

We need not lose our bearings to ease our feelings of anxiety. Through speech, through talking about something, we can allay anxiety. If some of us do not succeed in allaying anxiety because we have not used speech to drain off physical energy, if some of us lose our bearings, the way back from anxiety is also through speech.

Speech as Aggression

Speech is used both to prepare for aggression and as a substitute for actual physical contact in aggressive behavior. Linguistic systems include locutions associated with aggression. Some locutions, regardless of their origin and original use, are reserved almost exclusively for this purpose. Our oral verbal habits, including the vocal and the gesture, incorporate locutions that permit us to prepare for contact fight or to engage in an oral substitute for actual physical contact. Our words—or more properly our word forms—are able to raise the level of our blood sugar, raise hackles, and function as slings and arrows. Aggressive locutions may lead to sticks and stones, or inflict even more damage as their substitute.

Speech is also used to prevent aggressive behavior by serving as a valve outlet. When several persons assemble either to participate or listen to a good argument, opportunity is provided for controlled aggression. This may take place at "purely" social gatherings, at club meetings, or at discussion or debating groups. It takes place when we listen to or view programs in which men known to the general public meet the gentlemen and gentlewomen of the press. It may take place when an author meets his critics, or whenever a publicized position must be defended. Our aggressive feelings can then be released as we identify with a speaker in defending or attacking a position or a principle.

Beyond the language of strong feeling as we find in the terminology of swearing, our vocabularies include many terms that suggest their proximity to direct aggressive behavior. When we argue vehemently we engage in *verbal assaults;* when we argue for the sake of argument we may be *splitting hairs;* some thoughts are *razor edged* and others can *cut to the quick;* discussions that go out of control become *verbal free-for-alls;* some arguments become *ferocious* and others are *venomous;* and some speakers are prone to use *loaded words.*

A writer and lecturer noted for his emphasis on the need for adopting a scientific and objective view in our linguistic habits, has nevertheless admitted that he frequently *gnashed his teeth in rage* when, after he had spoken before a women's club on problems about which he wished to evoke thoughtful discussion, certain of the members remarked, "That was such a lovely address, professor. You have such a nice voice." (Hayakawa, 1941, p. 188) [2]

Silence too can be hostile, perhaps more so than most belligerent utterances. Merloo makes the psychoanalytic observation that "many hostilities are not verbalized at all. . . . Silence may be a symptom of hate and consuming melancholia" (1952, p. 117). Children of varying ages often exercise the tyranny of silence against their friends, their parents, and their teachers. Children who are punished for talking too much do not always succeed in avoiding punishment by their silence. There is little doubt, however, that the intentional silence of a child, or of an adult, is considerably more effective as a hostile manifestation than are words.

Not all hostility that is not acted out finds expression in verbal behavior or in silence. Sometimes pseudo conversation replaces silence and obvious aggressive speech. Some speakers insist on being objective, and talk about matters objective when the other members of a social group are warmly and comfortably subjective. Not infrequently hosts and guests at social gatherings talk to prevent silence. In social situations, unless all the members are old and good friends who have little need to put one another to verbal trials, silence may be fearful because it produces tension, discomfort, and apprehension. It is something to combat, perhaps because the speakers themselves so often resort to silence when their needs are to be hostile.

Concealment (Slips of the Tongue)

Beyond these broad purposes and functions of speech, there are others considerably more difficult to classify. *Slips of the tongue*, unless one

---

[2] In the 1949 revision (p. 118), Hayakawa changed the words describing his reaction to ladies from a women's club from frequently *gnashed his teeth in rage,* to *frequently been enraged.* One gathers that the reaction to the ladies is the same, but the author saw fit to choose somewhat less "loaded" words to describe his feelings.

has a Freudian inclination, are among these. For the Freudian, the slip of the tongue permits the speaker to say what he really has on his mind —or his sub-mind—rather than what he is socially expected to say. In his *Psychopathology of Everyday Life* (1920, pp. 93-94) Freud observes:

In the psychotherapeutic procedure which I employ in the solution and removal of neurotic symptoms, I am often confronted with the task of discovering from the accidental utterances and fancies of the patient the thought contents, which, though striving for concealment, nevertheless unintentionally betray themselves.

So, through a slip of the tongue a speaker may be aggressive, or derisive, or loving, or reveal a state of confusion, or perhaps even a new found clarification of a former confused state. All this can be done with a built-in defense of innocence of intent. Except for the psychoanalyzed, we do not in our culture hold the speaker responsible for recognizable tongue slips—for uttering what he apparently did not intend. One may gain quite a reputation, as did Professor Spooner, for being an unconscious wit, and so be safe even from the dean of his faculty or from a University Board of Trustees. All this, and still liberty if not license to utter the heart's if not the mind's desire, is served by the not-so-innocent slip of the tongue. Perhaps the reader may wish to ponder the possibilities of such tongue slips as "I'm sure you're glad to meet me," or, "It's kisstumary to cuss the bride," or "I must gurry to het the town down bus."

Other Functions of Speech

In the preceding pages we have considered some of the broad non-communicative or pseudo-communicative functions of speech. It is, of course, possible to double or treble our list by being specific rather than general in our considerations. Readers interested in such an approach and consideration may find it in Merloo's book *Conversation and Communication.* (1952)

Underlying the needs and functions served by speech and verbalization, Merloo includes the following: the need to give vent to emotion, the need to make sounds for their inherent pleasure and to avoid or escape from silence, the need for contact so that "interhuman" space is bridged, the need to communicate and be informative, the need to be aggressive, the need for individuation and self assertion, the need to control persons and situations by "verbal magic," the need to use words as defense mechanisms, and the need to withdraw and reject contact through silence. We have considered some of these purposes in some detail. We should like to re-emphasize in closing this chapter that in many instances and on many occasions, speech may have multiple purposes. We can be informative while being aggressive; we can enjoy the pleasure of a mouth full of words that can be soothing as well as controlling for a listener. We can be pseudo-communicative in order to avoid being hostile and enjoy the sounds we make in the effort.

REFERENCES

Freud, S. In A. A. Brill (Ed.), *Psychopathology of everyday life*. New York: Macmillan, 1920.

Hartley, E. L., & Hartley, R. E. *Fundamentals of social psychology*. New York: Knopf, 1947.

Hayakawa, S. I. *Language in action*. New York: Harcourt, Brace & World, 1941.

Hayakawa, S. I. *Language in thought and action*. New York: Harcourt, Brace & World, 1949.

Jespersen, O. *Mankind, nation, and individual from a linguistic point of view*. Cambridge: Harvard University Press, 1925.

Merloo, J. A. M. *Conversation and communication*. New York: International University Press, 1952.

Ojike, O. *I have two countries*. New York: John Day, 1947.

Ruesch, J., & Bateson, G. *Communication*. New York: W. W. Norton, 1951.

II.

BASIC
PSYCHOLOGICAL
PRINCIPLES

4

The Nervous Mechanism
And Speech

THE UNDERLYING PURPOSE OF THIS chapter is to review some of the accepted information as well as some recent theoretic formulations about the controlling neurological mechanisms for speech. Emphasis will be on the brain and its assumed functioning in the process that permits one person to talk to and be understood—arouse thoughts in, and be responded to—by another. Elsewhere in the text the communicative process is considered in some detail. In part, the communicative process indicates how the neurological mechanisms make it possible for a speaker who has a thought he would like to share to select symbols for his thought in appropriate words. These words cause a listener to transform what he hears into his own thoughts, which then become the basis of an overt action or become converted into another selection of words.

Penfield (1959, pp. 3-4), in the prologue to his and Roberts' book *Speech and Brain Mechanisms*, observes:

It is an astonishingly complex process that any speaker sets in motion. Consideration of it brings us, at once, face to face with the baffling problem of the nature of the *physical basis of the mind*. Without stopping for definition, let me say simply that I begin with what is called a thought. A succession of nerve impulses then flows out from my brain along the nerves in such a pattern that the appropriate muscles contract, while others relax, and I speak. An idea has found expression in electrical energy, movement, vibrations in the air. The boundary which separates philosophy from neurophysiology and physics has been crossed!

When that sound reaches your ear drums it is converted again into nerve impulses that are conducted along your auditory nerves and into your brain. This stream of nerve impulses results in a secondary mental proposition which resembles, but is far from being identical with, that of the speaker. It is a new perception. Again that strange *brain-mind frontier* has been crossed—crossed twice by each utterance.

THE MECHANISM OF SPEECH

In the process of evolution, the primary vocal organs developed in the first vertebrates that emerged from a water to a land habitat. With this emergence the gill respiratory mechanism lost its functional importance. Many of its parts were lost, but others remained and some were rearranged and modified into what finally became the primitive vocal mechanism to be found in such animals as the frog. This vocal mechanism further evolved and was elaborated, first in intimate relationship to the air-breathing organs of the higher vertebrates, and then in relationship to the digestive organs, as lips, mouth, teeth, tongue, palate, etc. Thus historically we can see that the speech function was extended to organs whose biological relationships were with other functions. Similarly, there is no part of the nervous system that serves exclusively for the production of speech. In the course of evolution, however, many parts of the nervous system have developed so that they make special contribution to the control of speech.

Speech, in contradistinction to the mere production of vocalized sounds, presupposes a control of the organs involved by a nervous mechanism supreme in its modifiability. Were it not for his brain which developed so that it became peculiarly capable of learning and taking advantage of accidental occurrences, such as sounds produced by organs that also serve the biologically fundamental but less distinctive functions of breathing and eating, man might have been limited to animal-like comprehension and ape-like noises. He could not, however, have achieved speech.

Before undertaking our major consideration—the functioning of the brain and its relationship to speech—we will briefly give an overview of the general anatomy and functioning of the human nervous system.

The nervous system (see Fig. 4-5) may be considered in three main divisions: (1) The central nervous system (CNS), (2) the cerebrospinal system, and (3) the autonomic nervous system (ANS). In keeping with our purpose of emphasizing functional relationships we will coordinate our discussion of the cerebrospinal nerves with the CNS.

THE NATURE OF NERVOUS ACTIVITY

Neurons

The basic unit for nervous activity is the nerve cell, or neuron. By studying this unit we should be able to appreciate the nature of nervous

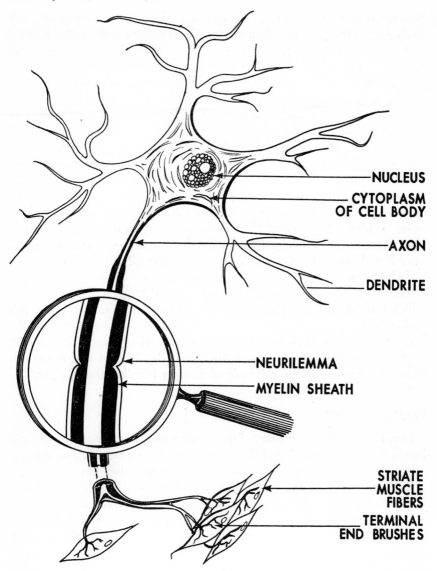

NUCLEUS

CYTOPLASM
OF CELL BODY

AXON

DENDRITE

NEURILEMMA

MYELIN SHEATH

STRIATE
MUSCLE
FIBERS

TERMINAL
END BRUSHES

Figure 4-1. A diagrammatic drawing of a neuron. At the top is the cell body and its numerous branchings, the dendrites. They make up the soma of the neuron. The axon, of which there is only one, extends downward. The point at which the axon leaves the soma is the axon hillock. Axons, and sometimes dendrites, may be covered with a myelin sheath and, outside the nervous system, a neurilemma. (From *Physiological Psychology* by Morgan & Stellar. 2nd Ed. P. 17. Copyright, 1950. New York: McGraw-Hill Book Co. Used by permission.)

activity as a whole. Neurons are constructed on a common plan, with variations occurring according to specific functions within the nervous system. A neuron consists of a cell body with branches, an axon and dendrites. Typically, a neuron has a long, thin process (the axon) that extends for a considerable distance from the main mass of the cell. Axons vary greatly in length as well as diameter, but they are nevertheless all extremely thin. The longest axon extends from a region in the small of the back to the tip of the toes. The diameter of an axon may be as small as one hundredth that of a human hair. Dendrites are usually extensively branched and are generally shorter than the axons. Many axons are covered by a fatty sheath known as myelin. This sheath serves to insulate the nerve fibers and so makes it possible for many fibers to run side by side in bundles without interference from the impulses that travel along adjacent fibers. Myelinated fibers conduct impulses much more rapidly than those without myelination. In the central nervous system a nerve fiber bundle constitutes a *tract*. Outside of the CNS such bundles are called *nerves*.

The axons of many neurons break up into end-brushes of fine branches which interlace with the dendrites or more directly envelop other cell bodies. Some neurons end in small plaques which may be applied to the dendrites or the cell bodies of other neurons. The place of junction at which an impulse may be transmitted from the axon of one nerve cell to the dendrites or to the cell body of another is called the *synapse*.

Synaptic Function

Despite the intimate contact of one neuron with another at the synaptic junction, there is no fusion of the protoplasm of the neurons. The synapse serves the function of transmitting a nervous impulse, but not all impulses that reach a synapse are transmitted across it. Thus, the synapse is in effect a barrier that a nervous impulse must overcome if the impulse is to be transmitted beyond the initial cell. The entire path transversed by an impulse, the path of neural activity, is determined by the synapses the impulse succeeds in surmounting and crossing as well, of course, as the synapses at which it is stopped.

It is believed that at some synapses—that is, at some interneuron junctions—transmission of the impulse is accomplished by chemicals secreted by terminals of the axons. Such mediating chemicals include acetylcholine, adrenalin, and perhaps others. These hormone products are presumably produced at the synaptic branches of the first cell. From a physiological viewpoint, therefore, whether or not an impulse will surmount a synapse depends in part upon the presence of an adequate amount of the transmission substance or neural hormone in sufficient quantity to make transmission possible.

The sensitivity or receptivity of the receiving neuron is another determinant of whether an impulse will be transmitted over a synapse. Receptivity is determined by a complex of factors that include the general condition of the blood, the hormones, the presence of enzymes that destroy neuro hormones, and particularly by the influence of other nerve impulses which may reach the synaptic junction at the same moment. In some instances concurrently arriving impulses may serve to facilitate transmission; in other instances they serve instead to impede or inhibit the passing of an impulse.

It should be apparent that the activity at a synapse is highly complex and that the precise nature of the process of transmission is as yet by no means certain. There are, however, several characteristics of neural action about which there is fairly common agreement.

1. When nerve impulses sweep along a nerve fiber, there is an accompanying burst of electrical activity. Most, if not all, neural activity is presumed in effect to be electrical and objectively measurable by electrical apparatus. Impulses sweep quickly along the insulated nerve fibers like an electric current; passage across neurons takes place as a result of a slower chemical process.

2. Neurons are apparently subject to fatigue. That is, immediately after an impulse has been transmitted through a neuron, a moment of rest seems to be required before the neuron is "ready" for another stimulation.

3. Neurons seem to be able to summate the strength of the stimulating impulses so that transmission may take place. In effect, it seems that though a single impulse may fail to be transmitted across a synapse, a succession of impulses, possibly by increasing the over-all electrical potential or amount of transmitting substance, may succeed in making the crossing.

Types of Neurons

A nerve fiber in a peripheral nerve may end either nakedly, as in the skin, or else may make contact with a sensory cell from which it receives stimuli. In either event, such a fiber conducts impulses toward the central nervous system and so is said to be *afferent* or *sensory* in character. A fiber which ends in contact with a muscle or gland which it stimulates into activity is said to be *efferent* or *motor* in character. Other fibers, known as *connectors*, serve to relay the impulses received by the sensory neurons to the motor neurons.

With this brief and perhaps over-simplified consideration of neural activity, we will proceed with a discussion of the reflex arc to demonstrate its occasional actual and more often theoretic application.

The Reflex Arc

Most of us have been directly involved in an examination to determine whether our reflexes are working properly. Usually the physician does not test all his examinees' reflexes. In the interests of time, and for special medical reasons, the physician is likely to confine himself to a few tests that usually include the knee-jerk reflex. In doing so, he is exciting a *pattern of movement* and assessing the pattern for its implications for the general health of the individual's nervous system. The physician may have forgotten the neurophysiological basis for his evaluation. If he has, he probably will recall that even though the entire route or pathway of a segmental or localized reflex may be within a small segment of the spinal cord, there is almost always concurrent and potentially competing

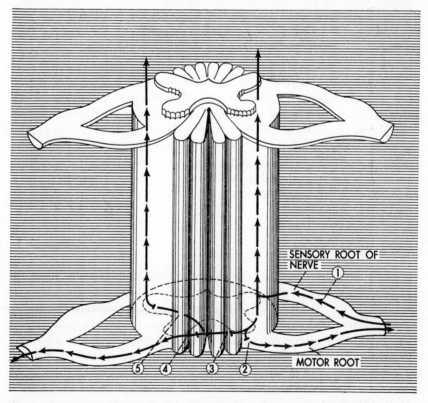

Figure 4-2. Path of the impulse in spinal reflex action. (From *College Biology* by W. Etkin. P. 191. New York: T. Y. Crowell, 1950. Used by permission.)

stimulation from other pathways and other levels of the nervous system. In effect, a simple reflex occurs because conditions in the nervous system as a whole permit its occurrence. With this in mind, we may consider the nature of a simple reflex.

· A sensory fiber conducts its impulses to the central nervous system where the impulse is passed through synapses to other neurons. In some cases the impulse is transmitted directly to a motor neuron and thus is carried to a muscle which it stimulates. It forms a neuron pathway through the nervous system that is called a *reflex arc*. Such a two-celled sensory-motor pathway constitutes the simplest possible reflex arc. Most reflex arcs are not so simple in higher animals. The incoming impulse passes to an intermediate (connector) neuron which then may distribute it to other such neurons or to motor neurons.

Further, the single afferent fiber may have several branches, each going to another intermediate neuron; these in turn may make several additional contacts. It is obvious that such a system permits of a very complex distribution of a single impulse. It is in this very complexity of distribution and routing of impulses that the fundamental importance of the central nervous system appears. The central nervous system should be thought of as an intricate intercommunicating arrangement of neurons so laid out in pattern as to permit the most complex reflex arcs to be routed through it. Such arcs may serve to throw large muscle groups into activity as a result of local stimulation or, on the other hand, to permit the activation of a given muscle by stimuli applied to any one of several regions. Thus, while we may diagrammatically present a simplified reflex arc as in Figure 4-1 with only one intermediate neuron, it must be understood that such a presentation is purely a convenient simplification. In Figure 4-2 we have a diagrammatic representation of what is more likely the case in an actual reflex path. The real significance of the central nervous system lies in the fact that it makes possible much more complex interrelationships between stimulus and response than the simple two-or-three-neuron reflex arcs.

Figure 4-3 should be studied because it represents a more complex and more usual reflex pattern than the simple two cell reflex arc.

THE CENTRAL NERVOUS SYSTEM (CNS)

The principal parts of the central nervous system are the brain, the spinal cord, and the cerebrospinal nerves. The cerebrum is the most anterior part of the central nervous system. It is enclosed and protected by the skull. The spinal cord extends along the back and is covered by protective bony arches of the spinal or vertebrae column. The cerebrospinal nerves extend from the brain and the spinal cord and go prin-

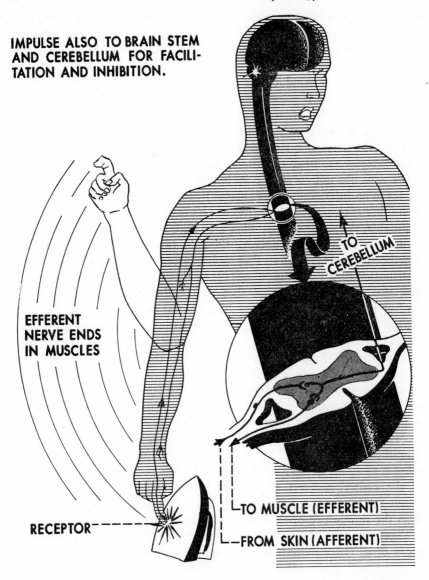

IMPULSE ALSO TO BRAIN STEM
AND CEREBELLUM FOR FACILI-
TATION AND INHIBITION.

TO
CEREBELLUM

EFFERENT
NERVE ENDS
IN MUSCLES

—TO MUSCLE (EFFERENT)

RECEPTOR- - - - - - -

—FROM SKIN (AFFERENT)

Figure 4-3. Diagram of reflex arcs indicating higher controls. (From *Speech Disorders* by Berry & Eisenson. P. 43. New York: Appleton-Century-Crofts, 1956. Used by permission.)

cipally to the skin and voluntary muscles of the body. Figure 4-5 is a diagrammatic representation of the Central Nervous System which highlights the implications for speech.

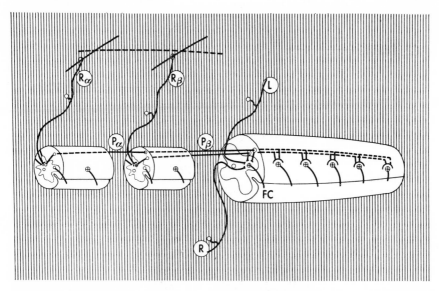

Figure 4-4. Diagram of the spinal arcs involved in scratch reflex (dog). L, receptive or afferent nerve-path from the left foot; R, receptive nerve-path from the opposite foot; Rα, Rβ, receptive nerve-paths from hairs in the dorsal skin of the left side; FC, the final common path, in this case the motor neuron to a flexor muscle of the hips; Pα, Pβ, proprio-spinal neurons. (From *The Integrative Action of the Nervous System* by C. S. Sherrington. New Haven: Yale University Press, 1948. Used by permission.)

The Cerebrum

An examination of Figure 4-5 will reveal the cerebrum and its anatomical relationship to other parts of the brain. The cerebrum—the largest part of the brain—consists of two symmetrical mirror-image hemispheres. The surface of the cerebrum is covered by a thin layer of matter containing cell bodies. Beneath this is a thicker layer of white matter consisting largely of myelinated fibers running to and from the cells of the gray cortex. Except for the cerebellum, the remainder of the nervous system has the gray matter as a central mass enclosed by the white matter. In this respect, the cerebrum and cerebellum represent a morphological reversal of the usual structural arrangement of the nervous system.

The Cerebral Cortex

The cortex, or outer covering of the brain, is characterized both by its gray surface and its deep and coarse folds or convolutions. This construction of the cortex provides additional area for the gray matter presumably to enable it to carry out its complex functioning relative to the

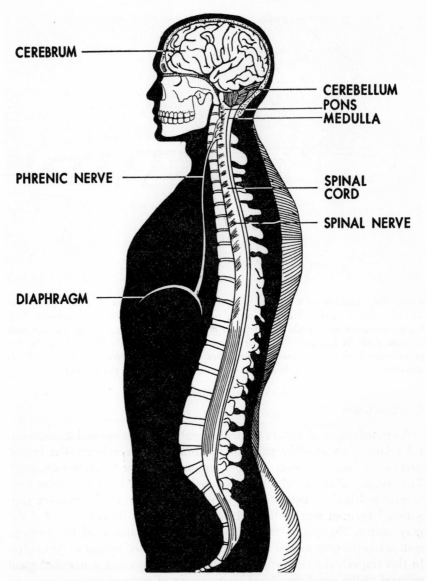

CEREBRUM

CEREBELLUM
PONS
MEDULLA

PHRENIC NERVE

SPINAL
CORD

SPINAL NERVE

DIAPHRAGM

Figure 4-5. The central nervous system in relation to speech. The *cerebrum.* Normal meaningful speech is dependent upon the integrative activity of the normal cerebrum. The *cerebellum* "sorts and arranges" muscular impulses that come to it from higher brain centers. Impulses are here correlated so that precise muscular activity such as is needed for speech becomes possible. The *pons* is a bridge of nerve fibers between the cerebral cortex and the medulla. The *medulla* contains the respiratory and other reflex centers. The *spinal cord* and its nerves control the respiratory muscles. The *phrenic nerve* emerges from the spinal cord in the neck region and extends to the diaphragm. It supplies the impulses which cause the diaphragm to contract in breathing. (From *Basic Speech* by J. Eisenson. P. 32. New York: Macmillan, 1950. Used by permission.)

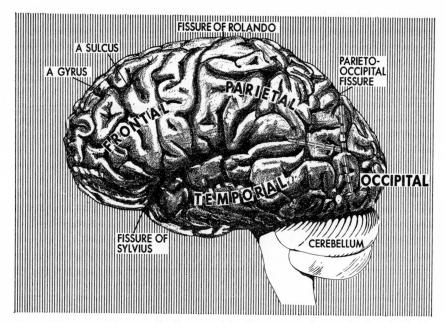

Figure 4-6. Lateral view of the brain, showing lobes. (From *Speech Disorders* by Berry & Eisenson. P. 50. New York: Appleton-Century-Crofts, 1956. Used by permission.)

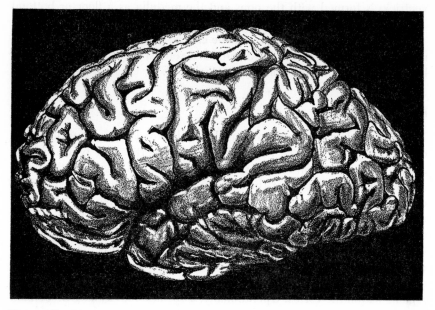

Figure 4-7. Diagram of a left cerebral cortex of a human brain.

reception, interpretation, and integration of stimuli and the organization
and expression of human behavior.

An examination of Figure 4-6, a left cerebral hemisphere, should provide an orientation to the major areas of the cerebral cortex and to some
of the terms that will be frequently used in our discussion of the cortex
and its functions. Compare Figure 4-6 with Figure 4-7 which is drawn
from an actual photograph of a human cerebral cortex.

The cortex, as we may note from the diagram and the photograph,
is somewhat like a conformation of gray cloth that has been rumpled so as
to produce elevations or ridges and indentations or valleys. A shallow in-
dentation or furrow is called a sulcus (plural sulci). The deeper indentations are referred to as *fissures*. These set off the cortex into the major
areas or *lobes*—frontal, temporal, occipital, and parietal. Another major
area, the *insula* or island of Reil, is buried in the lateral fissure and so
is not visible on the surface of the cortex.

The interior of the cerebrum consists of cavities or *ventricles*. Approximately in the center of each cerebral hemisphere is the narrow cavity
known as the *lateral ventricle*. Around the lateral ventricle lies the white
matter of the cerebrum. The white matter consists of masses of nerve
fibers which interconnect the areas of the brain.

The lateral ventricle communicates with another interior space in the
brain known as the *third ventricle*. This area, by way of a narrow channel,
is continuous with the fourth and last ventricle of the brain. The fourth
ventricle is formed with the pons and the medulla as a floor or bottom,
and the cerebellum as a roof.

The ventricles constitute part of the central canal system of the central
nervous system. They are filled with a cerebrospinal fluid which circu-
lates throughout the brain and the spinal cord.

Functional Areas

The physiology of the brain can be understood if we consider some
of the specialized centers. Part of the cerebral cortex may be considered
as having developed in relationship to the peripheral organs of the body.
According to the nature of the impulse, these areas may be referred to
either as sensory or motor projection areas. In general plan, the projection
areas receive or send fibers from lower brain centers which in turn
receive or send them to the peripheral organs. *Projection areas* may be
defined as regions of the cortex that communicate directly with lower
centers through nerve tracts. In contrast with these areas, the cerebral
cortex also contains *association areas*. These are connected only with
regions within the cortex. Operationally, association areas may be defined

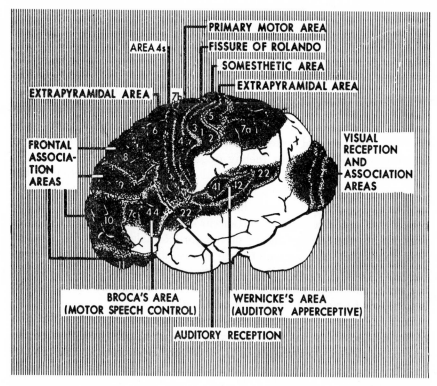

Figure 4-8. Localization areas in the cerebral cortex. (From *Speech Disorders* by Berry & *Eisenson.* P. 57. New York: Appleton-Century-Crofts, 1956. Used by permission.)

as regions of the cortex that integrate nerve impulses received from other cortical areas. Adjacent to each of the sensory (projection) areas are larger association areas. In the occipital and frontal lobes, the association areas are particularly large. Presumably, in the association areas interrelationships between the activities of the sensory and motor areas occur which make it possible for complex behavior, such as speaking, to be integrated and produced.

From the evolutionary viewpoint, the most primitive part of the cortex is the region covered by the temporal lobe. This area includes the hipocampus and the related area called the amygdala. These and related areas constiute the *limbic system* which is important in the control and recall of affective (emotional) behavior.

Figure 4-8 features some projection and association areas that have special significance for speech.

The Thalamus and Striate Bodies

The thalamus is a mass of cerebral tissue situated at the base of the cerebrum and projecting into and bounding the third ventricle. The thalamus has long been considered a great relay station for sensory stimuli. All visual, auditory, visceral, and somatic impulses either terminate in the thalamus or have synaptic connections there before continuing to the cerebral cortex. Because of this relay feature, the thalamus is known as the center for feeling or "affective behavior."

Penfield attributes an additional and a very different function to the thalamus in relationship to speech. Penfield believes that the thalamus is intimately involved in the intercoordination between areas of the cortex that are especially important in speech. Although Penfield does not indicate the precise nature of the cortico-thalamic involvement, he conjectures that the function of three cortical areas of special significance for speech are, ". . . coordinated by projections of each to parts of the thalamus, and that by means of these circuits the elaboration of speech is somehow carried out." (1959, pp. 207-208)

Penfield's conjecture of the role of the thalamus in the coordination of speech behavior has by no means been generally accepted by all interested clinical neurologists. It is, however, an interesting and provocative hypothesis worthy of consideration and, if possible, of experimental investigation.

The Striate Bodies. Beneath the white matter in the forepart of the cerebral cortex there lie three gray nuclear masses known collectively as the striate bodies. The great pathways going to and from the cerebral cortex pass through the striate bodies. In regard to speech, the striate bodies may be considered as part of a functional unit with the thalamus.

The Hypothalamus

Situated directly beneath the thalamus is the hypothalamus. The centers for the control of the visceral organs involved in emotional responses are here localized. Hypothalamic control over the visceral organs in emotional responses is indirect. This control is effected through fibers interconnecting the CNS with the ANS. For example, in anger or rage, the overt response of sneering is the result of the impulses coming from the thalamus and striate bodies; changes in heart rate and blood pressure are the results of the activities of the hypothalamic centers acting through the ANS.

The Cerebellum

The cerebellum or small brain is directly below and partly covered by the cerebrum. The cerebellum has many complex connections throughout the nervous system. Its principal sensory connections are with the fibers that convey muscle (proprioceptive) sensitivity from the muscles of the body and from the balance mechanism of the internal ear. The cerebellum also has elaborate interconnections with the cerebrum and so functions in the over-all coordination of voluntary movements. Precision of timing and the general tonus and character of muscular responses, whether reflex or voluntary, are presumably a result of the controls and impositions of the cerebellum. The finely-timed motor activity called speaking is an especially complex example of behavior served by the cerebellum.

The Brain Stem

The cerebrum and cerebellum are connected by extensive columns of neural tissue and central masses which are part of the brain stem. The posterior part of the brain stem (lower brain stem) is a somewhat flattened, cone-shaped mass known as the *medulla oblongata*. By way of an opening in the base of the skull, the medulla is continuous with the spinal cord. The anterior part of the brain stem, which includes the thalamus, is continuous with the cerebrum.

The Midbrain

The anatomical unit known as the midbrain lies immediately below the thalamus. The name *midbrain* has implications both for function and position. Its positional implication is evident from its anatomic relationship to the cerebral hemispheres and the brain stem. (See Figure 4-5.) Its functional implications are related to kinds of controls with which its centers are involved. By way of connections with the cerebellum and the medulla, the midbrain has centers which function in the regulation of muscle tone, body posture, and movement. By way of other centers, the midbrain is involved with functions that are integrated in the cerebral hemispheres, particularly of reflexes controlling the eye.

The Pons

The pons is the unit of the CNS that lies just below the midbrain.

This anatomic area serves as a bridge between the two sides of the cerebellum. Neural pathways to and from the cerebellum merge at the pons.

The Medulla

The medulla oblongata, or *bulb,* the flattened, cone-shaped mass referred to earlier, is an enlargement of the spinal cord. On the ventral side of the medulla there are two tracts of descending nerve fibers (the *pyramidal tracts*) that come from the cerebral cortex. These tracts cross over (decussate) at the narrower posterior end of the medulla. The medulla also includes sensory tracts going toward the higher centers. In addition, there are centers vital to biological existence that are involved with the control of respiration and circulation.

The Reticular Formation

A comparatively recent "discovery" regarding the functioning of the CNS is the reticular system. The reticular formation is a structure within the lower midbrain. It includes a highly complicated network of neurons which functionally may be divided into *ascending* and *descending* parts.

The ascending part of the reticular formation may be considered in effect a central station at which neural impulses arrive from many receptor organs including the ears, eyes, nose, and skin. For example, fibers from the retina of the eye arrive at the recticular formation by way of the thalamus. Impulses from the reticular formation are conducted to various parts of the brain including centers of the cerebral cortex.

As of now, research results on the functioning of the reticular formation do not permit of the presentation of a body of information about which there is sufficient unanimity to be considered established fact. According to Penfield the reticular system ". . . provides neuronal mechanisms which seem to be essential to consciousness and the integration of function in the cerebral hemisphere." (1959, p. 16) Figure 4-9 is a diagrammatic representation of the relationships of the reticular formation to other parts of the central nervous system. This is consistent with the observation of Krech and Crutchfield and others relative to the function of the reticular system. (1958, pp. 170-171)

In general, there is agreement that nerve impulses from the ascending part of the reticular formation serve *to arouse* or *alert* the cortex so that normal perception may take place. Experimental evidence indicates that if the ascending reticular system is temporarily or permanently prevented from discharging impulses to the cortex, the individual has great difficulty or is completely unable to respond to stimuli from the outside world.

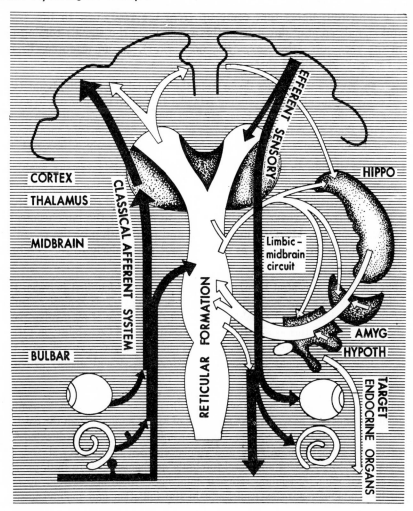

Figure 4-9. The reticular formation and its relations to other parts of the brain systems involved in learning. (From *The Central Nervous System and Behavior.* P. 289. Josiah Macy, Jr., Foundation, 1959.)

At worst, the experimental subject may go into a deep sleep, or lose consciousness; at best, he may have great difficulty in maintaining awareness of perceptual situations.

There is even less established information about the *descending reticular* system than the little that is generally accepted about the ascending system. It is probably safe to say that the descending reticular formation receives impulses from the cerebral cortex and in turn sends impulses to the numerous fibers that come up from the receptors. In this way, neural signals coming down from the cortex meet the signals coming up from the receptors (the ears, eyes, nose, skin). As an example, Krech and Crutchfield believe that:

> . . . an impulse that comes down from the occiptal lobes of the brain (the visual center) through the descending reticular formation can prevent impulses coming up from the ear from ever reaching the cortex. This can help us to understand the very common experience of not hearing someone speak to us when all our attention is directed at watching an object intently. (1958, p. 172)

Our brief discussion of the reticular formation anticipates the problem of integration of "high level" behavior. We shall, of course, return to this problem when we consider the cerebral cortex and its role in speech. For the moment, however, we should like to consider the conclusions of Magoun (1958, pp. 115-116) on the role and relationship of the reticular system to the nervous system as a whole and particularly to the cerebral cortex.

Within the brain, a central transcortical core has been identified between the strictly sensory or motor systems of classical neurology. This central reticular mechanism has been found capable of grading the activity of most other parts of the brain. It does this as a reflexion of its own internal excitability, in turn a consequence of both afferent and corticifugal neural influences, as well as of the titer of circulating humors and hormones which affect and modify reticular activity.

.   .   .   .

Influences of this reticular system which are directed spinalward modify central afferent transmission, as well as the activities of motor outflows from the cord, in particular those subserving posture. Reticular influences which are directed forward to the cephalic brain stem and rhinencephalon affect visceral and endocrine regulating systems and basal forebrain mechanisms for reward, punishment and emotion. Ascending reticular influences which are exerted upward upon the cerebral neocortex contribute to the initiation and maintenance of wakefulness and to the focus of attention.

These manifold and varied capacities of the reticular system suggest that it serves importantly, and in the closest conjunction with the cortex, in the central integrative processes of the brain. In no area do the findings seem more intriguing than in the new developments exploring its involvement in conditioned learning.

THE AUTONOMIC NERVOUS SYSTEM (ANS)

The autonomic nervous system consists of a complex of nerves extending throughout the body and connected at more centrally located masses called ganglia. Although we speak here of the autonomic nervous mechanism as a more or less separate system, structurally and functionally, it is closely related to the CNS. In the thoracic and abdominal cavities the autonomic ganglia receive branches from the spinal nerves and constitute the subdivision of the autonomic nervous system called the sympathetic system. The tenth cranial nerve from the brain is intimately associated with a set of autonomic nerves which together constitute the parasympathetic system. The importance of these two subdivisions of the autonomic system is that they control the internal organs and other structures not under the control of the will. The actions of the sympathetic and parasympathetic systems are generally opposed to one another; where one stimulates a set of organs, the other usually inhibits the same set. For example, the sympathetic system dilates the pupil of the eye, checks the flow of saliva, quickens the heart, and checks the movements of the stomach and intestines; the parasympathetic system, on the other hand, constricts the pupil, starts the flow of saliva, slows the heart, and increases the action of the stomach and intestines.

The autonomic nervous system has obvious importance in the maintenance of our biological existence. The ANS also has a significant role in the maintenance of our emotional and mental health. In turn, these states are reflected in the manner and often in the content of our speech.

THE CEREBRAL MECHANISMS FOR SPEECH

Cerebral Activity

With this general overview of the topography and hierarchy of the nervous system we shall shift our emphasis to a more specialized consideration of the brain mechanisms and the functions called language and speech. The reader should remember that in considering intellectual functioning we necessarily are dealing with theory, conjecture, and evaluations of evidence that may approach but cannot as yet be considered established fact.

Although a physicist may reduce or translate the speech process to sound, light, and electrical waves, such translation does not simplify the process. The understanding of a speech effort, as Dr. Wilder Penfield indicated (see p. 33), requires both a philosophic and scientific attitude.

Cerebral activity, however initiated, is in essence biophysical activity. In common with other neurons, the ten to twelve billion or more nerve cells of the brain are normally capable of developing the electrical energy which is needed for carrying out cerebral activity. This activity takes place as a result of the *orderly and controlled* transmission of nervous impulses from one insulated nerve cell to another. As it is everywhere else in the nervous system, transmission from one nerve cell to another requires the crossing of junctures (synapses) between neurons.

Bases of Knowledge of Brain Function

Much of our knowledge of how the human brain is presumed to function is derived on a negative basis. There is an extensive amount of literature on what happens to impair or destroy function, temporarily or permanently, as a result of damage or lesion to various parts of the brain. Disturbed functions, or dysfunctions, provide us negative information insofar as we learn what happens or is impaired in the event of an abnormal circumstance. The maintained functioning, however disturbed, affords us positive information of what the abnormal brain is able to do. From this information we conjecture about normal brains and about the functions of such brains in the performance of comparatively simple reflex and more complex learned behavior. As far as this behavior involves non-symbolic sensory and motor abilities, there is sufficient consistency between damage and dysfunction to warrant conclusions as to normal functional relationships. When we approach symbol behavior—the ability to produce and to interpret arbitrary auditory and visual patterns—no such consistency seems to exist. We cannot get direct evidence from experimentation with animals, because animals do not possess man's capacity for the level and complexity of integrative functioning required in symbol behavior. The evidence we have in regard to cerebro-cortical functioning comes to us from observations of two major research techniques. One is the technique of lesion or ablation; the second is the electrophysiological technique.

The observations of *lesions* or *ablations* provide us with negative evidence. When controlled ablations are experimentally imposed on animals, resultant immediate and ultimate dysfunctions or modifications of function may be noted. To the best of our knowledge, ablations intentionally performed on the brain of man are done so only when lesion is suspected or established on the basis of presumed dysfunction because of aberrant behavior. The observations following ablations on the brain of man, therefore, are based on abnormal brains. In any event, the information provided is of a negative nature. We learn what functions are disturbed or impaired following lesion or following ablation. This is not quite the same as establishing positively that a given cerebral area normally carries on a given function.

The electrophysiological technique may provide an approach to give us positive information as to the functions of cerebral areas. Experimental electrostimulation has been done with surgically exposed animal brains. Specific areas of the brain were stimulated with a mild electric current and the induced behavior recorded. In this way the animal brain has been functionally "mapped." This approach as applied to the human

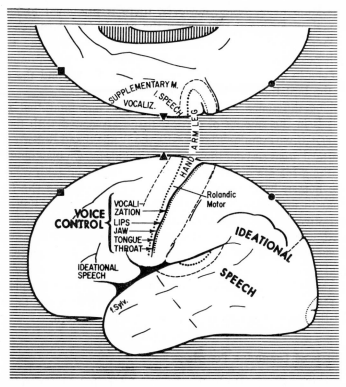

Figure 4-10. Speech mechanisms in the dominant hemisphere. Three areas are devoted to the ideational elaboration of speech: two areas, devoted to vocalization. The principal area devoted to motor control of articulation, or voice control, is located in lower precentral gyrus. Evidence for these localizations is summarized from the analysis of cortical stimulation and cortical excision. (From *Speech and Brain Mechanisms* by Penfield & Roberts. P. 200. Princeton: Princeton University Press, 1959. Used by permission.)

brain has been undertaken only with persons with some behavioral abnormality, for the most part with epileptic persons. The positive observations, though impressive, provide us with a "mapping" that may not necessarily hold for normal brains. Conclusions, therefore, should be considered tentative. (Penfield & Roberts, 1959, Chapters VII-IX)

Comparative Topography of the Brain

In external form and general appearance, the brain of a man resembles that of a dog. The brain of a chimpanzee is even closer to that of man in that the number and arrangement of the lobes are similar. The size of the cerebral hemispheres is relatively larger in man than in any lower animal. Within man's brain, however, there is presumed to be an organizational arrangement that makes the acquisition of speech possible for most human beings. Only in a very limited sense is the understanding of speech possible for the dog and the chimpanzee. The production of speech, even in a very limited sense, is apparently beyond the capacity of even the best trained chimpanzee.

A striking difference between the brain of man and that of other mammals is in the amount of cortical tissue associated with the evocation of voice. If we examine Figure 4-10, the Penfield and Roberts diagram of the cortical areas serving the speech mechanisms, we may note another distinguishing feature of the human cortex. Compared with other mammals, the human brain has a larger cortical area serving the functions of the mouth and the hand. If we are justified in concluding that, on a comparative basis, differences in functional areas of the brain are associated with differential development of special abilities, then the proportionally larger areas of the cortex that subserve voice, mouth, and hand functions may be associated with man's distinctive abilities for speaking and writing. We should, however, continue to maintain a critical reservation that there may be considerably more to cerebral function than even the instrument-aided eye can discern.

Localization of Language Function

Many contemporary students who are interested in the relationship of the functioning of man's brain to his unique ability to use language are not at all certain of just how this ability is accomplished and controlled. Most interested students are reasonably certain that they cannot accept the position of either the 19th or 20th century clinicians who believed that all parts of the brain were equal in potential and that the brain functioned as a whole for all activities. Many contemporary students are also unable to accept the extremely opposite position of the strict localizationists (Nielsen, 1947) who hold that the brain can be divided into many discrete and precise functional areas, including those for the various and related functions involved in the ability to use language. Specifically, strict localizationists believe that there are well defined areas of the brain responsible for the related functions of comprehension, oral language (speech), written language (reading), speaking, writing, arithmetic calculations, etc. Some localizationists are specific to a point of postulating if not demonstrating that there are different centers for functions such as the perception of animate objects and inanimate objects, the ability of naming, the use of grammar, and the perception of musical melody.

An interesting and new approach to solving the problem of localization of language function has recently been developed by Dr. Penfield and his associates at the Montreal Neurological Institute and McGill University. These clinicians and researchers have developed a brain-mapping technique with conscious patients employing electro-stimulation for the purpose of detecting and localizing abnormal brain tissue. This procedure has also been adapted to "explore and map" the speech areas. According to Penfield and Roberts speech mapping is carried out as follows (1959, p. 109).

> Recording electrodes are applied to the cortex for the usual routine study of the nature and position of electrographic abnormalities of the epileptic type. When this is finished, the recording electrodes are left in place while speech mapping is carried out. A stimulating electrode is then applied here and there to establish the limits of the cortex that are essential to normal speech. . . . In the speech areas, stimulation produces only local functional interference.

After the limits essential to speech are outlined, more precise localization of language function is determined through the same technique. Throughout the procedure the observer sits close to the patient so that he can see and be seen and can engage in conversation with the patient. The observer presents a series of card pictures to the patient who is directed to respond to each by identifying it and saying, for example, "This is a ship," "That is a dog," etc., or by writing his response on a sheet of paper. The operator who observes and listens to this exercise, applies his electrode to the cortex at one point and then another in the area being explored. If there is no interruption or interference in the function tested (naming, counting, reading, writing, etc.) a minute square of paper is dropped on the brain at the point where the electrode was applied and the result was negative (e.g., no interference with naming ability). If interference is produced (positive result), a numbered ticket is placed at the point of application.

The accumulated results of this "brain mapping" of several hundred patients have provided Penfield and his associates with information about the entire human cerebral cortex. Based on this information, they have made some observations they believe to be valid and statistically significant, and have come to tentative conclusions where the data permitted. They have "mapped" the cerebral cortex according to the generalizations they believe warranted by their findings. Figure 4-11 is one such "map."

Cerebral Dominance or "Control" of Language Function. In 1861 the French surgeon, Paul Broca, demonstrated by autopsy findings that one of his patients who lost the power to speak had incurred a lesion in the

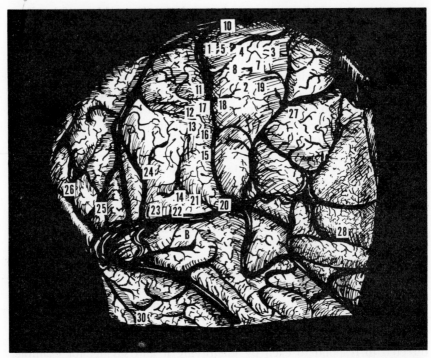

Figure 4-11. "Ticketing" of part of the left hemisphere of brain to indicate where Dr. Penfield obtained positive responses to electro-stimulation. (From *Speech and Brain Mechanisms* by Penfield & Roberts. P. 114. Princeton: Princeton University Press, 1959. Used by permission.)

third frontal convolution of the left hemisphere of the brain.[1] Because his patient had been right-handed, Broca and his students concluded that the function of speech was contralaterally controlled; that is, the capacity for speaking was controlled in the left hemisphere for right handed persons and so, presumably in the right hemisphere for left-handed persons. Unfortunately, Broca failed to distinguish between the motor aspects of language production and the ability to formulate linguistic symbols in anticipation of their production. Up to very recently most of Broca's students and clinicians assumed that both formulation and motor production of oral language (speech) were contralaterally controlled. Following Broca, observations of various types of productive and receptive (intake or comprehension of oral or written language functions) were believed to be controlled in the left hemisphere for right handed persons and in the right hemisphere for left handed per-

[1] For the interested reader, an English translation of the original Broca article is available. See J. Kann, *Journal of Speech and Hearing Disorders,* 15, 1950, pp. 16-20.

INTERFERENCE WITH SPEECH

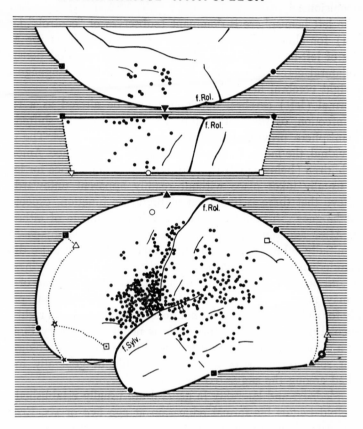

Figure 4-12. Electrical interference has produced interference with speech at these points in the left hemisphere. When the electric current has been applied to other areas, such as the frontal pole or the occipital lobe, no difficulty in speech has been noted. (From *Speech and Brain Mechanisms* by Penfield & Roberts. P. 122. Princeton: Princeton University Press, 1959. Used by permission.)

sons. On the basis of this assumption, a corollary belief was widely accepted that the establishment of handedness was somehow directly related to the development of cerebral dominance.

Laterality. Recent research and experimental evidence supports neither the assumption of contralaterality for language ability or the related proposition that the establishment of handedness was causally related to the development of cerebral dominance. The evidence of investigators

in the United States, England, and other countries permits of the follow-.
ing conclusions: [2]

1. The left hemisphere is dominant (subserves or "controls" language
function) for almost all right-handed persons as well as for a strong
majority of left-handed persons. A minority of left-handed persons may
have bilateral cerebral language control or may have language control
in the right cerebral hemisphere.

2. Normal (left) cerebral dominance may be altered as a result of
injury, infection, or some other type of damage and so shifted to the
right hemisphere, providing this hemisphere is not involved. The younger
the individual, the more likely it is that shift will take place. Among very
young children (below age two) shift of cerebral dominance for language
control usually takes place without readily apparent untoward effect.
We believe that there is limitation of linguistic function, especially for
abstract language, in children who incur brain damage of either hemisphere. After age ten, the shift and assumption of language function
by the initially subordinate hemisphere takes place with more difficulty.

3. Handedness in particular and laterality in general (eyedness, foot-
edness, and possibly even "earedness") is a result of a number of factors.
These may include hereditary predisposition, environmental pressures
(usually for right-handedness but not necessarily for uniform right laterality), special psychological factors such as negativism, injury limiting or
causing a change of inclined or established handedness, pathology of the
brain, or some other factor neither specifically or generally indicated
or implied among the suggested causes.

4. Handedness and laterality in general are usually established by the
time a child begins his formal education at age five or six. Except for
special reasons, handedness is maintained into adult life.

5. Cerebral dominance for language function is also normally established by the time a child is ready for school. The coincidence of time
for the development of handedness and cerebral dominance for language may be the basis for the assumption that the two factors are
causally related. Clinical evidence today supports the position that laterality for language function and handedness are independent factors.

The Role of the Non-dominant Hemisphere. The midline speech organs—the jaw, lips, tongue, and larynx—have representation in both
cerebral hemispheres. That is, both halves of these organs are represented

---

[2] Readers who wish to review some of the literature on the subject may consult
the following sources: J. Eisenson in L. E. Travis (Ed.), *Handbook of Speech
Pathology,* Appleton-Century-Crofts, 1957, pp. 459-463; W. Penfield and L. Roberts,
Speech and Brain Mechanisms, op. cit., Ch. VI; V. B. Mountcastle (Ed.), *Inter-
hemispheric Relations and Cerebral Dominance,* Johns Hopkins, 1962.

in each of the two hemispheres. From this point of view, one function of the non-dominant hemisphere is obvious. The nerve fibers from the non-dominant hemisphere participate in the control of motor speech activity. Beyond this, however, what is the role of the non-dominant hemisphere for language function?

We have already indicated that for virtually all right-handed persons and for a majority of left-handed persons, the right cerebral hemisphere is subordinate (non-dominant) for language function. This does not mean that the non-dominant hemisphere has no role in language function, or that it serves as a "spare" with latent ability to take over function only in the event of injury to the dominant hemisphere. We believe that the non-dominant hemisphere is importantly involved in all language functioning and that its contribution is probably of a more generalized nature than that of the dominant hemisphere. We agree in this respect with Weisenburg and McBride who observed that ". . . the non-dominant hemisphere is apparently concerned with normal language function but to a limited degree." (1935, p. 453) We should not infer that "a limited degree" implies either a low-level or an unimportant degree.

The research of the first-named author on the effects of damage to the right (non-dominant) hemisphere in right-handed persons strongly suggests that the quality of language functioning is impaired in these cases. This impression is based on the difficulties that right-brain-damaged adults have in giving good quality definitions for words and in dealing with sentence completion tests calling for the inclusion of abstract words. In general, persons with right-hemisphere damage have more difficulty in placing themselves at the disposal of other persons' linguistic formulations than in producing their own. These, in turn, tend to be more egocentric and concrete than we find in non-brain-damaged adults. Fluency of utterance, however, is generally not impaired. On the contrary, the clinical impression of the first-named author suggests that the person with right brain damage uses more words per idea than do persons free of cerebral involvement. On the basis of our research evidence we would be inclined to generalize that the right brain hemisphere is important for the appreciation of high-level, abstract language functioning.

Research evidence based on the results of intelligence tests generally indicate that damage to the non-dominant hemisphere is expressed in greater decrement in performance tests than in language ability. Non-verbal conceptualization is apparently impaired. We also have evidence that suggests that the non-dominant hemisphere as well as the dominant is involved in memory function—the retention and reproduction of experiences. Man's memories may be recorded and duplicated in both cerebral hemispheres. (Penfield, 1954, pp. 293-297)

The intimate relationship between memory and language provides a bridge for the belief that the non-dominant hemisphere serves man in recording his memories, and in producing them according to need, as well as in the formation of concepts and their representation in language symbols. The non-dominant hemisphere may be subordinate to the dominant one in its non-specific motor and sensory functions. It is certainly subordinate in regard to the comparatively specific aspects of language function such as are required in the understanding and production of language symbols. But it is by no means idle or a stand-by in regard to normal, general, on-going intellectual and linguistic behavior.

Localization of Language Function. Beyond establishing the dominance of the left hemisphere for language function for most persons, is it possible to localize specific sub-linguistic functions within the hemisphere? Are there separate centers for reading, writing, grammar, naming of objects, verbalization of ideas, as well as for arithmetic ability, music, and the reproduction of memorized language content? Are there different centers that control the release of language content according to level and degree of abstraction? Is affect-laden language that is expressive of our feelings and so emotionally "controlled" differently routed through cerebral centers from that for intellectual and more specifically meaningful language? We have already indicated that there are various schools of thought and that students of these schools would provide a variety of answers. These answers would range from a certainty that each language function has its own cerebral center or combination of centers for the control of each type of language function, to the position that maintains that it is simply not possible to localize language. (Weisenburg and McBride, 1935, p. 453).

Although we have quoted a conclusion of an investigation published in 1935, the general position that it is still impossible to localize language functions continues to deserve respect. There are, however, more moderate points of view that attempt to localize broad kinds of language function in different cerebral areas. Before presenting these viewpoints to which the authors of this text are inclined, we should like to emphasize that differences of opinion relative to the control of language function should not be confused with the localization of specific sensory and motor functions. It is possible to localize vision, smell, hearing, and movement of parts of the body. Clinical evidence has provided a basis for correlating cerebral area, and especially cortical areas, with non-language sensory and motor functions. For example, electrostimulation of cortical centers can induce or block movements of the hands or arms, or even evoke a laryngeal noise. There are, however, differences between seeing a word and reading it, between making a noise and producing a pattern of noises that has symbol significance. Where symbol behavior enters the picture, there is need for continual investigation. Some contemporary viewpoints on how the brain serves language will now be reviewed.

Traditional Localization Concepts. Clinicians who view the brain, and especially the brain cortex, as possessing the centers for language control, differ more in regard to the degree of specificity of function, number, and location of the centers than they do about the underlying concept in regard to centers. Traditionally, localizationists whether strict or "liberal," agree that intake stimuli (receptor events) are transferred by way of the lower centers to the supposedly higher centers of the sensory cortex. From these receptor centers the events are transmitted to some association areas where they are organized into "ideas" and then activate the motor system to some sort of output. This viewpoint was implied in our discussion (see pp. 44-45) of the projection and association areas of the cortex. This viewpoint emphasizes the importance of the association areas for complex, "high level" functions which are involved in symbol

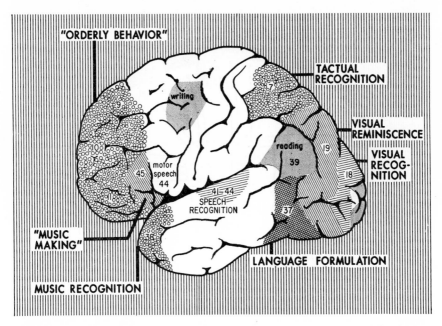

Figure 4-13. Composite diagram of the supposed "association" areas of the human cerebral cortex. Many neurologists believe that the cortex functions in some such way as indicated; some do not. The scheme is worthwhile mainly to provide hypotheses for further research and to help in thinking about the role of the cortex in learning and memory. (From *Physiological Psychology* by Morgan & Stellar. 2nd Ed. P. 514. Copyright, 1950. New York: McGraw-Hill Book Co. Used by permission.)

behavior in general and language behavior in particular. Figure 4-13 is a composite diagram that represents a moderate localizationist viewpoint. Implied in this representation is the notion that given association areas undergo excitation consistent with the type of stimuli received by the related projection areas.

At the risk of oversimplification, we may look at the various projection areas of the cortex as specialized signal centers and the association areas as transformation centers. Within the association areas the signals are organized and evaluated for their informational import and the derived information is transmitted throughout the brain for use by the organism as a whole.

Modifications of Traditional Localization.   A viewpoint of cortical locali- zation that considerably modifies the role of specific areas is held by Kurt Goldstein. According to Goldstein ". . . *each performance is due*

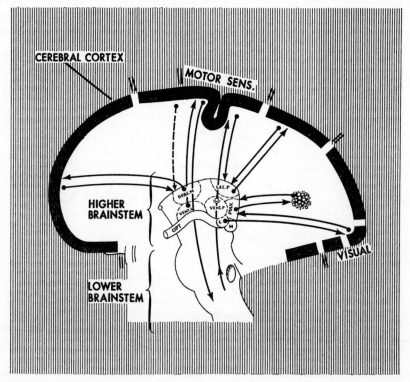

Figure 4-14. Diagram of connections between brain stem and cerebral cortex. This illustrates the hypothesis that each functional area of cortex forms a unit with some portion of the diencephalon of which it is the developmental projection. (From *Speech and Brain Mechanisms* by Penfield & Roberts. P. 19. Princeton: Princeton University Press, 1959. Used by permission.)

to the function of the total organism in which the brain plays a particular role. In each performance the whole cortex is in activity, but the excitation in the cortex is not the same throughout." (1948, p. 50) For Goldstein, the function of a specific cortical area is significant according to the influence it exerts on the excitation of the cortex as a whole and, by virtue of this influence, to the dynamic functioning of the entire nervous system.

Another viewpoint that is a considerable modification of traditional localization is held by Wilder Penfield. His concept of the communicative function of the brain is represented in Figure 4-14. Penfield stresses his belief that the large areas of the human cortex ". . . such as those in the temporal, the anterior frontal, and the posterior parietal lobes, have connections within the brain itself which enable them to carry out functions that may be described as psychical rather than sensory or motor." (1959, p. 19) All regions of the cortex are connected with subcortical gray matter by means of both specific and non-specific two-way nerve fiber projection systems.

Based upon their evidence from surgical excisions, Penfield and Roberts (1959) believe that there are three areas of the brain of special significance for speech. These areas, in order of importance, are the posterior or parieto-temporal, the Broca's area in the anterior, and the supplementary motor area in the superior part of the brain. (See Figure 4-15)

We may not at this time have succeeded in localizing language functions in general and oral language behavior (speech) in particular. It is possible, however, to arrive at a fair amount of agreement as to the parts of the cortex that are important for language function and, in broad terms, to assess the type of function with which each large area is involved. The posterior portion of the cortex is concerned with the reception and interpretation of visual events, including the evaluation of written words. The parieto-temporal portion is concerned with the reception and evaluation of auditory events; the anterior part of the brain, including Broca's areas, is concerned with productive language, including oral speech and writing.

The Integration of Language Function

Among the many unanswered questions about the brain mechanisms and language function there is the persistent one: "Where is language function coordinated and integrated?" Some students feel that the cortex as a whole serves the function of over-all integration as well as of specialization. Kurt Goldstein, as we have indicated, supports this view. Hebb, with strong reserve, holds that: ". . . the middle regions of one hemisphere, usually the 'dominant' one . . . appears to have some sort

SPEECH AREAS
EVIDENCE FROM EXCISION

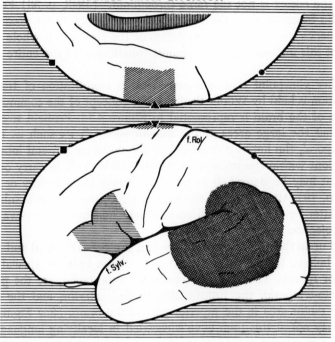

Figure 4-15. The three speech areas, according to Penfield & Roberts, are of different values. The posterior, or parietotemporal, area is the most important. The anterior, or Broca's area, is the next most important but is dispensable in some patients, at least. The superior, or supplementary motor, area is dispensable but probably is very important after damage to one of the other speech areas. (From *Speech and Brain Mechanisms* by Penfield & Roberts. P. 189. Princeton: Princeton University Press, 1959. Used by permission.)

of executive and organizing role that is essential to speech and some higher functions." (1959, p. 204)

From the time of Broca, many clinicians have attributed the coordinating and integrating function to Broca's area, and to the region anterior to it. Although there is little or no direct evidence to support this view, it continues to have its proponents. For example, Morgan and Stellar observe that though neither they nor neuroanatomists are certain how Broca's area is related to the rest of the frontal lobe and the remaining portion of the most anterior part of the cortex," it seems, however, to have been specially differentiated to be a center for coordinating speech." (1950, p. 515)

We are more inclined to accept Hebb's (1959, p. 286) observation in regard to the frontal lobe to the effect that:

. . . although the frontal lobe is the favorite place in which to localize higher functions when one is speculating about these matters, it is still true that there is no *proof* that any single higher function depends on this part of the brain. At least as good a case might be made out for the parietal and temporal lobes as the seat of man's distinctive psychological characteristics. . . .

Penfield and Roberts have taken a challenging view that higher functions may be coordinated and integrated in a sub-cortical, older portion of the brain which they localize in the *higher brain stem*. They hold that each functional area in the more recently evolved cerebral cortex has connections with areas of gray matter in the brain stem including the thalamus. Applying their assumption specifically to language function, Penfield and Roberts believe that:

Comprehension of speech occurs after receiving auditory impulses in both hemispheres and in the higher brain stem, and during the interaction of impulses between the higher brain stem and the left temporo-parieto-occipital region. Reading occurs after receiving visual impulses in both hemispheres and in the higher brain stem, and during the interaction of impulses between the higher brain stem and the left temporo-parieto-occipital region.

Productive speech occurs when, "following interaction between the higher brain stem and the left hemisphere, impulses pass to both cortical motor areas and thence to the final common pathway to those muscles used in speech. . . ." (1959, pp. 189-190, and p. 191)

Both in regard to localization and to integration of language function, Penfield and Roberts present their views with an attitude of confidence that many other students do not entertain. In contrast to their point of view, many students concerned with the brain mechanisms for language and speech still do not feel that we know how the brain stores language information or groups its functions related to language behavior. For example, Geschwind and Lambert assert: "Although it is certain that words or concepts are not 'stored' in the sense of occupying specific locations within the cortex, we simply do not know how such information is retained and utilized." (1958)

The reader should by now be impressed with the position of the authors that our present state of knowledge affords insufficient basis for localizing functions or the precise manner of the integration of those symbol noise patterns we refer to as speech, or the visible patterns we refer to as written words. Nor are we entirely certain of how information "stored" or received becomes a basis for language to be produced when the conditions are considered appropriate for some form of language output. If we were to take a position as to the integration of language function it would be that the cerebral cortex is one, but not the only, center for language integration and elaboration. Subcortical areas are unquestionably involved in integration. Some centers, cortical and subcortical, are apparently better receivers for certain kinds of impulses than others. The transmission and elaboration of information received may conceivably take place in a localized area of the cortex, or in the cortex as a whole (together with subcortical areas) depending upon the nature of the event and the condition of the organism. The organism is constantly exposed to many simultaneous stimulating events. Under some conditions we can listen to two or more persons at one time, each trying to provide different or differing information. Often, but not always, we are able to sort out one set of signals and translate this set into information. Later, when the noises have ceased, we may be able to recall (reproduce) another set of signals and respond to them. Occasionally the organism is unable to accept competing signals, and shuts itself off from the events to avoid the need for a response. It may be that given fibers, and given cerebral areas, can deal with more than one type of receptor event. Perhaps, in their wish to understand the nervous mechanism for language, some authorities have adopted a sense of economy, efficiency, and specialization that is properly neither economical nor efficient. Perhaps further consideration should be given the Lashley concept that any fiber in the central nervous system is capable of carrying information ordinarily originating in different "special" centers. It may be that the nervous mechanism has built-in emergency capacity that makes assumption of non-specialized function possible along with the usual relative specialization when "other things are equal." Undoubtedly this multi-functional concept applies better to so-called association areas than to given sensory and motor projection areas. Whatever the case may be, language function is somehow integrated in the central nervous system, and most probably in the cortex and the proximate subcortical areas. We are reasonably certain that language function is carried on as a result of the passage of nervous impulses normally in a manner both orderly and controlled through an electrophysiological system. The system must be embodied in a human organism. The human organism must mature physically and socially for a year or more before language function is acquired. Not all human beings, however, are capable of acquiring language or developing language behavior. Among those who do, differences are great both in regard to quantity and quality of language ability. Presumably these differences are related to capacities within the nervous mechanism as well as to the opportunities for stimulating the nervous mechanism so that capacity becomes ability. These matters are discussed elsewhere in the text.

REFERENCES

Eisenson, J. In Travis, L. E. (Ed.), *Handbook of speech pathology*. New York: Appleton-Century-Crofts, 1957.

Geschwind, N., & Lambert, W. *Report on an interdisciplinary seminar and conference*. Boston Veterans Administration Hospital, 1958.

Goldstein, K. *Language and language disturbances*. New York: Grune & Stratton, 1948.

Hebb, D. O. *The organization of behavior*. New York: Wiley, 1959.

Kann, J. A translation of Broca's original article on the localization of the speech center. *J. Spch and Hearing Disorders*, 1950, 15, 16-20.

Krech, D., & Crutchfield, R. S. *Elements of psychology*. New York: Knopf, 1958.

Magoun, H. W. *The waking brain*. Springfield, Ill.: Charles C. Thomas, 1958.

Morgan, C. T., & Stellar, E. *Physiological psychology*. (2nd ed.) New York: McGraw-Hill, 1950.

Nielsen, J. M. *Agnosia, apraxia, aphasia*. (2nd ed.) New York: Harper & Row, 1947.

Penfield, W. The functional organization of the human brain. *Proc. Amer. Phil. Soc.*, 1954, 98, 293-297.

Penfield, W., & Roberts, L. *Speech and brain mechanisms*. Princeton: Princeton University Press, 1959.

Weisenburg, T., & McBride, K. *Aphasia*. Commonwealth Fund, 1935.

5

Affective Behavior (Emotion) And Speech

CONCEPTS OF EMOTION

THE TERM EMOTION CAN BE used with such a wide variety and range of meanings that no writer should assume that his readers will understand his meaning or meanings without making his position clear. Before attempting to do so, we will present a few definitions or explanations to indicate the range if not the variety of meanings that may be associated with the term emotion.

According to Ruesch (1957, p. 14) ". . . the emotional state of an individual is conceived of as the sum-total evaluation of all events which occur inside the organism. . . . Emotions thus express the appraisal of existence from the inside out, while intellectual functions represent the view of the same events from the outside in." This view implies that there are two complementary aspects of experience, one (the intellectual) capable of objective evaluation and explanation, and the other highly individual and subjective and accordingly requiring a different (an analogic) evaluation and different principles of codification (linguistic explanation).

Frank (1954, p. 1) begins his essay on "Feelings and Emotions" with a statement showing awareness of the implications of the many, and often conflicting, meanings of the term *emotion*.

Feelings and emotions pervade all our lives. It is impossible to observe ourselves or others without being impressed by the extent to which our behavior is governed by emotions. Emotional reactions and responses color much of our political, economic, social, and personal activity. A wide variety of emotional appeals influences our votes, our purchases, our choice of recreation, our religious beliefs, and all our most cherished values. But we are confused about these reactions and responses of ours and our confusion is often increased by our language and the lack of a well-established terminology about emotions. (In this paper we cannot hope to resolve these verbal conflicts but we can try to make some clear-cut distinctions. For example, we may distinguish between an acute emotional reaction to immediate provocation, such as fear, and a chronic affective response, such as anxiety, derived from past experience but persisting into the present. Frequently we use the same word, namely feeling, for either or both of these and also for those pleasant, euphoric states and responses (sometimes called sentiments) of joy, happiness, and loving. Since feeling is an accepted colloquial expression, it will be used in this statement whenever it is not necessary to be rigorous or precise.)

Krech and Crutchfield (1958, p. 230) view emotion as a multidimensional term. "In its broadest psychological meaning the term *emotion* refers to a stirred-up state of the organism, reflected in three quite different ways: (1) emotional experience, e.g., the person feels angry; (2) emotional behavior, e.g., he curses and attacks his tormentor; (3) physiological changes in the body, e.g., the blood rushes to his face, the heart beats faster, etc. These three aspects are intimately related . . ."

Krech and Crutchfield, aware of the multiple meanings as well as the multidimensions of emotional experience, point to four "dimensions" that are common to them. These are intensity of feeling, level of tension, hedonic tone, and degree of complexity.

This contemporary concept of emotion was anticipated by the philosopher Spinoza who, almost three centuries ago, wrote ". . . by emotion we mean the modifications of the body by which the body's power of acting is increased or diminished, assisted or restrained, and also the consciousness of these modifications."

From the point of view of this text, the term *emotion* will be used to refer to a component of a complex reaction that an individual undergoes in a given situation. The component *emotion* is characterized by: (1) a marked change in the internal state of the organism, (2) awareness of the change, and (3) behavior indicative of an attempt to adjust to the given situation.

Emotions are *not* abstractions or disembodied states. Emotional reactions occur only as responses to situations and cannot be separated from the situations or experiences which evoke them.

AWARENESS OF CHANGE OF THE INTERNAL (PHYSIOLOGICAL) STATE

All behavior is accompanied by physiological changes. Unless there is a special reason for consciousness or awareness of physiological changes, most of us are inattentive to them. When the changes are marked, or unexpected, then we are more likely to become aware of them. We are not ordinarily mindful of the beating of our heart unless the heart misses a beat, or "pounds." We are not likely to become aware of respiratory activity unless the activity is suddenly or unexpectedly different. Certainly normal, well-adjusted persons pay little or no attention to the subtle, ever changing internal alterations of their organisms that are part of every moment's living and adjusting to ongoing and inner-going experiences.

Despite the lack of awareness of the specifics of physiological changes, we do have awareness of the total effect of such changes. Thus, we may verbalize the effects of the changes by saying that we feel *happy, sad, anxious, tense, apprehensive, excited,* etc. Such words indicate the more lasting effects to persons and to situations.

When the emotional reactions are more intense, we are likely to become aware of the specifics of the physiological changes. We may then become aware of physical (muscular) tenseness, of heart palpitations, dryness of the throat, panting, heavy breathing, sweating, and even of changes in body temperature. Marked physiological changes are often accompanied by involuntary overt motor activity such as trembling, and twitching and by vocal noises ("laughter" and cries).

Perceptions or awareness of these inner and overt changes often are dominating features of emotional reactions.

Homeostasis and Physiological Change

The nature of the physiological changes that constitute an integral component of emotional responses may be understood in terms of the concept of *homeostasis.* All mammals are born with the capacity for maintaining a dynamic internal equilibrium necessary for life. The mechanisms for homeostasis are involuntary and automatic and their ongoing effects ordinarily occur without conscious awareness of the organism. The same mechanisms that make the continuous and usually subtle changes for everyday living are also involved in the physiological processes and more marked alterations that prepare the mammalian organism for unusual or emergency situations. Often, but not always, these alterations are helpful in the organism's attempts at dealing with the situation. From the point of view of human behavior, the following observation of Frank (1954, pp. 4-5) is directly relevant.

When we meet with unusual situations that threaten or frighten or hurt us, these basic physiological processes and ongoing alterations are enlarged and accelerated, intensified beyond the usual "normal" limits of regular functional dis-

placements; they become stronger, more intense, or more extended and prolonged as the reserves and functional potentialities of the organism are called
into play. The organism is then capable of functioning more effectively in some
situations where a great exertion is necessary to fight or to escape, or it may be
handicapped by the very intensity of the emotional reaction, as in shock, panic,
or fainting.

In the face of danger (or what is perceived as dangerous) the organism responds with the *alarm reaction*, or *General Adaptation Syndrome*, as it has been
called by Dr. Hans Selye. The initial response to a threatening situation is a
quick visceral spasm with concomitant but limited physiological alterations. If
this initial reaction continues, however, it will be reinforced, by a cumulative
process, with adrenal gland secretions that evoke a circular process, or "feedback," as in the alarm reaction. The individual becomes fully mobilized for
action to run away or to fight. Sometimes his activities become disorganized
and he is unable to act in any coordinated, purposeful way.

EMOTION AND REORGANIZATION OF BEHAVIOR

Many students of the psychology of emotional behavior tend to view
emotions as disruptive and disorganizing forces which impair rather than
help the individual in his efforts at adjustment. Exponents of this viewpoint argue that emotional responses are characterized by predominantly
random, excessive, and largely useless motor as well as verbal behavior.
This view of emotions may be exemplified by the observation of Dockeray
(1933, p. 620) to the effect that ". . . emotion may be considered the
opposite of attentive or organized behavior. There are segments of the
total behavior which are largely organized, such as certain glandular
and visceral reactions; but the total picture is that of disorganization."

A related view of emotional behavior emphasizes the *reorganization*
rather than the disorganization of response patterns. An individual tends
to meet "new" situations in terms of his background of experience. If he
finds that his experiences are inadequate, or inappropriate, he attempts
to meet the situation with a modified response pattern, a new approach.
He is then reorganizing his response patterns. If he finally perceives that
his new approaches are without avail, and yet feels driven to do something either because he cannot or will not extricate himself from the
situation, then he may give way to disorganized behavior. Often this
very behavior serves to remove the individual from the situation that
evoked the emotional response and so permits a reorganization of patterns that tends to restore a comparative state of equilibrium. This concept of emotional behavior may explain the more intense emotions such
as fear, anger, and rage but not the less intense and hedonistically
pleasanter emotions such as joy, or the unpleasant emotions of sadness
and grief. Before turning our attention to the less intense affective states,

we will consider the disturbing emotions of fear and anger in some detail.

Fear

In an experiment with chimpanzees, Hebb (1949, pp. 241-245; 1953, pp. 259-276) demonstrated that *fear* may be evoked when the animals are confronted with strange and unfamiliar (unexpected) situations. Hebb confronted chimpanzees who were in their own cages with objects such as anesthetized chimpanzees, an ape head, and a window display dummy "human" head. The objects, placed in a box, were concealed from the experimental chimpanzees who were lured to the box by an offer of food. When the chimpanzees came close to the box, it was opened to reveal the aforementioned objects. Hebb attributed *fear* to the chimpanzees when they showed definite withdrawal behavior. Accompaniments to the withdrawal activity were signs of unusual excitement, such as screaming, threatening gestures, erection of hair, etc. These reactions were most consistently produced when the chimpanzees were confronted with the anesthetized chimpanzees and the disembodied heads. The reasons, presumably, were that the tested chimpanzees expected some responses from the experimental whole animal (anesthetized) chimpanzee and that they could not cope with the *lack of responsiveness*. The disembodied head evoked fear because it was *unexpected*.

The dynamics of the fear response may be understood in the light of the following explanation offered by Hebb:

1. On the basis of past experience (through past learning) the chimpanzees came to expect certain events when confronted (stimulated) by the objects used in the experiment. A chimpanzee expects to see a body attached to a head. A chimpanzee expects a reaction from another chimpanzee.

2. As a result of exposure (stimulation) to the experimental object, a sequence of neural events takes place in the chimpanzee's brain.

3. Neurologically, the immediate source and cause of fear is the direct consequence of *profound disorganization of cerebral processes*.

4. Psychologically, the fear response was evoked because strange objects (inanimate chimpanzees, disembodied heads) arouse perceptual and intellectual processes that are not compatible with pre-established and ongoing activities. (For the chimpanzees who had no experience with dummies and disembodied heads, the degree of unusualness, the strange and the unanticipated, did not prepare them for the experimental situations.)

The Hebb experiment is entirely consistent with what human beings know about the causes of their own fear. Mowrer (1960, pp. 166-169), in developing his unifying theory of emotions, holds that *fear* is a response to a stimulus which signals a *loss* in contrast to *hope* which is a response to a stimulus which signals a *gain*. Human beings fear the unknown. The unknown is often perceived as being potentially dangerous. Known situations, of course, may also be perceived as being dangerous or threatening. The common and essential component in fear-provoking situations, regardless of whether they are familiar or unfamiliar, is the assumption or the realization of the individual that he is inadequate. When an individual thinks that he lacks the power or the ability to deal effectively with a situation he is about to confront or one in which he is immediately involved, fear is evoked.

It follows from this explanation of the dynamics of fear that training and experience prepare the individual to meet potentially fear-evoking situations with patterns of responses that eliminate or reduce the likelihood of fear, or at least the intensity of a fear reaction that is disruptive rather than preparatory for emergency action. This is why some men voluntarily join military forces, and why military personnel are trained under simulated battle conditions. This is in part why it is possible to have fire-fighting forces and police. This is probably also why many villages continue to exist at the edge of active volcanoes, and why others exist and flourish where earthquakes become part of a way of life.

Anger

Most human beings are aroused to anger when they recognize that they are blocked or frustrated in attaining goals they consider attainable. Anger is not necessarily the invariable or the only possible consequence of the thwarting of an individual's goal. Some individuals may turn their backs on a potentially frustrating situation and so adjust by avoiding it and the resultant anger. Others may decide that the situation is really not within their capabilities and in the light of such a reappraisal, avoid anger. The emotion of anger is most likely to occur when an individual perceives, regardless of the "correctness" of his perception, the cause of his difficulty (the obstacle in the way of his goal), and cannot do anything about removing the cause or obstacle. Beyond this awareness, the likelihood of *anger* at a thwarting situation is increased if the individual considers the interposed obstacle to be there for the purpose of frustrating him, or somehow to be unfair or "deliberately malicious." With such awarenesses an individual may give expression to his feelings with aggressive or destructive behavior.

In general, one constant function seems to be served by behavior associated with the unpleasant, disturbing emotions, whether such behavior is apparently organized and directed at the disturbing situation or apparently "disorganized" and not so directed. This function is some-how ". . . such as to tend to put an end to the original stimulation. . . ." (Hebb, 1949, p. 254)

EMOTIONS AND HEIGHTENED FEELING

The scantily clad man on the cinder path who has just heard a pistol shot and is running with all the speed he can summon is physiologically in a state comparable to a man who is fleeing in fear. Because the scantily clad man is competing in a race for his alma mater, or his club, or his country he is in a state of heightened feeling motivated by such forces and sentiments as patriotism, competitiveness, and other possible dynamic factors that helped him to prepare to run as well and as fast as he could. In the absence of such feeling, unless the man happened to be a profes-sional runner with a monetary prize as his motivation, it is likely that he would not perform as well as might otherwise be possible.

Many stage performers and public speakers describe states that phys-iologically are comparable to fear before their performances. Some actors try to work themselves up to such states to insure good performances. As in the instance of the athlete, the physiological changes and the generalized heightened feeling are preparatory sets and are helpful in the execution of the anticipated activity. In a strict sense, therefore, these performers are not in a state of emotion, and certainly are not involved with a disturbing emotion.

There are instances in which the residual of heightened feeling be-comes disturbing to the individual. We have on more than one occasion seen a mother rush into the middle of a road to save her child from the imminent danger of an oncoming automobile. Having saved her child, the mother proceeded to whip him and shout "I'll kill you if you ever run away again." We assume that the forces that enabled the mother to move faster than she probably had ever moved before left physiological changes that were no longer useful for continued appro-priate behavior. The whipping and the "threat" were reactions that became part of a new emotionally disturbing state that probably in-cluded the dread of what might have happened had the mother failed in her attempt to save her child. In the instance we have described, heightened feeling that made appropriate action possible could not be spent or drained off in appropriate behavior, and so "spilled over" and influenced subsequent emotional behavior. The mother literally did not know what to do with her feelings. The child was on the receiving end of the not too well organized result. In very little time he too had heightened feelings and emotional reactions, especially if he was in-nocent of what had happened to him in the first place.

AFFECTIVE STATES AND EMOTIONAL EXPERIENCE

Most persons who are not especially concerned with distinctions between primary or "main" emotions, whether these be fear, anger, grief, and joy, as they are for Krech and Crutchfield (1958, Ch. IX), or fear, relief, hope, and disappointment, as they are for Mowrer (1960, p. 169), nevertheless have everyday experiences that they refer to as emotional. Most normal persons like or dislike others even if they do not hate; they entertain sorrow or grief, have feelings that they identify as sympathy, pity (they may or may not admit to envy); they enjoy humor, engage in laughter, cry or feel like crying, are occasionally overcome with awe of the beautiful or feel overwhelmed by the wonderful. Some sensory situations make them respond with positive pleasurable delight, and others with feelings of horror, disgust, and possibly pain. Beyond this, they have more enduring moods of sadness, and of well-being. Occasionally their feelings turn inward and they may then feel ashamed or guilty.

It may be of help in our discussion to make a more or less arbitrary distinction between the so-called primary, main, or basic emotions and the affective states that were referred to in the preceding paragraph. For the sake of argument, or perhaps to avoid fruitless argument, we may limit our use of the term emotion to the intense, essentially disruptive states and use the term affective states for the feelings that are less intense, generally more facilitating, and are associated with much of our day-to-day rather than our occasional extreme expressions of behavior. These affective states may be divided into two broad categories: (1) they are either *essentially pleasant,* constructive rather than disruptive, and motivate us toward maintaining or achieving behavior that we consider desirable or pleasant, or (2) they are *essentially unpleasant* and so normally are associated with behavior we wish to avoid or to terminate.

Most of the affective states, whether pleasant or unpleasant, are relatively enduring compared with the more extreme emotions. Most represent attitudes and predispositions to persons, to things, to situations in general that influence our relationships to the animate and the inanimate in our surroundings. When an affective state is established in relationship to somebody and to something, the state tends to be maintained and to color as well as predetermine our approach to similar somebodies and somethings.

THE CONTROL OF EMOTIONAL BEHAVIOR

In our discussion of the Nervous Mechanism and Speech we indicated that the thalamus and the hypothalamus include centers for the "control" of affective behavior (see p. 46). We also indicated that there are reticular influences which serve somehow to regulate and influence emotional behavior (see p. 48). These are general centers for the relatively intense emotional states. But because emotional reactions are specific to the motivating situations, cortical centers are necessarily involved in the specific form or expression of the emotional behavior.

Much of what we know about emotional reactions is based on experiments with animals in which strong reactions of fear and rage were evoked or the expected reactions were inhibited. Recent evidence of electrostimulation studies with humans tend to support the role of parts of the cortex in the evocation or inhibition of the expressive component of emotional reaction. We may sum up the results of such studies with the generalized observation that for the intense affective states, the initiation and control of emotional behavior is integrated and controlled within the cerebral structures that include parts of the cerebral cortex, the thalamus, hypothalamus, and the reticular formation.

THE EXPRESSION OF EMOTION

Language and Emotion

Most of us have had some occasion to say or to hear "There are no words to describe my feelings" or "Words cannot tell you how I feel." Such expressions are not necessarily euphemisms to cover up a lack of verbal facility. The more intense the feeling, the closer the feeling comes to an emotion, the more difficult it is for the state to be verbalized. The poet Wordsworth who held that "Poetry takes its origin from emotion recollected in tranquility" was aware that at best the poet can only describe and create an awareness of a state "kindred" but not equal to the original emotion. Thus, Wordsworth tells us in his *Poetical Works:* "The emotion is contemplated till by a species of reaction, the tranquility gradually disappears, and an emotion, kindred to that which was before the subject of contemplation, is gradually produced, and does itself actually exist in the mind."

Most of us who are not conscious or aspiring poets are more likely to speak our feelings rather than to wait and recollect them in tranquility. When tranquil we are not usually motivated to give verbal expression to our affective states. Perhaps we come closest to the poetic use of language in our vocabulary of slang. Although slang is spoken for many reasons and by members of many subgroups for different reasons,[1] one of its chief advantages over standard terminology or standard uses of

---

[1] The reader interested in the varied uses and purposes served by slang may wish to consult the Preface to the *Dictionary of American Slang* by S. Flexner and H. Wentworth (Crowell, 1960).

established terminology is that it indicates without a doubt the speaker's wish to be forceful, highly personal and expressive rather than accurate and intellectual. Thus, the adolescent during the 1960's may verbalize his approval of something or somebody by referring to it, her, or him (it hardly matters whether it is an it or a who, or whether it is animate or inanimate) as being *drooly, the greatest, reet, super, smooth,* or *way out.* During the 1950's the adolescent might have used terms such as *the cat's pajamas, nice,* or *keen.* Disapproval in the 1960's might have been expressed by such locutions as *creep, drip, goof,* or *square.* Ten years earlier the terms of disapproval might have been *boob, dope, jerk, sap,* or *weird.* Except as certain terms are more current within one subgroup than within others, the specific choice of word for approval or for approbation matters little. The distinction between a *creep* and a *jerk,* if any exists, is likely to escape most speakers and listeners.

Strongly affective language shows the same tendencies as slang to be characterized by vividness rather than by specificity of meaning. In general, the more emotionally charged the language, the less definite the meanings of the individual words. There is little logic in terms of abuse, or in the words men swear with rather than swear by. Terms of endearment are equally lacking in logic or in definiteness of meaning. By and large, however, we are more leisurely and more verbose if not more precise in how we express our tender feelings than in the expression of our dislikes and our hostilities. Those we hold dear have many names. In English, these names are often derived from Romantic influences in contrast with the Anglo Saxon influence prominent in the terms we use for those we dislike. The reader can put the last observation to the test by checking his list of terms used for "purring" and those used for "snarling." But whether he is purring or snarling, he will find that the more emotionally charged his speech, the less it is characterized by clarity and logic. These qualities give way to vividness as an expression of both the state of affect and the needs of the speaker. Love logically expressed may be intellectually interesting but probably is less satisfying and less convincing than the same state of feeling expressed with hyperbole.

Diversification of content characterizes the verbal utterances of persons in a state of heightened affect. The verbal flow of such speakers contains more words and a greater variety of words than do the utterances of persons in a state of "neutral" affect. At the other extreme the utterances of persons with lowered affect, including the mildly and the more severely depressed, contain few words and tend to include verbal reiteration (see samples of manic and depressive speech, pp. 373-374). These observations are consistent with the findings of the statistical studies of Zipf on the relationship between emotional states and articulatedness of meaning. (Zipf, 1935, p. 207 ff.) The observation is also in keeping with one made by Whatmough (1956, p. 212) to the effect that: "A relationship between frequency and affectivity is demonstrable, . . . Low frequency goes with high affectivity . . ." We shall find that the relationship between affective state and frequency of change (amount of diversification of speech content) holds for normal speech as well as for the speech of persons with affective disturbances. Moreover, not only the linguistic component but the attributes of the vocal component—pitch, loudness, rate—all show similar relationships.

Newman and Mather (1938) in their study of persons with affective disorders, found that patients in heightened states (mania) spoke with rich syntactic elaboration (high diversification of content). In contrast, patients in low affective states (the depressed) spoke with meager syntactic elaboration (low diversification of content). Other characteristics of the utterances of persons with affective disorders are summarized as follows in Table 1 (Newman and Mather, 1938).

Table 1.

Analysis of Speech Characteristics of 40 Patients with Affective Disorders

	Depression	Mania
Articulatory Movements	Lax	Vigorous
Pitch Range	Narrow	Wide
Pitch Changes	Step wise; infrequent	Gliding, frequent
Emphatic Accents	Absent or rare	Frequent
Pauses	Hesitating	Accented
Resonance	Nasal	Oral
Level of Style	Colloquial	Elevated
Syntactic Elaboration	Meager	Rich
Syntactic Techniques	Limited	Diversified
Initiation of Response	Slow	Quick
Length of Response	Short	Long

As a parting note on the subject of diversification of content, we shall cite the speculations of Jespersen (1928, p. 432) as to the nature and content of primitive speech.

. . . No period has seen less taciturn people than the first framers of speech; primitive speakers were not reticent and reserved beings, but youthful men and women babbling merrily on, without being so very particular about the meaning of each word. They did not narrowly weigh every syllable—what were a couple of syllables more or less to them? They chattered away for the mere pleasure of chattering, resembling therein many a mother of our own time, who will chatter away to baby without measuring her words or looking too closely into the meaning of each . . .

Simulated Emotion. Pronovost and Fairbanks (1939) and Fairbanks and Pronovost (1938) studied the relationship of pitch to simulated emotion. A uniform test passage was read by six competent actors to portray the states of *contempt, anger, fear, grief,* and *indifference.* Recordings were made of the readings and then played before a group of 64 observers who were given a list of twelve affective states which included the five that were studied. The additional states were *amusement, astonishment, doubt, elation, embarrassment, jealousy,* and *love.* The observers were asked to select (identify) the name of the affective state being simulated on each recording. The results indicated high percentages of accuracy for the identification of the simulated emotional state ranging from 84 percent for *contempt,* 78 per cent for *anger* and *grief,* and 66 per cent for *fear. Indifference,* which we would consider a neutral affective state, had the highest percent, 88, of correct recognition.

The experimenters—Pronovost and Fairbanks—analyzed the pitch characteristics of the key affective states with results indicated in the following table.

Table 2.

Pitch Characteristics of Key Affective States

Simulated "Emotion"	Median Pitch Level	Total Pitch Range	Inflectional Range	Pitch Change
Contempt	low	wide	moderate	moderate
Anger	high	wide	widest	most rapid
Fear	highest	widest	moderate	moderate
Grief	low	narrow	narrowest	slowest
Indifference	lowest	narrowest	moderate	moderate

In summary, the pitch changes of simulated strong emotions (contempt, anger, and fear) are wider in range and occur more frequently than they do in the more repressed states (grief and indifference).

In his *Psychology of Feeling and Emotion* (1936), Ruckmick reviewed some of the research on the relationship of vocal changes to emotional expression. For the most part, the studies were concerned with simulated emotions. That is, with the results of efforts of performers to suggest an affective state by reading material or in singing. The results generally indicated that there were definite tendencies for heightened feelings to find vocal expression at the higher end of the performer's pitch range, and neutral and depressed states to be expressed at the lower end of the pitch range. In general, Rucknick's survey as well as the findings of Pronovost and Fairbanks substantiated common observation that happy and angry persons who are giving voice to their feelings do so at higher pitch levels than sad or "indifferent" persons. Another observation in regard to the use of force is also supported in experimental findings. Skinner (1935) found that vocal expressions in happy states are characterized by an increase and in sad states by a reduction in the use of force. Skinner believed that force might be a more reliable index than pitch for differentiating the vocal reactions of happiness and sadness.

Visible Aspects of Emotional Behavior

The preponderance of evidence relative to the visible expression of emotional behavior strongly suggests that such behavior is learned and conforms to cultural patterns. The growing child learns how to purr and to sneer with facial expression as well as with words. He learns how to express approval by the way he looks and by the words and vocal tones he uses. He learns how to look pained and to sound pained. Along this line, B. F. Skinner (1957, p. 215) observes that "facial expressions of emotion are peculiar to a given culture. To some extent each verbal community has its own cry of pain (*Ouch!* or *Aie!*), its own form of laughter, its own verbal expressions of contempt . . . and so on."

This observation does not mean that children cannot express their basic emotions individually, or that there are no innate visible components for the different emotions. It does imply that as children mature and learn the ways of their culture, the ways in which their emotional states are normally expressed are modified and environmentally determined. This is why *simulated emotions* can be recognized. They follow patterns of expression that have been learned. In contrast, emotional expressions of very young infants are difficult to distinguish (Sherman, 1927) unless the observer is also permitted to see and so be informed about the situation that induced the emotion.

Coleman (1949) investigated the ability of adults to recognize emotions by means of motion pictures of facial expressions in natural and acted situations. He found that some emotional expressions were more readily identified from the eye region and others from the region of the mouth. In general, emotional expressions were more reliably identified when acted (simulated) than when they occurred as natural reactions to the experimental situations. Coleman's findings failed to support those prevalent in the literature, e.g. Dusenbury and Knower (1939), to the effect that women were better judges of emotional expressions than men.

On the basis of a survey of the literature on the recognition of emotional expression, Krech and Crutchfield (1958, p. 261) came to the following conclusions:

1. The evidence of common experience relative to the ability to recognize emotions is not consistently supported by experimental evidence.

2. The pattern of facial expression for a given emotion (or at least for an expected emotion according to the emotion-evoking experience) is highly variable among different individuals. This seems to be especially true for unpleasant emotions.

3. Posed or simulated emotions are more reliably recognized than spontaneous "true" emotions.

4. Certain facial features are more expressive of emotions than others. Dunlap (1927) found that the mouth provides more informative cues about an individual's emotions than do the eyes.

5. The accuracy of the identification of emotions increases according to the number of expressive cues to which observers may respond. Additional cues are provided by total bodily action (gesture and pantomime) as well as by vocal behavior. All such cues are determined by learning within a given cultural setting.

These conclusions are in keeping with those of Woodworth and Schlosberg (1954, p. 132), relative to cultural differences in facial expression. They hold that "one emerges from a study of this topic with the conviction that there *are* certain basic emotional patterns in man, but that different elements of these patterns are selected and stressed by specific cultures. This is especially true when facial expressions serve as a conventional means of communication."

Content-free Speech

Several studies strongly suggest that speaker affect can be determined from content-free speech. Starkweather (1956) filtered the content from the vocal component of a communication. He found that judges were able to identify aggressive and submissive speakers on the basis of the vocal component alone.

In another article in which Starkweather summarized the implications of several studies, including his own (1961), he generalized that: ". . . studies of content-free speech indicate that the voice alone can carry information about the speaker. Judges agree substantially, both when asked to identify the emotion being expressed and when given the task of estimating the strength of the feeling. Judgments appear to depend upon significant changes in pitch, rate, volume, and other physical characteristics of the voice, but untrained judges cannot describe these qualities accurately."

Soskin and Kauffman (1961) describe their studies on judgments of emotion in word-free speech samples. Their technique employed the use of low pass filters which isolated out the high frequency sounds which presumably carry the burden of semantic content. "The assumption is that suppressing the 'highs' by such a filter (low pass) leaves a remainder of contentless flow of voice which still retains some of the major affect cues." [2]

Soskin and Kauffman found that their subjects (judges) were able to agree that the "semantic free" speech conveyed such general states of affect as *contentment, hostility, anger, dejection,* and *grief.*

Cultural Influences of Emotional Expression

Social psychologists and anthropologists have provided us with considerable evidence that the expression of emotion is culturally determined. This is so for the manner as well as the occasion for emotional expression. We are probably aware of the differences between northern and southern Europeans. The differences are even more striking when comparisons are made, or implied, between Western and non-Western cultures. Klineberg (1938) studied the expression of emotions in several non-Western cultures. He notes that among the Maori of New Zealand copious tears are shed when friends meet after a long absence. Tear-shedding also occurs when warring parties get together to arrange a peace. Among the Japanese it is proper to respond to the scolding of a superior by smiling. A Japanese is also likely to smile if he has been awkward in his behavior to another. Thus, a waiter may smile if he has upset a dish on a diner. A father's announcement of the death of a member of his family is also likely to be accompanied by a smile.

In our own culture, patterns of emotional expression have changed with the times. Women today rarely blush and almost never faint. Victorian women blushed often and knew both when and how to faint, according to the exigencies of the social situations. In Western as well as non-Western cultures we still learn, by example or, as in the case of genteel Chinese women, by direct instruction as well as by example, how to express our emotional reactions in the presence of others. In a sense, this is merely saying that we learn expressive behavior whether it is visible or oral. When we wish to make others aware of such reactions, when we need to reveal our affective states, we do so through learned behavior. We are considerably less conforming and so more individual in our emotional expression when we are alone.

REFERENCES

Coleman, J. C. Facial expressions of emotion. *Psychol. Monogr.,* 1949, 63, No. 1, (Whole No. 296).

[2] Although this assumption would certainly not hold for languages in which intonational and other tonal changes carry semantic import, we believe that it—the assumption—is valid for American-English speech.

Dockeray, F. C. Emotions as disorganized response. *Psychol. Bull.*, 1933, 30, 620.

Dunlap, K. The role of eye-muscles and mouth-muscles in the expression of the emotions. *Genet. Psychol. Monogr.*, 1927, 2, 3.

Dusenbury, D., & Knower, F. Experimental studies of the symbolism of action and voice, II. *Quart. J. Spch*, 1939, 25, 67-75.

Fairbanks, G., & Pronovost, W. Vocal pitch during simulated emotion. *Science*, 1938, 88, 2286, 382-383.

Frank, L. K. Feelings and emotions. *Doubleday papers in psychology.* New York: Doubleday, 1954.

Hebb, D. O. *The organization of behavior.* New York: Wiley, 1949. Pp. 241-245.

Hebb, D. O. On the nature of fear. *Psychol. Rev.*, 1953, 259-276.

Jespersen, O. *Language: its nature, development, and origin.* London: Allen and Unwin, 1928.

Klineberg, O. Emotional expression in Chinese literature. *J. abnorm. soc. Psychol.*, 1938, 33, 517-520.

Krech, D., & Crutchfield, R. S. *Elements of psychology.* New York: Knopf, 1958.

Mowrer, O. H. *Learning theory and behavior.* New York: Wiley, 1960. Pp. 166-169.

Newman, S., & Mather, V. G. Analysis of spoken language of patients with affective disorders. *Amer. J. Psychol.*, 1938, 94, 913-942.

Pronovost, W., & Fairbanks, G. An experimental study of the pitch characteristics of the voice during the expression of emotion. *Spch Monogr.*, 1939, VI, 87-104.

Ruckmick, C. A. *Psychology of feeling and emotion.* New York: McGraw-Hill, 1936.

Ruesch, J. *Disturbed communication.* New York: W. W. Norton, 1957.

Sherman, M. The differentiation of emotional responses in infants, part II. *J. Comp. Psychol.*, 1927, 7, 265-284.

Skinner, B. F. *Verbal behavior.* New York: Appleton-Century-Crofts, 1957.

Skinner, E. R. A calibrated recording and analysis of the pitch, force, and quality of vocal tones expressing happiness and sadness. Doctoral dissertation. *Spch Monogr.*, 1935, 2, 1.

Soskin, W. F., & Kauffman, P. E. Judgment of emotion in word-free voice samples. *J. Comm.*, 1961, LII, 73-81.

Starkweather, J. A. Content-free speech as a source of information about the speaker. *J. abnorm. soc. Psychol.*, 1956, LII, 394-402.

Starkweather, J. A. Vocal communication of personality and human feelings. *J. Comm.*, 1961, XI, 2, 63-72.

Whatmough, J. *Language.* New York: St. Martin's Press, 1956.

Woodworth, R. S., & Schlosberg, H. *Experimental psychology.* (Rev. ed.) New York: Holt, Rinehart, and Winston, 1954.

Zipf, G. K. *Psychobiology of language.* Boston: Houghton Mifflin, 1935.

6

The Psychology of
Language Learning

WHAT IS LEARNING?

IT IS EXTREMELY DIFFICULT to define *learning*, although most readers will have a rather clear-cut idea of what is actually meant by the term. Yet it is surprisingly easy to cite examples of learning experiences. For example, learning to drive an automobile, learning to fly an airplane, learning to tune a television set, obviously constitute examples of learning. Perhaps less obvious, but certainly equally valid, is the acquisition of economic, political, and religious attitudes and information. Through learning, the individual becomes a Republican, a Democrat, or an Independent. Through learning, one can become—or cease to become— a Communist.

Other types of behavior seem to be partly the result of learning and partly the result of maturation. Thus language is, at least in part, learned. Yet the chronological predictability of the appearance and disappearance of certain types of language behavior in the development of the child suggest also a strong maturational factor.

Hilgard (1956) has offered the following provisional definition: "Learning is the process by which an activity originates or is changed through reacting to an encountered situation, provided that the characteristics of the change in activity cannot be explained on the basis of native response tendencies, maturation, or temporary states of the organism (e.g., fatigue, drugs, etc.)."

As Hilgard has noted, this definition is not formally satisfactory, because it contains many undefined terms. Nevertheless, as a definition it does distinguish between (1) the kinds of changes and their correlated antecedents which are included as learning, and (2) the related kinds of changes and their antecedents which are not classified as learning.

Hilgard, then, attempts to differentiate between changes in behavior that are the result of learning and those which can be the results of instinct or reflex, maturation, fatigue, and temporary changes in the nervous system.

Brogden (1951) has also dealt with the problem of separating learning from other forms of behavior changes. Feeling that acquisition is the primary phenomenon of learning, he has attempted to integrate all of the characteristics of acquisition in the following definition: "Acquisition is a progressive, incremental change in the proficiency of performance by an organism; the direction, rate, and extent of change in the proficiency of performance are functions of the rapidity for continuous presentation of the conditions under which measurement of the change in performance is made." (1951, p. 569)

Brogden defines transfer as follows: "Transfer is a change in the proficiency of a performance that is demonstrated, by appropriate control procedures, to be a function of a change in the conditions under which it was originally acquired or in the conditions under which a similar performance was previously acquired." (1951, p. 569)

Brogden defines retention as the difficulty in proficiency of a performance during reacquisition or retest from that during acquisition.

There is little question but what the mastery of any language must be regarded as an example of learning. Granting the assumption that individuals may have an intuitive need to use language, the fact remains that the type of language developed by an individual reflects the environment in which he lives. The nature of the language learned is, therefore, almost certainly an example of the learning process. This is not to say, however, that other elements do not enter into this process. Undoubtedly, one of the major elements that determine language learning is that of maturation. At times, it is difficult to establish whether the onset of language in the child is controlled by maturation or by experience. Undoubtedly both factors enter in. Because of the regularity of the appearance of certain events, however, it is tempting to feel that maturation probably sets the lower limit at which language forms may appear, and that learning then determines the utilization of the lower limit.

Inasmuch as it is difficult if not impossible to frame a completely acceptable definition of learning, it is certainly not surprising that differing concepts of the nature of learning have existed and still do exist. It is not, of course, the function of this text to review in detail the major learning theories. For such information, the reader is referred to Earnest

R. Hilgard's *Theories of Learning* or to O. Hobart Mowrer's *Learning Theory and Behavior* and *Learning Theory and the Symbolic Processes*. In addition, excellent reviews of learning theory appear regularly in the psychological journals.

For purposes of orientation, however, it is desirable that the present text undertake a brief review of the major streams in learning theory. Unquestionably, the two major sources of learning theory in American psychology have been the work of Pavlov and of Thorndike.

Pavlov is particularly known for his work in conditioning. Figure 6-1 exemplifies the classical conditioning situation of Pavlov. In his experiments, an unconditioned stimulus (natural stimulus) such as food was presented to a hungry subject, typically a dog. Upon the presentation of the natural stimulus, the dog would make an unconditioned response, in this instance, salivation. Pavlov discovered that if a neutral stimulus, that is, a stimulus that previously had no particular association with the response, were presented shortly before or in temporal overlap with the natural stimulus, the salivation response would after some trials be shifted forward in time and would be made to the formerly neutral stimulus. Thus, if a light were presented shortly before the appearance of the food, the dog ultimately would salivate to the appearance of the light alone.

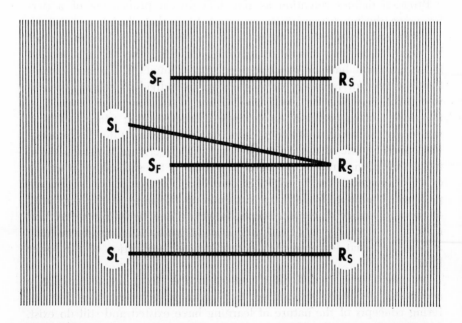

Figure 6-1. Classical Conditioning of Pavlov. S_F = Stimulus—Food (Unconditioned). S_L = Stimulus—Light (Conditioned). R_S = Response—Salivation.

In Pavlov's terminology, the natural stimulus, i.e. food, became known as the unconditioned stimulus, and the neutral stimulus, i.e. the light, became known as the conditioned stimulus. Pavlov and his followers saw this process as the basic process in learning. It is convenient to think of this type of learning as essentially a stimulus substitution. That is, as such learning takes place, the response remains essentially the same but is made to a new stimulus. Hence the term stimulus substitution.

Just as Pavlov is primarily associated with *classical* conditioning, so Thorndike is associated with the concepts of learning that have evolved from so called "trial and error" learning, from *instrumental* conditioning. Ordinarily, in instrumental conditioning there are two conditions of stimuli presentation. One is recognized when the conditioned (new or learned) response is made; the other, when the conditioned response is not made.

During the course of his long and active life, Thorndike's position with respect to learning was not static. Thus, at one early stage in his career, Thorndike (1913) believed that if an appropriate response to a stimulus were rewarded, the response would be strengthened, that is, would occur more frequently, or more predictably, or for a greater length of time. On the other hand, he felt that if an inappropriate response were not rewarded (or perhaps punished), that this response would be weakened. Responses, then, were reinforced (made stronger) or not reinforced (made weaker).

More specifically, if a hungry rat, after hearing a tone, made a response that secured food, the food-producing response would be strengthened. On the other hand, any response made by the rat in the same situation that did not produce food would be weakened. To Thorndike, at least in the early stages of this formulation, a bond or connection between the stimulus and the response was either made stronger or made weaker.

It is easy to see that just as Pavlov's concept of learning may be viewed as stimulus substitution, so Thorndike's early concept of learning may be viewed as response substitution.

Mowrer (1960) has reviewed brilliantly much of the subsequent development in learning theory as it has related to and varied from these two points of view. He has stressed that both Thorndike and Pavlov and their followers sought to account for all learning in terms of these two points of view. Strong experimental programs tended to support both points of view. Unfortunately, each school was faced with at least one inexplicable learning process.

Pavlovian theory could not explain why the final behavior of a rat in avoidance learning may be quite unlike the behavior which the rat shows in response to the unconditioned stimulus, in the event that this latter stimulus is not successfully avoided. That is, the final response was different from the original response. This finding tended to challenge the belief that learning is simply stimulus substitution.

At the same time, Thorndike's notion that learning is instead simply a matter of response substitution has also been challenged. In avoidance learning, the subject soon learns to be afraid of a formerly neutral stimulus. This learning of a fear response occurs too rapidly to be based on trial and error. Indeed, the fear learning is more easily explained as classical conditioning. The subject evidently reacts to the danger signal purely and simply because that signal has been made contiguous to the feared event.

Mowrer notes that out of demonstrations of the types summarized, the suggestion arose that perhaps Thorndike and Pavlov were both correct —that the theories of both were necessary to explain all of learning. This was the first two-factor conception of learning. Some learning was explained essentially as stimulus substitution, à la Pavlov; other learning, as essentially a response substitution, à la Thorndike.

Unfortunately, even the new two-factor theory could not deal adequately with the stamping out of a habit. As explained earlier, Thorndike (*circa* 1915) held that if the connection between a stimulus and a rewarded response were modifiable, then the connection between the stimulus and a punished response was weakened. Actually, Eisenson (1935) later found that the mere occurrence of a response tended to maintain it, even in instances in which the response was punished. Mowrer (1960, p. 5) concludes that

. . . it is obvious, even to casual observation, that the most immediate and reliable effect of behavior is neither punishment nor reward but rather the stimuli (sensations) associated with the occurrence of the behavior itself. Now, if these response-correlated forms of stimulation are followed by an event such as an electric shock, they will by the principle of conditioning themselves become capable of arousing fear which can be allayed only if the subject inhibits the response which arouses them. In other words, if a response has been "punished," when the subject starts to repeat that response it will arouse proprioceptive, tactile, visual, and other forms of stimulation which will act as danger signals and will tend through the fear they elicit to block the response.

This particular explanation of punishment was first evoked to explain situations in which the warning was external—as a light, or bell—but it was soon realized that the situation was no different in principle if the warning stimuli were internal, that is, products of the subject's own behavior. In the first instance, the fear becomes related to the external stimulus and the subject tends to retreat from that stimulus. In the second instance, the fear becomes related to internal or self-produced stimuli and the subject tends to inhibit these stimuli. In the first instance punishment results if the subject does not actively make an appropriate avoidance response; in the second instance, if he does not inhibit a response.

This version of the two-factor theory was also inadequate. First, it did not adequately deal with secondary reinforcement. Second, it failed to modify Thorndike's bond theory of habit. To meet these objections, Mowrer evolved the present two-factor theory of learning. In this theory, those internal stimuli that tend to be punished result in an inhibition of an action, and those internal stimuli that are rewarded result in facilitation of an action. Of course, it was also recognized that rewarded, independent stimuli would produce an approach response; punished, independent stimuli, an avoidance response. Finally, Mowrer (1960) suggests that ". . . the tendency to facilitate a particular group of stimuli, is what is ordinarily termed as habit."

Figure 6-2 outlines this conception of learning. The likely response to independent fear-producing stimuli is flight; to response-correlated fear, inhibition. Again, the likely response to independent hope-producing stimuli is approach; to response-correlated hope, facilitation. Mowrer's conception enables him to account for positive or negative learning in relation to either external or internal stimuli.

It is particularly important to note that although Mowrer terms his

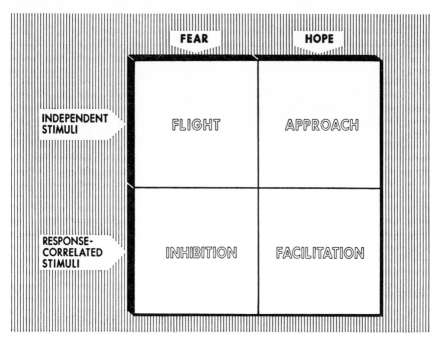

Figure 6-2. Two-Factor Learning Theory. (after Mowrer)

present theory a two-factor theory, the theory is no longer two-factor in the original sense. As now framed, the theory is entirely a sign-learning as opposed to a response-learning point of view. Mowrer, however, continues to regard it as a two-factor theory in that it deals with both decremental (need-reducing) and incremental (need-increasing) stimuli.

FACTORS AFFECTING LEARNING

Fortunately, irrespective of the theoretical position that one takes with respect to the nature of learning, it seems possible to agree on the effects of certain elements in the learning situation on the learning process. Hilgard (1956, p. 485), for example, has summarized the situation in these words: "It turns out, however, that many of the quarrels of the theorists are internal ones, not very important in relation to immediate practical problems; there are, in fact, a great many practically important experimental relationships upon which the theorists are in substantial agreement." He adds, somewhat cheerfully, that, ". . . advice for practical people today need not wait for the resolution of these theoretical controversies."

At this point, it seems appropriate to summarize some of these points of practical agreement rather than to continue to examine points of theoretical disagreement. This summary will be in terms of learning in general, although applications will be made to the more narrow area of language learning. The first factor to be discussed is that of motivation.

Although it is very common to think—at a somewhat superficial level, it is true—in terms of such dichotomies as reward and punishment, or reinforcement *vs.* non-reinforcement, the plain truth is that we do not have full understanding of what is rewarding and what is punishing. Somewhat circularly, reward can be inferred if the "reward" results in approach or facilitation, and punishment can be inferred if the "punishment" results in avoidance or inhibition. But such observations beg the question of *why the what rewards,* or of *why the what punishes.*

A truism, easy to accept but difficult to apply, is that motivation cannot be observed directly. Motivation can only be inferred. Yet, once we have inferred a motive, in a particular situation or instance, we are then prone to explain behavior in similar instances by treating our inferred motive as if it had objective reality.

Drive-Reduction Theories

According to Hilgard (1956, p. 409): "The commonest interpretation of reinforcement . . . can be traced back to Sherington's preparatory and consummatory response. It now goes by the name of the *drive-reduction* theory." At present, the theory is particularly identified with the writings of Hull (1943). This theory suggests that at any given moment, the subject will determine, perhaps consciously, perhaps unconsciously, what his needs may be. This decision will be controlled by his previous experiences, his capacities, and his present situation. These determinants will relate to biological processes, the general and the immediate environment, and previous habits of response.

In a narrow sense, the drive-reduction theory holds that deprivation —particularly of a biologically important factor such as water—produces an active condition of need in the organism. This need is reflected as a drive, a condition that may be interpreted psychologically as producing tension and physically as producing characteristic stimuli. The result is a willingness to act. If the deprivation is increased, the willingness to act is presumed to be increased; if the deprivation is decreased, the willingness to act is presumed to be lessened. In these terms, primary reinforcements are those that satisfy a need and thus reduce drive. Hence the term "incremental reinforcement" has come to mean punishment, because it results in an increase in need. Likewise, the term "decremental reinforcement" has come to mean reward, because it results in a decrease in need. It is probable that the terms *incremental* and *decremental* will continue to have wide usage, even if the drive-reduction theory of motivation is eventually found to be more limited in scope than commonly supposed today.

As has just been suggested, the need-reduction theory of motivation has not gained total acceptance by contemporary psychologists. Hilgard (1956) states that there are indeed some learning theorists "who have come to believe that, as a motivational model, the need-drive incentive pattern is actually misleading." Miller (1959) and Spence (1956) have also expressed serious reservations with respect to the drive-reduction concept as the exclusive motivation for learning. So, even in terms of primary reinforcement, explanations other than drive-reduction must now be sought.

Secondary Reinforcement

In addition to primary reinforcement, secondary reinforcement has also been recognized as a key element in the learning process. In secondary reinforcement, a formerly neutral element in a situation takes on reward or punishment effects of its own. Although disagreement exists as to the permanency of secondary reinforcement by itself, its immediate efficacy in learning situations has been effectively demonstrated. Thus the buzzer that presages the presence of food (primary reinforcer) may itself take on reward properties (secondary reinforcement). Once these formerly neutral stimuli have acquired a reward or punishment effect, they in turn can be used to motivate learning. Of great significance, particularly in the practical learning situation, is the finding that secondary reinforcers need not be drive-reducing.

As Hebb (1949) has pointed out, drive or motivation may determine the activity level of the subject but may not control the nature of the activity. Drive, then, is a basis for learning, but is not the sole determinant of learning. In this connection the experiment of Campbell and Sheffield (1953) is very pertinent. These experimenters kept experimental animals in a constant environment under two conditions: one in which food was always present, and one in which food was never present. In terms of the drive-reduction theory, one would have expected great activity in the rats during the period of food withholding, and relatively little activity during the period of food abundance. Campbell and Sheffield found, however, that there was little difference in activity in the two situations so long as the environment was kept constant. If, however, cues such as light and sound were introduced into the situation, the activity level of the hungry rats became greater than did the level of the well-fed rats. This experiment serves to point up the importance of the distinction between willingness to act (activity level) and direction of activity (cues and total situation).

We are reasonably confident today that a motivated subject in general learns more rapidly than a non-motivated subject. At the same time, we recognize that over-motivation can slow down learning, particularly if fine discrimination is involved. Finally, we believe that motivation which grows out of the task itself is preferable to motivation that is imposed in an external fashion. The issue of reward *vs.* punishment will be dealt with later. At this time, may it simply be noted that in general reward seems easier to control than does punishment.

The particular reinforcements that are effective in a particular learning situation constitute the specifics of learning. As Shelton, Arndt, and Miller (1961, p. 369) have said:

"The teacher who deals with students who already have many acquired drives, is faced not with a vague problem of motivation but with the problem of eliciting and reinforcing the behavior he wishes to develop. He must discover that for which the individual student will work. The presence of motivation or drive is not in itself sufficient to bring about learning."

Intermittent Reinforcement

In addition to selecting the most effective reinforcement, the teacher must also face the problem of when and in what pattern to administer the reinforcement. It is of great practical import whether the reinforcement should be constant or intermittent.

It has been demonstrated in situations that range, for example, from the relatively simple reinforcement of a rat in a maze to the relatively complex situation of shocking or not shocking an individual in a galvanic-skin-response situation, that intermittent or partial reinforcement produces a stronger type of learning than does 100% reinforcement. Indeed, so widely accepted has this point of view become, that the literature now recommends specific amounts of reinforcement, as for example 40% reinforcement, in certain learning situations.

To the conventionally trained learning theorists, the effectiveness of intermittent reinforcement has always been somewhat perplexing. Intuitively, it seems that the more consistently a response is rewarded the stronger this response would be. A partial answer is suggested in the following interpretation. Habit strength is frequently measured against the criterion of extinction. How is extinction defined in those test situations in which intermittent reinforcement is found to be more effective than 100% reinforcement? Typically, extinction is defined as the failure of the learned response to occur in the absence of reinforcement. Extinction thus becomes a particular measure of learned response failure.

If the subject has learned that a particular response will always be rewarded, then the non-rewarding of this response may well prove frustrating. On the other hand, if, in the learning process, the desired response is not always rewarded, but rewarded only intermittently, then the subject will probably not be frustrated by the sudden onset of unrewarded performances. That is, a subject trained by intermittent or partial reinforcement will be less frustrated by instances of non-reinforcement than will a subject trained by 100% reinforcement. Thus, if learning is measured against extinction, it is not surprising that partial reinforcement apparently produces greater learning than does 100% reinforcement. This is not to say, however, that the habit strength of partial reinforcement learning is greater than that of 100% reinforcement learning. This is only to say that resistance to extinction may be greater.

This concept is of extreme importance in the learning of speech and particularly in the learning of new and revised speech and language habits. It seems quite possible that many of the reinforcements of the user of language, of the stutterer for example, may be intermittent rather than complete. Does this intermittency of response strengthen or weaken the habit that is formed? What effect does this have on the teaching of a new response? Should we reward it intermittently or should we reward it 100%? Complete experimental answers to these questions are not presently available. Nevertheless, data now available begin to suggest the kinds of answers that we need.

Delay in Reinforcement

Another problem to be faced is the timing of the reward or punishment in relation to the response. In general, reward or punishment should be administered as quickly as possible after the response in order to secure maximum reinforcement or non-reinforcement effects. Nevertheless, it has been possible to demonstrate in the laboratory and in life that delayed reinforcements can also be effective. In the laboratory animal situation, the maximum effective time for reinforcement after response seems not to exceed some 30 seconds. One explanation for this possibility is the strong probability that any stimulus received by the nervous system reverberates in the system for a few seconds (of reverberated life). Reinforcement during the reverberation period may still be effective. In the human, particularly after the symbolic system is well developed, reinforcement may be delayed for almost unlimited lengths of time. But the fact that delayed reinforcement is possible even without an elaborate symbol system is of major importance in the learning of speech. It is quite probable that if all reinforcement had to be immediate, that is, to coincide with the existence of the objective stimulus or performance, the speech act in its present form would not emerge nearly as early as it does in the life of the infant.

Conflict

The effect of conflict on learning is well recognized. In the first place, conflict may reduce the amount of learning that takes place. This reduction of the amount or rate of learning may be accounted for in terms of such factors as a reduction in the potential activity level, a degrading effect on the relative effectiveness of cues, an impairment of discrimination factors, and a reduction in the predictability of reinforcement. Thus one effect of conflict may simply be that of reducing the amount of learning that takes place. The seriously disturbed child may simply not learn to use speech. But another effect of conflict may be to change the type of learning. Dollard and Miller (1950) have stressed the effects of approach-avoidance conflicts on learning. Stuttering, for example, has been treated by Sheehan (1958) as a type of verbal behavior that may be learned and maintained in double approach-avoidance conflict situations.

The true nature of conflict has not been particularly well established. An explanation offered by Mowrer (1960), and one that is reasonably compatible with the facts as now known, is that any one response or any one situation may involve a great number and variety of stimuli, some of which may at a particular point in time be pleasantly or unpleasantly conditioned. Thus, as the subject concentrates now on one and now on another set of stimuli, first one emotion or attitude will predominate and then another. This could easily account for the back-and-forth vacillations sometimes seen in a conflicted organism, as for example, the stutterer, and also explain why it is that such an organism is said to be of two minds. Perhaps conflict is the normal state of affairs. Perhaps only when all or at least a clear majority of the stimuli associated with a particular response or place become positive or negative does the individual become one-minded, unified, and organized.

Specific Training Factors

According to Dael Wolfle (1951), the following factors are known to be instrumental in determining the effectiveness of training: (1) knowledge of results, (2) avoidance of habit interference, (3) variety of practice materials, (4) methods used in training, (5) knowledge of principles involved, (6) effectiveness of guidance.

The evidence as to the importance of knowledge of results to the subject in a learning situation is overwhelming. Perhaps the classic experiments of this type were the early experiments of Thorndike (1927) and the later work of Trowbridge and Cason (1932) in line drawing. In the Trowbridge and Cason experiment, blindfolded subjects were asked to draw three-inch lines under four conditions: (a) no feedback from the experimenter, (b) a nonsense syllable said by the experimenter after each line, (c) a "right" or "wrong" response from the experimenter after each line, and (d) a descriptive response from the experimenter after each line in which the degree of error was precisely described. The experiment clearly demonstrated that no learning (increase in accuracy of the lines) occurred under conditions of no feedback or of nonsense syllable feedback, that learning did occur when the right or wrong evaluation was made, and that learning occurred still more rapidly when the discriminative response was given. In short, the more precise the knowledge of results, the greater the amount of learning.

Of great interest is the fact that the subjects who received no information nevertheless tended to standardize a response. This standardization, although not necessarily an improvement over the original line-drawing efforts, probably represents an attempt to duplicate internal standards of performance. Thus, in articulation problems, as has been suggested by Van Riper and Irwin (1958), one reason for the stability of an articulation error may be the fact that the child has ceased to pay attention to external feedback and is simply concentrating on his internal stimuli.

There are two possible explanations—not necessarily inconsistent—of the importance of knowledge of results to learning. One, of course, is that without such knowledge, it is impossible to modify subsequent performance meaningfully. The other explanation is that such knowledge is, in and of itself, rewarding. Skinner (1961) in his teaching-machines theory emphasizes this latter explanation. Van Riper and Irwin (1958) have developed a concept of voice and articulation therapy that emphasizes the importance of information feedback.

Irrespective, then, of precisely why knowledge of results is effective, we know that such knowledge is one essential to many learning situations.

Another factor cited by Wolfle (1951) is that of habit interference. The principle involved here is quite simple. Learning tends to be slower, more laborious, and less certain if it is necessary to master a number of alternative responses to approximately the same stimulus situation. The key word in the preceding sentence is *approximately*, for this problem does not occur if stimuli are markedly different or completely identical. This observation leads directly to the subject of discrimination and generalization.

It has been well established that both humans and animals, if placed in a learning situation, are able to function in both a generalized and a discriminate mode. We shall deal first with the generalized mode.

Assume that an experimental subject has learned to push a bar whenever he hears a thousand cycle tone. Now if the experimenter varies the frequency of the tone to either 1001 or 999 cycles, and presents this new tone to the subject, the subject will respond essentially as he did to the original tone. In experiments in which the effect of varying the frequency of the tone on the reaction of the subject has been thoroughly studied, it has been found that generally the more unlike the original tone the substitute tone is, the less likely the subject is to react to the substitute as to the original. Nevertheless, the effect described is gradual; the fall-away in response is plotted as a typical bell-shaped curve. This means, then, that in a wide variety of situations, subjects will react to stimuli that are reasonable approximations of the original stimuli as if they were the original stimuli.

At the same time, as is shown in Figure 6-3, the further the stimulus tone deviates from the original stimulus tone the more deviant the response tends to be. Note also that if the deviation is great enough, the subject may fail to respond at all. There is thus a limit to the degree of generalization; this limitation is related to the fact that individuals are not only able to generalize but also able to discriminate.

If two stimulus patterns A and C, as shown in Figure 6-4, are presented, the experimental subject will have no trouble discriminating between them. If he is asked to make one response to A, and another to C, no conflict will be involved. On the other hand, if two such patterns as represented by B and C are presented, the subject may find it difficult

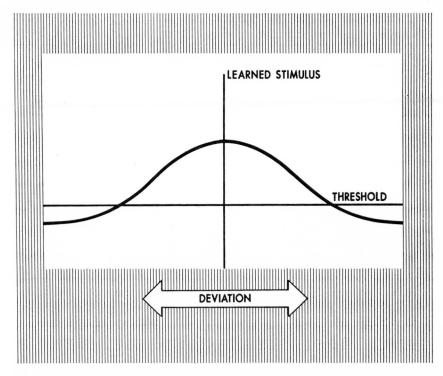

Figure 6-3. Stimulus Generalization.

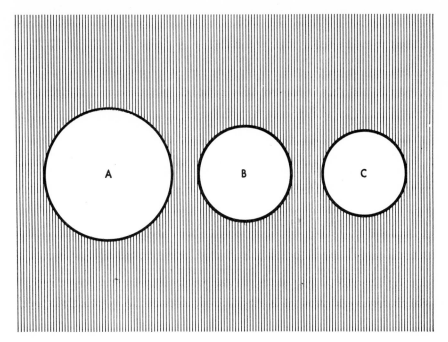

Figure 6-4. Stimulus Discrimination.

to decide which of the two patterns is present. His abilities both to discriminate and to generalize produce this conflict. This kind of interference with learning has been referred to under such terms as habit interference, negative transfer, and proactive and retroactive transfer.

Wolfle (1951) cites evidence to support the following two hypotheses concerning habit interference: (1) the greater the similarity between the two stimulating situations, the greater should be the similarity between the two responses if habit interference is to be avoided; (2) the greater the similarity between the two responses, the greater should be the similarity between the two stimulating situations if habit interference is to be avoided.

From these hypotheses it follows that both the stimulating situations and their responses should be made either as little alike as possible or as much alike as possible if learning is to proceed without such interference.

Habit interference arises when partially overlapping stimulus patterns are expected to elicit differentiated responses. In learning oral language, it is not surprising that homonyms—words having the same pronunciation but different meanings—are frequently confused. In this instance, identical stimulus patterns, so far as the isolated word is concerned, are expected to elicit different responses. Only when the homonym is introduced in context does the pattern become differentiable. And even in context the overlap of the basic word may still be confusing. The same phenomenon can also be observed as the child learns to say words that are the same except for one or two sounds. For example, *stroking* and *striking*, or *sliding* and *slicing* present a sufficient overlap of stimulus pattern to cause habit interference.

The evidence seems to suggest that the greatest habit interference occurs when two habits are partially learned and of approximately equal strength. This observation not only suggests why this problem occurs in the learning of language, but also suggests a remedy if the problem becomes severe. The preventive treatment is to withhold training on one of the competing systems until the other is well learned.

Another factor that influences learning is the variety of practice material. Careful experimentation has verified what one would intuitively expect: that is, practice materials should encompass so far as practicable the depth and breadth of the situations in which the learning is to be applied. This principle strongly suggests that speech improvement and remedial speech activities should be confined neither to nonsense syllables nor to isolated words, but should include actual speaking activities.

In the acquisition of skills, learning techniques may emphasize either the end product or the process. As children learn speech in the normal situation, the end product is emphasized. In remedial speech and speech improvement, it is sometimes desirable to emphasize the process as well. At present, evidence is not available which would enable us to generalize with confidence about the relative merits of the two techniques. As Wolfle (1951) has said:

It cannot be concluded, however, that emphasis on process is always desirable. A skilled act involves both motor and sensory components. On the motor side, skill consists of precise timing, coordination, and control of effort. On the sensory side, it requires a response to small changes in the stimulation. In some acts the controlling stimuli are self-initiated. The cutoff operator studied by Lindahl and the rifleman studied by English are examples. Although these subjects utilized other sensory data, their skill consisted of precise movements that were in large part controlled by the kinesthetic impulses aroused by the movements.

In some other acts the controlling stimuli are not self-initiated. Examples are: learning to follow in ballroom dancing, learning to parry an opponent in boxing or fencing, etc. Skill in these acts consists of coordinating one's movement with cues that are not self-initiated.

The way in which we learn these two kinds of skill and the best methods of teaching each may be quite different. Careful experimentation in this area is needed before we can know the best methods of teaching all possible skills.

The views of various learning theorists with respect to the relative effectiveness of reward and punishment cannot be brought into agreement. At an intuitive level, it would seem that reward and punishment are essentially equals and opposites. From this viewpoint, then, either would be equally effective: reward to facilitate behavior and punishment to inhibit behavior.

Later research by Thorndike (1932) did not confirm this equal and opposite concept. Indeed, Thorndike found punishment relatively much less effective than reward in modifying behavior. Despite some realization today that it would be possible to interpret Thorndike's data somewhat differently, the consensus still prevails (Hilgard, 1956) that reward is more effective than punishment as motivation for learning.

Even if, at a theoretical level, it does become possible to establish that punishment and reward are equally effective, in the practical situation the overwhelming social advantage of relying on reward seems to work against the wide, habitual use of punishment.

In addition to the factors already mentioned, several other variables enter into the effectiveness of learning. Space does not permit the development of each of these. In general, however, it should be noted that:

1. Tolerance for failure—in the sense of not permitting failing episodes to block future effort—can best be learned through the experiencing of both success and failure, through the discovery that one failure is not final.

2. The setting of a realistic goal—a goal compatible with ability time, or importance, for example—is preferable to either too high or too low a goal.

3. Active participation is usually more effective than passive observation, although Mowrer (1960) insists that it is possible to learn without doing.

4. Knowledge of the principles involved usually improves transfer of learning to new situations.

5. Repetitive practice seems essential for the learning of highly skilled acts.

6. Learning is dependent upon basic neurological prerequisites.

7. And, finally, individual differences in previous experience and in ability make tremendous differences in the learning process. The best learning aid is a good student.

LEARNING WITHOUT "DOING"

Of considerable theoretical and practical importance is the question of whether or not behavior can be learned by an individual without the individual ever executing the behavior in any active or voluntary meaning of the act. In the original discussions of learning, it was frequently asserted and popularly held that practice makes perfect. Interestingly enough, even this popular assertion carried with it a large measure of error. For example, in such a simple situation as dart-throwing, when one recognizes that a high percentage of the early throws do not hit the target and that a high percentage of the later throws do hit the target, one would almost be justified in concluding that what one has learned is not what one has practiced.

Mowrer's position with respect to this question of the possibility of learning without doing is this: He feels that a habit is essentially the facilitation of an action that produces pleasant stimuli. If it is possible to produce these stimuli in the subject without the subject actively performing the act, then the act can be learned without being "done." How is such stimulation—such learning—possible? Several examples suggest themselves.

A familiar example of this type of learning is that of teaching the dog to shake hands. One may begin by grasping the dog's paw with one's hand, shaking the paw up and down, releasing the paw, and then rewarding the dog with some tidbit. If this sequence of events is repeated several times, the dog may come to associate the internal stimuli from the paw movement with the possibility of reward to come. The active dog, then, who has come to like the hope engendered by these passive paw-moving sensations, may spontaneously move his own paw up and down. He is actively producing stimuli that have previously been produced passively. To the degree that the dog performs the act actively, to that extent has there been learning without active participation on the part of the dog.

In the field of speech, the situation is somewhat clearer. By bombarding the subject with particular speech sounds and by making this bombardment pleasant, either by expressions of affection while it is being done or by appropriate rewards during or subsequent to the act, the auditory stimuli growing out of the bombardment can take on a favorable value. Thus, without ever having made the sounds himself, the youngster may be in position to recognize these auditory stimuli when first he makes them himself, and, having recognized them, to have a habit.

In the learning of speech, it is extremely important that the type of acoustic events that we want the subject to learn be reinforced. To the extent that this can be done successfully, to that extent can the first appearance or production of a sound by the individual represent learning.

To hold, however, that one can learn without doing is not to say that one can learn that which cannot be done. That is, although one can learn that which he has not done, he is able to learn only that which he can do. This distinction becomes of considerable importance in certain learning situations. For example, can the chimpanzee be taught to use English? Apparently, despite the application of all that is now known about learning, the answer is "no." Why? Because the chimpanzee, we think, does not have the neurological equipment for speech. Not having the speech potential, he cannot complete the learning act.

In the education of the language handicapped, this question ceases to be of only academic importance. Speech pathologist and patient alike may be wasting time if the one seeks to teach the other language responses that, in the present circumstance, are impossible. Only those responses that can be made can be learned.

Of course, this is quite different from saying that a response that has not been made cannot be made. It is this difference, perhaps, that makes it possible for parents, teachers, and workers with the handicapped, to continue to make apparently fruitless efforts. Perhaps, in the individual case, the only valid test of what cannot be done is to discover what cannot be learned.

UNLEARNING

Thus far, of course, we have been dealing with the subject of learning. Of great interest to the teacher, the reformer, and the speech therapist, is the subject of unlearning. How do you unlearn habits, skills, and attitudes that have once been learned? You will recall that the original

Thorndikean explanation of unlearning was a stamping out of the bond between stimulus and response, although the precise nature of how this stamping out was to be accomplished was not stated. But if one accepts the point of view that all learning is sign learning, then the two basic mechanisms of unlearning almost automatically become those of counter-conditioning and extinction. Pavlov had demonstrated earlier that if a conditioned stimulus, as for example a light, is for a long period of trials not followed by food, then the animal ceases to salivate in the presence of the light. This dropping out of a previously established response is known as extinction. It was also established by Pavlov that if the conditioned stimulus, if related or if learned in conjunction with a pleasant response, were modified so as to be followed by an unpleasant response, the process known as counter-conditioning would result. In this process the original response fails to occur or is unlearned.

How then may unwanted language habits be unlearned? One approach is that of counter-conditioning. If any reward attached to the unwanted response can be recognized and if a certain unpleasant consequence can be substituted, the undesired language response can be eliminated. Less dramatic, but perhaps more effective in the day-in-and-day-out situation, is the application of the extinction process. In this instance, failure ever to reward the unwanted response would ultimately insure its deletion from the individual's responses. But the use of extinction in the practical language situation is not easy. A basic problem is that of determining the reward. Sheehan (1958), on the one hand, and Appelt (1929), on the other, have suggested two radically different interpretations of the reward resulting from that language behavior known as stuttering. To Sheehan, stuttering is rewarding because it is associated with a feeling of relief; to Appelt, stuttering is rewarding because it becomes a mechanism of self-justification for certain failures. So, finding the reward in and of itself is a difficult process in many instances. Once found or isolated, the withholding of the reward may prove equally difficult. In summary, it is not surprising that unlearning—except in the laboratory —is a difficult process. Let us hope that with increased knowledge of learning the necessity for unlearning will be lessened.

LEARNING LANGUAGE

It is possible to study the development of language from at least two viewpoints: the development of language by man and the development of language in the child. This section is concerned with the latter emphasis, that is, with how the child learns to use the language current in his environment.

It has been commonly asserted that the child learns language in either two or three stages. Russell (1927), for example, has upheld a two-stage development, the two stages being receptive and expressive use of language. Myklebust (1954), on the other hand, has described a three-stage development, the stages being, in order of genetic development, inner, receptive, and expressive. Inner language is defined as that language an individual uses autistically, that is, uses to talk to himself; receptive language, as that language an individual uses to understand others; and expressive language, as that language an individual uses to make himself understood by others. Myklebust believes that by 8 or 9 months the infant has enough inner language to begin to understand some of the spoken language he hears. By 12 or 13 months he begins to use language expressively.

In terms of learning theory, it has been somewhat easier to account for the receptive use of language than for the expressive use. Explanations for the acquisition of receptive language run somewhat as follows. A particular symbol, as for example the word *water,* becomes associated with a glass of water in such fashion that at least part of the reaction actually evoked by the glass of water becomes evocable by the stimulus *"water."* Thus, if a word is repeatedly heard in a temporally contiguous relationship with a physically present object, person, or idea, a part of the meaning of the object, person, or idea will become attached to the word.

But the explanation of the emergence of expressive language has not been clear. One possible explanation, of course, has been in terms of some version of Pavlov's classical conditioning. But it has been extremely difficult to devise an explanation for the first production of a word in these terms. It will be remembered that, so far as classical conditioning is concerned, learning was regarded as essentially a stimulus substitution. That is, that which was already in the repertoire of the individual was transferred to a new stimulus. But if the response is not present in the behavior of the individual, the possibility of such transfer seems remote! Since babies do not come equipped with ready-made words, classical conditioning could not very easily account for the expressive use of language.

The other alternative in conventional learning theory was some version of Thorndike's trial-and-error learning. In this conception, it was assumed that the individual would make a series of responses to a stimulus until it made one that was appropriate, that is, was reinforced. Here it was assumed that an infant more or less accidentally says *water* —or at least an utterance that the parents may accept as *water*—and then has his utterance reinforced, perhaps by being given a glass of water. Presumably the reward predisposes him to repeat the process. This explanation is simply a variant of Thorndike's "babble-luck" theory which presupposes that the infant in the course of babbling has the luck once in a while to make a noise that to others sounds like a word. Such a noise or word elicits attention or other rewarding behavior on the part of the parents. In this way, supposedly, the responses or the habits involved in speech are learned.

As one thinks coldly about the possibilities of this process actually taking place, one is forced to agree somewhat with Mowrer. Although not illogical or even impossible, it is highly improbable.

Mowrer (1960) has attempted to resolve this difficulty—that is, the improbability of the random emergence of the word—by suggesting that the auditory stimuli that compose a word become emotionally pleasant to the child even before he makes it because he hears it produced by a loved one in affectionate relationships. This point was given earlier discussion on p. 22. As noted, the stimuli—the words—are made pleasant and meaningful to the individual even before he makes any attempts to produce them himself. Thus, in the first production of the stimulus complex by the child he will recognize and enjoy his own production. The effect of this spontaneous and immediate recognition of his own saying of the word heightens the probability that he will single out this particular complex again. Perhaps the details of this explanation will become clearer if Mowrer's own explanation of the steps involved in teaching a bird to talk are reviewed here. As noted in the earlier discussion of the emergence of speech sounds, Mowrer has stated that the steps in teaching a bird to speak are: (1) make a pet of the bird; (2) make certain characteristic noises as one takes care of the bird; (3) these noises become "good" sounds and in the course of its own at first random vocalizations the bird will eventually make somewhat similar sounds; (4) by the principle of generalizations some of the derived satisfaction or pleasure which has become attached to the trainer's sounds will be experienced when the bird itself makes and hears like sounds. And when this begins to happen, the stage is set for the bird's learning to talk. Explanation: In learning theory initially neutral sounds by virtue of temporal contiguity with primary reinforcements have acquired secondary reinforcing properties.

This conception, as it now stands, is somewhat different from the trial-and-error approach of Thorndike. In particular, the randomness of the Thorndike concept is now reduced by Mowrer's presumption of a favorable feeling toward the word. This theory does not, or at least it so seems to the authors, completely explain the trial element of Thorndike's theory. That is, the explanation of how the correct stimuli are first produced by the child is still not entirely clear.

The explanation, as thus far given, accounts for the production of the sound by the infant, his recognition of the sound, and his pleasure in the recognition. Now, if in addition to the elements already described, the parents respond to the word production in ways that reinforce the behavior in a primary sense—as, for example, by bringing water when *water* is said—the infant will begin to use the word purposefully. Thorndike's law of effect thus enters into this second stage in the development of expressive language.

To review and summarize, Mowrer's concept of language learning assumes that certain auditory stimuli become pleasant to the child and acquire secondary reinforcement properties. The child—by a process that is still not entirely clear—makes these sounds himself and, because of his conditioning, recognizes what he has done and enjoys it. At this stage, the sound is still being made for the enjoyment of making the sound itself. Now, if the sound production is given primary reinforcement, the infant begins to use the sound in a truly expressive sense.

Once the child begins to learn language, the related functions of generalization and discrimination become tremendously important. Indeed, the importance of these processes is almost too obvious to need development here. Perhaps a few examples will suffice. As has been well established by the work of Moses (1939), for example, no one individual ever reproduces a sound in exactly the same way. It is still more true that different individuals do not produce the same sound in the same way. If the tendency to generalize were not fairly real, it would follow that each of us would have to learn to react not to a general phoneme of English, as for example the [t] phoneme, but to all the individual variants of the [t]. This would probably constitute a hopeless learning situation. Indeed, it almost seems safe to say that, were it not for this ability to generalize, the learning of language would not be possible. If you were not able to interpret the word *hungry* as said by your brother as being the same as said by your teacher, as being the same as said by the President on TV, language would be impractical.

Yet, vital as generalization is to the development of language, discrimination is equally so. For, if we could not discriminate at all, it would be impossible for us to develop—or recognize if we could develop—different phonemes. English is usually regarded as having some forty-odd phonemes. If no discrimination were possible, these some forty phonemes would all sound the same. We would lack the building blocks with which we make the morphemes of English.

Discrimination enables us to recognize different phonemes, different morphemes, and different morpheme combinations. Generalization enables us to recognize the common phonemic or morphemic element in utterances of different speakers and of the same speaker at different times. Discrimination makes language possible; generalization makes it practical.

It is clear, then, that difficulties in the process of learning language are many. Perhaps operant conditioning and teaching machines as exemplified by Skinner (1961) may indicate the threshold of a new element in language—and other—learning. But, until this or some other breakthrough is achieved, language learning will probably proceed haphazardly as it has in the past. The desire and need of man for language are apparently sufficient to carry him through the inadequacies of our present language learning techniques.

REFERENCES

Appelt, A. *Stammering and its permanent cure*. London: Methuen, 1929.

Brogden, W. J. Animal studies of learning. In S. S. Stevens (Ed.), *Handbook of experimental psychology*. New York: Wiley, 1951. Ch. 16.

Campbell, B. A., & Sheffield, F. D. Relation of random activity to food deprivation. *J. comp. physiol. Psychol.*, 1953, XLVI, 320-322.

Dollard, J., & Miller, N. E. *Personality and psychotherapy*. New York: McGraw-Hill, 1950.

Eisenson, J. Confirmation and information in rewards and punishments. *Arch. Psychol.*, 1935, 181.

Hebb, D. O. *The organization of behavior: a neuro-psychological theory*. New York: Wiley, 1949.

Hilgard, E. *Theories of learning*. New York: Appleton-Century-Crofts, 1956.

Hull, C. L. *Principles of behavior*. New York: Appleton-Century-Crofts, 1943.

Johnson, W. Introduction: the six men and the stuttering. In J. Eisenson (Ed.), *Stuttering, a symposium*. New York: Harper & Row, 1958.

Korzybski, A. *Science and sanity*. Lancaster, Pa.: International Non-Aristotelian Library Publishing Co., 1933.

Maier, N. R. F. Reasoning and learning. *Psychol. Rev.*, 1931, XXXVIII, 332-346.

Miller, N. Liberalization of basic S-R concepts. In S. Koch (Ed.), *Psychology: a study of science*. New York: McGraw-Hill, 1959.

Moses, E. R., Jr. Palatography and speech improvement. *J. Spch Disorders*, March, 1939, IV, 103-114.

Mowrer, O. H. *Learning theory and behavior*. New York: Wiley, 1960.

Mowrer, O. H. *Learning theory and the symbolic processes*. New York: Wiley, 1960.

Myklebust, H. R. *Auditory disorders in children*. New York: Grune & Stratton, 1954.

Myklebust, H. R. Aphasia in children. In L. E. Travis (Ed.), *Handbook of speech pathology*. New York: Appleton-Century-Crofts, 1957. Ch. 15.

Russell, B. *Philosophy*. New York: Norton, 1927.

Sapir, E. The status of linguistics as a science. *Language*, 1929, V, 207-214.

Sheehan, J. Conflict theory of stuttering. In J. Eisenson (Ed.), *Stuttering, a symposium*. New York: Harper & Row, 1958. Ch. 3.

Shelton, R. L., Arndt, W. B., & Miller, June. Learning principles and teaching of speech and language. *J. Spch and Hearing Disorders,* 1961, XXVI, 368-376.

Skinner, B. F. Teaching Machines. *Scientific American,* 1961, CCV, 90-102.

Spence, K. W. *Behavior theory and conditioning.* New Haven: Yale University Press, 1956.

Thorndike, E. L. *Educational psychology, vol. II: the psychology of learning.* New York: Teachers College, Columbia University, 1913.

Thorndike, E. L. The law of effect. *Amer. J. Psychol.,* 1927, XXXIX, 212-222.

Thorndike, E. L. Reward and punishment in animal learning. *Comp. Psychol. Monogr.,* 1932, VIII, No. 39.

Trowbridge, M. H., & Cason, H. An experimental study of Thorndike's theory of learning. *J. gen. Psychol.,* 1932, VII, 245-258.

Van Riper, C., & Irwin, J. V. *Voice and articulation.* Englewood Cliffs, N.J.: Prentice-Hall, 1958.

Wolfle, D. Training. In S. S. Stevens (Ed.), *Handbook of experimental psychology.* New York: Wiley, 1951.

7

How Linguistic Forms
Acquire Meanings

LANGUAGE UNITY

LEONARD BLOOMFIELD (1926) IN A FREQUENTLY cited statement describes an act of speech as an utterance. As has been repeatedly recognized, both in common-sense, day-to-day observation and in rigidly controlled scientific investigation, the standard utterances within a given speech community tend to be essentially alike. The particular concern of this chapter is the study of (a) those oral linguistic forms which are essentially alike and (b) those stimulus reaction features which are respectively alike in two or more successive utterances. In this sense any community that uses like—or nearly like—utterances is a speech community. The complete sum, the totality, of utterances that can be made in a speech community is the language of that speech community.

Bloomfield (1926) suggests that the language act may be conveniently analyzed under the following three headings:

A. A person reacts to certain stimuli.
B. This reaction may be in the form of speech.
C. This speech in turn stimulates his hearers (or himself) to certain reactions.

Within a given language community, the A, B, and C of the above breakdown acquire a close intracorrelation. Social habits beginning in infancy and continuing throughout life ensure the development and maintenance of these relationships. Bloomfield (1926) emphasizes that the stimuli, classified as A, and the reactions, classified as C, are very closely linked, as each person acts differently as a speaker or as a hearer. On the other hand, the linguistic features, classified as B, must be treated separately. As noted by Weiss (1918), the significant item in the above analysis of the speech process is that the reaction, C, may be either the adequate *reaction* to the total situation, or, on the other hand, may become the adequate *stimulus* for either another speech reaction or, for that matter, some other type of reaction.

Perhaps it may be well to make these concepts more specific. A given individual, John, may be exposed to the stimuli from his daily newspaper. As a result of these stimuli, John makes an utterance. Hearing this utterance, Jim reacts. Jim's reaction may be another utterance or may consist of some action such as walking out of the room. Whether Jim replies verbally or non-verbally, new stimuli have been presented to John, who may now react verbally or non-verbally himself. Or he may go back to his newspaper.

It follows that the linguistic forms of a language must have common signifiance to the users of a language if the A-B-C type of relationship is to prevail predictably. Unless the linguistic forms used by John and by Jim have a high common core of significance, A-B-C type relationships cannot be continued cooperatively. Of course, the degree of identity of significance is never 100 per cent. Yet this lack of completeness of identity should not blind us to the highly significant core of agreement that does obtain among the members of a language community. The important question then becomes: How do linguistic forms acquire their common meaning? Or, somewhat rephrased: What is the process that enables symbols, whether auditory, visual, or tactile, to function with such predictability? This is the question that this chapter will seek to answer.

Later we shall attempt to develop a more complete explanation of this predictability. For the moment, it may be worth noting that the social acts of man probably provide the essential basis for predictability of significance. Mead (1934, p. 7) defines a social act as one which involves "the cooperation of more than one individual, and whose object is defined by the act." It is, therefore, quite possible that the significant symbol— the symbol with predictable significance to users within a language community—arises primarily within such cooperative social acts. On the other hand, it has been strongly urged that symbols can arise also from competitive behavior. Morris (1946, p. 33), for example, defines the comsign in the following terms: "A sign which has the same signification to the organism which produces it that it has to other organisms stimulated by it will be called a comsign." He stipulates, however, that "it is by no means clear that comsigns can arise only in cooperative social behavior. Competitive and even symbiotic social behavior may be sufficient to account for the genesis of some comsigns."

Certain design features in communication have been discussed on pp. 108-9. Here, for purpose of emphasis, it is convenient to recognize two elements in the linguistic expression system, that is, in the B of the A-B-C analysis of Bloomfield. The two elements usually recognized in this expression system are *phonemes* and *morphemes*.

The phonemes are the basic elements of the expression system. Each phoneme, actually, consists of a *class* of very similar (but by no means identical) sounds. Each phoneme—or class—is usually treated as one sound and represented in phonetic transcription by one symbol. Each phoneme class tends to be distinctive, in the sense of differentiating one word from another. Phonemes, then, are the acoustical building blocks of the language. Depending upon the system of classification used, and upon the narrowness of transcription, the number of phonemes recognized in English will vary. In general, however, we may say that in English there are approximately 45 or 46 essential phonemes (Van Riper & Irwin, 1958).

These phonemes or sound-building blocks of a language may be put together in different sequences. The sequences within a given language are not randomly determined; certain sequences occur with much greater frequency than do others. Indeed, as pointed out in Kantner and West (1941), certain sequences are incompatible and do not occur at all. *Phonology* is the study of phonemes and of the sequences of phonemes (Gleason, 1955).

Since a phoneme is regarded as the minimum acoustic element of oral language, it follows that the phoneme is the element in the sequence that differentiates one thing as having been said from another thing that was not said. Thus the words *bit* and *bat* are differentiated from each other by their respective vowel phonemes.

Phonemes are features of the oral language, of the language as spoken. Phonetic transcription attempts to represent the phonemes of spoken language. A crudely analogous basic unit of the written language is the grapheme. But, from the standpoint of the present analysis, it must be kept in mind that the written language is really not an independent entity; it is a dependent extension of the spoken language.

As indicated earlier, the second division in the expression system of a language is the morpheme. Morphemes enter into a close, significant, predictable relationship with the content of language. In linguistics a morpheme is defined as a word (or stable part of a word) that conveys meaning. Morphemes are typically composed of one phoneme—as in the word *a*—or several phonemes—as in the word *encyclopedia*. *Grammar* is the term applied to the study of morphemes and their combinations.

From the standpoint of the present chapter, the importance of the distinction between morphemes (grammar) and phonemes (phonology) is that morphemes typically have meanings and phonemes typically do not.

Some partial exceptions to this distinction must be noted. Since it is the phonemic sequence that determines the particular morpheme, it may be argued that the phoneme does contribute to meaning. But this argument does not contradict the notion that the isolated phoneme is essentially meaningless, and that the isolated morpheme is essentially meaningful. In this connection, it should be recognized that an occasional phoneme acquires permanent morphemic characteristics. For example, "sh" has come to mean "Be quiet." But the meaning thus acquired is as a morpheme and not as a phoneme.

It should also be mentioned that sequence in and of itself is a heavy-handed determiner of meaning. Phonemes by themselves, as already developed, are essentially meaningless. Phonemes in proper sequence become morphemes. Isolated morphemes have some meaning. Morphemes in accepted sequence have considerably more meaning. Meaning, then, is in part a function of the symbol: that is, the morpheme; it is also in part a function of the sequence in which the morpheme appears.

To carry the idea of sequence somewhat further, Stuart (1946) insists that not until the appearance of nouns was real language possible. Stuart contends that nouns and nouns alone make propositions possible. Actually, it is not desirable to push Stuart's distinction too far, because even ancient grammarians quite clearly recognized that adjectives and substantives are closely connected. The classical terms for the two classes, nouns and adjectives, indicate the closeness of this relationship. The *nomen adiectiuum* (adjective) is simply the noun that is added to the *nomen substantium* (noun) in order to suggest some special quality which the noun displays in the particular situation to which the speaker refers: thus, black hair as opposed to gray hair.

Nevertheless, Stuart's insistence on the importance of propositionality is well taken. Eisenson (1957) has repeatedly stressed the importance of propositionality as opposed to non-propositionality in the speech of the stutterer and in the speech of the aphasic. Thus, to the extent that propositionality is proportionate to meaning, to that extent does the difficulty of the stutterer with fluency increase, to that extent does the difficulty of the aphasic exist.

Lerea (1958), writing partly as a speech pathologist, partly as a psychologist, and partly as a linguist, comments that it is possible to explain linguistic meaning as the sum of at least two components: lexicon and structure. Lerea adds that "the lexical meaning" of the word may be found in any dictionary. This lexical meaning, in the sense that Lerea is using the term, is the significance of the isolated word symbol. Of more importance, in the present context, is the term "structural meaning." Usually the term structural meaning refers to the relationship between the lexical elements in a particular utterance. Many examples of the effect of such relationships occur in English. In the example given by Lerea, the following statements occur:

1. The man found the black boot.
2. The bootblack found the man.

Obviously, the above sentences contain identical morphemes. Yet the two sentences would suggest to most users of English two entirely different meanings. Why? Simply because meaning in English is partly a function of morpheme and partly a function of morpheme sequence. The example here given is contrived to show the importance of sequence. Although contrived, it is not isolated in principle. The example, in short, should be considered as representative rather than as exceptional.

In oral language, variation in the use of stress also makes frequent and important contribution to meaning along with choice of morpheme and morpheme order. For example, note how the meaning of the following sentence changes, depending on the stress that is employed. In the examples as printed, the word parts to be stressed are shown in italics.

1. We like light *house*keeping.
2. We like *light*house keeping.

Clearly, the morphemes in sentence No. 1 and sentence No. 2 are identical and in the same order. Yet, in oral usage, the stress pattern tells the listener that No. 1 refers to a form of conventional residency and No. 2 to an occupation with marine overtones. On the printed page, differences in morpheme division may also give a visual clue.

Another example follows. The same code will be followed as in the above example. But, in this instance, the reader may make his own interpretation.

1. I saw a *black*snake pit.
2. I saw a black *snake*pit.

SYMBOLS: WHAT THEY ARE AND WHAT THEY DO

Semantics is concerned with the relations between the symbols of a language and their meaning. This definition should be carefully set apart from the definition of *general* semantics which is related to the many ways in which the meanings of words and other symbols change the responses of human beings to their environment and to each other.

It is probably desirable to review the distinction between symbols and signs. Whatmough (1956, p. 19) states: "Of symbols there is nothing in the nature of things that gives them the meaning stated; that is something *we* have given them, by agreement or convention, so that the symbol acquires a certain arbitrary character." Whatmough is here stressing the arbitrary nature of the true symbol. We must re-emphasize that there is no essential, basic, fundamental, necessary, inherent relationship between a symbol and its meaning. The relationship is arbitrary. It is a "created-by-man" relationship. It is a relationship that exists only among the users of a given language, among the speakers of a given language community.

Oddly enough, once a symbol has been designated by a language community, it tends to sound right. A table is called a table because a table is a table. Of course, if a table had been called a *glomph* by early speakers of our language, the argument would run that a glomph is called a glomph because a glomph is a glomph.

As indicated, once a symbol-referent pattern is established, it tends to be both accepted and relatively permanent. Yet language is not static. And one strong factor making for change is a linguistic form that is truly confusing to the users of a language. In such instances, one can predict that over sufficient time either the symbol or its referent will be changed.

Now a sign is something different from a symbol. Of signs, Whatmough (1956, p. 19) says: "A sign has a direct relation to its object, like water dripping from the trees is a sign of rain; but the *word* rain (which obviously is not rain or a sign of rain, for I can say it indoors or for that matter I can say it repeatedly even outdoors without getting wet) is a symbol of 'rain' or 'raining.'" Whatmough here stresses the basic difference between a sign and a symbol. The symbol has no inherent relationship to the meaning; the sign has a direct relationship to its object or its meaning. It follows, then, that it is extremely important to keep separate the symbol and the sign as one examines the ways in which linguistic forms acquire meaning. The symbol acquires its arbitrary meaning in a variety of arbitrary ways. The sign reveals its meaning in a series of non-arbitrary situations. The recognizer of a sign and the recognizer of a symbol have both achieved a learned experience. Essentially identical principles of learning, as developed in chapter 6, have made these experiences possible. But, although the learning principles are similar, that which is learned is quite dissimilar. The symbol-meaning is arbitrary; the sign-meaning, inescapably determined.

Morris (1946, p. 50) makes somewhat this same distinction, in his case using the terms *signal* and *symbol* as somewhat analogous to *sign* and *symbol*. Morris first quotes from Suzanne Langer: "A sign [that is, a signal] indicates the existence—past, present, or future—of a thing, event, or condition. . . ." Thus a term which is used as a sign evokes appropriate action in the presence of its object; a term that is used as a symbol need not evoke such action.

Morris then continues this discussion by stating that signals [signs] announce their objects while symbols lead their interpreters to conceive their objects. He concludes, on the basis of this distinction, that the symbol is on the whole a less reliable term than is a sign. He further points out that when a term is not reliable, behavior becomes naturally hesitant. In summary, then, (a) signs indicate existence more closely than do symbols, (b) signs are likely to be less general than symbols, (c) signs and behavior are more closely tied together, and (d) the effect of both signs and symbols depends upon motivation. Having drawn this distinction between the sign and the symbol, and recognizing that in linguistic form we are dealing primarily with the symbol rather than with the sign, we must also recognize the danger of concentrating on what Morris calls the spoken-heard sign.

It is probably true, as many linguists have insisted, that the spoken language is the basis of symbolic function. It is also true, however, that in our age, an age in which such visual media as cinematography and still photography, television, printing, and painting flourish, it is extremely important not to neglect the visual sign. Fortunately, the analysis here presented, although framed in terms of the spoken-heard symbol, appears to be equally true of all symbols. The printed word, the trademark, the arbitrary tonal or visual symbol of the radio or television show —each derives its symbolic function in a manner analogous to that of the spoken word. Of course, visual signs, like heard signs, have a non-arbitrary relationship that differentiates them from visual symbols.

How are symbols actually used, whether these be visual or heard symbols? One important use of the symbol is that of eliciting a specific meaning. Eisenson (1957) stresses that most intelligent and normal human beings learn to use language symbols with sufficient proficiency to elicit specific responses. That is, these individuals learn to express specific ideas through symbols according to the needs of various situations. In this sense, a symbol, a short sequence of symbols, or even a long sequence of symbols, may be said to have *cognitive* meaning. That is, it stimulates information—whether true or false—as do statements from textbooks, from mathematics, and from commentators.

In addition, however, symbols may also be used to elicit emotional responses, whether mild or strong, whether sweet or harsh. Such use may be referred to as the *emotive* use of symbols. It is perhaps obvious that in a particular sequence of symbols, both a specific and an emotional meaning may be conveyed, although typically one or the other of these may predominate.

In addition, a third use of symbols is frequently recognized in which the symbol is used to give a request, a command, or an order. This usage of symbols is referred to as the *directive* usage. These three usages, then, the cognitive, the emotive, and the directive, are the three broad applications of symbols that are typically recognized.

In addition, however, certain specialized uses of symbols have been recognized. There may be some question as to the legitimacy of these additional functions, but there can be little question of their existence. The first of these may be called the *ambi-meaning* use of symbols. Here, the evoker *seeks deliberately to put his morpheme sequence together in such fashion as to create a possibility of different interpretations in the mind of his listener.* If such ambi-meaning results accidentally, we have simply poor cognitive use of language, poor directive use of language, or poor emotive use of language. But if such ambi-meaning is the intent of the evoker, then we have a deliberate, specialized function. Under what circumstances would ambi-meaning be the intent of the evoker? In situations in which the evoker is unable or unwilling to commit himself, and in which he may feel an inability or unwillingness of his listener to commit himself, it may be desirable for both evoker and reacter to deal in morpheme sequences of ambiguous reference. More high-level political utterances and academic profundities than we like to admit can be classified as ambi-meaning in nature.

Another classification is the *quasi-meaning*. Phatic communion [1] is one example of this type of interchange. In such usage, highly conventionalized morpheme sequences are presented in situations in which the complete sequence is recognized as having a conventionalized meaning, this conventionalized meaning not necessarily being the true referent either of the individual morphemes or of their order. Fortunately, morphemes are used in this quasi-meaning sense in such stylized fashion that both evoker and reacter usually recognize the intent and situation. If taken literally, such quasi-meaning would frequently be impossible to comprehend. That is, even an observer who is familiar with the lexical meanings of the isolated symbols and the usual effects of sequence on the symbols, would be unable to interpret correctly the reactions to such quasi-meaning communications. For example, a current teenage expression is: "piling up the z's." Like most such expressions, this one will probably have a blessedly short existence. Users of English may have difficulty in interpreting this example of quasi-meaning. For those who

[1] "The term *phatic communion* Bronislaw Malinowski gave to speech which is used to establish the bonds of social communion between individuals. Greetings, pretty compliments, pleasantries, jests, all serve to create a pleasant social atmosphere." (Black & Moore, 1955, pp. 162-3)

are curious, the phrase means "sleeping." A heavy-handed adult explanation of this transient literary blight is that it is based on the representation of sleep in cartoons and the funnies by a series of z's.

Finally, the *contra-meaning* of symbols must be recognized. Again, in certain instances, perhaps for humor, perhaps for threat, the evoker will employ a phoneme sequence in a situation in which the exact opposite of the usual signification of the phonemes and their sequence would indicate. Usually, total context plus, in oral speech at least, inflection and facial expression, reveal the contra-meaning use of symbols. This is a dangerous technique. If used well, it is effective. If used poorly, its effects can be disastrous. The sleepy hostess who, long after midnight, says, "I'm so sorry that you have to go," is sometimes an example of this phenomenon.

If one tries to generalize and to pull together larger functions of symbols on the basis of the specific uses here indicated, one recognizes, of course, that language is used to communicate. But, as indicated on pp. 20-1, this is probably not the basic use of language. Perhaps more fundamental is the fact that language enables man to see reality symbolically. To the general semanticist, a disturbing aspect of this function is that symbolic reality may misinterpret objective reality. If such symbolic distortions are not recognized as such, the reaction of humans to their physical environment and to each other will be complicated. To the general semanticist, this is the problem that grows from this usage of language.

As a consequence, users of linguistic forms will derive at least two kinds of satisfaction from the successful employment of these forms. First, there will be what may be termed an objective value. Thus, in the successful use of linguistic forms, the evoker and the reacter may achieve these definite advantages. As Black and Moore (1955, p. 7) state: "(1) Words introduce a refined method of analysis into thinking. (2) They provide a basis of inference, of reaching conclusions not demonstrable to the senses. (3) They make it possible for the mind to conceive the complex rational systems of the world (science, metaphysics, logic, etc. with their many subdivisions)." Perhaps more simply, the objective value of a language enables the user to express his wishes in such way that he may receive them. Such language represents a tremendous extension of the individual's control of his environment.

But, in addition, the successful use of linguistic forms brings subjective values. As will be recalled from the preceding chapter, linguistic forms—as morphemes and language sequences—can acquire secondary reinforcing values. Certain words feel and sound "good." Certain words feel and sound "bad." By verbalizing, then, an experienced user of a language can achieve real subjective satisfactions.

COMMUNICATION: A SYMBOL FUNCTION

It is, of course, recognized that communication is a major function of language. Indeed, to the naïve observer of the language process, communication is the sole function of language. Surprisingly enough, however, there is considerable disagreement as to the mode of communication in symbolic function. Whatmough (1956), for example, suggests that in linguistic communication meaning is conveyed from one person to another. This tends to suggest that linguistic symbols, linguistic forms, may be thought of as buckets that somehow or other pick up meaning from the mind of one person, carry this meaning to the mind of another person, and there spill it. There is probably a certain accuracy and cogency in this bucket brigade concept of communication.

Yet it seems likely that the mode of transfer may be accurately viewed in the following sense. Rather than defining the transfer of meaning as being something that occurs from one person to another person, it may be more accurate to regard it, as has Mowrer (1960), as a transfer from one sign to another sign. This distinction emphasizes that if we are to communicate effectively with another individual, that other person must already have—and have neatly related to appropriate linguistic symbols— those meanings with which we shall be dealing. That is, unless the respondent, the reactor, already has meanings related to the symbols used by the evoker, communication stumbles. Examples of this difficulty occur daily in our attempts to communicate with Communist leaders. Words such as "democracy," "freedom," and "elections" seem to have no common significance. Thus, the communicative act may be viewed for the most part as merely changing the signs to which particular meanings are attached, merely shifting or transferring meanings from one sign to another.

HOW SYMBOLS ARE LEARNED

The basic learning process by which symbols acquire arbitrary meaning has been discussed in chapter 6. Essentially, what we have is a variety of symbol learning or conditioning. As described previously, if the linguistic form occurs in a situation contiguous to an already established meaning, or experience, the individual ultimately will react to the new symbol as to the old symbol or as to the complete experience.

In the life of the child, this learning experience ordinarily occurs in one of two situations: a formal explanatory situation, or a repeated contextual situation. In the formal explanatory situation, a parent, teacher, peer, or TV ad man seeks to define the meaning of a new or unfamiliar word. In these formal explanatory situations, the word is usually isolated clearly in order that recognition of the symbol will be complete. This isolation may take the form of repeating the word visually or audibly several times, of spelling the word, of saying it with a peculiar voice or inflection, or of printing it with unusually large letters. Thus the linguistic form to be learned is carefully isolated. Concurrently a meaning is related to the symbol. This meaning may be verbal, that is, the new symbol is related to a previously understood verbal sequence. For example, in explaining the word *orange,* the teacher may explain that it is a color, that it is a color something like red and something like yellow. Or, in the demonstration type definition, the teacher would isolate the term *orange* and then point out examples of orange in the child's environment. This formal explanatory situation remains important throughout life. Perhaps it is of greatest importance in infancy and early childhood, but it is a learning experience that most of us continue to experience in later years.

The second major form of learning linguistic forms is the repeated contextual experience. In this circumstance, the listener experiences the new word in a variety of situations. If he is fortunate, these situations will have certain similar elements and certain dissimilar elements. Ultimately, he is able to piece together the similar and separate out the dissimilar and then grasp what the new word means. This is perhaps the more usual way for older children and adults to relate an arbitrary significance to a linguistic form. After hearing a new symbol used in several different contexts, the experienced user of a language will feel some confidence in the meaning.

Both the formal explanatory and the repeated contextual approach usually involve a second phase, that of usage of the symbol. The second phase is most clearly evident in the formal learning situation. The teacher, after completing the explanation, usually suggests that the learner attempt usage of the new form in either a structured or a non-structured situation. In the contextual situation, opportunity for usage usually is not given. Such usage frequently comes spontaneously, and may result in unfortunate experiences. For example, the TV-devoted, young daughter of one of the authors referred only to "decorator colors." Any color that she mentioned in a room, in a car, in a landscape, was a "decorator color." Out of her contextual experiences, probably in TV, she had apparently learned the idiom or phrase "decorator color" as one symbol meaning color.

As the above example suggests, an important aspect of usage is the act of *monitoring* and—if necessary—correction. Language learning is not complete until usage has been checked against the standards of the language community. Self-monitoring is the final test of language learning.

REFERENCES

Berry, Mildred, & Eisenson, J. *Speech disorders*. New York: Appleton-Century-Crofts, 1956.

Black, J. W., & Moore, W. E. *Speech*. New York: McGraw-Hill, 1955.

Bloomfield, L. A set of postulates for the science of language. *Language*, 1926, II, 153-164.

Eisenson, J. Aphasia in adults. In L. E. Travis (Ed.), *Handbook of speech pathology*. New York: Appleton-Century-Crofts, 1957. Ch. 12.

Gleason, H. A. *An introduction to descriptive linguistics*. New York: Holt, Rinehart, and Winston, 1955.

Kantner, C. E., & West, R. W. *Phonetics*. New York: Harper, 1941.

Lerea, L. Assessing language development. *J. Spch and Hearing Res.*, 1958, I, 75-85.

Mead, G. H. *Mind, self, and society*. Chicago: University of Chicago Press, 1934.

Morris, C. *Signs, language, and behavior*. Englewood Cliffs, N. J.: Prentice-Hall, 1946.

Mowrer, O. H. *Learning theory and the symbolic processes*. New York: Wiley, 1960.

Stewart, G. R. *Man, an autobiography*. New York: Random House, 1946.

Van Riper, C., & Irwin, J. V. *Voice and articulation*. Englewood Cliffs, N. J.: Prentice-Hall, 1958.

Weiss, A. P. Conscious behavior. *J. Philos. Psychol. Sci. Meth.*, 1918, XV, 631-641.

Whatmough, J. *Language*. New York: New American Library, 1956.

8

Speech and Thought

THE RELATIONSHIPS OF SPEECH and thought are fascinating, vital, provocative, and—for the moment—not completely resolvable. No one is quite
prepared to say precisely what happens as you begin to decide whether
to drive or take the bus to college, attempt to solve a problem in the
laboratory, try to understand the meaning of a conversation that you had
this morning, or seek to make up your mind about which of two people
you should marry. In each of the above instances you must—it is to be
hoped—think. But in the above instances must you also speak—at least
implicitly—to yourself? If you spoke differently, would you think differently? If you couldn't speak, could you think at all? These are the
kinds of questions this chapter seeks to answer.

At one extreme is Watson who, in his famous *Behavior: An Introduction to Comparative Psychology* (1914), describes thinking as implicit
movement of the speech musculature. At the other extreme is Wertheimer
who, in his widely recognized *Productive Thinking* (1945), takes little
notice of the verbal or speaking aspects of thinking.

It may ultimately prove to be true that individual differences among
people make impossible a single, definitive answer to these questions.
That is, it may be that for some people thinking is a verbal process; perhaps for others, at other times or in other activities, a non-verbal process.
Some of the more important relationships between speech and thought
will now be introduced and developed.

The first viewpoint to be examined will be Watson's suggestion that
speech and thought are identical. Next to be discussed is the belief that
speech and thought are closely related, but not identical. The third
viewpoint to be considered here is that speech and language are simply
the expression of thought. Finally, the notion that speech and thought
are not particularly closely related will be brought forward.

THOUGHT AS IMPLICIT SPEECH

Watson (1914) stated that thoughts, ideas, and images are merely implicit verbal responses. He described the thought process as actually consisting of slight movements of the speech apparatus. Thinking was thus viewed as slight movements of the speech apparatus, and so as sub-vocal talking. This concept stimulated investigators to attempt to secure a record of the thinking process by using pick-up instruments on the speech mechanism. Early attempts made use of relatively crude techniques such as tambours and lever systems applied to the tongue. The results were inconclusive, since slight speech movements occurred during some but not all sub-vocal speech, and since the pattern of a whispered phrase was usually not the same as the pattern of the same phrase when it was merely thought.

More sensitive recording techniques were introduced. Electromyograms, that is, recordings of the electrical component of muscular activity, were made from various speech muscles while subjects performed relatively simple thinking tasks, such as reciting silently from memory. In situations such as these, EMG's were sometimes picked up from the tongue and lips. Unfortunately, EMG's were not always found in the speech muscles and, still more unfortunately, were sometimes picked up in non-speaking areas such as the arms.

It was perhaps natural that proponents of this viewpoint would attempt to record EMG's from the forearms of mutes who used manual signs in communicating. Interestingly enough, it was found that in many mental activities—such as memorizing—EMG's were picked up from the forearms, suggesting the possibility of "sub-manual" as well as sub-vocal speech (Max, 1937).

Some of the experiments suggested that the electromyographic activity—whether "sub-vocal" or "sub-manual"—tended to vary directly with the apparent tension of the subject. But hearing subjects, who served as controls, failed to display similar electromyographic activity, even under tension (Max, 1937).

In general, however, as noted by Woodworth and Schlosberg (1954), the evidence for implicit speech always being present during thinking was not very convincing.

THOUGHT AND SPEECH AS CLOSELY RELATED

Many scholars who have examined the relationships between thought and speech regard the two as separate aspects of an essentially single process. That is, although they do not regard thought and speech as identical, they do believe that the two interact so intimately as to make the one usually affect the other.

In particular, it has been frequently suggested that the organization and structure of a given individual's native language will pre-determine the organization and structure of his thinking. Sapir (1929, p. 210) has stated this idea in the following words:

. . . Human beings do not live in the objective world alone, nor alone in the world of social activity as ordinarily understood, but are very much at the mercy of the particular language which has become the medium of expression for their society. It is quite an illusion to imagine that one adjusts to reality essentially without the use of language and that language is merely an incidental means of solving specific problems of communication or reflection. The fact of the matter is that the "real world" is to a large extent unconsciously built up on the language habits of the group.

Sapir is thus suggesting that much of our perceptual experience, even of the external world, is determined not exclusively by such physical stimuli as light and sound but also by our learned language behavior.

The same basic idea has been expressed with equal vigor by Nolan D. C. Lewis in the preface to *Language and Thought in Schizophrenia* (1946, pp. vi-vii):

Every language used by a people has its own characteristic framework of established distinctions, its shapes and forms of thought into which, for the one who learns that language as his "native tongue," are cast the contents of his mind, his mass of acquired impressions, and his knowledge of the environment. This is brought about as a result of external influence; it is imposed from without, and is associated with the process by which the individual acquires the material of expression itself. It is not a product of his free, undirected, internal forces; his mind has been led to view the things and to group them in certain ways and to contemplate them consciously in those particular relations.

This same theme is developed by Benjamin Whorf (1941, p. 251): "We cut up and organize the spread and flow of events as we do, largely because, through our mother tongue, we are parties to an agreement to do so, not because nature itself is segmented in exactly that way for all to see. Our language, then, may affect even our perception of language." Thus, predication, as a test of true language behavior, is most likely to be employed by a scientist whose language manifests predication.

In essence these writers are suggesting, as noted by Whatmough (1956), that we are bound hand and foot by our linguistic habits, "that our model of the universe is merely our language, English or Navaho as the case may be." Stated in perhaps more familiar terms, the world of reality can be perceived only through symbols; the symbols available and the probabilities of their relationships place blinders on the perceptive process. In this sense language may be thought of as the window through which we view the world; the world we see, then, is in large part a function of the particular window through which we look.

Not all scholars accept the pre-determining influence of language. To some, it seems equally reasonable that the kind of world we live in will determine the kind of window that we build. Whatmough (1956, p. 84) has stated this most succinctly:

> There is a specious half-truth, but no more, in the view that meaning is controlled by the very grammatical structure of a particular language. It seems more likely that in standard average European the structure of language has been made to correspond with what the speakers of it have discovered about their universe, and that what they believe about it depends not only upon the structure of the universe itself but on free inquiry.

LANGUAGE AS EXPRESSION OF THOUGHT

Another, and at least somewhat different, point of view is that speech is essentially the expression of thought. In this sense, which may not be too different from that of Whatmough (1956), language is neither part of nor controller of thought; it is, rather, a vehicle, a tool, an instrument of thought. Lewis (1946, pp. v-vi) states:

> All students are agreed that language is the expression of human thought. It is "natural to man." From the highest civilized persons to the most belated primitives, all men speak in some fashion and are able to interchange such thoughts as they possess. . . . In the broadest sense, it might include, besides audible signs of thought such as words and sentences, all the other ways of communication—gestures, postures, facial expressions, and so on. If language is but the instrument for the expression of thought, it then comes to be just what the users make of it.

It is worth noting that, in his statement, Lewis is careful to extend the meaning of language to include not only the audible but also the visual means of communication.

LANGUAGE AND SPEECH NOT ESSENTIAL TO EACH OTHER

A possible point of view, of course, is that language and speech are not essential to each other. Much of the theorizing that has been done on this point has been concerned with the thinking and language abilities of animals. In its most straightforward form, the argument takes this form:

> Animals think.
> Yet, animals do not have language.
> Therefore, language is not necessary for thought.

Obviously it is possible to challenge this argument on at least two points. One may deny that animals do think; or one may deny that they do not have language. A second argument, that animals do have language but do not think, and that therefore thought is not necessary for speech, is seldom developed, partly because it poses a mutual contradiction and partly because it is not particularly germane to the argument.

Do animals think? The answer to this question is partly a matter of definition. If one defines thinking functionally—and emphasizes change in behavior that is not trial and error—it seems possible to establish that animals think. Hobhouse (1901), Yerkes (1928), and Köhler (1927) have all demonstrated evidence that animals think—in the functional terms referred to here. But if one defines thinking in terms of higher orders of abstraction—whether symbolic or sub-symbolic—it becomes increasingly difficult to establish that animals think. Certainly, if one defines thinking in terms of duplicating the mental processes of man both in kind and degree, the case becomes clear that animals do not think.

The answer to the question, "Do animals think?" varies, then, more in terms of the definition of thinking employed than with the evidence that is available. There is considerable agreement about the data; there is considerable disagreement about the definition.

To the authors of this book it seems most reasonable to conclude that animals are capable of at least a crude kind of thinking. For example, Muenzinger's work (1938) with what he has termed vicarious trial and error (VTE) offers an interesting example of at least a simplified type of thinking in animals. In running a maze a rat may, at crucial points of decision, turn his head back and forth in the directions of possible choices but not actually move in any of the directions. It has been observed that these VTE are typically not present in the initial trials of the rat nor in those trials made after the response has been learned. Rather, the VTE occur primarily in the pre-fixing trials. Why? One interpretation is that in the initial trials the rat does not have enough information to make sampling of his impressions helpful, and that after he has learned the maze, there is no need to sample his impressions. In the pre-fixing stages, however, the extra stimuli apparently help him to think.

Mowrer (1960) suggests that the stimuli resulting from VTE are sought "not for information inherent in them but because they are conditioned to affective states which will then serve to guide the subsequent course of overt behavior." Mowrer concludes that animals can apparently make plans for future action when such plans are based upon spatial arrangements.

The second assertion in the basic argument holds that animals do not have language. Again, it must be remembered that this is partly a matter of definition. Certainly, as will be developed in considerable detail (see pp. 157-9), animals—at least in some interpretations—communicate with each other. According to Mowrer (1960) and to Darwin (1873) animals vocalize in at least four conditions: if trapped, if mother and young are separated, if seeking a mate, and if fighting. In addition, certain predators vocalize when making the kill. It is suggested that animals remain basically quiet in order to survive. Many domesticated animals vocalize more freely than wild animals. This increased vocalization may represent the security and—particularly in the case of the dog—the responsibility of belonging.

Morris (1946) then raises the question of whether or not language is unique to man. He avoids a clearcut answer to this question. Morris concludes that language behavior is sign behavior and that language signs rest upon and never completely take the place of the simpler signs which they presuppose. Thus he interprets the continuity between man's and animal's use of signs to be as real as the discontinuity, and the similarity of human and animal signs-behavior to be as genuine as the difference.

Why then do animals other than man not talk as man talks? Several factors suggest themselves. First, as is clearly implied in the Hayes' (1952) description of the ape who lived in their house, many animals lack the voluntary control of the speech mechanism necessary for a multiphonemic language. Thus, as has been developed elsewhere in this book, one cannot *learn* what one cannot *do*. Second, the intellectual ability of animals in general is probably inadequate to the full needs of a complex oral language. Finally, the social development of animals does not require an elaborate symbolic representation. As Mowrer (1960, p. 162) states:

A subtle interplay of neurological and social evolution does seem to have provided the conditions for the development of the symbolic attitude and fully articulate speech. Language is thus truly a miracle, not only in terms of what it can do but also in terms of the improbability of its emergence.

Irrespective of the validity of the above explanations, it must be agreed that, by any complete test, animals do not have language. It is difficult if not impossible to demonstrate predication in the speech of animals. It seems fair to agree with Lewis (1946, pp. v-vi):

Moreover, man is the sole possessor of language as such. A certain degree of power of communication, sufficient for the comparatively restricted needs of their gregarious intercourse, is displayed also by many species of the lower animals; but these types of response are not only greatly inferior in their degree to human language, they are also so radically diverse in kind that the same name cannot with justice be applied to both.

If, then, the reader cares to accept the conclusions suggested, namely, that animals do think and that animals do not have language, it follows that at least a primitive type of thought is possible without language.

At least a limited amount of evidence is available from human behavior to suggest that thinking is possible without language. Meyers (1948) reported that dysphasic patients, in spite of a severe loss of speech due to cerebral lesions, were not significantly inferior to normals in the solution of non-verbal problems similar to those used by Yerkes. An interesting example of the retention of the ability to solve non-verbal problems by an aphasic with almost complete loss of propositional speech was observed by one of the authors. Upon returning to his office with the aphasic after a coffee break, it was discovered that the "absent-minded professor" had left the keys to the office in the office. Even before the speech man could find speech to explain the predicament, the speech-handicapped member of the pair perceived the situation, dashed through an adjoining open office, climbed out on a ledge, walked along the ledge to the open window of the locked office, and came through and opened the door.

The work of Duncker (1945) and of Wertheimer (1945) in configurational theories of thinking has revealed that much human thinking is based upon referential restrictions that are governed by essentially non-verbal restrictions.

CREATIVE THINKING

Unfortunately, too little is yet known about the essential elements of creative thinking. It seems almost a truism that language facilitates such thinking. Yet it is interesting that Leeper (1951), in his excellent chapter on cognitive processes, treats inventive concept formation without specific reference to language.

According to Leeper (1951), inventive concept formation is favored especially by: (1) certain species characteristics, (2) adequate motivation, (3) long-continued effort, (4) relevant knowledge and skills, (5) definition of the functional value the solution must serve, and (6) favorable "directions." Inventive thinking often is handicapped, on the other hand, by the lack of these. Several studies call attention particularly to the hampering influence of (1) too strong motivation, (2) a "functional imbeddedness" of elements needed for the solution, and (3) faulty "directions."

And Graham Wallas (1926) also fails to list language as an isolated prerequisite to creative thought. The four stages of creative thought listed by Wallas are: preparation, incubation, illumination, and verification, in which the stages may overlap in time.

Language, if one avoids the traps of extreme definition and isolated example, may be regarded as an exceedingly useful, if not necessary, ingredient to thinking. Unfortunately, not only can it not be established that language is a prerequisite to thought, but it must also be frankly admitted that the use of language in any given instance is not in and of itself evidence of creative thinking. Much of our daily use of language may be regarded as automatic, over-learned, stereotyped redundancy. Such reflexive language frequently serves in our culture as an acceptable—perhaps preferred—substitute for reflective thinking. Yet, although language—in extreme view—may be neither a prerequisite for nor a guarantee of thought, it is difficult to overemphasize the facilitative relationships of speech and thought.

REFERENCES

Darwin, C. *The expression of the emotions in man and animals.* New York: Appleton-Century-Crofts, 1873.

Duncker, K. On problem-solving. *Psychol. Monogr.,* 1945, LVIII, No. 270. (Translated by L. S. Lees from 1935 original.)

Hayes, K. J., and Hayes, Cathy. Imitation in a home-reared chimpanzee. *J. Comp. Physiol. Psychol.,* 1952, XLV, 450-459, 108 ff.

Hobhouse, L. T. *Mind in evolution.* New York: Macmillan, 1901.

Kohler, W. *The mentality of apes.* New York: Harcourt, Brace & World, 1927.

Leeper, R. Cognitive processes. In S. S. Stevens (Ed.), *Handbook of experimental psychology.* New York: Wiley, 1951. Ch. 19.

Lewis, N. D. C. Preface. In J. S. Kasanin (Ed.), *Language and thought in schizophrenia.* Berkeley: University of California Press, 1946.

Max, L. W. Action current responses of the deaf during awakening kinesthetic imagery and abstract thinking. *J. comp. Psychol.,* 1937, XXIV, 301-344.

Meyers, R. Relation of thinking and language: an experimental approach, using dysphasic patients. *Arch. Neurol. Psychiat.,* 1948, LX, 119-139.

Morris, C. *Signs, language, and behavior.* Englewood Cliffs, N. J.: Prentice-Hall, 1946.

Mowrer, O. H. *Learning theory and the symbolic processes.* New York: Wiley, 1960.

Muenzinger, K. F. Vicarious trial and error at a point of choice. *J. Genet. Psychol.,* 1938, LIII, 75-86.

Sapir, E. The status of linguistics as a science. *Language,* 1929, V, 207-214.

Wallas, G. *The art of thought.* New York: Harcourt, Brace & World, 1926.

Watson, J. B. *Behavior, an introduction to comparative psychology.* New York: Holt, Rinehart, and Winston, 1914.

Wertheimer, M. *Productive thinking.* New York: Harper & Row, 1945.

Whatmough, J. *Language.* New York: New American Library, 1956.

Whorf, B. Languages and logic. *Technolog. Rev.,* 1941, XLIII, 250-252 ff.

Woodworth, R. S., & Schlosberg, H. *Experimental psychology.* New York: Holt, Rinehart, and Winston, 1954.

Yerkes, R. M., & Yerkes, D. N. Concerning memory in the chimpanzee. *J. Comp. Psychol.,* 1928, VIII, 237-271.

III.

THE COMMUNICATIVE PROCESS

9

The Communicative Process:
Schema and Design

In some of our earlier discussion we anticipated definitions of communication which we shall now specifically verbalize. In a broad sense, communication is any act by virtue of which one organism evokes behavior from another. Thus, the frightened hen's clucking that sets her brood into flight is communication. So also is the roaring of the lion that produces fright and flight in other animals. Even the reflexive crying of an infant is communication when mother or another member of the environment responds to the crying, though the infant's noises were a result of a discomfort state and did not, at the outset, anticipate attention.

Our chief concern in this chapter is with an exposition of *intentional* communication. By this we mean the use of symbol behavior that not only triggers other behavior but does so with the initiator usually able to anticipate the nature of the reaction to his behavior. This does not imply that the evoked reaction will be consistently what the initiator anticipates. Usually, however, the reaction is somehow related to the intention and anticipation of the initiator's symbol efforts, even if the relationship is a negative one. A beckoning word or a gesture may not always produce the desired positive result. The respondent may turn away rather than come to the beckoner, but the reaction is nevertheless related to the initiator's symbol (in this case a gesture symbol) behavior.

SEQUENCE OF OCCURRENCES IN COMMUNICATIVE SITUATIONS

The nature and type of reaction is determined by many factors. Among these are the inclinations and abilities of the presumed respondent to engage in a communicative act; the familiarity of the respondent with the over-all communicative code as well as the selected linguistic symbols addressed to him; the presence or absence of other persons who may or may not be co-respondents; the sensory, motor, and intellectual capacities of the presumed respondent; and other factors we shall consider later. For the present, we should like to present a schematic sequence that summarizes the major steps or stages in a communicative undertaking. We shall assume at this time that we are dealing with a one-to-one (person-to-person) communicative situation. The first part of the scheme will present what we believe usually takes place when a Speaker (A) decides that he wants to say something to a person who has been selected by the Speaker to be his Listener (B). Speaker (A) is probably better designated as Speaker (about-to-be-Listener). In any "normal" situation a speaker is also a Listener in that he reacts to his own pre-verbal and verbal behavior. This will be considered in Steps 3 and 4 of our present discussion. Similarly, Listener (B) should be designated as Listener (about-to-be-Speaker). We shall work on the assumption that both members in the about-to-be-established communicative cycle are able and willing persons who, at the outset at least, want to talk.

Occurrence 1.   Speaker Response to a Provocative Situation [1]

As a result of internal or external stimulation an event occurs which somehow provokes Person A to wish to say something that will involve Person B. In the sequence of occurrences A is destined for the role of Speaker A and B for the role of Listener B. An example of an internal event would be the awareness of a twinge of pain in the knee joint which, for reasons beyond this awareness, provoke the announcement "My arthritis tells me we're about to have a change in the weather." Another example of awareness of an internal event provoking a verbal announcement might be "Is that your stomach or mine that just growled?" To be certain, in both of these examples, the internal event alone did not stimulate or provoke the initial communicative effort. Some need in the situation, some element in the over-all situation and relationship between A and B, induced the evocation. Most adults do not ordinarily utter words or even word forms aloud whenever they become aware of internal changes. There is, however, a difference between an event which begins with awareness of a beneath-the-skin change and one where a clear external event excites verbal expression. External events such as

[1] The discussion that follows is an adaptation of W. Johnson's article on the normal communicative process "The Spoken Word and the Great Unsaid." *Quarterly Journal of Speech,* 32, 1951, pages 419-429.

the witnessing of an automobile crash, or a beautiful sunset, or a bolt of lightning are also usually accompanied by awareness of internal changes, but these events are initially externally induced. What is said is more likely to be related to the external aspect of the event than to the internal changes that are part of the response to the event. So, as a result of either internal or external stimulation, or as a result of both, an individual capable of saying something in regard to the event decides to say something to another individual who is presumed to be capable of reacting to what will be said. A communicative effort is now under way.

Occurrence 2. The Occurrence of Neurological, Physiological, Mental, and Affective Reactions

In effect, Occurrence 2 was anticipated in Occurrence 1, and is not a discrete step or stage, especially when the provocative event begins with awareness of internal changes. Where the event begins with a predominantly external event, the second step succeeds the first. It is unlikely that any of us has awareness of the neurological changes that take place as a response to a provocative event. We are more likely to become aware of the neuromuscular expression of the neurological impulses. We may become aware of a change in attention; we may become aware of new awarenesses; we may become aware of a change of thought, or the beginning of thinking. Some events will be accompanied by an awareness of feeling that accompanies the other changes. These are all internal reactions that are about to produce other reactions in Occurrence 3.

Occurrence 3. Evaluations of Reactions

Reactions begin to be evaluated as soon as the individual is aware of their occurrence. So, of course, are the reactions to the reactions. An individual may at the moment he is making a response wonder *why he is making such a response* and question himself "Why do I feel this way about such and such?" Reactions of the first order, and reactions to reactions (indefinite order) are evaluated in terms of the individual's established habits, attitudes, and wishes as well as in terms of his general physical and personality make-up and more specifically in terms of his neurological, sensory, and intellectual capacities.

All of the above paragraph is in effect a particularization of another way of saying that during Occurrence 3 an individual reacts with his capacities to a complex situation he apprehends and evaluates. The reactions have not yet reached a verbal state, though it is likely that considerable private or inner symbolization, or at least image manipulation has taken place. More conventional verbalization takes place in the next stage of the sequential and overlapping events in the communicative process.

Occurrence 4.   Translation and Selection of Inner Events into Verbal Behavior

At the stage of Occurrence 4 the individual begins to select words in preparation for external production. In assessing the events at this stage we should be mindful of Skinner's observation (1957, p. 11): "The speaker and listener within the same skin engage in activities which are traditionally described as 'thinking.' The speaker manipulates his behavior, he reviews it, and may reject it or emit it in modified form." If, as we have assumed, there is an intended Listener, the same events take place, except that the ultimate verbal selection is determined by what the initial Speaker anticipates the Listener will be able to understand. The Speaker entertains many possible verbalizations in terms of his own verbal habits, and his anticipations of the verbal habits of his Listener.

Occurrence 5.   External Verbal Behavior

At this stage the Speaker engages in overt verbal behavior. He now says something that can be heard and seen. These selected, organized sound and light waves (the words and the accompanying gesture and pantomime, or the accompanying action) may be immediately modified and reorganized according to the responses he begins to get from the listener. If, for example, the Listener seems not to have heard the Speaker, the same words may be uttered more loudly, or gestures may be more emphatically employed to reinforce the words. If the Listener seems to have heard, but not understood, other verbalizations may be tried. Occasionally a Speaker may realize that he has used an inappropriate verbal system, that the Listener did not understand the language as a whole and so could not respond to the selection of uttered words. If this is realized, gesture may replace words, or the Speaker may try another linguistic system if he has such at his command. If the Speaker still fails to get a response he may continue trying new selections of verbal patterns, or may decide to give up the communicative effort. What he does depends upon many factors, including the kind of person he is, his linguistic abilities, and the purpose and needs the communicative effort was supposed to serve. If all the Speaker intended to engage in was an interchange of social verbalizations, he may not deem it urgent to get a response to "Fine day, isn't it?" If, however, he had lost his way in a strange city and needed directions, he might well continue his communicative effort.

Listener (Speaker) Occurrences

At this stage the intended or anticipated Listener begins to be involved in a series of events that parallel those of the initial Speaker. There is, however, an important difference between them at the outset. The Listener did not have the Speaker's freedom of choice as to the subject of the communication—at least not at the start. If the Listener shared the external provocative event, if, for example, he as well as the Speaker observed a sunset or an automobile accident, or attended a television newscast, he would begin his reactions with an exposure to an immediately similar stimulating situation. If he did not share such an experience, then the external provocative situation is limited to the verbal products of the initial Speaker.

The Listener-about-to-be-Speaker does exercise a choice comparable to that of the initial Speaker. It is the choice of deciding whether to become overtly engaged in the communicative sequence with the initial Speaker. This choice has many possible determinants which include: (1) the Listener's general attitude toward talking with others; (2) the Listener's specific feelings and attitude in regard to the particular Speaker, if he knows the Speaker; or (3) the Listener's attitude about "getting involved" in talking to persons he does not know; (4) the amount of time the Listener has in the light of other impending situations; (5) the Listener's ability to comprehend the linguistic code employed by the Speaker; (6) the Listener's ability to respond in the same linguistic code or in another that the Speaker-about-to-become-a-Listener may be presumed to be able to understand. Beyond these factors there are many more of a general nature and of a nature directly related to the provocative situation that will determine whether a given communicative effort will be short-lived or will continue. Some provocative verbal situations invite and encourage prolonged communication while others evoke terminal verbal or non-verbal reactions. Inclinations to talk vary with the mood and the time of the day as well as with the exigencies of a given situation. A verbal situation that may induce prolonged conversation at one time may die for want of a verbal response at another time, even though the same persons may be involved.

Now, for the sake of completing our exposition of the communicative cycle, we will indicate what takes place with our Listener.

Occurrence 6.   Beginning of Listener (Speaker) Response to Provocative Verbal Situation

At this stage the Listener is, within the limits and with the privileges just considered, in a state comparable to that of the Speaker at the outset of the communicative cycle. The Listener who is about to be a Speaker, experiences physiological, neurological, mental, and affective reactions stimulated by the verbal and non-verbal behavior of the initial Speaker and to the initial external (non-verbal) provocative situation if he shared it.

Occurrence 7.   Listener (Speaker) Evaluation of Reactions

At this stage the Listener is engaged in evaluations comparable to those of the Speaker at Occurrence 3. The Listener's evaluations include his reactions to the Speaker, his internal reactions, as well as his reactions to his own reactions. The Listener evaluations are determined in large measure by forces which are products of his own attitudes, habits, and wishes, and his personality as a whole. They are also pre-determined by his sensory, neurological and physiological make-up.

Occurrence 8.   Listener (Speaker) Selection of Responses

At this "point" in the sequence of events the Listener (Speaker) makes his choices as to the role he is to play in the communicative process. He may decide to get involved, but *just for a moment,* and so behave verbally and non-verbally in a manner to indicate this inclination. He may decide to engage in prolonged verbal communication, and say something to encourage this eventuality. He may decide to avoid involvement, and say nothing but behave non-verbally so that the communication comes to an abrupt halt. So, in terms of the Listener (Speaker's) need, wish, and opportunity to continue or to terminate the communicative process, and in terms of his capacities and experiences, the Listener (let us assume that he decides to be a Speaker) selects and translates his responses as the initial Speaker did in Occurrence 4.

Occurrence 9.   Listener Becomes Overt Speaker

At this stage the initial Speaker (Listener) and Listener (Speaker) exchange roles. In effect, the erstwhile Listener (Speaker) becomes the second Speaker (Listener). He now behaves overtly, verbally and non-verbally, in response to and in anticipation of a response from the first

Speaker (Listener) who, if he is playing his role properly, has become a Listener (Speaker). The new Speaker produces his selection of organized responses, and his over-all behavior suggests that he expects a reaction. Sometimes, as an immediate result of the reaction he observes to his responses, the new Speaker modifies what he has said or what he was about to say. He may try to maintain the communicative interchange, or seek to terminate it. If he succeeds in continuing the communicative cycle he must be prepared once again to become a Listener (Speaker) as part of a second interchange of roles with the first Speaker. The number of such role interchanges varies with the specifics of the initial communication, and with a host of variables that include the needs, habits, wishes, attitudes, personalities, etc., of the two speakers. The direction a communicative cycle takes after it has been initiated is subject to so many variables that even with an intimate knowledge of the persons involved, prediction, except within broad limits, is tenuous. Even the most talkative individual must occasionally be terse, and even the most laconic must occasionally evoke more words than he might like.

DECODING AND ENCODING

In any communicative attempt the persons are involved in two on-going processes of decoding and encoding. The situation which provokes or maintains communicative effort is *decoded* by each speaker in turn. His own internal reactions are also decoded so that he learns what they mean to him. Following the decoding there is an *encoding*. During this process the reactions are put into a private symbol system, and then into a conventional symbol system, one that the Speaker hopes may be understood and responded to by the listener. Thus, a maintained communicative effort may be summarized as . . . $\approx$ *Decoding - Encoding - Decoding* $\approx$ . . . or, to indicate the simultaneous and overlapping aspects of the ongoing events, the process might be more accurately represented as: . . . $\approx$ Decoding ----- Encoding ----- Decoding $\approx$ . . .

$$\text{Encoding} \qquad \text{Decoding} \qquad \text{Encoding}$$

Table 1 is a more detailed representation of the occurrences which take place in a communicative effort.

APPROXIMATION OF CONTENT OF COMMUNICATIVE EFFORT

Elsewhere in this text the reasons for approximation of meaning and of understanding in communicative efforts are considered in some detail (see Ch. 7). We should like here to summarize why one participant in a communicative cycle, at best, can only provoke the other into understanding approximately what he wants understood, or why one partici-

Table 1.

Schematic Representation of the "Normal Communicative Process"
(Adapted from W. Johnson, "Speech and Personality" *Etc.* Winter, 1949, Vol. 6, #2, 84-102)

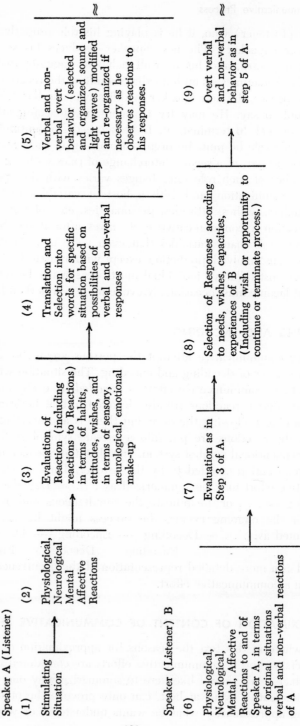

Speaker A (Listener)

(1)
Stimulating Situation

(2)
Physiological, Neurological Mental Affective Reactions

(3)
Evaluation of Reaction (including reactions to Reactions) in terms of habits, attitudes, wishes, and in terms of sensory, neurological, emotional make-up

(4)
Translation and Selection into words for specific situation based on possibilities of verbal and non-verbal responses

(5)
Verbal and non-verbal overt behavior (selected and organized sound and light waves) modified and re-organized if necessary as he observes reactions to his responses.

Speaker (Listener) B

(6)
Physiological, Neurological, Mental, Affective Reactions to and of Speaker A, in terms of original situations verbal and non-verbal reactions of A

(7)
Evaluation as in Step 3 of A.

(8)
Selection of Responses according to needs, wishes, capacities, experiences of B (Including wish or opportunity to continue or terminate process.)

(9)
Overt verbal and non-verbal behavior as in step 5 of A.

All of above, at best, results in an approximation of shared communicated meanings.

138

pant can succeed in sharing only partially the information he wants shared. Approximation of understanding—partial rather than full sharing of information *when there is intention for understanding and sharing— results from differences between the communicating participants along the following lines:*

1. Differences in experience relative to the initial provocative situation if it is a non-verbal one or to the verbal situation, or to the combination of the two: For example, to most persons who do not live in the San Francisco area, there is likely to be some initial confusion between high fog and clouds and between golden hills and browned-out hills. There are other related differences to conditions of weather that induced Mark Twain to observe that the coldest winter he could recall was a summer he spent in San Francisco. Such observations can have special significance only for persons who have lived in and have attitudes about the northern California city. The implications of Mark Twain's remark are quite different for those who knew only the words of his utterance but are without benefit of the experience of a summer in San Francisco.

2. Existing differences in perception, apperception, motivation, intelligence, ability and inclination to engage in abstract behavior: There is no need to discuss all of these factors. Most are apparent, so that an example of one of these differentiating factors should be sufficient for our purposes. An intelligent, discerning adult is likely to have richer experiences than a dull adult. If he is motivated to share his experiences, he will usually have greater developed ability to relate his experiences than would a dull person. His potential ability will not be exercised if his attitude or his immediate concern or his motivation is negative to the situation. The phrase *to the situation* very importantly involves the other fellow, the second participant in the communicative effort.

3. Linguistic ability: This factor is highly correlated with intelligence, but is not inseparable from intelligence. Other things being equal, a person with good linguistic facility will be better able to communicate his thoughts, wishes, feelings, and intentions than a person with lesser linguistic facility. Obviously, comprehension as well as expression, decoding as well as encoding, is a function of linguistic ability, facility of expressions, and an inventory of meanings for comprehension.

4. Varying experiences with specific words or with common locutions, and with words and locutions having varying implications according to region: Words, as we all have come to appreciate, are the vehicles for many possible meanings and for shades of meanings. Some words and some phrases are used in special and perhaps restricted ways in different communities. A communicative effort may fail to be understood, or be misunderstood, because a "wrong" word was used in a given community. The item of food you get when ordering *baked potato* in a northern

city of the United States will not be precisely the same item you are likely to get when the order is placed in a southern city. The reaction to a locution including the word *bloody* will vary considerably according to whether it is uttered in London or Chicago.

5. Personality differences: Differences between essentially normal participants in a communicative undertaking increase the margin of approximations. When one or both of the participants is markedly deviant or is frankly aberrant, there as an increased likelihood that what one participant intends will *not* be received by the other. The reasons for this widening of approximation of meaning and intention are considered in detail in our discussion on personality and speech. For the present, we may summarize and generalize, perhaps over-generalize the influence of personality differences and deviations by observing that an individual who cannot assume an attitude that permits placing himself at the disposal and point of view of another will have difficulty in producing or in receiving an intentional communication.

6. Sensory defects: The perception of an apple tree in bloom is different for a person who is near-sighted or far-sighted according to whether he is wearing corrective eyeglasses. Habitual perception of such objectively concrete situations as trees, bodies of water, the sound of the wind and the sounds made by non-human, non-speaking live creatures vary according to individual sensory capacities. Thus, the apple tree in bloom has distinguishable branches and flowers for the person with normal vision; the "same" tree is a foggy shaped mass to the person with near-sighted, uncorrected vision. It is still something else to a far-sighted individual or to one who is astigmatic. The perception and meanings of the phrase *apple tree* are different. The specific meaning apprehended by the near-sighted listener for the term *apple tree* is different when spoken by a normal-sighted speaker from that which is heard by the near-sighted, astigmatic, or far-sighted listener.

7. Neurological defects: A child born with a damaged brain learns differently—acquires meanings differently and probably acquires fewer meanings for situations—than does a normal, non-brain-damaged child. An older child or an adult with adventitious brain damage may incur modifications and impairments of meanings for his earlier acquired verbal and non-verbal experiences. When the impairments are severe, the difficulty in communicative behavior becomes quickly apparent, and individuals suffering from such communicative impairments are referred to as *aphasic*. When the impairments are relatively mild they may modify the manner of articulation, the melody of speech, or the facility and precision of word choice. All of these modifications make for differences in communication which widen the margin of approximation between the participants in a communicative effort.

8. Defects of Speech: Significant defects of voice or articulation that distract a listener from *what* is said to the *manner* of the saying may make a difference that widens the margin of approximation in a communicative effort. Usually, unless the defects of speech are so severe as to make intelligibility extremely difficult,[2] the speaker despite his deviant speech becomes intelligible after a brief "tuning-in" period. If the communicative effort is a short one, an individual with defective speech may fail to be understood if the time for the "tuning-in" to him exceeds the time of his utterance.

This relatively condensed discussion of some possible differences between the members involved in a communicative engagement was intended to highlight factors that result in approximations rather than precise interchanges of thoughts and/or feelings. Even with the best of intention, and the most highly developed skills in speaking and in listening, all one participant can do is to produce a pattern of verbal behavior that reflects an evaluation and symbolization of his reactions for a response. This response may take the form of verbal behavior or of direct action. In a communicative engagement, both participants must make adjustments to the over-all linguistic conventions and to other cultural influences that modify and control the form and manner, as well as the content of the interchange.

CHARACTERISTICS OF THE HUMAN COMMUNICATIVE SYSTEM

Much of what is discussed in this book is based on the assumption that man is the only being capable of communicating by means of abstract symbols. The expression of this developed capability, though unique in its form and multiplicity of functions, nevertheless has many features that are present in the communicative behavior of animals. We will be able to appreciate the richness and the potential of human oral language (speech) and the limitations of animal communication by a consideration of the features that characterize human oral linguistic signals. Our discussion will be based on the theoretic design-features of the linguist Hockett. (1958, 1960)

The Vocal-Auditory Channel

The first design feature of the human communicative system is that it ordinarily employs a vocal-auditory channel. (Extra-ordinarily, a substitute for this feature is the visible-visual channel employed in gesture

[2] Here too, difficulty in intelligibility is not solely a matter of speaker behavior. Some listeners can quickly understand what a speaker is trying to say while co-listeners fail of comparable understanding.

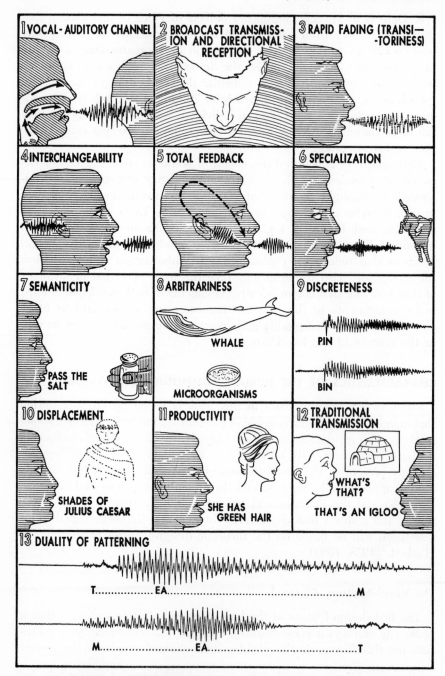

Figure 9-1. Design features of communicative systems. (From "The Origin of Speech" by C. F. Hockett. P. 91. *Scientific American,* September 1960.)

systems.) The vocal-auditory channel permits the organs not directly involved in speech production or speech reception to be free for other purposes. So, a human being may talk while he works, or a man may dig a hole, or chop a tree, or hammer a nail, or drive a car, and yet be able to talk either about what he is doing, what he had done, or what he intends to do, or about a matter unrelated to his present, past, or future activities. What one man may do while talking, another may do while listening. Speaking and listening may go on concurrently with other activities. This may be the basis for the waggish observation that some women sew to give themselves something to think about while they are talking.

Broadcast Transmission

Human beings can "broadcast" their messages within "earshot." Normally, unless there are competing signals or interfering noises, it is possible for a listener or listeners to locate the source of the linguistic signals and so to "tune in" and listen. Mechanical devices serve to increase the range of the signals and the distance between sender and receiver.

The oral linguistic signal is transitory. At least, this was the situation until man devised means of recording and storing messages for future transmission. Unless there is mechanical storing, and except as the produced messages impress the minds of the speaker and listener, the initial signals fade away even as they are produced. The effects of the signals, however, are storable and reproduceable through memory and recall. Further, most human linguistic systems are translatable into written systems so that the articulate components may be permanently stored. Direct mechanical imprinting has the advantage of permitting the recording of the vocal as well as the articulate and visual components of human linguistic signals to be reproduced for future purposes.

Interchangeability

Within limits, and with varying degrees of accuracy, a speaker of a language can reproduce any linguistic message he has received and understood. Variations occur according to relative experiences, background, and other individual and subjective factors that make communication of meanings approximate rather than exact. By and large, however, most messages that are received and understood by one listener can be re-transmitted to other listeners who employ the same linguistic system. In this way the roles of the speaker and the listener can be *interchanged*. This is not the case with many lower animals that have rudimentary signal systems. Hockett cites as an example the courting behavior of the stickleback fish which is individual and discrete for the male and the female. Though the behavior of each stickleback triggers (cues and evokes) behavior in the other, the behavioral events (the communicative signals) are different and the roles are not interchangeable. To some degree, of course, non-lingual and pre-lingual communicative behavior is different among human beings. The roles of the infant and the mother are not interchangeable, though the behavior of one triggers behavior in the other. The infant who extends his arms to be held usually evokes holding behavior from his mother. When symbols begin to replace signals, then roles begin to be interchangeable. Ultimately, as Hockett points out, ". . . any participating organism equipped for the transmission of messages in the system is also equipped to receive messages in the same system, and vice versa." (1958, p. 578). The interchange of messages and the interchange of roles is learned behavior. Human beings are not born with a system of symbols. Most of them are, however, born with a capacity for learning one or more symbol-linguistic systems.

The basis for learning oral linguistic symbol systems is inherent in man's *total feedback system*. The sound patterns that are produced are responded to in the act of production. Feedback may be auditory, tactile, and kinesthetic. So, sound patterns can be stored, recalled, and reproduced according to the stimulating occasion.

Specialization

The patterns of signals used by man are specialized in that their primary if not entire purpose is communication. The words uttered by a speaker create disturbance in the surrounding air, but the act of producing the words does not serve a fundamental biological purpose. In contrast, the noises and sudden flight of a bird serve a purpose for the bird. Incidentally, this behavior may set other birds in flight. But the first bird began his flight because he needed to fly, and not presumably because he had a need to set other birds in flight. Similarly, the panting, tongue-protruding, open-mouthed dog is not intentionally signalling or informing another dog or a human observer that he is warm. The dog's mouth is open and his tongue is protruding to permit him to cool off and so to maintain a comfortable body temperature. One human may incidentally, and usually unintentionally, inform another that he is warm by the way he acts. But when one human being *wishes to inform another* about how warm he feels, he selects appropriate words for conveying this information.

Discreteness

The human vocal and articulatory mechanisms can produce a wide range and variety of sounds. We can approximate the extent of human sound-making ability by listening to a young infant while he is engaged in vocal play. During the first few weeks of his life, when he is relatively uninfluenced by the dominant human noises of his culture, the infant's sounds range far and wide. During this period the infant is an internationalist in his vocal and articulatory behavior. As he grows older, the infant's sounds become more selective until finally, even in his vocal play, he begins to sound like the people around him. In the process of selection the infant somehow learns to make discrete and different sounds. By the time he is six or seven, most of the sounds used by the child in his speech efforts resemble closely the articulatory efforts of older persons. Thus, his *t*'s and his *p*'s sound like *t*'s and *p*'s and can be distinguished from the cognate *b*'s and *d*'s. These sound differences become semantically significant, so that a child learns to distinguish *tip* from *dip*, and *pie* from *by*. Similarly, he learns the distinction between *lip* and *lap*.

Minor sound distortions within words tend to be resolved in the direction of one or another word, *according to the prevailing sounds within a given linguistic system.* Within each system, differences between sounds are functionally absolute. The differences determine and permit a listener to distinguish one possible word from another. Distortions in sounds must be resolved by the listener in favor of one word or another. The speaker does not produce a new word, or the listener understand a new meaning, because a distorted sound within a word falls somewhere in between two conventional articulatory products. If sounds are distorted, the listener tries to guess the intended word on the basis of the context in which the word was used. If the context does not help him, then the listener simply fails to understand what was said.

Duality of Patterning

An oral linguistic system comprises a selection of key sound elements which are "distinct" insofar as they can be discerned, isolated, and separately produced by the speaker of a particular language. These key elements or *phonemes*, discussed under the heading of *Discreteness* (see also Chapter 7), have no meaning as separate entities. When the sound elements are combined, the smallest individually meaningful units uttered are *morphemes*. Morphemes consist of one or more phonemes signifying a minimal unit of utterance in a linguistic system. A linguistic system combines at once an arrangement of phonemes and an arrangement of morphemes. For example, the word *hat* is a morpheme consisting of three phonemes. The word *hat* is distinguished from the word *sat* by the difference in the first phoneme; it is distinguished from the word *ham* by the difference in the last phoneme. The *-un* of *unfit, unlike,* and *unless* is a morpheme. The *-ess* of *priceless* and *fearless* is a morpheme. Each of the just enumerated words contains two morphemes.

Productivity

The flexibility of human linguistic systems permits even the meanest of men to produce utterances that can be understood even though, in total, they have never (or at least probably never) been produced or heard before. Other creatures such as the gibbon have sound calls, but these calls are limited in number and are not combined to make new calls. Man can combine and arrange sounds and sound units to make words, can arrange and rearrange the words to give expression to his feelings and to convey his thoughts. Within the conventions of the structure of his linguistic system, he can be almost indefinitely productive. If he abides by these conventions he can be creative and share his verbal creations with listeners. If he is fortunate, what he produces can be appreciated as well as understood.

Traditional Transmission

The conventions of a linguistic system are transmitted culturally rather than genetically. Man, if he has normal intellectual and sensory capacities, is capable of learning one or more languages. The one or ones he learns are culturally determined. Most Americans learn to speak American-English because they are exposed to American-English and, directly or indirectly, this is the linguistic system they are taught. To what extent other sound-making creatures possess acquired rather than genetically-determined systems is still not known. Some birds, such as the American mockingbird, are apparently able to imitate the calls of other birds, though they seem to have their own native calls as well. For the most part, however, sound-making animals have characteristic calls according to a species. The uniformity of these calls suggests the possibility that their initial sound-making system is genetically determined, even though some species of animals can acquire the calls of other animals.

Animal Communication

Several of the design features which we have considered are present in the communicative systems of some insects, in birds, and in the primates. No sub-human communicative system, however, incorporates all of the design features of human speech. Differences and similarities are summarized in the following table (after Hockett).

Table 2.

Design Features of Human and Sub-human
Communication

	Bee Dancing	Western Meadow-lark Song	Gibbon Calls	Language Human Oral
Vocal Auditory Channel	No	Yes	Yes	Yes
Broadcast Transmission	Yes	Yes	Yes	Yes
Interchangeability and total feedback	Limited	Doubtful	Yes	Yes
Specialization	Doubtful	Yes?	Yes	Yes
Discreteness	No	Doubtful	Yes	Yes
Duality of Patterning	No	Doubtful	No	Yes
Arbitrariness	No	Possible, but limited	Yes	Yes
Displacement	Yes	Doubtful	No	Yes
Productivity	Yes	Doubtful	No	Yes
Traditional Transmission	Probably No	Doubtful	Doubtful	Yes

Arbitrariness

Except possibly for a relatively small number of onomatopoetic words, human language shows little direct relationship between the verbal forms and the meaning or meanings the verbal forms acquire. There is also possible exception in the size of the opening of the mouth for the vowel and, at least for some words, in an element of meaning. For example, *bit, wee, little* are words that refer to *smallness*. But the word *big* contains the same vowel as the word *bit*, and yet conveys an opposite meaning. There is a larger mouth opening for the diphthong of *tiny* than for the vowel of *huge*. Essentially, linguistic systems are arbitrary, or become arbitrary, in regard to semantic denotations and implications.

Almost all of the verbal forms we use acquire meanings through associations rather than through the manner of articulation or as a result of the quality of the audible product, or of any other quality or aspect of a word. It is possible, of course, that if there were direct relationships between verbal forms and meanings, that communication would be more precise. A word might then mean what it sounds like, or feels like, or moves like, etc. Perhaps words such as *slide* and *slip* and *trip* suggest meaning by the articulatory action required for their production. On the other hand, arbitrariness imposes no limitation on linguistic meaning, and so verbal forms may acquire many meanings, and subtle shades of meaning, that would not otherwise be possible. Thus, the word *big* contains a small vowel, and *nightingale* is a long (large) word for a small bird, while *stork* is a relatively small word for a relatively large bird. There is nothing inherently sweet about the word *sugar,* or inherently sour about the word *lemon.* But man may learn to respond to the word *sugar* with reactions as reliable as if the word had a direct or inherent meaning, just as he may pucker or salivate at the sound as well as the sight of a cut *lemon.*

Displacement

Man, as we indicated earlier, is able to talk about things that are far removed from him in physical space or in time. His oral linguistic system permits him to talk about things in the past, in the immediate or remote future, or about things that might have been or might at some future time come into being. The bee, in its dance, can apparently get other bees to do something at a place distant from where the initial dancing took place, but he must be present and lead them on. No creature except man, however, can displace himself and his listeners through his oral noises. Only man can talk about otherwheres and othertimes, and project his listener backward or forward in space and time while he and they remain relatively immobile.

REFERENCES

Berlo, D. K. *The process of communication.* New York: Holt, Rinehart, and Winston, 1960. Ch. 2.

Cherry, C. *On human communication.* New York, Wiley, 1957.

Hockett, C. F. *A course in modern linguistics.* New York: Macmillan, 1958. Pp. 574-580.

Hockett, C. F. The origin of speech. *Scientific American,* 1960, 3, 203, 89-96.

Miller, G. A. *Language and communication.* New York: McGraw-Hill, 1951.

Ruesch, J., & Bateson, G. *Communication.* New York: W. W. Norton, 1951. Ch. 11.

Saporta, S. *Psycholinguistics: a book of readings.* New York: Holt, Rinehart, and Winston, 1961.

Skinner, B. F. *Verbal behavior.* New York: Appleton-Century-Crofts, 1957. Ch. 4.

10

Communication Among Animals

By William Etkin, Ph.D.

Albert Einstein College of Medicine
and The City College of The
City University of New York

BROADLY CONSIDERED, COMMUNICATION is not only important to social organization but is the essence of the socialization process. To justify this statement we must consider what we mean by the terms social and communication as related to animal behavior. We consider animals to be social when they remain together in groups as a result of behavioral responses to each other. Thus sheep in a herd are genuinely social because they stay in the group as a result of their reactions to one another, whereas insects gathered around a light at night are not because they stay together by virtue of a common response to this environmental factor. In other words, the existence of the social group presupposes that the members provide stimuli which evoke responses in other members of the group by which the group is held together. The provision of stimuli eliciting social responses from other members of the group is what we mean by communication. Clearly such stimuli need not be (vocal) nor need they have other characteristics of human speech such as being a mutual exchange, depending upon learned symbols, etc. In this chapter we wish to examine animal communication thus broadly conceived, in the hope that such an examination will widen the scope of our thinking about human communication. We shall see that modes of communication other than speech are of importance in the social life of man and that speech itself shares many attributes of animal communication. Finally we shall consider the basis for the great gulf which does exist between speech as the primary mode of human communication and the forms used by animals.

FUNCTIONS OF ANIMAL COMMUNICATION

Elicitation of Direct Response

In part the phraseology we used above to define communication will be readily understood from our common experience with human communication. Thus the statement "Give me a pencil" is ordinarily an adequate stimulus to evoke the appropriate social response. But our naïve thinking about speech is much too limited even with respect to the idea of stimulus-response relation. In human speech the stimuli are of almost infinite variability, and the motor responses likewise may take many different forms. In the simpler communication system of animals, the motor activities are largely stereotyped or limited in their variability. Correspondingly the stimuli need be of relatively few kinds. Not only is the repertory of stimulus-response relations thus very limited in animal communication but the characteristic motor responses such as feeding, courting, attacking, etc., are each accompanied by an emotional tone or orientation as a prominent part of the response. It is, therefore, an important function of stimuli in animal communication to elicit not only motor responses but an emotional pattern as well. Animal signals thus tend to approximate our cries or exclamations such as "Help" and "Scat" rather than the communication of ideas.

Physiological Coordination

Related to the underlying emotionality of animal response is a second functional characteristic by which animal communication tends to differ in marked degree from speech. Animal signals often tend to guide or direct developmental and physiological processes, thereby inducing co-ordination with respect to these processes among the members of the group. These are, of course, long-term effects and correspondingly the signal system is often characterized by perseverance over long periods. Anyone who has watched a male pigeon courting a female must be struck by the persistence and repetitiveness of his activities. We know now that such signalling operates more deeply than merely evoking acceptance or rejection on the part of the female; it also serves to influence a gradual development of the female toward the phase of her reproductive cycle wherein she becomes receptive to a male.

Many animal signals thus serve physiological coordination, sometimes in a more obvious and more immediate manner. When a frightened gull utters its alarm cry and flies off, not only do the others of the flock take to flight but they also take up the alarm cry and soon the air is filled with fluttering wings and alarm notes which bring all the birds into a state of high excitement. Psychological developmental processes may also be influenced by persistent communication methods, as we shall discuss more fully under the heading of "socialization" later in this chapter.

KUMPAN THEORY AND ANIMAL COMMUNICATION

Modern zoology has developed new insights into the integrative mechanisms in animal societies as a result of studies of animal behavior under natural conditions. This study is known as ethology (Tinbergen, 1951). We will present a brief summary of the ethological theory of instinctual behavior which forms the basis for an understanding of some aspects of animal communication.

Ethological Theory of Instinct

Ethologists regard instincts as complex behaviors which are organized in centers within the central nervous system. As such they are largely fixed by the developmental capacities of the nervous centers and little affected by experiences during the animal's lifetime (learning). These centers tend to accumulate a driving force or energy specific to each center (action specific energy). Normally, this energy is not discharged because a blocking mechanism, called the internal releasing mechanism (IRM), prevents such release until a stimulus, acting upon the IRM, opens the block. Each IRM is released only by a specific type of stimulus that fits it individually more or less as a key fits a lock. In general, such stimuli, called releasers or signals, are characterized by being simple, conspicuous and highly specific so that they operate with maximal efficiency in releasing the instinctual activity when, and only when, the occasion is appropriate. An example may be taken from the life of the English robin in which the male secures a territory in the spring and defends it against other male robins (Lack, 1953). The defense behavior of such a bird is a complex stereotyped response involving singing, posturing, and pursuit as well as physical attack upon the intruder. Experiments show that such territory defense behavior is given not only to another male robin but to a dummy, even if the dummy is deprived of head, wings, legs, etc. In fact the response is given even to a bundle of red feathers thrown into the territory. Yet a dummy robin, complete except that the breast had been dyed brown, is not attacked at all. Thus we see that the stimulus that releases the attack response is not really a rival male in the sense we would think of a rival (i.e., a live bird potentially capable of taking over the territory) but a single feature of the rival, namely its red breast. It will be noted that though simple, this feature is efficient in the sense that it normally appears in the robin's experience only in connection with real rivals. Moreover, it is the most conspicuous aspect of the rival.

The Kumpan Relationship

It has been found that many complex behaviors that play an important role in the lives of insects and lower vertebrates (particularly fish and birds) are released by such innately fixed releaser signals. Not all are, of course, quite as simple as the above. In fact, other behavioral signals such as song play a role in releasing territory defense in the robin. However, the red breast of the robin was chosen as an example because it illustrates another principle basic to a communication system founded upon innate releasers. It will be noted that each male robin bears on its breast, so to speak, the distinctive sign that releases the rivalry-fighting behavior of other robins. Other species of birds in the robin's environment do not have this red breast nor do other species respond to the flashing of the red breast with attack behavior. Each species of song bird that defends territory in a region in the spring responds to a different signal, and in each species that signal is displayed by the males only of the species. In many species the specific stimulus includes the characteristic song of the species which thus functions primarily, though not exclusively, in regulating the interactions of males with each other. In short, rivals respond to each other with appropriate "rivalry behavior" because the social releasers for such behavior are "built into" the structure and behavior of the species.

Members of a social species may interact with each other in many different ways. Thus males interact as territorial rivals; males and females pair up in mating; parents and their young have their own patterns of behaviors toward each other; members of a migrating flock are companions in flight, etc. In each of these interrelations the animals similarly have special peculiarities of structure and behavior that serve to elicit appropriate responses from their companions. Such interactions have been designated *Kumpan relations* (from the German word for companion—Lorenz, 1957). Many of these kumpan interactions are instinctually controlled by built-in signals which, despite their apparent purposefulness, are purely mechanical in their actions. This is illustrated by the ease with which imitators can "fool" the animal. Thus, parent song-birds are stimulated to feed their young by the way the babies open their mouths (gaping) and by their peeping calls. The parents respond equally well, however, to the gaping of foreign young. The European cuckoo and the American cowbird take advantage of the automaticity of these feeding responses by laying their eggs in the nests of songbirds. The parasitic birds develop more rapidly than the songbird's own young, and by out-gaping them receive all the food. The behavior of the parent bird may thus be as mechanical as the activities of the wooden bird in a cuckoo clock which performs its appointed task no matter how far off time the clock is running.

It is obvious that for a releaser to be of maximal effectiveness it should be conspicuous and distinctive enough not to be confused with other available stimuli. The responding organism tends to evolve in the direction of being sensitive to one or a few highly distinctive characteristics of the appropriate object in its environment. For example, dragonflies whose eggs must develop in water are stimulated to lay eggs by a shimmering surface. In their natural environment such a reflecting surface is found only over open water and thus the response is given appropriately. However, in cities dragonflies have been known to lay eggs on the surface of a freshly tarred roof.

With social releasers an additional factor makes its appearance. The two kumpans in the relationship tend to evolve in correlation with one another so that stimulus and response fit together more and more perfectly. Thus the releasing organism becomes more and more conspicuous and distinctive in respect to the releasing stimulus which it produces and, at the same time, the responding kumpan becomes more and more sensitive to this particular stimulus. Where social releasers are structural characteristics, their conspicuousness is assured by the development of bright color, or large or unusual shapes, etc. We thus recognize that many structural features of animals such as plumes, wattles, stripes, etc., which, superficially considered, seem to be useless are, in fact, highly functional as releasers of social behavior from the animal's kumpans.

Ritualization

Behavioral characteristics used as releasers tend to evolve in the direction of conspicuousness and distinctiveness by a process called ritualization. The courtship display of most birds and many mammals includes stiff and peculiar postures, strutting, and other mannerisms which are conspicuous by their very oddity. Thus, the turkey gobbler performs a slow "formal" dance around his lady love with the wing on the near side held down and the tail fanned out and twisted to face his lady.

Of course, these postures show off his fine feathers to greater advantage but they are conspicuous in and of themselves as anyone who has seen the performance of a pure white albino turkey can testify. In the Indian antelope the dominant male expresses his position in the herd by folding his ears back against his head in a position made conspicuous by its very awkwardness and uselessness. The effectiveness of animal structures used as signals is greatly increased by the manner in which they are displayed. Thus ritualization of social signals is an important item in the efficiency of animal communication.

Mammalian behavior is notably lacking in the rigidity and stereotyped action patterns so often found in lower vertebrates and insects. However, despite the flexibility with which response patterns are carried out there are many instances in mammalian behavior which are at least analogous to the responses to social releasers in lower organisms. Baby monkeys are soothed and quieted by contact with the soft cloth "skin" of an artificial mother even though in other respects the model is very different from a real monkey (Harlow, 1958). Anyone who has had a dog knows how automatically its pursuit behavior is released by any running animal or person, a behavioral response that clearly is a relic of the pack-hunting activity of the ancestral wolf.

With respect to human behavior it is, of course, difficult to establish critical evidence for the existence of any innate releasing mechanisms. But certain elements of the human communication system are clearly suggestive of such a factor. To many zoologists human beings seem to have drive systems that respond specifically to signals produced by others, releasing generalized moods and types of behavior such as aggressiveness, friendliness, relaxation, sexuality, or parental care much as they do in animals. The smile of the adult has been shown to evoke friendly relaxation in even very young infants. Ritualized postures in man are often strikingly analogous to those which animals use in like circumstances as we see in such descriptive phrases as "cock of the walk." Human gestures and facial expressions as in threat, dominance, and subordination are much the same in all cultures and closely analogous to the comparable expressions of animals. Thus in many birds lowering of the head signals subordination and tends to inhibit aggressiveness of the kumpan. Bowing is widely used in the same way by peoples of many cultures. The direct stare is a sign of hostility in animals as in man and many animals establish dominance relations by, as we say, "staring each other down." Whether such responses have important components that are innate or not in humans is, of course, not clear. It is significant, however, that in both human beings and animals similar signaling systems are the basis of the communication of the "emotional-tuning" of individuals to one another.

LEARNING IN ANIMAL SIGNAL SYSTEMS

Psychology students are generally quite familiar with various forms of conditioning in relation to learning in animals and nothing need be said here on that subject. However, animal behaviorists have become aware of other aspects of the learning process which are not as widely studied in psychology. Because they are of especial significance in animal communication, some general concepts in this area will be briefly considered now.

Specificity

Animal learning capacities often are remarkably specific and limited in time and range (Thorpe, 1956). A particular species of animal may show great learning ability in one respect but very little in other aspects. For example, digger wasps after making a nest-hole cover it over for camouflage. They then fly one or two circles over the area and go off to hunt prey for their young. They may be gone as long as several days. Yet they return directly to the spot they had left. Experiment shows that in their brief orientation flight they "memorized" the position of the hole with respect to neighboring landmarks. Yet wasps like other insects have very little capacity for learning other items. As an example of the high specificity of learning in the area of communication, we may cite song learning in birds (Lanyon, 1960). Though in some birds "knowledge" of their species' song is innate, others need some learning experience to be able to sing the complete song. In such birds it has been found that a brief exposure to their own song during their first few months of life while they themselves are silent, enables them to produce the perfect song of their species many months later when they become mature. Interestingly, only their own species' song is thus quickly picked up. Foreign patterns are generally either not learned at all or learned only to a limited extent.

Imprinting

A special aspect of the time and type specificity in animal learning is the ability of some young birds which normally follow their mothers to learn to identify them (Lorenz, 1957; Thorpe, 1956). Actually, as experiments show, they learn to follow the first large moving object to come into sight during the first few hours after hatching. They can thus be induced to follow a human being, a box, etc., as though it were their parent. This phenomenon is called imprinting. After the bird is just a few hours old, its susceptibility to being imprinted decreases sharply. Such time-limited learning abilities are not restricted to the young. Ewes which have just given birth learn to identify their own from all other lambs during the few minutes that they normally spend cleaning the newborn by licking it (Blauvelt, 1955). They cannot be induced to develop this maternal attachment toward a lamb at any other time. One of the more surprising effects of imprinting on socialization is seen in the delayed appearance of effects. Doves of one species imprinted to another by being raised in the nest of that species will accept as mates only individuals of the foster species when, many months later, they mature. Thus we see that different animals may show special capacities for learning particular signal systems, and these capacities may be limited to one period of their lives. Sometimes the effects of learning are not expressed until a much later period.

Phenomena that are, at least superficially, analogous to imprinting are easily discerned in respect to human socialization. The importance of early experience in human socialization is indeed a favorite topic of psychological research and psychiatric evaluation. The attachment to childhood memories of places and persons is commonly conceded to be strong in man and perhaps such emotional experiences as falling in love find their explanation along these lines. Variations in sensitivity to learning experience in respect to speech will be considered elsewhere in this book.

Socialization

We have previously discussed the physiological effects of persistent signal-exchange between kumpans in developing sexual coordination, etc. Here we should note the related effect of reiterated signals upon the socialization of animals living in a group. Familiarity with surroundings is of utmost importance in the life and survival of animals (Etkin, in press). For social animals this includes recognition of other members of the group and of their status in the dominance hierarchy of the group. Having an assured place within a familiar organized group is of extreme psychological importance to social animals. When deprived of their in-group feeling they are put under great tension which is reflected in their endocrine system as well as in their behavior. One of the chief ways in which an animal develops and maintains this in-group feeling is by the interchange of mild stimuli with other members of the group. Play, which is common in the young of group-living mammals and some birds, functions in this capacity. In their rough play puppies and young monkeys seem to become thoroughly familiar with their peers as individuals and gradually establish dominance-subordination relations with them. As a result, animals that play together stay together in a stable, hierarchically organized group. The behavior of these animals is extremely hostile toward individuals which are not members of their own in-group.

In addition to play we find other modes of stimulus interchange in different groups. Thus monkeys and apes groom each other. This searching and picking through each other's hair and skin is very widespread, often forming an all-engrossing activity for many hours a day. Of course, it promotes cleanliness but it appears to be far more intensively cultivated than can be accounted for on this basis. The exchange of grooming courtesies appears to be an important socializing factor promoting the strong in-group feeling that characterizes these animals. It appears obvious that play among children serves much the same socializing functions for human beings as it does for monkeys. In older persons socialization is promoted by a variety of visiting, club, ceremonial and other activities in different cultures as befits the needs of humans to maintain cooperative social relations throughout adult life. In man, each social group tends to produce a pattern in some measure specific to itself. The group transmits to individuals raised in it a sense of belongingness dependent upon these peculiarities, whether of dress, diet, speech or any of a thousand and one other sources of cultural variability. Variations in the traditions of the group that serve to isolate one group of the species from another are indeed not unknown in animals. Recent studies on the Japanese monkeys indicate that different bands among them have peculiarities in behavior and food preferences which are transmitted to the offspring as traditions which are distinctive for each group. But, of course, nowhere among animals is this cultural isolation as pronounced as it is in man where it shows itself so conspicuously in local variations of speech.

CHARACTERISTICS OF SPEECH SHARED WITH
ANIMAL COMMUNICATION SYSTEMS

To this point we have discussed animal communication with only the briefest reference to analogous phenomena in non-language areas among humans. Though, as we have seen, such communication plays a significant role in human social life, it is clearly overshadowed by speech as a means of communication. The subject of speech is, of course, the subject of the body of this book. But it is worthwhile here to consider briefly how speech as a means of communication functions with respect to those aspects achieved by animal communication systems.

Speech, as indicated earlier, occasionally seems to have the character of a social releaser. The chuckling and cooing of a mother to her infant and of the infant to its mother is a sound pattern (may we call it speech?)

which has all the earmarks of a social releaser. It communicates an emotional orientation and appears to be independent of learning since, though the formal phrases used may be culturally conditioned, these are not the essential elements. Rather it is the tone, facial expressions, and other qualities associated with the speaking which communicate the endearment. Foreigners have no difficulty communicating in this way with babies, however lacking they may be in our language. Similarly we express and evoke in others pleasant and cooperative attitudes or their opposites, not necessarily by the words we say but by those other qualities of speech which seem to be rather general human responses, probably at least in part unlearned. The hero of the TV western who reminds the less heroic character of his need to "Smile when you say that" is an expression of this insight. The well-bred hostess continues to be her cordial self even to the brash young man who smiles sweetly as he says "Thank you for a boring evening." Of course, we cannot be sure of the extent to which the response to such tonal and gestural qualities is innate and to what extent conditioned. Yet it would be doctrinaire to deny a priori that a significant role for innate releasers is involved.

The physiological stimulation of the visceral mechanisms of the body that, as we have seen, follows persistent repetition of emotion-releasing signals finds close analogies in human crowd behavior. As we have mentioned above, birds in flocks arouse each other to a high pitch of excitement by the effects of their alarm cries on each other. Small birds under such conditions even become aroused to the point of attacking (mobbing) hawks. Similarly, human crowds can be aroused to a lynching or other violent action by the autocatalytic effects of their own shouts without anyone really knowing what the basis of the excitement is. The Nazis characteristically carried this principle to a studied perfection with their organized "Sieg heil" responses at rallies. But not only may violent emotions be thus communicated and coordinated within the group by repetitious exchange of signals but peaceful cooperative in-group feelings may be so developed in a group. The contagion of laughter in a shared joke thus helps speaker and members of the audience identify with one another. Choral responses of other kinds likewise serve to coordinate the emotional orientation of members of the group in many other occasions as in political, religious, and social groups. The physical character of sounds that are alarming or soothing to humans and to animals generally seem to have much in common (Collias, 1960). Thus alarm cries are almost universally high pitched and loud (e.g. screams); threat notes are commonly low pitched but harsh (e.g. growls); and sounds serving attractive and approach functions are low pitched, soft and repetitive (e.g. cooing). It is worth noting that the higher the pitch the more difficult it is to localize the origin of the sound so that alarm cries do not betray the position of the caller as much as do threat and attractive calls.

As we have seen, sensitivity to early childhood experiences is commonly accepted as of fundamental importance in human behavior in a way analogous to imprinting and other time-limited learning propensities in animals. The extent to which human language learning is time-limited is a significant problem discussed elsewhere in this book. Here we may point out that the emotional attachment to the mother tongue, like many imprinted attitudes of animals, may be expressed only after long latent periods. It was Santayana's opinion that a poet could be truly creative only in the language of his childhood for only there was the full subtlety of emotional expression open to him.

The socialization function of animal communication in such activities as play and grooming is closely paralleled in human relations by speech phenomena. Babbling in the young is well recognized as a form of play, and the exchange of baby talk between parent and child is part of the socialization process. In addition, the almost ubiquitous phenomenon of idle chatter and small talk among adults is strikingly similar to the grooming behavior of monkeys. It is a gentle massage of the mind, repetitious, slightly stimulating, and in general promoting warm interpersonal relations. The matter of the transmissal of information is strictly secondary although we do recognize that the revelation of little personal secrets is not a defect in gossip. It is part of its essential capacity for expressing shared emotionality. People who insist on intellectual content in cocktail conversation are simply not entering into the spirit of the mental grooming involved. They should spend an afternoon watching apes at the zoo placidly grooming each other by the hour. Perhaps much of newspaper reading, radio listening, TV watching, and light literature reading is appreciated for the self-assurance the quiet verbal stimulation gives human beings whose emotional lives so much depend upon socialization by verbalization.

DISTINCTIVE CHARACTERISTICS OF SPEECH AS A SYSTEM OF COMMUNICATION [1]

Reciprocity and Feedback

One of the most distinctive characteristics of human speech is that it is basically, though of course not necessarily, a reciprocal exchange of signals between people. As we have seen, animal signals are generally mere expressions of the animal's own mood. The use of these signals

[1] Note. The logical differentia of human speech signals are considered elsewhere in this book.

to other animals is, in a sense, not the controlling or determining factor in their production. The sender himself is not usually affected by them nor does the effectiveness of the communication depend upon a reply from the recipients. The sender commonly pays no attention to the effects of his message. Thus for the most part there is lacking the reciprocal interaction of sender and receiver so characteristic of human communication. People do, of course, sometimes talk aloud to themselves but this is so inappropriate that we commonly regard such behavior as bordering the pathological.

When we speak of animal language we generally mean the phrase metaphorically, as in the "language of the bees." The worker bee that has found a good food source signals the distance and position of that source by the kind of dance it performs upon returning to the hive. Yet this signaling system, complex as it seems to us, is hardly to be confused with true language since it is evident that the sender bee is simply producing stimuli without the possibility of entering into a reciprocal exchange of stimuli with the other bees of the hive. They neither answer nor question the sender nor does the sender check on their response.

On the other hand, reciprocity is not entirely lacking in all animal communication. Even the fly-away or alarm signal given by birds, though generally given as a signal of whose effect the sender takes no notice, is reported in some instances to have a measure of reciprocity (Lorenz, 1957). Among certain crows, the sender of an alarm may fly back and circle around repeating the alarm until all members of the flock take to flight. The continued progress of the courtship behavior in many lower vertebrates depends upon a reply being received from the mate. In Japanese monkeys observers have noted that certain cries are directed to particular individual companions. In a sense these may be considered examples of reciprocity in animal communication. Human speech may, therefore, be said to differ generally but not absolutely from animal communication by being a reciprocal interchange of signals.

Specificity of References

A second general characteristic of human communication deficient in animal systems is that of its capacity for specific reference. Animal systems generally signal only the over-all nature or significance of their referents. Thus the alarm cry indicates danger, generally of a predator, but does not specify the kind, direction of approach, or other characteristics of the attack. It is up to the recipients to determine this for themselves having been put on the alert by the alarm. But here, as in respect to reciprocity, the distinction between man and animal communication is quantitative, not absolute. Many birds, particularly ground-living birds, have a different alarm cry for an aerial predator than for one on the ground. Perhaps the most extraordinary example of specificity of reference in animal signals is that of the bee dance mentioned above. But it is doubtful if even this can be regarded as fully specific in the information conveyed since much the same dance is given to signal the position of food or of a swarming site (Lindauer, 1961). The response thus depends on the "needs" or mood of the recipients. Thus the signal says in effect that whatever it is we are all excited about is to be found at such and such a place rather than that food is to be found there. As far as is known there are very few items about which bees signal in this way so that the bee, like other animals, is very strictly limited in its ability to give signals that have specific references.

The phonemic system used in human communication by speech provides a far better basis for conveying specific meanings than does any animal system. Even with only 40-50 phonemes, the variety of signals that can be produced is indefinitely large. Yet it is clear that the methods of communication used by animals are inherently capable of conveying much more in the way of detailed information than they do, in fact, achieve in animal behavior. The limitation in the transmissal of information by animals lies not in the method used but in the mind that uses it. If animals could talk as we like to imagine, would they really have much to say?

Closely related to the specificity of reference is the flexibility introduced into language by the change in referents resulting from change in context. The meaning of a term is contingent upon the other words associated with it. The term "father" changes in reference when modified by "my," "your," or another adjective. Animal signals on the other hand generally have only one referent, irrespective of the context in which they occur. But again this is not an absolute differentiation. Monkeys have been trained to react to contingent stimuli, i.e., to pick blocks of different shapes, depending upon the color of the tray upon which the blocks have been placed. Other examples of contingency in referents can be found in courtship or territory defense where the signal varies in meaning according to attendant circumstances.

SPEECH AS THE INSTRUMENT OF MAN'S MIND

The main point that emerges from the above discussion is that there is no one function of human communication by speech that is not shared to some extent by animal systems. By speech, man does many of the same things that animals do at much the same level, particularly the communication of emotions and attitudes. But with respect to other functions, particularly the communication of specific items of information, man operates at an enormously more advanced level. This does not mean that man is to be viewed as merely a slightly more advanced animal. Such a point of view was popular among biologists of fifty years ago. The study of animal behavior has, however, done much to break down this gradualist evolutionary viewpoint and to emphasize that man, though an animal and a product of animal evolution, is very different in some fundamental behavioral activities from any other animal. The uniqueness of man must be sought not in the special characteristics of speech as a technique of communication but rather in the nature of the mind that makes use of speech as its chief instrument of communication. Indeed the effective use of sign language by the deaf or dumb (*vide* the story of Helen Keller) is sufficient to point out that however useful the special characteristics of speech are to the development of human mentality, they are not of its essence, for the human mind clearly can at least continue development with symbol systems other than speech sounds. Speech, we believe, does not make the mind human, rather the human mind creates speech.

It is hardly possible here to attempt to characterize the special properties of the human mind in any detail, but a few points bearing directly on the relation of speech to this problem may be made.

The animal mind is very much restricted to the here and now. Of course, animals have memories and can respond in a learned manner to cues even after long lapses of time. But the cues must be presented to the senses of the animal at the time if they are to evoke the response. Animals seem unable to call forth from within themselves the stimuli to which to respond. For them, out of sight (or other sense) is out of mind. Even the chimpanzee is surprisingly limited and is almost entirely situation bound. This was dramatically illustrated in Köhler's studies (1927, 1959). After the animals were thoroughly familiar with the use of boxes as aids in retrieving fruit hung beyond their reach, Köhler removed the boxes to the hall outside. Later he allowed the animals to play with the boxes just before entering the experimental room. When faced by the problem in the room they looked around for instruments to use in reaching the fruit. Failing to see any boxes, all the animals except one tried to get the fruit by leaping, etc., and were completely frustrated. One animal after long delay and many vain attempts finally solved the problem by what Köhler considered a sudden insight. Running into the hall he brought in one of the boxes. There is nothing to indicate that animals lower in the scale can solve any such problem, for it is well known that delaying the response to a stimulus even a few minutes usually makes it impossible for the animal to give the correct response. Even the bee in its dance is responding only to the hive stimuli as evidenced by the fact that the dance is given only in the hive situation and not to bees met outside. Of course, the kind of response the bee gives to the hive situation is determined by its recent experience as in learning situations generally.

Because the human mind has as its content things past and future as well as present, it has been described as time-binding. The stimuli to which it responds are not limited to things within the range of its senses. Man can thus deal with a vastly greater number of specific items than can animals, and it becomes possible therefore to communicate by specific identification of innumerable referents. A vocal system of communication using the variations of a fair number of phonemes and elaborated by other items in context then becomes a suitable technique for such use.

Another peculiarity of the human mind relevant to language is its capacity for thinking in terms of purpose and of cause and effect. This is, of course, derivative of the time-binding capacity since it depends upon the capacity for recognizing antecedents and consequences. Our use of language is permeated with causality. In relation to human beings we think in terms of purpose. In such thinking we impute to one another the capacity to plan and foresee the consequences of acts and to associate past, present, and future. So ingrained is this so called "teleological" thinking that we tend to extend it to animals or even to inanimate objects. It required a severe discipline that took many years to develop before students of animal behavior recognized clearly the teleological fallacy and avoided imputing purposefulness and foresight to animals. For example, it is difficult to talk about the alarm cry of a species without implying that it is given "in order" to warn others. Yet, as we have seen, the evidence indicates that in its alarm cry the animal is only expressing its own mood, not deliberately warning others. Today, with the characteristic inertia born of success, some scientists carry the avoidance of teleological thinking to their consideration of human behavior, and wish to exclude purposiveness from human psychology in the name of scientific objectivity. A more reasonable understanding would seem to be to recognize the great gap that exists between the minds of man and of the animal in this regard.

It is in the light of this great difference between the human mind and that of the animal that we may understand the central position of reciprocity in human communication and its almost complete absence in animals. In our speech we anticipate the consequences of our signals and expect signals back which communicate not merely the present condition of the communicant but also its purposes.

Speech may thus be viewed as the unique method of communication evolved by man to suit the uniqueness of his mind. By its great flexibility it permits man to produce a variety of signals commensurate with the richness of his imagination. At the same time the ability to think in terms of causality and purposiveness (time-binding) enables man to expand enormously his use of reciprocal communication for the co-ordination of social activities.

In summary of the comparison of animal and human communication we may conclude that:

1. Both animals and man accomplish certain functions of communication in a similar way. These common functions center largely around the transmission of moods or states of emotionality from one individual to another. In addition to conveying information of immediate significance, such transmission may serve to coordinate physiological functions and establish and maintain socialized in-group feelings. These functions may be attained by signals and symbols originating from specialized (ritualized) postures, movements, or vocal signals. The study of animal society has shown that such communication is basic in the social process in both man and animals.

2. Though human speech signals and symbols afford a richer repertory for communication than any system possessed by animals, the essential difference between human and animal communication does not lie in the capacities of the instrument of communication used but rather in those of the mind using it. Because the human mind is time-binding and thus can develop purposiveness, it uses its signal system (speech) at a level widely separated from that of animals in two regards. Through speech, human beings transmit a wealth of specific reference and engage in a reciprocal interaction with each other.

REFERENCES

Blauvelt, H. Maternal-neonate relationship. In Schaffner, B. (Ed.), *Group processes*. New York: Josiah Macy, Jr. Foundation, 1955.

Collias, N. An ecological and functional classification of animal sounds. In Lanyon, W., & Tavolga, W. (Eds.), *Animal sounds and communication.* Washington, D. C.: American Institute of Biological Sciences, 1960.

Etkin, W. *Social behavior and organization in vertebrates.* Chicago: University of Chicago Press, in press.

Harlow, H. The development of affectional responses in infant monkeys. *Proc. Amer. Phil. Soc.*, 1958, 102, 501-509.

Köhler, W. *The mentality of apes.* New York: Humanities Press, 1927. (Reprinted: New York, Vintage Books, 1959.)

Lack, D. *The life of the robin.* London: Penguin Books, 1953.

Lanyon, W. The ontogeny of vocalizations in birds. In Lanyon, W., & Tavolga, W. (Eds.), *Animal sounds and communication.* Washington, D. C.: American Institute of Biological Sciences, 1960.

Lindauer, M. *Communication among social bees.* Cambridge: Harvard University Press, 1961.

Lorenz, K. Companionship in bird life. In Schiller, C. (Ed.), *Instinctive behavior.* New York: International Universities Press, 1957.

Thorpe, W. H. *Learning and instinct in animals.* Cambridge: Harvard University Press, 1956.

Tinbergen, N. *The study of instinct.* Oxford: Clarendon Press, 1951.

11

Information Theory and the Psychology of Speech

By Milton Valentine, Ph.D.
University of Colorado

HISTORICAL BACKGROUND

BEGINNING IN 1948, SHANNON'S EXPOSITIONS (1948, pp. 379 and 623) have enabled us to become aware of some of the possibilities inherent in considering information and the exchange of information in a quantifiable way. The basic discovery by Shannon and others that information is subject to the same mathematical-statistical interpretation as heat, facilitates not only the handling of various control and computer systems but the description and interpretation of a number of phenomena in the social sciences as well. In the field of speech, for example, applications of information theory or the model of the communication processes upon which much of information theory is based have found application in such diverse areas as group discussion, speech pathology and audiology, and public address, as well as in the mass media.

Perhaps because of its mathematical origin, information has had an immense appeal. Not only engineers and mathematicians, but psychologists (Attneave, 1959), linguistic scholars (Gleason, 1955), artists and musicians (Hajny, Weiss, & Miro, 1962), speech scholars, and a great many others have been attracted by the elegance and apparent fruitfulness of some of the information theory concepts. A part of the appeal lies in the actuarial model of human behavior which allows some prediction of human responses in a way which can never be duplicated by "intuitive" or "clinical" models. Another appeal lies in the possibility of quantifying variables which have previously defied quantification.

Obviously, any theory with impact and possible application in so many different areas is a significant event—provided the applications are not mere marginal notes or questionable dilettante speculations. Information theory, unlike some other general theories, does have some built-in checks on its possible misapplication. It can be applied only where the mathematics are appropriate; like all good "maps" it must fit the territory. A second check on misapplication of information theory is that it purports to predict and describe communication events. A great many things, including certain aspects of human speech, can be considered communication events. As a result, a large body of data is available against which to check the theory. It is important to remember, however, that most of the work done in developing information theory has *not* been done in the area of human communication. Indeed, some information theorists regard the application of the theory to human communication as impossible because of the complexity of the events to be described (Gallegher, 1962). A mathematician might say that the similarity (more technically "isomorphism") of human communication and, say, binary digit transmission, has not been established.

The purpose of this chapter, therefore, must be to provide the student with a reasonable introduction to information theory and to some of the attempts to apply it in the area of human speech.

Fortunately, in spite of the esoteric sounding vocabulary of some of the material, many of the basic ideas in information theory are only old friends wearing new and sometimes scientifically more practical clothing.

DESIGN OF INFORMATION THEORY

Information theory developed against a background which might be described as the engineer's model of a communication or control system. (see Figure 11-1.) An idea (1) is encoded (2) and sent out by a transmitter (3) as a signal over some particular channel(s) (4) which is invariably characterized by some interfering noise (5). The signal (plus noise) is picked up by a receiver (6), decoded (7) in some way, and, hopefully, an idea similar to that which started the process is stimulated in the mind of the person to whom the communication was addressed. In order to be even somewhat sure of this, however, "feedback" from the receiver to the sender must be provided for; this, of course, reverses the entire process; the original sender becomes the receiver; the original receiver, the sender; and more noise and possibility for error is introduced. Such a concept is hardly original with engineers, although in their efforts

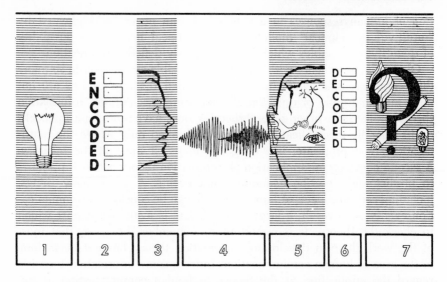

Figure 11-1. The engineers' model of communication. An idea (1) is encoded, translated into language (2), sent out by a transmitter (3), as a signal over some particular channel or channels, for example audible and visual, (4), which are invariably disturbed by some noise (5); the signal and the interfering noise are picked up by a receiver (6), decoded in some way (7), and, hopefully, an idea similar to that which started the process is stimulated in the mind of the person to whom the communication was addressed.

to evaluate radio communication equipment (which gave rise to the field of speech testing in audiology), they were forced to it. The model of communication is strikingly similar to the paragraph in George du Maurier's *Peter Ibbetsen:*

Language is a poor thing. You fill your lungs with wind and shake a little slit in your throat, and make mouths and that shakes the air; and the air shakes a pair of little drums in my head—a very complicated arrangement with lots of bones behind—and my brain seizes your meaning in the rough. What a roundabout way and what a waste of time!

From the engineer's point of view, du Maurier ignores the encoding and decoding processes (perhaps significantly related to semantics among other things) and the necessity for "feedback." The fact that "feedback" cannot safely be ignored can be illustrated in three ways. The testing of communication equipment during World War II which gave rise to speech testing in audiometry by the simple expedient of regarding the listeners as independent variables (rather than as dependent upon the equipment) and keeping the equipment constant, emphasized the inherent, "two-way" nature of communication. In control of gun-fire, for example, it is as important to know where the shell hit as where the gun was aimed in order to correct the aim for the following shot. Even closer to most students of speech: the obvious necessity for the speaker to have some concept of how his audience is reacting, "feedback," in order to adjust appropriately to it, and the recently developed concept that certain problems in cerebral palsy and aphasia may be related to interference with the "feedback" processes rather than to disturbance of the motor-output (Tustin, 1952, p. 54 and ref. 20).

The basic communication model, then, is not unfamiliar. Shannon, following Brillouin, defined that which is communicated so that behavior is modified, information, as "negative entropy." This is a formidable and mathematical way of saying that information is that which tends to eliminate confusion or random activity. Reasoning from this premise, Shannon argued that *the amount of information contained in a given message depends upon the number of alternative possibilities which the message eliminates.* This idea, too, is an old friend. Consider this situation. You have gone to the airport to meet a friend. On arriving you hear your name being called, so you go to the passenger service counter and receive the following message from your friend, "Unable to make 3 P.M. flight." Now you are in a quandary. Is your friend coming? At all? When? If so, by the same air-line or by another? Very few alternatives have been eliminated by his message. For the same six words, however, he could have eliminated all confusion: "Sorry. Arrive Midwest Flight 802 today." Now most of your questions are answered; the second message is more specific, it eliminates most of the alternatives.

In more mathematical language, Shannon's definition of information reads: the amount of information varies as the logarithm of the number of possible alternatives.[1]

From Shannon's basic definition a number of important deductions are possible. One of these is the remarkably elegant "coding theorem." Notice that all communication channels are noisy, and all communications subject to error. In order to prevent error, some "check" or "feedback" may be provided but this, in turn, involves a noisy channel. How noisy some

---

[1] For several reasons the logarithm here intended is the $\log_2$ rather than the more generally familiar $\log_{10}$. The actual formula for information most widely used is: Amount of information $= \log\left(\dfrac{S + N}{N}\right) 2TW$ or $2TW \log \dfrac{S + N}{N}$. Translated into conventional verbal symbols the formula means: "The amount of information in a speech wave is proportional to the duration of the speech, to the range of frequency components involved, and to the logarithm of the number of discriminable steps in amplitude. (Miller, p. 45) Thus, in order for a speaker to increase the amount of information he is attempting to present, he must do one or more of the following: 1) talk longer; 2) talk with a wider range of frequencies (greater variety) in the speech spectrum; or 3) talk so that there are finer distinctions in the intensity of his utterances.

channels can be is readily illustrated by the childhood game of sending a whispered message around a circle of children and comparing the end result with the original message. To avoid some errors we might have the same message sent again and again until the final message was reasonably accurate. In practical situations, however, such a way of getting redundancy is expensive and time consuming. Clearly, we would like to send messages as rapidly and accurately as possible. Shannon's theorem, not precisely stated here, guarantees that the capacity of a channel, even a noisy one, is equal to the fastest rate at which the channel will handle information with a pre-set degree of accuracy or reliability. Consider that during time "T" a number of distinct messages can be sent "N"; then, $\log_2 N(T)/T$ can be shown to give the rate of transmission for the particular channel. Now the surprising thing which follows is that, assuming all other factors to be constant, we can send messages with as low a probability of error as we wish, provided we are willing to slow down our rate of transmission! Error can never be wholly eliminated, but it can be reduced to an infinitesimal level. The general conclusion appears to be true for even the noisiest channels.

REDUNDANCY

Another aspect of the problem raised by noise contamination of the message is that redundancy (repetition of the signal) can be used to reduce errors. (The reader may be interested in thinking through the relationship of this statement to the previous paragraph.) Both noise and information can assume a variety of forms. For example, information may be encoded as speech sounds, Morse code, or the presence or absence of a voltage (as in some binary computers); noise may occur as the rustling of papers, radio static, or any random disturbance of the signal in the channel. Since noise seems to be universal, it is not surprising to find that redundancy is present in all languages in order to insure the reduction of errors. In English a number of types of redundancy can be illustrated. There are rules of syntax which govern the way in which symbols can be related: for example, pronoun must agree with its noun in gender, number, and case. Knowing this rule, we may deduce the gender, number, and case of a noun even when it has been garbled by interfering noise. If the users of a language do not agree upon such rules of syntax, or do not practice them, the possibility for error becomes much greater. Another form of redundancy in English is the structure of the language itself. English sentences tend to be constructed on an "actor-action" basis, just as the phonetic elements of the language tend to be assembled on a "consonant-vowel-consonant" basis. Neither of these tendencies is universal, but the knowledge of them makes it easier to

guess the identity of a missing element in a word or sentence. Some pho-
neticians add another form of redundancy by arguing that the phonetic
process of assimilation adds an additional element which helps the hearer
to guess the identity of sound even when the sound itself has been
destroyed by noise. A study by Misak (1958) indicates that many listeners
can identify a missing consonant sound correctly even when large por-
tions of the following vowel as well as the sound itself are eliminated.
There are, of course, many other forms of redundancy which help reduce
the possibility of error provided that they are known and agreed upon
by sender and receiver. From the mathematician's viewpoint most languages partake of the properties of "Markov chains," that is: the occurrence of any one signal (letter, sound, etc.) limits the possible signals
which may come after it, the occurrence of any two signals limits still
more the possibilities for the following signal, and so on. In this connection the reader will be interested in trying the experiment suggested
as exercise 1 at the end of this chapter. Mathematical "check-codes" represent another form of redundancy designed to eliminate error (Hamming, 1950).

Redundancy has another form as well—semantic redundancy. If we
say "Throw the !!!!!! out the window," the noun is limited to the class
of things which can be thrown out the window, unless of course we are
speaking metaphorically. In this latter case the number of logical meta-
phors is also somewhat limited by the context in which the message
occurs.

ABBREVIATION

While redundancy is a necessary part of language there must be a
counterforce to prevent messages from becoming too long, too repetitious,
and therefore too slow for practical use. This anti-redundancy is abbreviation. Zipf (1949) and others have shown various kinds and patterns
of abbreviation. Abbreviation can be phonetic, semantic, or syntactic,
or all three. In any case the users of the abbreviations must agree on
the terms of use, or agree to accept incomplete information.

The over-generalization which is inherent in pronoun substitution is
one undesirable form of abbreviation because important information is
lost or sometimes deliberately hidden. "They" are "ruining the country,"
for example, may occur from laziness, impatience, or downright dis-
honesty.

A good many abbreviations belong to the class called "definitions."
Definitions can be considered as being either extensional (extensive or
pointing) definitions or denotative (dictionary) definitions. These aspects
of symbols are discussed elsewhere. One interesting use of this concept

in communication was developed by Wendell Johnson (1944). He conceived that an "extensional agreement index" could be determined by having people enumerate things belonging to particular classes represented by words. Suppose we were to ask one hundred people—is expresident Harry Truman a liberal? If fifty say "yes" and fifty say "no" we have the smallest possible agreement among the people asked, and the word liberal would have little application or ability to communicate meaning within such a group. Fortunately, such disagreements do not occur for frequently used words in everyday life.

Miller (1951, p. 111) discusses an "intensional agreement index" determined by counting the number of important words (nouns, verbs, adjectives, adverbs) used in various definitions of a given abstract term. Comparative studies show that workers in the field of biochemistry agree on terms about eight times better than workers in the field of psychology. For example, there is almost no disagreement about the definition of DNA but considerable disagreement about the definition of learning or emotion. (Biochemists might do no better than psychologists in agreeing about definitions, however, if the words selected were "life," "energy," and "matter".) One interesting application of the intensional agreement index in the field of speech was to the area of stuttering (Wepman, Bock, Jones, & Van Pelt, 1958). The study used formal definitions of stuttering and found that these statements were in only slightly more agreement than would have been suggested on the basis of chance, largely because statements about the cause of stuttering were included within the definitions.

APPLICATIONS: LINGUISTIC HABITS

Efforts to solve the problem of vagueness in ordinary speech and language are probably bound to have only limited success. Redundancy can balance abbreviation, definition can balance vagueness only to a limited degree. Noise will always be present. The typical solution is to devise new languages when older languages do not fit. Computer designers and programmers devise languages, complete with syntax and semantic rules for special problems. Linguists have for years devised international languages such as Interlingua or Esperanto. In some ways the most interesting feature of such attempts and of invented or "local" languages in general is the effect of the language on the users. Neither sociologists nor mathematicians are surprised by the observable fact that the language used to "encode" a problem in part determines the solution. The Sapir-Whorf hypothesis that language helps to determine the way in which "reality" is seen has been amply illustrated by the semanticists.

In "The Status of Linguistics as a Science," Sapir (1929, p. 214) argued that "we see and hear and otherwise experience very largely as we do because the language habits of our community predispose certain choices of interpretation." Translated into other terms, there is a very human tendency to become attached to the "map" and make the "territory" fit the map rather than the reverse. The philosopher Nietzsche observed that the very structure of a language may make things "run easily for one philosophy, while making another philosophy quite impossible." Since individuals using the same language tend to view "reality" in the same way (and to re-enforce each other's views), it is not surprising to find that certain linguistic features can be used to separate various social groupings. Shaw's *Pygmalion* makes this point in terms of English social classes: "The moment an Englishman opens his mouth he makes some other Englishman despise him." The surprising thing is how general such a tendency is, especially when studies in the context of information—communication theory. Two examples of effects related to communication and language are considered here since they are problems of some concern to students of speech. The first relates to the phonetic structure of language as a reflection of the patterns of identification of the users. Incomplete studies by Valentine and others have shown that in several bilingual communities in Colorado the number of articulatory errors made in English by Spanish-speaking American children is greater when their social group choices are more nearly within the Spanish-speaking community than when their choices were within the English-speaking community (Avery, 1958). Similar results have been reported in other areas and with other language groups. Factors of education, contact, parental home-language, and so on, have been reasonably well controlled in such studies. What is surprising is not the phenomenon but that it occurs in such small units as the phonemes of everyday speech, and it underlines the probable importance of speech as a determining factor in a whole variety of relationships.

Prediction

The second example is more directly related to information-communication theory. Some years ago Bell Telephone Company was confronted with the problem of predicting how many telephone channels would be needed to connect two cities of known size. For cities of middle size the number of messages was found to be given, roughly, by the following formula:

$$M = k\ \frac{p_1 p_2}{d} \quad \text{or} \quad = \frac{k}{d}\,(p_1 p_2)$$

where M stands for the number of messages, k for a constant, p_1 and p_2 for the populations of the two cities, and d for the distance between them. Considerable work in sociometry can be related to this formula. The studies of Loomis (1946) and others provide an admirable example of how this concept may be applied to communication phenomena and related factors in large groups. In this study families in a small German village were studied for political affiliation and for visiting relationships. Families were classified according to the previously determined political belief of the head of the household. Nazi 21, Social Democrat 23, Communist 6, other 11. The results of the study are shown in Figure 2. The arrows represent the channels used, and the numbers at the arrow points represent the number of times a visit occurred in the direction shown, while visits within the group are shown by circular arrows. Thus, there were 32 visits by Nazi family members to Social Democrats, but only 25 by Social Democrats to Nazis. An information-communication theorist would refer to this as "traffic density." Since the number of visits to be expected might be assumed to be similar to the number of telephone calls anticipated between groups of given size, although no one has made the application, one might argue that some version of the message formula might be applicable to Loomis' data. Zipf (1945, 1949), Miller (1951, pp. 261-2), Steward (1947), and many others have demonstrated that the likelihood of messages passing from one person to another is roughly inversely proportional to the distance between them. Distance, however, may be thought of as geographic distance, or in terms of distance in what Kurt Lewin called "social space" (1935). This application was actually made by several University of Colorado graduate students to Greek letter organizations on the campus. The number and direction of telephone calls between a number of Greek letter organizations were recorded, and treated by means of the "message" formula. Obtained results agreed rather well with those predicted. The determined "d" was greatest when the high-status and low-status organizations were exchanging messages, least when high or low status organizations were calling within their own group. Status ratings were determined independently from studies which had been run on an entirely different basis by another department.

Group Functioning

Such applications suggest another possible use of the information-communication theory concepts in an area of special significance to students of speech—the general area of leadership and group functioning. Studies at the Ohio State University by Shartle and others, and at Massachusetts Institute of Technology by Bavelas and others have made important contributions to our knowledge of group functioning and communication patterns.

Consider two contrasting organizations assigned similar tasks. Group A is organized and required to communicate along the more or less traditional lines of the so-called "inverted-Y" pattern. Group B is organized and required to communicate as an "open" or "star-wheel" group. For most tasks, set Group B will solve the problem faster, with higher morale, and greater accuracy than Group A. If a linear pattern, Group C, is added, one of the reasons for Group A's non-success becomes apparent, a reason which is related to the communication network itself. In Group C the center individual, since he is central, is in a position to control more of the group's communication than anyone else, and becomes the leader; the individuals on either end of the line, since they are at the ends, tend to become uninterested and consequently less productive in terms of the assigned task. Notice that in Group A the communication network is similar to Group C, and the general problems of morale or involvement and productivity are similar in these two groups. In Group B, however, the pattern is different: everyone is involved, morale is high and productivity is at a maximum. The student is urged to observe these phenomena for himself with the Bavelas demonstration described at the end of the chapter. The student is cautioned, however, against over-interpreting his findings. Under certain conditions, especially when the central individual in the communication network knows the solution to the problem in advance, Group A will prove superior to Groups B and C.

One basic factor affecting human organizations is communication. By using communication as the independent variable as has been suggested, a number of interesting observations can be made on both large groups and individuals. Consider the large groups first. One application of Shannon's theorem suggests that information will be lost due to noise in the channel under all conditions. Now consider a large organization as an information relaying entity. At each station (each individual) the message must be decoded, receded, retransmitted, just as in the whispered message sent around the circle of children. Even where the message is written it must at least be placed in the envelope for retransmission, and there is always the possibility that it may be lost or temporarily mislaid. The "line loss" in transmitting any message is thus greater when a larger number of individuals are involved. Studies of the psychology of rumor or mass hysteria have shown how messages are changed under such circumstances in terms of the perceptions of the senders and receivers, but the nature of the communication network also has an effect. In studies of group communication in hierarchies it can be observed that in inverted-Y type organizations there is a greater tendency for each individual, when possible, to withhold certain aspects of information to

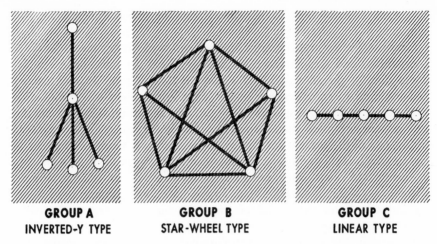

GROUP A   GROUP B   GROUP C
INVERTED-Y TYPE STAR-WHEEL TYPE LINEAR TYPE

Figure 11-2. "Inverted-Y," "Star-wheel" and Linear patterns of group communication.

be transmitted, or to interpret such information in such a way as to be more favorable to himself or to make his appear to be more valuable to the organization. This tendency is less marked in "star-wheel" type groups. Moreover, in the inverted-Y type organization a greater percentage of communications relate to the "staff" rather than the "line" functions of the group than in the star-wheel type group (Hertz & Lesser, 1951). The format of information-communication theory has proved successful in providing an elementary model for such studies; for studies of the individual it may prove even more useful.

Individual Verbal Functioning

Suppose that the "threshold" of an individual is to be studied. Almost at once certain factors become apparent. The better the individual knows the "code" and understands the "syntax" of the message to be sent, the more able he will be to cope with the "noise" which is always present. The individual apparently "sets" himself to respond, and his set may be effective, or ineffective, partly depending upon his knowledge. The better he knows the code the more noise he can tolerate. He will also be affected by the group of which he sees himself a part, by his emotional state, and by his tolerance for uncertainty in the situation. Radio telegraphers have, as a group, lower auditory thresholds than individuals not so trained; persons under stress may "over-react" to very slight stimuli and totally ignore louder ones; individuals who recognize and accept the possibility of error tend to do better than those who do not. In all these cases the number of *probable* alternatives has been affected, thus changing the amount of information carried by a particular signal. The abbreviation for the class of phenomena has acquired different value and enumerations. Now consider, as one example, an individual with aphasic language disturbances.[2] If his problem is primarily one of out-put or expression, we may think of it as a loss of the syntactical elements for communication. The contextual restrictions of ordinary speech have less force for the aphasic; perhaps he must learn again how to combine sounds into syllables, syllables into words, words into sentences, sentences into paragraphs. Little words (say, prepositions and conjunctions) do not come easily and must be searched out with difficulty. For the expressive aphasic the rules by which signals are fitted together have been impaired. Another possibility is that the aphasic is not readily able to behave verbally within the old set and pattern of conventions and linguistic rules which govern his community. For a receptive aphasic the situation is, perhaps, like that of a listener to a very noisy channel—he does not receive enough information to narrow down the group of possible messages; he is confronted by signals which, because of the distortions introduced by his own nervous system, convey very little information. He is assisted by context, however, because context applies a limiting factor to the number of possibilities. To a receptive aphasic the word in isolation may be impossible, yet he may perceive and repeat a word in context even when he cannot perceive and repeat the parts of that word.

A somewhat similar analysis may be made of the problems of an individual who is hard of hearing. He, too, learns to depend upon context, and upon the probable alternatives.

The analysis of anomia by Wepman and others (1958) provides a summary statement which suggests some possible relationships between aphasia and the communication-information theory here discussed.

. . . it was hypothesized that anomia may be characterized by the use of all but the most general (and hence most frequent) words in the language . . . such a patient has suffered disruption of the voluntary control of those . . . words which carry essential information to the listener . . .

In other words, anomia results when the "memory-bank" for all but the best-learned (most frequently used) words and syntactical rules is destroyed.

Channel Overloading

Perhaps the most potentially fruitful application of information-communication theory in the field of speech relates to the mass media of com-

[2] Aphasic disturbances are impairment of language function which are associated with cerebral damage after the establishment of conventional *verbal behavior*.

munication. Here a great body of actuarial data is potentially available, data of a type which seems to be readily adaptable to the general theory under discussion. As a final illustration of possible inter-relationships between information theory and the field of speech, consider four concepts derived from information theory and some illustrations of them derived from various aspects of the study of speech and communication in the mass media broadly conceived, and then from other aspects of speech.

An over-loaded channel adds to the noise and hence to the loss of information. Almost everyone who has a mail-box is in a good position to illustrate this statement by simply observing what happens to other than first-class mail. Certain large administrative organizations have found it necessary to resort to special announcements in addition to regular news-letters, in addition to bulletin boards, in addition to word of mouth communication, simply because the paper channel has been overloaded with so much trivia that it is consistently ignored by the employees. Some groups have found a partial solution to this problem through the medium of "briefing"—using the appeal of the individual standing before a group presenting information in as clear and concise a manner as possible. This method has had wide use in the military and various business organizations, perhaps influenced by the Hollywood picture of a movie-star before the bombing-mission map. Such a solution to the overloaded channel has a number of advantages: first, a person is generally more interesting than a piece of paper; second, more "information" (including the speaker's feelings about the topic and his character) can be provided in a briefing because of the greater band width of face-to-face communication than that possessed by a piece of paper (recent studies of the believability of news show that news is more likely to be believed when presented over television than when presented by newspaper); third, the individual making the presentation becomes more involved or committed to the group and the idea by the very act of making the presentation; fourth, and most important, the briefing allows the speaker to adjust to the feedback from the audience, to clarify and adjust to their misunderstandings and their needs. There are significant disadvantages to briefing. All the advantages depend upon the ability and willingness of the speaker to make use of them. No written record is available, and in spite of the greater "band-width" of the oral-visual channel for some purposes, it will not handle detailed information without considerable redundancy. (Students of public speaking might consider the various forms of redundancy in the several forms of outline suggested in the standard textbooks.) Studies of the effectiveness of personal presentation suggest its effectiveness for certain purposes, but any teacher who has read an examination covering a lecture can also point out its limitations.

Another possible parallel to the over-loaded channel is the behavior of the child with a speech problem who has been "over-taught,"—he simply closes off the channel.

A channel can be overloaded or noise can be increased in another way —if redundant messages arrive in poor or untimed sequence. This can be shown in the study of attempts of various groups to inform the public about events or arguments thought to be important. Consider the problem of the chairman of, say, the Peach Festival. He sends out announcements to newspapers—the story appears from one to three days later— to the local radio station—the story appears on the same day—and he appoints a committee to "spread the word"—rumor of this type may take more than a week to pass through a reasonably small, homogeneous community. The harried chairman, unless he has timed these messages to arrive together, will not get maximum effect from his campaign and may receive calls for a week after the Festival asking what has happened. Furthermore, the messages may arrive differently, simply because the channels are different as the receiver sees them. It is one thing to find in your mail box a note reading "You will see the Dean of the College in his office at 4:30 on Thursday," and quite another to have the Dean ask in a friendly voice, "Please come by the office about 4:30 Thursday." Some of the difference is due to reaction to the written message as opposed to the spoken one. The hypothetical "Peach Festival" mentioned by a newspaper story buried in the classified section is one thing, the same program given five minutes on the six-o'clock news broadcast is another. One study of a campaign to insure the licensing of X-ray technicians backfired simply because the audience received negative impressions based upon the insistence of the presentation and because it was presented at the same time as that of a major advertising program by a large electrical company.

INTENTIONAL REDUNDANCY

A second corollary in information theory might be stated as follows: while noise cannot be eliminated, its effects can be reduced by the choice of a code which introduces redundancy into the message as efficiently as possible. Such use of redundancy requires that the possibility for error be recognized and accepted. It is interesting and somewhat frustrating to note how many individuals refuse to accept just this possibility—they "believe their ears" under any and all circumstances and violently resist any suggestion that error is possible.

Admitting the possibility for error, a number of redundancy schemes are possible. Mathematically, such devices as Hamming codes and Bose-Chaudhuri codes have been developed and are relatively well understood. For speech, however, the situation is less clear. One well developed scheme involves the use of simple, concrete language. This is effective from the information-communication theory viewpoint for two reasons: the use of simple language enlarges the potential audience, and the use of short, simple words and sentences assures that every potential reader will have the maximum possible knowledge of both the semantic and syntactic aspects of redundancy. Such books as Flesch's *The Art of Plain Talk* and *The Art of Readable Writing* exploit these principles. There is, naturally, a serious check on such applications of redundancy. The writer or speaker who limits himself to seven-word sentences may be more readable or listenable, but he will also discover that the number of concepts which he can express is limited and the degree of precision with which he can express them is more limited. Other forms of redundancy have been referred to earlier: restatement and enumeration of examples are two common forms used in the preparation of speeches, the effects of which have not been widely studied in a quantified way.

A more clinical illustration of the need for redundancy and clarity in communication may be found in the area of hearing. There is considerable evidence to suggest that the auditory threshold as presently determined is subject to a variety of effects resulting from the internal criteria for response established by the subject (Swets, 1961). As was previously suggested, individuals who regard their "hearing" as poor or inadequate may demand a higher degree of certainty before they will respond to a signal than individuals without such a set; they may also demand more signal intensity or less noise than is usually necessary. One might speculate that some change in the patient's internal response criteria may be significantly involved in auditory training.

ENCODING FOR KNOWN RECEIVERS

A third deduction from information-communication theory is that if behavior is to be changed the messages must be encoded in ways appropriate to the receivers. Festinger discriminates between messages which are intended to be instrumental and which require feedback from the group and messages which are consummatory and serve their purpose only by expressing the feelings or ideas of the sender. In either case the general deduction holds. If the language of the speaker is not understood or is misinterpreted by his hearers, his instrumental communication ceases to influence, except perhaps negatively. For consummatory communication the generalization is less obvious but still true. Consider an individual who is receiving therapy in which a goal of the treatment is to allow him to express his feelings. Whether the therapy is determined by language, relationship, or some combination of methods, the patient must express himself in symbols which are genuinely related to his emotions. A child, whose natural language is play, must be encouraged to play out his feelings. Simply talking about them will not usually be enough.

The process of appropriately coding information may relate to such obvious factors as word or example choice or to somewhat more subtle factors such as organization. One study of how coding may affect audience responses was reported by Hovland and his associates in 1949. This was a study directed to the question: when the bulk of evidence supports one argument, is it more effective to present only one side of the argument or to introduce arguments opposed to the point being made? The actual study was made in connection with the Army program to convince the troops that the end of the war in Europe did not necessarily mean an early end to the Pacific war. The results of the study suggest that the presentation of both sides of an argument is more effective with listeners who are opposed to the viewpoint being presented. Apparently the coding feature which indicates that the sender realizes or understands the possibility of disagreement is more effective with hostile listeners than a mere one-sided expression of opinion, however well presented.

NECESSARY NOISE

A fourth deduction relates to the influence of noise or errors in communication. The elimination of all noise or all error would probably be an undesirable thing. Strange as this may sound after previous discussion, the presence of noise in communication channels forces the group to repeat messages and to subject them to analysis. Shaw's work with group problem solving in 1932 supports this argument that the redundancy inherent in group effort provides a safeguard against errors since the process of repeating and recoding messages was likely to bring errors or misinterpretations to light. Stated in more theoretical terms, a noiseless circuit would reduce errors but might also lead to an undesirably high degree of uniformity in behavior. In a continually changing world, a group composed of individuals with one, uniform, reinforced view of that world would soon perish. Gaylord Simpson, a biologist, notes that when the number of varieties within a species becomes too small the species is doomed to extinction. This might possibly mean that when the number of modes of adjustment to changing reality becomes too small the group is in danger, and when communication is so effective that only one form of behavior is possible within it the group is finished.

The presence of a reasonable degree of noise in the circuit has another less abstract advantage. Where noise forces recoding, it is likely to break down fixed ideas and result in new solutions to old problems.

Our discussion of information theory, which began on a rather unpleasant note, thus ends on a somewhat hopeful one. While it is true that noise cannot be avoided and information can never be communicated in its entirety, the use of energy to send information, to recode and decode it, to overcome noise, has its own compensations.

For the field of speech, the use of information theory promises a new and potentially valuable way of regarding old problems and a way of treating mathematically variables which were not previously subject to such treatment. However attractive such a prospect may be for students of so incredibly complex a subject as speech, it must be remembered that no one system or model can provide all or even most of the answers.

The exercises that follow are intended to give the reader an opportunity to apply some of the principles of information theory in a "practical" or at least easily workable situation.

EXERCISES

1. Assemble a group of friends and ask them to guess letter by letter a message which you have devised. Keep a count of the number of guesses required to identify correctly each letter and space. Remember that the information carried by any one letter or space depends upon the number of alternatives eliminated by the occurrence of that letter or space. How do you account for the fact that the initial letter of each word does not carry the most information? Explain why the last word or letters of the message can usually be guessed all at once? For purposes of comparison you might try this sentence: There is no reverse gear on a motorcycle.

2. Cut a number of cards into jig-saw patterns like those used by Bavelas and shown below. Now distribute the pieces of cards in random order to three groups of five members each. Instruct the groups that they are

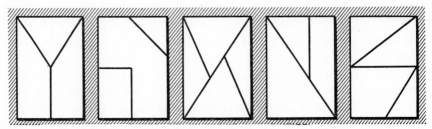

Figure 11-3. Bavelas' card patterns (modified).

to assemble cards of an approximate size, and that members can exchange pieces until the task is completed. Make sure that all the groups understand that they can exchange pieces only along the lines indicated by the arrows in the diagram. Compare the morale, speed, efficiency, and satisfaction of "inverted-Y," "star-wheel" and other groups.

3. Develop a plan for determining the percentage handicap of an individual with an articulation problem. Base your analysis upon the amount of information carried by each phoneme. What are the limitations of such a procedure?

4. In terms of information-communication theory, why are educational programs on radio and television generally rather unpopular?

5. Can a group leader maintain his position if he is not at the center of a communication network? Why?

REFERENCES

Attneave, F. *Applications of information theory to psychology.* New York: Holt, Rinehart, and Winston, 1959.

Avery, J. Sociometric choices and articulatory behavior among bilingual Spanish-Americans. Unpublished paper, University of Colorado, 1958.

Flesch, R. *The art of plain talk.* New York: Harper & Row, 1946.

Gallegher, F. Some applications of simple coding theory. Public Lecture, U.S. Bureau of Standards, Boulder, Colorado, Feb., 1962.

Gleason, H. A. *An introduction to descriptive linguistics.* New York: Holt, Rinehart, and Winston, 1955. Pp. 280-283.

Hajny, J., Weiss, W., & Miro, G. Communication in architecture, painting, and music. Public lecture, University of Colorado, March, 1962.

Hamming, R. W. Error-detecting and error-correcting codes. *Bell System Technical Journal,* 1950, XXIX, 147 ff.

Hertz, D. B., & Lesser, S. L. People in groups. *Scientific American,* 1951, CLXXXIV, 26-38.

Hovland, E. I., Lumsdaine, A. A., & Sheffield, R. *Experiments in mass communication.* Princeton: Princeton University Press, 1959.

Johnson, W. Studies in language behavior. *Psychol. Monogr.,* 1944, LVI, 2.

Lewin, K. *A dynamic theory of personality.* New York: McGraw-Hill, 1935. Pp. 66-68.

Loomis, C. P. Political and occupational cleavages in a Hanoverian village, Germany. *Sociometry,* 1946, IX, 316-333.

Miller, G. A. *Language and communication.* New York: McGraw-Hill, 1951.

Misak, J. Recognition of certain consonant sounds when varying amounts of the sound are eliminated. Unpublished paper, Stanford University, 1958.

Sapir, E., *Language,* 5, 1929, 207-214.

Shannon, C. E. A mathematical theory of communication. *Bell System Technical Journal,* 1948, XXVII.

Stewart, J. Q. Empirical mathematical rules concerning the distribution and equilibrium of population. *Geograph. Rev.,* 1947, XXXVII, 461-485.

Stogdill, R. M. Leadership, membership, and organization. *Psychol. Bull.,* 1950, XLVII, 1-14.

Swets, J. A. Is there a sensory threshold? *Science,* 1961, LXXXIV, 3473, 168-178.

Tustin, A. Feedback. *Scientific American,* 1952, CLXXXVII, 3, 48-55.

Valentine, M. Speech therapy and the cerebral palsies. Proceedings: University of Colorado Medical School Rehabilitation Conference, March, 1960, 18-22.

Wepman, J., Bock, R. D., Jones, L. V., & Van Pelt, D. Psycho-linguistic study of aphasia: a revision of the concept anomia. *J. Spch and Hearing Disorders,* 1958, XXI, 4, 468-477.

Zipf, G. K. The meaning-frequency relationship of words. *J. gen. Psychol.,* 1945, 251-256.

Zipf, G. K. *Human behavior and the principle of least effort.* Reading, Mass.: Addison-Wesley, 1949.

IV.

APPLICATIONS:
THE INDIVIDUAL

12

The Development of Speech
In the Child:
First Sounds to First Words

SOUND PRODUCTION

BEFORE A CHILD CAN LEARN to use an arbitrary array of oral sounds as
a form of symbol behavior, he normally lives through a series of pre-
lingual overlapping stages of sound production. Each stage serves important functions and has lasting significance. Each stage serves the physical, emotional, and intellectual needs of the child. In turn, if we are
dealing with a normal child, his speech status is likely to be an excellent
index of his physical, intellectual, and emotional status. Together, these
factors constitute the status of the child as an acting and reacting personality.

FACTORS RELATED TO SPEECH SOUND DEVELOPMENT

Differences that may make a difference in the ultimate speaking and
linguistic abilities of the child begin to appear during the first six months
of the child's life. Even at this early age, changes take place that are
related to the infant's establishment of himself as an independent organism. Some children are more proficient in the sounds they produce
than others; some resort to sound play more often than others, and some
show earlier selectivity than others in their sound play. Our evidence
about the early sound play of children suggests that by the end of the
first year it may be possible to make predictions about later language

development. Among the infants who show variety and control of sound production, we are likely to find more than a chance representation as they grow older of children with better than average language ability. The infant with a good phonemic storehouse is likely to become the child with a good lexical storehouse. By and large, speech sound development is likely to be positively related to intelligence and to the occupational status of the parents, with children of professional parents showing earlier and more rapid development than children from parents in "laboring" occupations. Differences, especially in control of consonant sounds, begin to become apparent after eighteen months. After this age, differences also become apparent in speech sound development between boys and girls, with girls showing better control of distinct speech sound types than boys (Irwin, 1957).

In the very early sound-making of infants, the production of front vowels predominates, with a variety of [æ] especially prominent. According to Irwin (1957), ". . . the major trend of vowel mastery by the infant lies with the back vowels. The increment in the use of back vowels begins to appear about the 6th month and is quite prominent after a year." In interesting contrast is Irwin's observation that though infants below six months of age produce mostly front vowels, their consonant production is mostly back-of-the-mouth in the velar and glottal areas. Irwin's findings do not support the general belief that front consonants such as [b], [p], and [m] are the earliest ones produced and brought under control by infants.

Negative Factors: Inadequate Stimulation

Aside from mental retardation, there are two factors that are negatively related to speech sound development and to later language development. One is lack of stimulation, and the other is brain damage. Irwin's data supports the general observation that children who have spent a considerable portion of their time in orphanages do not speak as well as those brought up in the usual family setting. As early as six months the sound development curves of infants in orphanages are inferior to those of infants brought up in their own homes. The presumed reason for this unfavorable difference is the lack of stimulation for speech sound play provided in orphanage settings. The effects and implications of stimulation for vocalization and sound production are given weight by the observations and theoretic formulations of several psychologists and psychiatrists (Goldfarb, 1945; Miller & Dollard, 1941). The orphanage infant, as any infant deprived of the attention and affection of an adult, is likely to continue to be retarded in all forms of behavior that develop as a result of social stimulation and imitation.

Babbling, we may presume, is brought forth more as a result of adult stimulation than imitation. Later stages of pre-lingual sound production, as we shall soon consider, call for identification and imitation as well as stimulation.

Brain Damage

Children with brain damage and cerebral palsy show marked retardation in their speech sound development compared with normal children. In a study by Irwin (1955), cerebral palsied children took until age five and a half to reach the speech sound proficiency reached by most children at age two and a half. The cerebral palsied children at five and a half showed a striking deficiency of consonant sound production and control, a decrement of back vowels, and a preponderance of front and middle vowels.

SPEECH SOUND PROFICIENCY

The observations of Irwin and his associates on the sound production of infants are based on the appearance of distinctive sound types in their spontaneous utterances. Another approach to speech sound production is based on manifest ability of children to produce speech sounds proficiently in words. Templin (1952, 1953) tested for speech sound proficiency by asking school age children to repeat test words read by the examiner. Pre-school articulatory proficiency was checked either through the repetition of presented test words or in verbal utterances evoked in the identification of pictures.

Templin's findings indicate that most children reach the equivalent of adult articulatory proficiency between the ages of seven and eight. In keeping with the findings of Irwin on infant speech, girls were observed to develop articulatory control earlier than boys. On the average, the girls are about 95 per cent correct in their articulatory efforts at about seven years of age while boys on the average require another year for equal articulatory proficiency. Vowels and diphthongs are accurately produced by both sexes at a very early age. By three years most of the children studied by Templin could correctly produce the vowels and diphthong sounds of American-English in 90 per cent of their verbal utterances.

Ruth Metraux is another observer of the speech of young children whose findings relative to sound production are essentially along the same line as Templin's. Metraux (1950) studied the speech products of children at seven pre-school age levels from 18 to 54 months. She observed that by 30 months the vowel production of children was 90 per cent or more correct and that consonant production was 90 per cent or more correct by 54 months. The children observed by Metraux were all average or above in intelligence who were in attendance at the Guidance Nursery of Yale University. In general, research findings on the speech sound proficiency of young children indicate that most sounds are controlled (produced with the equivalent ability of the non-speech defective adult) by age seven or eight. Girls reach articulatory proficiency about a year earlier than boys. Children of average or above intelligence reach speech sound proficiency earlier than do children who are below average in intelligence. The factors of age and intelligence, we will later learn, are also related to linguistic (verbal) proficiency.

Before discussing linguistic proficiency we will review the stages of speech production that may be observed in pre-verbal development of infants and pre-school-age children.

STAGES IN THE DEVELOPMENT OF SPEECH

The Undifferentiated Cry

The first reactions of the newborn infant to his environment are reflexive, total bodily responses. The infant reacts as a whole to the stimuli that come to him out of a world full of whirling, buzzing confusion. Crying, the infant's first vocal activity, is part of a purely reflexive total bodily response to chemical-nervous stimuli within his organism. Expiration of breath sets the vocal cords into vibration and gives rise to the birth cry. The cries which follow and which may be caused by sensations of pain, hunger, thirst, heat, cold, or other sources of discomfort, are also reflexive, total bodily responses which lack specificity and direction. The nature of the irritant does not significantly alter the character of the response. This lack of differentiation persists, in a very large measure at least, through the first month of the infant's life, and sometimes through part of the second month.

Blanton (1917) studied infant crying under conditions in the infant which included the following states: hunger, responses to noxious stimuli such as rough handling, circumcision, lancing and care of boils, sores, etc., and fatigue. She observed that the cries in response to any one of these states were not uniform for all infants. Differences were noticed to exist in regard to vowels and consonants produced, timbre, and degree of intensity. The cries, however, were used interchangeably by the same child. For example, the cry as a response to noxious stimuli was fundamentally the same as the cry in response to hunger, with an exaggeration in degree of intensity. A possible exception is the colic cry. Blanton described it as starting abruptly on a tone three to five octaves above the adult female voice, and sliding through a "modified chromatic scale to within range of the middle octave." The differences in the colic cry can be accounted for by its muscular innervation. The muscles of the abdominal walls are rigid and tense. The extraordinarily high degree of muscular tension is probably shared by the body as a whole, including the muscle folds that control the action of the vocal cords. This would explain the unusually high pitch of the cry.

In general, we might conclude that even the fondest and most sensitive of mothers is unable to determine by listening to her child's crying just what he needs or wants during the first month of his life. The mother has to *see* her child as well as hear him before she can decide whether to feed him or bring him a change of linen.

Despite the lack of differentiation in the early crying of the infant, there is one important similarity between such crying and later speech stages. Most of the reflexive crying of infants is produced on expired breath. Beyond this, the respiration of infants in their reflexive crying is characterized by short, quick inhalations and comparatively slow, prolonged expiration. The reflexive cries of the infant during the first month or two include sounds that resemble the front vowels and the back consonants they will later produce as they learn the language of the adults in their environment. Vowels predominate in the undifferentiated reflexive sound production of infants.

Differentiated Crying

Differentiation in the sounds of crying may become discernible after the first month of the infant's life. The crying continues to be a total bodily response to situations. The type of bodily response, however, begins to vary with the situation, with the nature of the stimulus or combination of stimuli. For example, the sensation of hunger—caused, among other things, by a contraction of the muscles of the stomach—results in changes of *all the muscles of the body,* including those involved in the production of the crying sounds. These changes, when accompanied by vocalization, give rise to the type of cry which we come to recognize as a hunger cry characterized and distinguished from others by its rhythms. So, also, skin irritations, thirst, pressure, etc., give rise, because of special types of total bodily responses, to characteristic cries which accompany the responses.

At the beginning, these responses are more or less fixed, and may be considered as pattern-responses, that is, complexes of movements which occur from time to time, and which are called forth by certain types of stimulus situations. The pattern-response as a whole is usually directly adaptive in that it modifies or "controls" the environment of the infant so as to result in the satisfaction of a need or a want. The intake of food or water, or the avoidance of a painful pressure, are examples of such satisfactions. The uttered sounds are merely elements in the pattern-response. They arise from the innervations of the muscles of the throat and mouth and are characteristic of the total pattern-response. Because of this they become identified with the stimulating situations or conditions that evoke the sounds.

A mother tuned in to her child, because of the characteristic qualities of the sounds, may learn to recognize his varying cries and to react to them as signals that announce his changing needs and wants. Even though the varying cries are produced without symbol or indicative intention on the part of the infant, they may serve as signals and so may result in signal reactions on the part of an observer. In this manner they may become the basis of a sound-reaction system between the child and a listener-observer.

Babbling

Following the stage of differentiated reflexive crying, but not entirely abandoning it, most infants enter the babbling or vocal play stage. This may begin as early as the third month for some, and by the fourth month for most normal children.

For the most part, sounds are produced at random. With increasing frequency, however, as the infant matures, occasional sound repetition may be heard. Repetition may be interpreted as an indication that some sort of "feedback" through the tactile, kinesthetic, or auditory sensory avenues, or through a combination of two or more, is being established. Something is beginning to happen which permits for sound reproduction, without which an oral language system could not be developed.

The trained listener can begin to distinguish specific sounds and combinations of sounds in the infant's babbling and vocal play. Some of these sounds may resemble fairly closely the sounds produced in the speech of the listener. He should certainly be able to recognize the vowel [æ] as in *hat* or a reasonably close approximation of this vowel. He should also be able to hear some back-of-the-mouth consonants such as [k] and [g], and possibly some front consonants such as [p], [b], and [m]. The order of these sounds was considered earlier in our discussion of Orvis Irwin's research. (See also Winitz & Irwin, 1958.) We might point out that Irwin's findings differ from those of older reports in that Irwin reported the appearance of back consonants before those articulated in the front of the mouth. It might also be pointed out that the older studies were for the most part based upon observations of one or two children whose sounds were immediately transcribed by the listener-reporter. The observations of Irwin and his associates are based on a comparatively large number of infants (forty or more); they employed trained observers whose observations were compared for reliability. Further, the sound products of the infants were recorded on tape, and were (and still are) available for re-evaluation. These points are mentioned not to deprecate the observations of earlier students, but to emphasize that the Irwin studies reviewed in this text are considered objective and worthy of the attention we have given them. If the observations differ from those of earlier reports, we are inclined to accept those which are results of investigations carried on directly by Irwin or by his associates.[1]

The infant who has arrived at the stage of babbling also shows responsiveness to the sounds of others around him. He may coo or gurgle in response to a pleasant voice or a "happy" sound; he may cry or stop his own vocal play in response to an angry or "unhappy" voice. He may appear momentarily to interrupt his own vocal and oral activity in response to another's efforts. In short, during the period of vocal play, the child is *listening* as well as producing sounds. These activities reveal the development of responsiveness to externally produced sounds as well as to self-initiated sounds. The babbling of the infant, especially during the latter period of vocal play, is an important preparatory period for later articulate utterance.

Though the oral and vocal activities are still a by-product of other behavior and so an aspect of a total pattern response, it is a much better differentiated response than the crying of the first two or three months. Beyond this, the infant is "practicing" sounds that he will later produce in his articulate speech efforts. To be sure, he will discard many sounds that are not included in the linguistic system or systems of his environment. But some sounds will definitely remain and become part of his phonemic inventory as he learns to speak. The babbling stage usually continues until the end of the fifth or sixth month for most normal infants.

The speech development of the congenitally deaf child differs from that of the normal hearing child beyond the babbling stage. The deaf child does not continue babbling for as long a time as does the hearing child. The speech of the deaf child does not progress to the lallic (self-imitative) and echolalic (imitative of sound patterns, or words of environ-

---

[1] The interested reader might wish to investigate and compare the studies of W. Preyer, *The Mind of the Child* (New York, Appleton, 1890) and J. Sully, *Studies of Childhood* (London, Longmans, 1896) with those reported here. He might also wish to investigate the discussions of early sound development in M. W. Lewis, *Infant Speech*, 2d ed. (New York, Humanities Press, 1961) and W. F. Leopold, "Patterning in Language Learning" (*Language*, 5, 1953-1954, pp. 1-14). Along related lines, the reader might also wish to study the article by R. W. and Joy B. Albright, "The Phonology of a Two-Year-Old Child" (*Word*, 12, 3, 1956, pp. 382-390).

ment) stages because he cannot hear the sounds he makes, and so cannot reproduce heard sounds. Whatever self-imitation in sound production does occur is probably determined by the ease of kinesthetic production and the pleasure derived from the production of the sound. The self-reward of pleasurable aural reaction which is present and so important in the hearing child, is lacking in the deaf child.

Lallation

Lallation [2] may be defined as the repetition of *heard sound complexes or syllables.* This stage begins usually during the second six months of the infant's life. At first, the only sounds produced are those the child has himself produced in his babbling. The infant reproduces those sounds which are pleasurable for him. The first step in lallation, very likely, is the production of a sound complex or syllable which occurred originally because of a motor reflex process involving the vocal mechanism. In this respect it is no different from babbling. The important difference is that during the lallation stage the child's response to the sound he has produced results in self-imitation. Successful imitation presumably is a source of pleasure, and so serves as an incentive for further repetition. Thus auditory and kinesthetic impressions become associated with states of pleasure and satisfaction, and the infant learns that he can imitate sounds that he has himself produced. After he has learned to imitate many sound combinations of his own accidental, motor-reflexive making, he has laid the foundation for his next step in the development of speech, echolalia.

During the period of lallation, the child's responses to the sounds of others seem to become more selective. He will not interrupt his own oral play merely because some adult is speaking to him or is near him. If he is occupied with his own play activity, he may ignore or seem to ignore the efforts of adults to respond to them and their "vocal play." The child is likely, however, to demonstrate displeasure through "angry noises" if his activity is forcibly interrupted or if a play object is taken from him. In an important sense, the child's vocal and oral products are beginning more and more to be selective responses to different external situations. The child is using sound-making in a manner which may be interpreted as showing his relatedness to events around him. Children who do not show this behavior are likely to be children who will be retarded in speech.

[2] This should not be confused with the term denoting a disorder of speech characterized by defective articulation or sound substitution.

Echolalia

Echolalia is the imitation by the infant of sounds which he hears others make, but which he does not comprehend. It is like lallation in that the child produces those sounds which are pleasurable for him. It is unlike lallation in that another individual provides the stimulus for the repetition of a sound. The lallation and echolalic periods are of tremendous importance because during these stages the child acquires a repertoire of sound complexes which ultimately he will be able to produce at will, and which he must have before he can learn to speak, or acquire a language, in the adult sense. The echolalic stage of speech begins at about the ninth or tenth month of infancy. Echolalic behavior, varying with circumstances, may continue indefinitely throughout life.

Verbal Utterance

Before the child can acquire a language he must have verbal understanding. By verbal understanding we mean responding with certain appropriate bodily movements to words or phrases pronounced by others. Verbal utterance—the establishment of conventionalized speech patterns as specific responses to socially presented stimulus patterns—usually begins during the first half of the second year. The acquisition of a language is based upon the same dynamics of learning that cause the child to repeat a sound he himself has made, in the lalling stage, or to echo a sound someone else has made, in the echolalic stage. A pleasurable reaction follows closely upon the utterance of the given word form.

The first word form is uttered, in all likelihood, as an accident, without the child realizing or knowing that the sound or sound complex has any special meaning or indicative potential. For example, the child may and probably does produce the sound complex which we recognize as *mama,* many, many times purely as an affective or motor-reflex response. But *mama* does not become a word until that wonderful time when the mother hears the child utter that sound, and elated, goes immediately to him. Then if the mother repeats the sound, not without satisfaction to herself, and the child imitates the mother's sound (echolalia), a word-form becomes transformed and elevated to a word. Thus, the sound complex *mama,* becomes associated with satisfaction; and finally, *mama* is uttered to bring about the source of satisfaction. We should note, however, that the first imitation is that of the child's sound by the mother, and that the original "word" is most likely produced accidentally, or at least involuntarily, by the infant, as a part of a total pattern response, with vocal and oral expression accompanying motor expression. The mother's imitation is, of course, confined to the audible expression or sound complex. This sound complex is in turn imitated by the child. In the process of reciprocal imitation the overt motor activities which give rise to the given sound complex disappear, so that finally, all that remains is the audible word *mama*. Hereafter, whenever the child says *mama* at the sight of his mother, or says *mama* in order to get his mother to come to him, he may be said to be truly speaking because he has *established conventionalized speech reactions as specific responses to socially presented stimulus* patterns and has learned to use these specific responses as stimuli for responses on the part of other persons.

After the child's first few voluntary words there generally is an interval before further progress can be noted. During this interval which may be as long as two months, there is usually a great increase in the comprehension of oral language. In the matter of "words" the small child's comprehending vocabulary is many times that of his evocative or speaking vocabulary. Though the ratio of the differences decreases with the age of the child, the comprehending vocabulary always remains larger than the speaking vocabulary.

We have now reached the stage in the development of infant speech in which the child is learning a language. Before continuing with an analysis of the acquisition of language, we will pause to review the steps in the development thus far.

1. *Crying.* The first *oral response* is the birth cry, which is an accompaniment of a motor-reflexive, totally a bodily response to a new environment. This is an undifferentiated cry, and cannot be discerned from the cries which are reactions to pain, or hunger, or thirst. *Differentiated crying,* that is, crying that can be *recognized as indicative of the presence of a specific need or want,* does not occur for two or three weeks. Differentiated crying is also a vocal and oral accompaniment of a total body response to a more specific type of situation.

2. *Babbling* is heard about the end of the second month. Babbling is a type of vocal play in which a great variety of sounds, more than are present in any one individual language, may be heard. Vowels appear first in babbling, followed in order by back and then front consonants.

3. *Lallation,* or sound imitation, usually begins in the sixth month. The child imitates his own sounds.

4. *Echolalia,* the imitation of sounds made by others, but not understood by the child, is the next step. This begins about the ninth month and lasts, in a modified form, throughout the life of the individual.

5. *Verbal utterance* brings the child to the stage where he is engaged in acquiring language. In this stage the child is establishing a repertoire of conventionalized speech reactions as specific responses to socially

presented stimulus patterns. This stage usually starts at about the beginning of the second year. It may, however, begin a month or two earlier, and sometimes not until as late as the third year.

It must not be thought that the several stages are discrete, one beginning where the other abruptly ends. There is considerable overlapping in all of the stages. A child may still babble after he has acquired a considerable vocabulary of real words.

SPEECH AND THE EMERGENCE OF THE CONCEPT OF SELF

Even in our relatively brief review of the stages of speech development, we are able to note that all stages, except the very first, are characterized by an underlying process of *differentiation*. Growth and development are differentiating processes. At first the child, on a reflex basis, produces differentiated crying. Later his responses reveal differentiation between internal and external stimulating situations. Still later and for an indefinite time, the individual as a child, an adolescent, and a post-adolescent acquires a differential vocabulary that enables him to respond to verbal symbols and to react with verbal symbols to different symbols. Throughout this maturational process, the individual is developing a *self*. In psychoanalytic Freudian terminology, the changes that begin with undifferentiated reflexive crying and culminate in the stage of verbal utterance represent stages in the direction from primary narcissism to object-related expression. (Glauber, 1958)

When a child learns to use words, he is able to communicate with his environment without direct contact or direct manipulation. He can engage in mental manipulation, in mental trial "activity," and he can test the results of anticipation by mental trial behavior. He can deal with situations not *here*, at times that are *not now*. He can reach out for objects and persons at considerable distances beyond his physical grasp. Such anticipatory behavior is the beginning of thinking. The memories of the behavior, and the awareness of the influence that can be exerted over the environment through language give rise to a consciousness and to a conscience. If this happens, the child has reached a stage in which he has not only the advantage but the responsibilities that come with the acquisition of language. He has developed an ego and a self, and must learn to be able to deal with both. Language is the medium through which this new mature and responsible behavior becomes possible.

One of the awesome realizations that comes with the acquisition of language is physical separation from the mother—the child's primary love object. The use of language reduces the need for direct physical contact between the child and the mother. This awareness, especially if it is reenforced by the mother in the form of a remark such as "Tell me, don't tug at me," may make the child reconsider whether learning to speak was worth the effort. Physical separation brought about by the child's learning to speak may also be traumatic for the mother. She may not be ready for the child's reduced physical needs of her. The mother may also be in conflict because of her realization of her child's need for an increased measure of physical separation, and her own anxious reaction that her child is no longer an infant, and has outgrown some of his baby needs. Fortunately, most children and most mothers soon learn to use language to bridge gaps and minimize the effects of physical distance. For most mothers and children, verbal contact replaces direct physical contact, and both are able to mature through language.

Before concluding this part of our discussion on the development of speech, we should like to emphasize that the child who is beginning to communicate through speech is not ready or able to abandon the many expressive non-communicative functions that speech served before he learned to use words. Oral gratification, pleasure in vocal play, the expression of varying states of feeling, continue as basic needs that must be served through speech. If adults who are either unsympathetic or unwitting impose communication as the sole function to be served through speech, the child is not likely to be an effective person or a proficient speaker. In fact, it is our belief that too early or too frequent imposition of communication on the child may result in making the child one who will be defective in speech.

CONDITIONS NECESSARY FOR SPEECH DEVELOPMENT

In the preceding pages we presented some objectively obtained information and some subjective evaluations of what seems to be taking place when an infant becomes ready to acquire language and to develop verbal behavior. We could probably have been considerably more objective if infants were more available and better controlled as experimental subjects. Because they are not, many of our conclusions are necessarily made by implication. At the present, we should like to consider the implications of a study by Mowrer relative to conditions necessary to establish "speech" in the so-called talking-birds. (1952, 1950) Based upon his analysis of the literature on talking-birds and his own close observation with a small number of birds, Mowrer (1952) generalized that birds capable of learning to "talk" do so only when the human teacher becomes a *love object* for them. In practice, Mowrer found that the first step in "teaching" a bird to talk (to imitate the sounds of a human being) is to make a pet of it. For Mowrer this means that the bird must be cared for in such a way as to ". . . deflect the interests and emotional attachments of the bird away from members of its own species to another species, namely *homo sapiens*. This is commonly done by isolating the bird from its own kind and making it dependent for food, water, and social attention and diversion upon its human caretakers."

The second step in "teaching" a bird to talk is for the caretaker to make some characteristic noise as he tends to the bird. The noise, Mowrer points out, need not be or even resemble conventional speech symbols. ". . . any kind of a noise will do—be it a word, or phrase, a whistled or sung fragment of a tune, a nonsense vocalization, or even a mechanical sound. . . ." The only essential feature of the noise is that it can be one which is consistently and intimately associated with the human being who is serving as the trainer as he engages in his caretaking functions. "As a result of the association of these sounds with the basic satisfactions for the bird, they become positively conditioned, i.e., they become *good sounds;* and in the course of its own, at first largely random vocalizations, the bird will eventually make somewhat *similar* sounds." In time, through the process of generalization, sound-making *per se* will enable the bird to derive some of the satisfaction originally attached to the care-taker's activities *and* sound-making behavior. When this conditioned state is established, the time and circumstances are right for the bird to begin to "talk." The bird with a capacity for making sounds that resemble those used in human speech has arrived at a time of *speech readiness.*

In the manner just outlined, Mowrer succeeded in training two parrots, a Mynah bird, two common crows, two Western magpies, and several Australian parakeets to talk. We do not, of course, know why a bird should want to "talk" or make sounds that approximate those made by human beings. Mowrer offers a possible explanation based on psychoanalytic theory to the effect that the bird, because of its "love" for its human trainer and caretaker, identifies with him and tries somehow to be like him. Because it is obviously easier for a bird to sound like a human being than to look like one, this is the choice made by a bird in a human rather than a bird environment. This accomplishment must be satisfying for the bird, otherwise it would not be acquired and maintained.

If we draw parallels between a bird's learning to "talk" and an infant's learning to speak, the following may be noted. The infant has better equipment for sounding like a human being than even the most capable of the so-called talking-birds. The infant can identify with more features of human behavior than just sound making. He can in time perform and do, as well as sound, like his trainer and love-object. The bird is made dependent by being brought up by human beings. The infant is born dependent and continues to need human beings for his basic biological needs longer than any other living being. The infant cannot escape from his caretaker and survive. His needs, biological and emotional, and his physical equipment make identification urgent if the infant is to develop normally. Speech then can be expected from almost all infants who are physically and mentally normal, *providing that the environment provides normal stimulation and satisfaction and that the identification with one or more caretakers is readily possible for the child.*

Earlier we pointed out that the incidence of vocalization during early infancy is influenced by the amount of attention—physical contacts and human noise contacts—to which the child is exposed. The "mothered" baby vocalizes more than does the infant given physical care but not maternal attention (Brodbeck & Irwin, 1946). Beyond this, there is evidence to believe that the difference in proficiency in speech develop-ment between boys and girls may be related to the greater ease of iden-tification a girl can make with the mother—the parent more likely to be home and the more talkative one—than can the boy. Dorothea McCarthy theorizes that a girl can more closely approximate the vocal pitches of the mother than can the boy those of the father. "Echo-reaction" is both easier and more satisfactory for the girl who identifies with the mother than it is for the boy who identifies with the father. To be sure, most children of either sex are exposed to male and female adult voices. The girl as well as the boy is exposed to the father's voice. The difference in influence is explained by McCarthy (1953) as follows:

It may be argued that the girls also experience the father's voice about as much as do boys, but they probably feel less need to imitate and to identify with him than do boys, for they are already making good progress in echoing the speech of the mother, and are finding considerable security and satisfaction in so doing.

To be sure, McCarthy's position is a theoretic one, and may be difficult to establish by experimental evidence. In any event, the theoretic posi-tion attempts to explain on the basis of identification the established facts that girls speak earlier and are more proficient speakers than boys and that boys have more defects in speech than do girls.

SPEECH PROFILE OF THE CHILD BEGINNING TO SPEAK

Though the development of speech is characterized by progressive differentiation and relative order, not all children who arrive at the stage of verbal utterance sound alike. Some children articulate words so that they sound—are pronounced—much the way the same words would sound if pronounced by proficient adult speakers. Others produce what might be generally termed reasonable facsimiles of adult pronunciations,

By and large, the child who is beginning to speak is more likely to produce a reasonable facsimile pronunciation than he is one that would be recorded by a dictionary as standard. It might be of some help to know how the "typical" child speaks and sounds from the profiles that follow. These profiles are based upon the studies of Ruth Metraux (1950) which were cited earlier in this chapter.

The 18-month-old child is characteristically uncertain and inconsistent in his pronunciations. He usually makes his words "intelligible" by the production of a proper vowel, a medial consonant, and appropriate vocal inflection.

The child's voice is not well controlled and tends readily to become high pitched and to sound strained. He seems to be engaged in frequent experimentation with his vocal pitch. Often there is "a variety of vocal overflow with little or no phonetic value, such as a laugh, sigh, or whisper."

Easy, apparently unconscious repetition of words or parts of words occurs "more frequently than not" in the speech flow of the child.

The 24-month-old child is a "telescopic" speaker. Phrases are likely to be telescoped so that they sound like long, single words. Words are usually pronounced to include an initial consonant, though not necessarily an appropriate one, an appropriate vowel and a final consonant. Medial consonants are likely to be slighted.

The voice of the two-year-old shows improved control compared with what it was at a year and a half. Although straining and squeaking is not uncommon, the pitch is generally lower.

Repetition of whole words and phrases is a strong and almost compulsive feature of the two-year-old child's speech. Syllable repetition is also likely to be present. Responses may be initiated with the sound "uh" /ʌ/ before the "right" word is evoked.

The Metraux speech profiles are based upon a study of children all average or above in intelligence who were in attendance at a Guidance Nursery at Yale University. Any comparisons made between a "real" child and the "typical" child of the Metraux study should be with this point in mind. We would suggest that doubts in comparisons should be settled in favor of the "real" child. In any event, it should never be overlooked that it is extremely unlikely that any child is aware of what speech schedule he is supposed to observe. His articulatory and linguistic proficiency is likely to follow an order determined by his own physical development and over-all psychological and social maturation, as well as by the adequacy of environmental conditions. Each child is, however, a law unto himself, and follows an order determined by an over-all complex of influences peculiar to himself. But no child is likely to develop speech, or have much to do with verbal behavior, unless this form of behavior provides basic satisfactions and pleasures at least sufficient to balance out those that were possible for him before he undertook the responsibilities of speaking.

REFERENCES

Blanton, M. G. The behavior of the human infant during the first thirty days of life. *Psychol. Rev.*, 1917, 24.

Brodbeck, A. J., & Irwin, O. C. The speech behavior of infants without families. *Child Developm.*, 1946, 17, 3.

Glauber, I. P. In Eisenson, J. (Ed.), *Stuttering: a symposium.* New York: Harper & Row, 1958.

Goldfarb, W. Effects of psychological deprivation in infancy and subsequent stimulation. *Amer. J. Psychiat.*, 1945, 103.

Irwin, O. C. Speech development in the young child. *J. Spch and Hearing Disorders*, 1952, 17, 3.

Irwin, O. C. Phonetic equipment of spastic and athetoid children. *J. Spch and Hearing Disorders*, 1955, 20, 1.

Irwin, O. C. In L. Kaiser (Ed.), *Manual of phonetics.* Wood-Holland Publishing Co., 1957.

McCarthy, D. A. Some possible explanations of set differences in language development and disorders. *J. Psychol.*, 1953, 35, 155-160.

Metraux, R. W. Speech profiles of the pre-school child 18-54 months. *J. Spch and Hearing Disorders*, 1950, 15, 1.

Miller, N. E., & Dollard, J. *Social imitation and learning.* New Haven: Yale University Press, 1941.

Mowrer, O. W. The autism theory of speech development and some clinical applications. *J. Spch and Hearing Disorders*, 1952, 17, 3.

Mowrer, O. W. *Learning theory and personality dynamics.* New York: Ronald Press, 1950.

Templin, M. C. Speech development in the young child. *J. Spch and Hearing Disorders*, 1952, 17, 2.

Templin, M. C. Norms on a screening test of articulation for ages three through eight. *J. Spch and Hearing Disorders*, 1953, 18, 4.

Winitz, H., & Irwin, O. C. Syllabic and phonetic structure of infant's early words. *J. Spch and Hearing Res.*, 1958, 1, 3.

13

Language Development
In the Child

FIRST WORDS

SOMETIME DURING THE SECOND HALF of the second year of life, most children have begun to utter words that resemble those used by adults in their environment. The resemblance is along two dimensions: the words uttered by the child sound like those used by adults; the words are evoked in situations comparable to those in which adults would use them. The child has arrived at the productive end of symbol behavior. Earlier, perhaps as early as eight or nine months, many children learn to associate events and objects and persons with what they will much later learn to call arbitrary sound symbols. Some even learn to produce a few arbitrary sound combinations to identify and, much more importantly, to bring about certain events.

Phonetic Aspects of First Words

The child's first words almost always incorporate sounds he has made during his pre-lingual speech stages. According to Seth and Guthrie (1935, p. 92) "The child's first words are in part, at least, vocables of his own invention which are the direct outcome of the sounds of his babbling or lalling, especially insofar as his parents or nurses adopt them and help him to apply them to a meaning or psychological context." Usually the child's early attempts at words are modified by the older members of the environment so that they become approximations if not precise replications of conventional words. In some instances, the members of a family accept the child's approximations. This results in "private" or family words for some objects, persons, or situations. It is more likely, however, that when a sound complex becomes a word—a name for a something—it also begins to resemble the standardized or conventionalized (adult) pronunciation of the word. This achievement, if the child is identifying with an older speaker, is the goal as well as the token of the child's effort. As such it is rewarding to both the child and the older speaker.

First words are likely to be either monosyllables or duplicated monosyllables such as *papa, mama, dada* or *by-by*. McCarthy (1946, p. 503) on the basis of a survey of the literature on this subject concludes that: "In regard to the form of the first word there is rather striking agreement in the literature that it is usually a monosyllable or a reduplicated monosyllable. . . . Certainly the commonest words heard in the nursery of the child who is just beginning to talk are of the reduplicated monosyllable type." Lewis (1951, p. 125) estimated that 85 per cent of "first words" are either monosyllabic or reduplicated. According to Lewis, 39 per cent are monosyllables and 46 per cent are duplicated monosyllables.

Several explanations have been offered for the tendency for sound duplication in the "first words" of children. One conjecture is that reduplication arises out of the child's attempts to imitate the sounds of nature and so account for the *moo-moo, bow-wow* words. These, presumably, are of an onomatopoetic nature and as such provide a "natural" association between sound and meaning.

Another explanation is that many so-called onomatopoetic words are learned by young children from older children and adults. They are imitative not of the things that make these noises but of the older persons who use these noises to designate the things that allegedly make them. The so-called onomatopoetic words are learned in imitation of adults, with whom children can identify, rather than of the animals with whom identification is more difficult, and less rewarding.

A third explanation is that reduplication is a carry-over from the earlier stages of speech development, particularly of the lalling and echolalic stages. The reduplicative tendency may also represent articulatory inertia and so express a tendency of the speech musculature to continue in the direction and manner in which an act was initiated.

Whatever the explanation or explanations may be, linguistic reduplication is not limited to the speech of young children. This characteristic is found in many adult languages. Reduplication is also a feature of adult songs and of many ballad refrains. The young child may simply be doing naturally what many adults contrive to do in their literary and musical efforts.

Affective Implications of First Words

First words, whether or not they are names for persons, are likely to have personal references. The first words are likely to be associated with the child's needs and wishes, or with his responses to the needs and wishes of older persons in his environment. According to Seth and Guthrie (1936, p. 96) the personal import of first words ". . . is to be expected in view of the child's dependence upon his social environment not only for the acquisition of language, but also for more practical assistance. But the principal reason for it is the tendency of parents the world over to attach the child's first articulate utterances to themselves."

The child's first words have highly affective implications. This is not surprising if we appreciate that the child understands and responds to the affective components of oral language—the changes in voice quality and melody—before he understands the intellectual implications of words. Many children who are retarded in language and articulatory development are nevertheless able to produce the speech melody of their linguistic environment. A second factor to appreciate is that the first words *directed at the child* by adults are likely to be heavily laden with affect. Expressions of affection, words of warning, admonitions, exhortations, etc., are all strong with feeling. The child, as we have suggested, responds with his own affect to the words he hears and to the situations in which the words occur. Thus, the connotative meanings of adult words may at first be better understood by the child than the denotative and more limited meanings. When in turn the child utters his first words he is expressing his own affective attitude—his wishes or desires or fears or attitudes—about the word and the related situation. Shirley (1938) says that the words used by children from ages two to five continue to be laden with affect and to relate most often to the mother, home, father, and siblings. Half or more of the concepts of the words seem to be related to and arise out of the common needs of the children. This finding supports the general observation of students of children's language that the underlying function of early language is to express desires, feelings, and needs.

The Word-Sentence

A single word utterance such as *mama* is in reality a sentence, in that it is used to express a complete thought, to communicate the child's reactions about mama at the time the word is uttered. Vocal expression and inflection assist in making a sentence of a single word. Thus, any one word may be used to express a multitude of meanings. For example, "mama" may mean "I want my mamma," or "Mama, give me the doll," or "Mama, I love you," or "Mama, pick me up," or even "Mama, you're something of a bother, I wish you'd go away and leave me alone." When we realize that the mother has become associated in the child's experiences with each of these particular types of affectively colored situations, and that these associations have become strengthened and fixed through repetition, we no longer need to wonder why the child expects his mother to do just what he wishes by his mere utterance of a single word.

Mothers usually have a way of knowing what the child wishes at the given moment by reading into the verbal utterance the specific situation that surrounds it. If a mother and her child are playing with a doll, the mother is very likely to hand the doll to the child when the child says "mama" properly inflected and modulated. If the mother has just left the child after playing with him, and the playing has been of such a nature that the child as well as the mother have derived pleasure therefrom, the ability of the spoken word "mama" to recall mother to continue the fun is easily understood. Should the mother *return* because of the child's utterance, another meaning of the word "mama" comes into existence. Thus, the many possible meanings of any one word may be multiplied according to the number of situations in which the object and the name for the object are likely to appear. The appearance of the object and its associated name must create a state of satisfaction for the child if the connection and so the meaning is to become permanent.

The first words are most likely to be nouns with wish-fulfilling import. The several sentence meanings expressed by the word *mama* are all of this nature. The child is not particularly interested in having the members of his environment know that he has mastered a name for an act or object; his utterance is intended rather to indicate his desire or attitude in regard to the particular act or object.

The Sentence

Not only does the child use isolated words as sentences, but his understanding of a sentence, in the adult sense, is dependent upon the position of the particular known word in the sentence. Thus, if the recognized word stands out because of its initial position, or because it is stressed when the entire sentence is enunciated, the child will react to the word and appear to understand the entire sentence. A little girl, when ten months of age, was taught to point to her ear, eye, nose, or mouth on command. At first only the word associated with the desired action was uttered, so that when the child heard *ear*, she placed her hand on her ear—if she was so minded at the given moment. Later the particular command word was included in a phrase or sentence, but always in such a position or so stressed that it stood out boldly. "Baby puts her hand on her *ear*" was understood and obeyed. The child, however, completely ignored a poorly trained relative who said, "I'll bet the baby can't put her hand on her ear when I ask her." Even if she could, this particular baby did *not*. The word *ear* was so obscured in the aunt's lengthy and skeptical request that the child was probably not able to pick out the key word and to respond to it. A sentence, especially if it is long, tends to make individual word understanding more difficult by obscuring the identification of words which might be understood if isolated. Because of this, the sentence has a word value to the beginning speaker while words which may be isolated or individualized have sentence value.

The single-word-sentence-stage is likely to continue for several months after the child begins to speak. At about fifteen months, possibly earlier for children who are precocious in their language development, some children begin to combine disconnected words into sentence units. Most children, however, are not likely to advance beyond the one-word sentence until they are two years of age and, according to Seth and Guthrie (1935, p. 107) not until they have functional vocabularies of from 100-200 words.

The early multi-word sentences are most likely to consist of a noun and a verb with full subject-predicate implications. "Baby eat" or "Baby walk" are typical noun-verb combinations which may be produced by children between fifteen and twenty-seven months of age. Persons who insist that a sentence must literally sound like a sentence to be a sentence might well argue that the mere combining of words does not constitute a sentence. Such persons would probably insist that most children do not use complete sentences until they are three years of age. Templin (1957, p. 144) observes that by three years of age children's utterances begin to conform to the grammatical structure of a language.

The senior author's daughter began to combine words at fifteen months. "Mama go 'way" was her first conventional sentence. The sentence was used to express several ideas, each one differentiated from the others by inflection. "Mama go 'way" sometimes merely expressed the notion to any adult person present that the child was aware that her own mother was not among those in sight. When uttered plaintively, the words expressed a desire for her mother to return. Occasionally the sentence was pronounced with an upward inflection on the last sound, and meant "Did mother go away?" or "Will mother come soon?" At sixteen months the child spoke the sentence "Doggy says bowwow." The longest combination of words uttered by the child before the end of the sixteenth month was "Doggy says bowwow, heigh dog." The child raised her arm in a gesture of greeting when she uttered the last two words.

The sentences of children under two years of age are characterized by an economic peculiarity: articles, prepositions, conjunctions, etc., are usually not used. For example, a sixteen-month girl said "Mama hat" on seeing her mother put her hat on before leaving the house. As a rule the child is satisfied to put the verb next to the noun, omitting entirely any word expressing relationship. Occasionally the child below two years of age seems to be using articles or prepositions in some sentences. The likelihood is, however, that in such sentences the article or preposition is used as an integral part of another word, usually of the verb, rather than as a separate word. A child may hear such combinations as *to go*, *to dress*, and *to eat* so frequently that they are responded to and used functionally as single word units.

Parts of Speech in the Vocabularies of Children

The first word to appear in a child's vocabulary, as we have indicated, is generally a noun, the name of a person or thing. Verbs may follow shortly after the nouns; adjectives, adverbs, and pronouns are late in appearing. Articles, prepositions, conjunctions, make their appearance last, and are often omitted even after they have been learned. Interjections form a large portion of the vocabulary of the younger child. It must be remembered, however, that any and all of these words can be shifted, from a functional point of view, from one word category to another. We have already mentioned that the word *mama*, when uttered alone, has sentence value, and may have several meanings besides the designation of the child's mother. The word *mama*, for the sake of ease of classification with a dictionary as a guide to classification, may be considered to be a noun. It is likely to be a noun if we consider the most likely form in which the word is used. According to McCarthy (1946, p. 503) ". . . if only the form of the word is considered in terms of the most frequent occurrence of the forms, the first words are characteristically nouns or interjections."

Nouns, interjections, and verbs precede the other word categories probably because these words, alone or in utterances that approximate conventional sentences, most easily express the child's feelings about his own needs and his reactions to the potencies of words, or really, his potency as a user of words. These word forms get done what needs to be done! Beyond this, words in these categories are likely to be spoken by older persons with greater emphasis than other words in a flow of utterance. They stand out more, because of the likelihood that they will be the stressed words, and so the words that carry the essential meanings in a sentence unit. Later in our discussion we will again consider the proportions of word categories in a child's developing vocabulary.

LANGUAGE DEVELOPMENT

Information as to language development of young children comes to us from three types of studies. The first type is essentially biographical. Some students of language, interested in developmental aspects, have been biographers for their own children. An example of such a study is the work of the Sterns (1928). A second approach is that of the longitudinal studies that have produced developmental norms. In the United States, Shirley (1933), Gesell (1925), and Gesell, Thompson, and Amatruda (1938) have published representative longitudinal studies that provide normative data for language development in the young child. Buhler and Hetzer (1935) are responsible for another significant study of this type. For those of us who feel that biographical studies, especially when parents are Boswells for their own children, may suffer from an excessive degree of subjectivity or, even if free from such fault, probably present developmental pictures of precocious children, the long term studies of large groups of children present obvious virtues. A third approach employs a procedure calling for taking samples of the speech of many children within an age group, with the children selected on bases which presumably make them representative of the population of children at large. The studies of McCarthy (1930) and Templin (1957) are examples of the third category. In our discussion of the language development of the young child we shall lean most heavily on the third type of study.

McCarthy (1930) published the results of a study on language development in children which became a model for several later studies. McCarthy's procedure was to record 50 verbal responses from each of a group of 140 children. She secured a representative population sample by using paternal occupation as the criterion for selection. McCarthy evoked verbalizations from her subjects by stimulating them with selected toys and books. The toys included a little red auto, a cat that squeaked, a telephone with a bell, a little tin mouse, a music box, and a small ball. The books included one with animal pictures and one with illustrated Mother Goose rhymes.

The data from McCarthy's investigation was subjected to analysis along four basic lines: (1) length of response, (2) complexity of sentence structure, (3) function of the response, and (4) proportions of the various parts of speech within the response.

The general plan and procedure established by McCarthy was employed with individual and relatively minor variations by Day (1932) who studied 80 pairs of twins. It was also used by Davis (1937) whose studies included comparisons of single children with siblings, with twins, and with only children. More recently Templin (1957) employed the McCarthy procedure for children within the 3-8 year age group.

Templin secured normative data on several language skills and studied the interrelationships among the skills. Her sample included 240 boys and an equal number of girls ranging between 3 and 8 years of age. The children were divided into eight sub-samples of 30 boys and 30 girls according to age as follows: half year intervals between 3 and 5 years, and full year intervals between 5 to 8 years. Templin selected each sub-sample so that it would constitute a representative sample according to the father's occupation as classified on the Minnesota Occupational Scale.

The skills studied by Templin included articulatory proficiency, sound discrimination, vocabulary, and verbalizations. We have already referred to some of the findings in our discussion of the development of articulatory proficiency in children. We shall make several references to Templin's and some of the other named studies in our consideration of language development.

Vocabulary Development

Recognition Vocabulary.   Most adults know or recognize a considerably larger number of words than they are themselves able to employ in either their writing or speaking vocabularies. This difference begins at the outset when the infant begins to develop verbal behavior and to establish verbal habits. Infants, we recall, respond to language and so develop behavior toward language before they arrive at the stage of verbal utterance. Most children can play "Peek-a-Boo" or "Where's Baby" months before they can say the name of the games that adults assume amuse the infants. By eighteen months most children have acquired a dozen or more meaningful words—sound combinations used in recurring situations in anticipation of more or less specific responses. At this age, it is still not possible, except for extremely precocious and verbal children, to measure the differences between recognition and productive vocabularies. Assessments are more possible during the third year (Ammons and Holmes, 1949). Templin's study was made with children from ages 3 through 8.

Templin measured *vocabulary of recognition* using the Ammons Full-Range Picture Vocabulary Test for children from 3 through 5 years of age and the Seashore-Eckerson English Recognition Vocabulary Test for her 6-to-8-year-old subjects.

The Ammons test calls for identification of a picture from several on a page. The item to be selected by the child is announced by the examiner. The child is required merely to point to the picture he selects. The Seashore-Eckerson test is a multiple choice inventory.

Templin found that the 3-to-5-year-old children showed a steady increase in their mean recognition scores for the Ammons picture vocabulary items. Boys did somewhat better than girls at age 3 while girls did somewhat better than the boys at ages 4 and 5. The differences, however, were not statistically significant at any of the ages.

Children who, based upon father's occupation, belonged to the upper socioeconomic status groups had higher recognition vocabulary scores than did the children from the lower socioeconomic status groups. The differences tended toward statistical significance. The results for the pre-school children are summarized in table 1.

Table 1.

Mean Scores on Ammons Vocabulary Test for Boys and Girls, Upper and Lower Socioeconomic Status Groups, and Total Subsamples, by Age

| | Boys (N=30) | | Girls (N=30) | | USES (N=18) | | LSES (N=42) | | Total Subsample (N=60) | |
CA	Mean	SD	Mean	SD	Mean	SD	Mean	SD	Mean	SD
3	13.4	3.4	12.3	2.9	13.4	3.5	12.6	3.1	12.8	3.2
3.5	15.5	2.8	14.6	2.7	16.1	2.6	14.6	2.7	15.1	2.8
4	16.8	3.0	17.0	3.0	17.7	3.4	16.6	2.8	16.9	3.0
4.5	18.4	3.6	18.6	2.8	19.9	2.8	17.9	3.2	18.5	3.2
5	19.4	3.3	21.5	3.2	20.7	3.1	20.3	3.6	20.4	3.4

The results employing the Seashore-Eckerson English Recognition Vocabulary Test permit a projection of actual number of words recognized to a presumed number of words known.[1] Templin found that her children between 6 and 8 years of age continued to show regular and substantial increments in their vocabulary recognition ability from year to year. Boys have larger recognition vocabularies than girls at each of the ages from 6 to 8, but the differences are not statistically significant. Boys have a recognition vocabulary of 8.9 thousand words at age 6; 13.5 thousand at age 7; and 18.3 thousand at age 8. For girls the estimates

[1] In estimating vocabulary, each basic word and each compound word is considered to represent 505 words in the Funk and Wagnall Unabridged Dictionary, while each derived word is considered to represent 4,450 words. (Seashore and Eckerson, 1940)

are 8.1 thousand at age 6; 12.9 thousand at age 7; and 18.0 thousand at age 8. The estimated recognition vocabulary scores are greater for children from the upper socioeconomic status groups than they are for the children from the lower socioeconomic status group. Templin believes that the substantial difference in the estimated basic vocabularies between the two groups of children according to socioeconomic status ". . . is probably related, at least in part, to the difference in intelligence between the two groups." (Templin, 1957, p. 112)

Vocabulary of Use. Estimates of the size of a vocabulary of use for a substantial number of children must necessarily be based on samples of utterance under a given set of conditions. Templin (1957), using materials similar to those of McCarthy (1930), evoked 50 consecutive responses from 480 children. *The number of different words* used in the 50 utterances was taken as a measure of the size of the use vocabulary of the children. The Templin findings show that both boys and girls increase their use vocabularies at each succeeding age level. Templin found that her children used a larger number of different words than did Davis (1937) in an earlier study. Templin's 480 subjects used a total of 6,144 different words in their 50 verbalizations compared with a total of 2,033 different words for the Davis subjects. Interestingly, however, there is considerable similarity in the words most frequently used. Davis reported that 175 words were used 100 or more times; Templin reported that 178 words were used 100 or more times by her children.

Children from upper socioeconomic status groups as a whole (all age groups combined) used significantly more different words (mean total of 138.9) than did the children from the lower socioeconomic status groups (mean total of 127.3). Templin found a positive correlation between level of intelligence and the number of different words used. She observes, however, that "correlations between intelligence and the vocabulary measures were somewhat lower than reported by other investigators. In the correlations of intelligence with the number of different words used in the 50 remarks, a sharp break in the magnitude of the correlations occurs at 5 years." (Templin, 1957, p. 120). The correlation dropped from .57 at age 4.5 to .27 at age 5, and continued to be low (.26, .28, and .20) for ages 6, 7, and 8. (Templin, 1957, p. 118). Templin is not inclined to believe that her finding in regard to the low correlation between intelligence and number of different words used for 50 utterances has general significance. She is more inclined to the view that for children between ages 5 to 8 a larger sample of speech is needed than 50 utterances to reflect or be representative of the total number of words these children can use. Though a 50-utterance sample may be adequate for pre-school children, it is not enough for the older children. "That the sample of speech is too small is a more likely explanation than that the relationship between the number of different words used and intelligence decreases during the early developmental period." (Templin, 1957, p. 119)

Parts of Speech in Children's Vocabularies.   The first words, as we have already indicated, are likely to be nouns, or at least have nominal forms. Verbs may be heard shortly after several nouns are under control. Adjectives, adverbs, and pronouns appear after nouns and verbs, as sentence units constitute characteristic utterances. Pronouns appear later, followed by prepositions, conjunctions, and articles. The last categories may not be uttered regularly even after they begin to be present. These, apparently, are the luxury words, the ones the child as well as adults who may have need of economy of communicative effort are most likely to omit in a stream of utterance. Interjections, according to McCarthy (1946, p. 508), form a large portion of the utterances of the child beginning to talk. Templin (1957, p. 101) finds a smaller proportion of interjections. It might be interesting to compare McCarthy's and Templin's findings as to proportions in parts of speech in the vocabularies of children from thirty-six to fifty-four months of age. Tables 2 and 3 (Templin, 1957, p. 101) permit such comparisons.

McCarthy found a decrease in the proportion of nouns to other parts of speech from 18 months through 36 months. From 36 months to 54 months the proportion of nouns is relatively stable. Templin found comparatively little change in the proportion of nouns from ages 3 through 8. According to Templin (1957, p. 102), "The differences in the characteristic proportions of the various parts of speech when calculated on the total number of words and the different number of words used are the result of the restrictions imposed by formal language structure." Stability, apparently, in regard to the various parts of speech, begins to become established soon after the child uses complete sentences.

We may note from Table 4 that there are some differences in percentages for the parts of speech with increasing age. The percentage of pronouns decreases after age 3 while the other parts of speech either remain relatively unchanged or show a slight increase. These changes reflect normal vocabulary growth. The English language has comparatively few pronouns to be learned, but new nouns, adjectives, verbs, and adverbs may be acquired throughout life. The vocabularies of mature and superior speakers and writers tend to show proportionate increases in these parts of speech. Articles, conjunctions, and prepositions are, of course, relatively stabilized with the pronouns.

Table 2.

Mean Percentages of Various Parts of Speech Used by Subjects 3 to 8 Based on Total Number of Words Uttered

CA*	Noun	Verb	Adjective	Adverb	Pronoun	Conjunction	Preposition	Article	Interjection	Miscellaneous
3	17.7	22.6	6.3	10.0	19.4	1.5	6.5	6.8	2.1	7.1
3.5	17.1	23.0	6.9	9.9	19.2	2.3	6.9	6.5	1.8	6.5
4	16.3	23.1	6.7	10.1	20.3	2.8	6.9	6.8	1.3	5.7
4.5	16.5	23.6	7.7	10.0	18.9	2.5	6.8	7.3	1.2	5.6
5	16.1	23.5	7.5	10.6	20.0	2.6	6.7	6.7	0.8	5.4
6	17.1	25.0	7.6	10.0	19.3	2.6	7.6	7.0	1.0	3.1
7	17.0	24.0	7.3	10.4	18.0	3.3	8.0	7.9	1.4	2.8
8	17.0	24.3	7.4	9.1	17.8	3.7	7.9	8.1	1.2	2.9

* N=60 in each age group.

Table 3.

Mean Percentages of Various Parts of Speech Used by Subjects 3 to 8 Based on the Number of Different Words Uttered

CA*	Noun	Verb	Adjective	Adverb	Pronoun	Conjunction	Preposition	Article	Interjection	Miscellaneous
3	25.5	23.4	8.8	11.5	12.1	1.1	5.8	2.2	2.0	7.6
3.5	23.8	24.1	9.8	11.6	11.4	1.6	6.6	2.0	2.0	7.2
4	24.2	24.0	0.3	12.2	10.4	1.6	6.0	1.7	1.6	8.0
4.5	25.0	23.3	10.9	12.4	10.5	1.4	5.5	1.7	1.4	7.9
5	23.7	23.9	11.0	13.4	10.4	1.6	5.7	1.7	0.9	7.7
6	25.9	24.4	12.1	12.8	9.2	2.2	5.9	1.6	1.3	4.8
7	26.0	24.1	11.9	12.9	9.2	2.2	6.1	1.5	1.7	4.2
8	27.4	24.2	11.9	12.4	8.7	2.5	5.6	1.5	1.3	4.5

* N=60 in each age group.

Table 4.

Mean Per Cent of Each Part of Speech by Age and Sex
(Based on Total Number of Words Used)

Age in Months	Sex	Noun	Verb	Adjective	Adverb	Pronoun	Conjunction	Preposition	Interjection	Miscellaneous
18	B	43.6	16.7	5.1	5.1	12.8	.0	.0	16.7	.0
	G	51.5	13.1	10.7	8.5	9.8	.6	.0	5.5	.3
	All	50.0	13.9	9.6	7.9	10.3	.5	.0	7.6	.3
24	B	49.3	15.3	5.8	3.7	15.0	.0	2.0	3.4	5.4
	G	35.5	22.6	11.6	8.0	14.5	.7	4.1	2.2	.8
	All	38.6	21.0	10.3	7.1	14.6	.5	3.6	2.4	1.8
30	B	25.4	24.9	14.4	6.3	21.0	.5	4.3	1.5	1.8
	G	26.0	22.3	14.3	6.9	17.6	2.5	4.9	3.8	1.7
	All	25.8	23.4	14.3	6.7	19.0	1.7	4.6	2.8	1.8
36	B	23.6	23.5	15.4	7.8	21.3	1.1	5.4	1.5	.6
	G	23.2	22.5	16.7	6.3	17.3	3.7	8.4	1.5	.5
	All	23.4	23.0	16.1	7.0	19.2	2.4	6.9	1.5	.5
42	B	18.5	25.3	15.1	8.4	19.7	3.0	6.7	2.4	1.0
	G	18.5	27.0	16.6	7.0	21.8	1.3	5.8	1.6	.5
	All	18.5	26.0	15.7	7.8	20.3	2.3	6.3	2.0	.8
48	B	19.7	26.8	13.7	6.7	20.5	3.3	7.3	.9	1.0
	G	20.4	25.3	15.4	5.2	22.5	3.8	6.2	.6	.6
	All	20.1	26.0	14.6	5.9	21.6	3.6	6.7	.8	.8
54	B	19.4	25.0	14.4	7.7	21.1	4.0	6.7	.9	.9
	G	19.3	25.3	16.1	6.3	19.9	3.5	7.6	1.4	.6
	All	19.3	25.1	15.2	7.0	20.5	3.8	7.1	1.2	.8

ANALYSIS OF VERBALIZATIONS AS INDICATORS OF LANGUAGE MATURATION

Several investigators have considered length of verbalization (utterance), the complexity of the utterance, grammatical accuracy as well as the proportion in parts of speech and the number and types of different words known as indicators of level of maturity in language development. We shall refer briefly to some findings and suggest some possible implications.

Length of Response

A basic problem in evaluating oral verbalization is to decide *how long is a response.* Even the most proficient adult speakers do not always speak in well defined grammatical sentences unless they are reading from manuscript. In determining length of response for children it becomes necessary, therefore, to lay down some ground rules, at least for the purposes of a given investigation.

Davis (1937) considered that her subjects produced a unit of utterance when: (1) The child came to a complete stop after a verbal effort. A *stop* was indicated by a marked inflectional change either downward or upward. (2) The child otherwise indicated that he did not intend to go on with the utterance. The utterance was not considered complete if one simple sentence was immediately followed by another without the child's pausing for breath ". . . if the second statement was clearly subsidiary to the first." (Davis, p. 44).

Templin (1957, p. 76) found increases in mean length (number of words) in a response at each age interval. Increments were also found by McCarthy (1930) and Davis (1937). Templin's children, however, showed larger increases than either of the other investigators. Templin's children at age 6 had a mean length of response approximating that of Davis' group at 9.5 years. Templin makes the following observation which we consider important in regard to the obtained differences in length of response (1957, p. 77):

That longer utterances have been found in the present study is particularly important since the method of obtaining the data so nearly duplicated that of the McCarthy and Davis studies. Factors of sex, intelligence, age, and socioeconomic status are comparable in all three. Since no one person gathered data for a majority of the children in the present study, it is not likely that the obtained difference is merely a reflection of the influence of a particular examiner. . . . It is more likely that the greater amount of linguistic stimulation and the increased permissiveness in child-adult relations in the environment of the present-day child are important factors in determining the results.

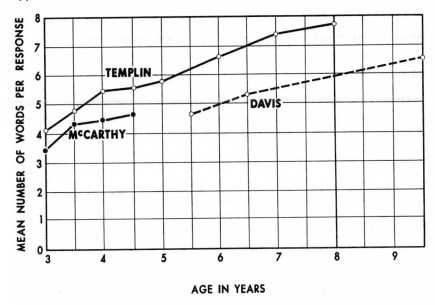

Figure 13-1. Comparison of mean number of words in 50 remarks by age as reported by McCarthy, Davis, and Templin. (From *Certain Language Skills in Children* by M. Templin. P. 76. Minneapolis: University of Minnesota Press, 1957.)

Templin found practically no significant differences in length of utterance for boys and girls except at age level 5. This finding contrasts with that of Davis who found that girls have longer utterances than boys at 6.5 and 9.5 years.

In regard to socioeconomic status, there is general agreement in the various studies we have cited that children from the higher groups have a greater mean length of utterance than do children from the lower groups.

Complexity of Utterance

Templin found a consistent increase with age in the use of remarks (sentences) which are complex and elaborated. This developmental index did not vary significantly according to sex. Although there were no significant differences between the children according to socioeconomic groups, the trend was for the children in the upper group to use more advanced types of sentence structure than those in the lower group.

GENERAL FACTORS RELATED TO LANGUAGE DEVELOPMENT

Intelligence

Throughout our discussion of the language development of children we have presented factors which are related to over-all verbal maturation. Templin's data supports earlier findings to the effect that there is a substantial positive relationship between language development and intelligence. This support comes directly from studying the relationship between vocabulary and intelligence and indirectly between the aspects of language development studied and the differences for children in the upper and lower socioeconomic groups.

Another body of data to support the generalization that language development and intelligence are positively related comes to us from evidence on the age of onset of talking. Although there are exceptions for both bright and mentally retarded children, by and large, bright children begin to talk earlier than children of normal intelligence, and they in turn as a group begin to talk earlier than retarded children. The correlations, in general, hold not only for age of onset of speech but for all the maturational criteria we have discussed. These include articulatory proficiency, size of vocabulary, and type and complexity of utterance.

Table 5 summarizes some of the findings in the literature and permits comparisons of children within a wide range of intelligence as to the age of onset of true speech.

Table 5.

Findings Relative to Age of Onset of First Word
According to Levels of Intelligence

Investigator	Type of Population	Age in Months of First Word
Terman	Gifted children—I.Q. above 140	11
Buhler	Children from upper socioeconomic backgrounds	10
McCarthy	Normal children	15.3
Mead	Undefined population of feebleminded children	38.5

Socioeconomic Status

In the studies of McCarthy, Day, Davis, and Templin to which we have made previous references, consistent favorable differences were found for the children from the upper socioeconomic groups in regard to all aspects of language development studied. Compared with children from the lower socioeconomic groups, those from the upper groups begin to speak earlier, have larger vocabulary increments at the age intervals studied, use sentences earlier, and develop earlier sentence maturity.

There is, of course, little question that most children whose parents are from the upper socioeconomic levels have hereditary as well as environmental advantages. By and large, *though with very important individual exceptions,*[2] the children from the upper groups have inherited better intellectual potential than the children from the lower groups.

Sex Differences

McCarthy (1946, p. 551) observed that "one of the most consistent findings to emerge from the mass of data accumulated to date on language development seems to be a slight difference in favor of girls in nearly all aspects of language that have been studied." This statement should be contrasted with Templin's (1957, p. 145) observation:

The more precocious language development of girls is frequently referred to in the literature of child development. The present study has not entirely substantiated this, especially at the separate age levels. When the performance of boys and girls is compared over the entire age range, girls tend to receive higher scores more frequently than boys, but the differences are not consistent and are only infrequently statistically significant.

On the basis of 230 comparisons, Templin found that girls received higher scores 133 times, boys 84 times, and no differences occurred 13 times. It would seem then that the girls, at least up to age 8, continue to have an edge over the boys.

If Templin's findings relative to decreased and inconsistent differences between boys and girls is indicative of a trend, we may well ask, why the change? One conjecture is that differences between male and female roles at home are not as great as they once were, so that it is easier for a male child to identify with mother, still the more talkative of the parents, than was the case a decade or more ago. Radio and television may also supply stimulation to young children without respect to sex differences.

[2] Exception should also be made for children who are brought up in times of economic stress, and for children whose parents are political refugees and who must enter occupations beneath their intellectual and actual or potential vocational levels.

Another possibility that deserves consideration is the change in the way children are brought up. Nursery schools and kindergartens no longer emphasize sex differences in play activities. Perhaps Templin's (1957, p. 147) observation comes to the heart of the matter: "It may also be that over the years differences in language ability of the two sexes have actually become less pronounced in keeping with the shift toward a single standard in child care and training in the last few decades."

Twins

The incidence of twinning in the population is sufficiently high (about 1.1 per cent) to deserve separate consideration relative to language development. In our consideration we should become aware of how twins, biologically as well as environmentally, are different from children born as singletons. Some of the factors we believe to be directly relevant to our study include the following:

1. Twins have a greater infant mortality rate than do single-born children and at least 50 per cent are born prematurely. (Nelson, 1959, pp. 305-307)

2. The over-all physical and developmental schedules of twins are slower than those of singletons. This may in part result from the increased proportion of premature births and in part from the adverse pre-natal and co-natal conditions associated with twinning. (Lorimer, 1952; Berry & Eisenson, 1956, p. 110)

3. Identical twins are mirror-images of one another. This mirror-imaging includes the hemispheres of the cerebrum, a circumstance which may be related to the higher proportion of left-handedness in twinning and may have possible implications for environmental interreactions.

Day (1932) replicated McCarthy's procedures with a population of 80 pairs of twins. Day found that compared with singletons, the twins were retarded in all aspects of language development as judged by the McCarthy criteria. Using length of response as a specific basis for comparison, Day found that pre-school age twins had age interval increments approximately half that of singletons.

Davis (1937) extended the study of Day to twins at higher age levels. She found twins to be retarded in language development when comparisons are made with single children. The differences, however, decreased after the children began to attend school.

Both the Day and Davis findings seem to support the conclusion that as far as language development is concerned, twins tend to create adverse environmental conditions. One twin is not as good a stimulator for the other as an older sibling might be. Parental attention is divided, and so necessarily is language stimulation. Perhaps unfortunately twins are satisfied with one another's social stimulation, so that there may be less need for the seeking out for older persons. Beyond this, twins are known to develop idioglossia—oral and pantomimic private or "secret languages" which serve adequately for their early "communicative" needs, but which may not be understood by other members of their environment, parents included.

Although we cannot ignore the environmental implications in the retarded language development of twins, even the tendency to catch up after school entrance may not entirely make up the early retardation. Time also helps to overcome the initial effects of the possible adverse physical conditions associated with excessive prematurity and high incidence of birth trauma which some investigators (Zazzo, 1952; Nelson, 1959, p. 305) have found to be associated with twinning. We may conclude then that initial retardation of twins as to onset of speech and their retarded development during pre-school years may be explained on a combination of atypical physical and environmental conditions.

Position in Family

In contrast with the negative implication of being a twin as a special environmental influence, is the positive advantage as far as language development is concerned, of *being an only child*. McCarthy (1946, p. 560) reports that "Of all the groups studied, only children, especially only girls, seem to be most precocious in all aspects of language development." In part this superiority may be explained by several related factors. There is a positive relationship between being an only child and being a member of a family from the upper socioeconomic levels. There is also a positive relationship between being an only child and being somewhat higher than normal in intelligence. However, McCarthy points out that the linguistic superiority of the only children is ". . . out of all proportion to what would be expected on the basis of their age, sex, and socioeconomic status alone." The superiority, we believe, comes from the advantage if and when it is provided of association with adults and the greater opportunity this provides for language practice under favorable conditions. For example, McCarthy (1930) found that the median percentile rank on length of response was 70 for children who associated chiefly with adults compared with 52.5 for those who associated chiefly with younger children. Smith (1935) found that children used longer sentences and in general more advanced patterns of language development in situations involving adults than in those involving conversations with other children.

Bilingual Background

If bilingualism as an environmental influence could be evaluated as such, and not as part of a complex of related factors, its implications for language development would be less involved. We should, at the outset, distinguish between bilingualism as an initial environmental influence, and the conscious learning, or teaching, of a second language even for pre-school children. In most American homes, exposure to one language is the norm. Second languages are learned as *foreign languages* in school. Parts of Canada are bilingual, but there is preference in most homes for either French or English. The social status of the language is not uniform throughout the bilingual Canadian areas. Some European countries are more nearly truly bilingual than Canada, yet it is not unlikely that there is some status significance for one language. The status of the language, of course, reflects the attitude of the speaker and the sub-culture toward the particular language. Furthermore, it is likely to make quite a difference whether in a given family a language is learned by a child from a nurse engaged for that very purpose, or from exposure to an adult with unequal ability in the two or more languages that he or she may speak. The child who is exposed to bilingual influences through parents who are considered foreigners in their community, or in the larger culture, has a different attitude toward the influences than one who was taught two languages from infancy, one by parents and the other by a nurse.

In the United States many bilingual children come from homes with limited economic, social, and educational advantages. But some come from homes with educational and cultural advantages that outweigh the early economic limitations. It should become apparent, therefore, that there can be neither firm nor widely applicable conclusions as to the influence of a bilingual background on the language development of children in general. With such reservations, we can consider some specific findings.

Ten per cent of the children in McCarthy's (1930) study were bilingual. With mean length of response as a criterion, these children were found to be more advanced in language development than would be expected on the basis of their age, sex, and paternal occupation. Reflecting on this finding McCarthy (1946, p. 566) says: "It may be that the handicap is more readily detectable in articulation and in quality of speech than in quantitative measures like length of response." We gather that McCarthy, despite her findings, considers bilingualism a handicap for over-all language development.

Seidl (1937) studied bilingual children of Italian parentage. He found that the scores of the children tested were 5 to 6 points below average on verbal intelligence and were 10 to 12 points lower than their performance scores.

Smith has been responsible for several comprehensive investigations on the influences in the Hawaiian Islands of bilingualism on language development. In 1939 Smith concluded that Hawaiian children from non-Caucasian (Portuguese excepted) homes are seriously retarded in language development. At the time they enter school these bilingual children have general language proficiency equal to that of most 3-year-old children with monolingual backgrounds. In a more recent study Smith (1949) investigated the language status of Honolulu children who spoke Chinese and English. The children ranged in age from 37 to 77 months. She found that as a group the children had below average-sized vocabularies in either Chinese or English. Furthermore, *even when the vocabularies of the two languages were added together, only two-fifths of the children exceeded the norms for monolingual children.* On the basis of her data Smith concludes that ". . . only the superior bilingual child is capable of attaining the vocabulary norms of monoglots and that a name for a large number of concepts is more desirable than two names for many of a smaller number of concepts."

Smith's conclusion for her 1949 study suggests the need for a new line of investigation for assessing language development in children as well as the more or less established language abilities of adults. The new approach would not stop at word counts but attempt to go beyond such measurements to an appreciation of the depth of the concept for a word. Related to this we would suggest that investigators attempt to determine *how many meanings their subjects know for the words they seem to know.*

REFERENCES

Ammons, R. B., & Holmes, J. C. The full range picture vocabulary test, III. Results for a pre-school population. *Child Development*, 1949, 20, 5-14.

Berry, Mildred, & Eisenson, J. *Speech disorders.* New York: Appleton-Century-Crofts, 1956.

Buhler, C., & Hetzer, H. *Testing children's development from birth to school age.* New York: Farrar and Rhinehart, 1935.

Davis, E. A. The development of linguistic skills in twins, singletons with siblings, and only children from age five to ten years. *Univer. Minn. Inst. Child Welf. Monogr.*, 1937, No. 14. Minneapolis: University of Minnesota Press.

Day, E. J. The development of language in twins. *Child Developm.*, 1932, 3, 179-199.

Gesell, A. *The mental growth of the preschool child.* New York: Macmillan, 1925.

Gesell, A., Thompson, H., & Amatruda, C. S. *Infant behavior.* New York: Mc-Graw-Hill, 1934.

Lewis, M. M. *Infant speech.* New York: Humanities Press, 1951; London: Routledge and Kegan Paul, 1951.

Lorimer, F. Trends in capacity for intelligence. *Eugenics News,* 1952, 37, 17-24.

McCarthy, D. The language development of the preschool child. *Univer. Minn. Inst. Child Welf. Monogr.,* 1930, No. 4. Minneapolis: University of Minnesota Press.

McCarthy, D. In L. Carmichael (Ed.), *Manual of child psychology.* New York: Wiley, 1946. Ch. 10.

Nelson, W. E. *Textbook of pediatrics.* (7th ed.) Philadelphia: Saunders, 1959.

Seashore, R. H., & Eckerson, L. D. The measurement of individual differences in general English vocabularies. *J. educ. Psychol.,* 1940, 31, 14-38.

Seidl, J. C. G. The effect of bilingualism on the measurement of intelligence. Unpublished doctoral dissertation, Fordham University, 1937.

Seth, G., & Guthrie, D. *Speech in childhood.* London: Oxford University Press, 1935.

Shirley, M. M. Common content in the speech of preschool children. *Child Developm.,* 1938, 9, 333-346.

Smith, M. E. A study of some factors influencing the development of the sentence in preschool children. *J. Genet. Psychol.,* 1935, 46, 182-212.

Smith, M. E. Some light on the problem of bilingualism as found from a study of the progress in mastery of English among preschool children of non-American ancestry in Hawaii. *Genet. Psychol. Monogr.,* 1939, 21, 121-284.

Smith, M. E. Measurement of vocabularies of young bilingual children in both of the languages used. *J. Genet. Psychol.,* 1949, 74, 305-310.

Stern, C., & Stern, W. *Die Kindersprache.* Leipzig: Barth, 1928.

Templin, M. *Certain language skills in children.* Minneapolis: University of Minnesota Press, 1957.

Zazzo, R. Situation gémellaire et dévelopmentale. *J. Psychol. norm. path.,* 1952, 45, 208-227.

V.

APPLICATIONS: GROUP COMMUNICATION

14

Basic Psychological Factors
In Group Communication

For more than two thousand years the chief source book on the psychology of communication was Aristotle's *Rhetoric*, supplemented in largely derivative treatises by Cicero, Quintilian, and a host of later rhetoricians. These works were to some extent based upon the observation and analysis of contemporary speakers, but they were also largely subjective, introspective, and even impressionistic. Not until early in the present century did changing concepts and quantitative studies open up a new stream of psychological research for application to the processes of oral communication. From Walter Dill Scott's pioneer work (1906) relating psychology and speech, to the most recent publication, contemporary textbooks in public speaking, discussion, debate, and radio and television communication, are now constructs of classical rhetorical theory and modern psychological investigation. To a lesser extent the same is true of modern textbooks in oral reading and acting, although these are beyond the limits of our present concern with direct, original, informative, or persuasive oral discourse.

In the interest of simplicity, this section of our book begins with a consideration of psychological factors common to all oral communication, and then treats in separate chapters the special circumstances and forms in which that communication takes place:

Chapter 15, *the face-to-face situation*, as in group discussions, committees, and conferences, where in a structured or unstructured discourse many speakers may participate, with a constantly shifting focus of attention from one to another.

Chapter 16, *the co-acting situation*, ranging from classroom lectures to political campaign speeches, where one speaker addresses many auditors, and there is a relatively fixed focus of attention upon him.

Chapter 17, *the radio and television situation,* where a variety of forms of direct discourse may be employed, but always involving one or more speakers addressing an unseen audience.

In the interest of economy, factors common to all three communication situations, though sometimes in varying degrees, will be treated in detail in this chapter, and merely referred to or summarized in later chapters.

THE ACT AND ART OF COMMUNICATION

It is important to distinguish between the act and art of oral communication, for we are here primarily concerned with the latter. The act of speech is simple vocal utterance; it may be performed by the untutored, crudely and ineffectively, as well as by those schooled in the art, effectively, intelligently, and responsibly. But since man first communicated with man, the act has engendered the art. Jebb (1876, II, 370), for example, affirms that "It was of the essence of Greek oratory . . . that its practice should be connected with a theory. Art is the application of rules . . . and the Greek conception of speaking as an art implied a Rhetoric." The unschooled act of verbal communication may reflect only a knack; the best communication is based upon a compend of theory.

As we have previously noted, it was Aristotle, *c.* 336 B.C., who set down the earliest extant complete and systematic theory of rhetoric, or scientific rationale for oral discourse. Essentially the peripatetic Greek conceived of rhetoric, or communication, as an instrumental discipline, a powerful social force by means of which man could interpret, control, modify, or adapt to his environment. Aristotle did not deal with transmitting information as a specific end of speech, but limited its purpose to persuasion: "So let Rhetoric be defined as the faculty [power] of discovering in the particular case what are the available means of persuasion." Aristotle and later classical writers structured the discipline of persuasive discourse around five canons: *invention,* the source and substance of ideas in a speech; *disposition,* the structure and sequence of the discourse; *style,* the specific language used in communicating; *memory,* the recall and retention resources of the speaker; and *delivery,* the vocal and physical attributes of speaking.

While eighteenth- and nineteenth-century writers maintained these canons in structuring their treatments of rhetoric, they restated the classical doctrines for a new society, and adapted to newer understandings of the behavior of man. This was notable in George Campbell's *Philosophy of Rhetoric,* 1776, strong psychological orientation in establishing the ends of speech as (a) to enlighten the understanding, (b) to please the imagination, (c) to move the passions, and (d) to influence the will. This division of purposes was influenced by the prevailing faculty psychology of his day, especially as it attempted to distinguish between belief and action, a dichotomy no longer in psychological fashion. Greater insight into human behavior was reflected in Campbell's definition of persuasion as argument or logic based upon desire: "To say that it is possible to persuade without speaking to the passions, is but, at best, a kind of specious nonsense."

Early twentieth-century rhetoricians, such as James A. Winans, adopted the psychological concept of attention as a determinant of action, and later writers, notably William Norwood Brigance, incorporated more of the findings of contemporary psychologists to expand the concept of desire, or motivation, as the heart of the persuasive process.

From this point on, students of the art of communication drew with increasing frequency from the researches in the behavioral sciences. As Wallace (1954, p. 125) wrote, the field of speech "cannot deal fully with either the act or the art of communication unless it knows all it can about the behavior of the speaking and listening individual, the behavior of individuals in group situations, the psychology of motives, emotions, and attitudes, the psychology of the speech-handicapped person, and the methods of tests and measurements." Beyond this draft on the funds of psychological research, students of communication must also, on occasion, become acquainted with related studies in linguistic behavior, logic, ethics, and semantics, as well as those in physiology, anatomy, and neurology, in literary history and criticism, and in general culture. As a consequence, the standard research bibliographies in speech have been drawn about equally from the humanities, the natural sciences, and the social sciences. The references and additional readings cited in chapters of this book attest to the almost universal resources employed for the study of speech, as well as to its singularity among the academic disciplines.

Both the act and art of communication, then, are concerned with the behavior of man communicating with man for reasons practical, cultural, or aesthetic. The chief sources for our understanding of man's communicative behavior are the traditional concepts of rhetorical theory as modified by the contemporary contributions of the behavioral sciences. As we shall try to exemplify, these disciplines provide the conceptual framework, the analytical and critical methods, and the evaluative techniques for any comprehensive study of oral communication.

SPEAKER-LISTENER RELATIONSHIPS

We commonly identify only two elements in the communicative process, speaker and listener, but it is really more complex. The traditional rhetorical analysis has always recognized four distinct elements: the speaker, the speech, the individual listener or the audience, and the occasion for speaking. Harold Lasswell (1946, p. 121) identified similar elements commonly phrased in a formula question: "*Who* says *what* to *whom, how,* and with *what effect?*" Considering communication as an electronic system, Shannon and Weaver (1949) isolated source, transmitter, channel, receiver, and destination.

When these several approaches to the communicative process are articulated we may describe it something like this: Any oral communication act (whether in face-to-face groups, co-acting groups, or via the mass media) begins with an idea, concept, or proposition in the mind of the communicator. He then encodes the idea into a communication consisting of a set of audible (and sometimes visible) symbols and transmits it, with light and sound waves as his channel. The receiver is an individual listener (sometimes a member of an audience group) who decodes the symbols into terms meaningful to him, and the communication, or at least a facsimile of it, reaches his mind and elicits some kind of response. This response may be covert only. It may also be overt, in clearly distinguishable physical movement or vocal response, apparent to the communicator and acting as a "feedback" from the impact of his initial communication. Thus his further communication may be affected by his own reaction to his hearer's response.

This simple tracing of the communicative process (based on our detailed analysis in Chapter 9) shows how much more complicated it is than the commonly conceived speaker-listener interplay. We now explain in some greater detail three of the elements in that relationship.

1. *Individuals may play either specialized or alternating roles in the communicative process.* In face-to-face groups, such as committees, each member may play alternating roles, sometimes acting as communicator, sometimes as listener. Especially in informal discussions, the transitions from one role to another may come irregularly and rapidly. In co-acting groups, on the other hand, individuals commonly have specialized roles: one stands on a stage or behind a lectern, consistently communicating in a "solo performance," while the others are auditors, normally all attending and responding to the single stimulus of the speaker. Except for overt responses, such as applause, shouts of "hear, hear!" and the like, the communicative behavior of the listeners is limited both by custom and by the degree of their polarization (psychological and

physiological orientation toward the speaker). In communicating via the mass media the speaker normally plays a specialized role, but his listeners, gathered in small groups in living rooms, taverns, or automobiles, play alternating roles, sometimes attending to him, sometimes distracted by other stimuli and ignoring him.

2. *Response from the listener is the ultimate goal of all communication.* Earlier in this book we dealt with the nature of psychological response, commonly manifested in muscular or glandular activity when one or more sense organs are stimulated. Response is what the individual does when he reacts to a stimulus. Thus we use the term response as the goal of all communication. The speaker wants the listener to respond, preferably in a way that will implement the speaker's specific purpose. But, and this was the reason for introducing Campbell's concept of an intellectual-emotional duality a few pages ago, if we understand response to be physiological reaction to a speaker's words, then there is no real psychological difference between such terms as belief and action or conviction and persuasion. Each one is merely a special way of describing response, but all are response. It is true, of course, that some levels of response are easier to achieve than others; for example, "I *understand* what you are saying," "I *believe* what you are saying," and "I will *act* upon what you are saying," may often represent a sequence of increasingly difficult response-goals for the communicator.

3. *Individuals respond most readily when they are highly involved in the purpose of the communication.* At some point in any communication situation the basic purpose becomes clear to everyone. In a face-to-face situation, such as a committee meeting, that purpose is the "group task," normally understood in advance, but often recalled by the chairman's opening remarks: "Our assignment is to prepare a slate of officers. . . ." or in an informal group: "I believe that we all agreed to discuss this evening the kind of foreign policy which . . ." The more intensively group members are committed to and involved in the group task, the more likely it is that they will participate freely and work toward the group's goals. To achieve this positive orientation toward the purpose of the communicative situation may require, as we shall see later, a careful selection of group members, a collective approach to agenda planning, and specific encouragement for members to assume active group roles. In the co-acting group situation, such as for a persuasive speech, the speaker's specific purpose may not always be understood in advance, and he may even want to conceal it during part of his speech. In any event, the speaker's message should seem as important to his hearers as it does to him; unless the hearers have a sense of personal involvement or at least interest in his subject, they are unlikely to respond to his purpose-proposition.

THE IMPACT OF COMMUNICATION UPON BEHAVIOR

We have already observed that response is the aim of all purposeful communication. As Hovland, Janis, and Kelley (1953, p. 12) state this premise for their psychological studies of opinion change, communication is "the process by which an individual (the communicator) transmits stimuli (usually verbal) to modify the behavior of other individuals (the audience)." But how are these modifications in behavior manifested, and how can they be measured and evaluated? Psychologists generally agree that *attitudes* and *beliefs* are key indexes to behavior and that both are measurable in such ways as to reflect the influence of communication upon behavior.

Attitudes

One of the most useful definitions of attitude is Allport's (1935, p. 906): "a mental and neural state of readiness, organized through experience, exerting a directive or dynamic influence upon the individual's responses to all objects with which it is connected." An attitude toward any person, object, or situation, is thus a tendency to respond, either favorably or unfavorably. Attitudes may be as general as a favorable response to "physical fitness" or as specific as an unfavorable response to a particular person.

Some writers classify pairs of attitudes, such as personal and social, or general and specific. Especially significant for communication is the distinction between *dominant* and *latent* attitudes. Dominant attitudes are those that are active at the moment; they tend to give the individual a psychological "set" or readiness to react in a patterned way when confronted with a general problem or a specific stimulus situation. It is the dominant attitude that the communicator hopes to touch off when persuading an audience; more difficult is the task of securing a response by connecting a proposition with the latent attitudes of his hearers.

Attitudes are not a part of the individual's native psychological equipment; they are acquired or developed throughout his life. Like other mental or emotional patterns of behavior, they are learned, modified, or discarded as the individual reacts to his environment and his experiences. A child may develop a dislike for certain foods, but later come to like them as his taste matures. The same child may also acquire from his environment an unfavorable attitude toward other racial or religious groups, but subsequent pleasant experiences with individuals in those groups may modify or destroy that attitude.

Beliefs

In contrast to the generalized nature of an attitude, a belief is the acceptance of a specific proposition. An individual may have a general attitude of religious tolerance, but be quite categorical about the question "Do you believe in God?" Although beliefs may be covertly held, we commonly identify them by an individual's verbal utterances. Skinner (1957, p. 88) implies a progression in a listener's behavior from attitude to belief, describing the latter as "the probability that he will take effective action with respect to a particular verbal stimulus."

Men are born without beliefs. We commonly say that beliefs are socially determined; while they may be based partly upon personal experiences, they depend more largely upon the advice, testimony, and influence of others. Even traditional beliefs in a family or a sect are social in character since they have been transmitted from one generation to the next.

It is important to note that all men tend to formulate beliefs about most situations they encounter; both problems and people are perceived with meaning and interpretation, even though with limited evidence. As Krech and Crutchfield (1948, p. 86) observe: "Man is an organizing animal. . . . As soon as we experience any facts, they will be perceived as organized into some sort of meaningful whole. This is a universal characteristic of the cognitive process and not a weakness of the impatient or prejudiced individual . . ." It follows that the establishment of a belief involves some thinking on the part of an individual; this is not necessarily true about an attitude. The difference is that individuals verbalize their beliefs and prefer to be able to state supporting reasons. There is something unsatisfactory even to the believer in confessing that "I don't know why, I just believe this is true." Thus the individual tends to rationalize, or to organize reasons for, his beliefs, a procedure he seldom follows in justifying his attitudes.

Generalizations About Attitudes and Beliefs

In concluding our discussion of attitudes and beliefs as they relate to communication a number of general observations are pertinent:

1. Attitudes and beliefs are in large part products of an individual's general culture, including his family, religious, and educational backgrounds. So long as an individual remains in the context of this culture these same influences tend to preserve existent attitudes and beliefs, by exerting social pressure for conformity.

2. Attitudes and beliefs are also products of what the individual thinks are pertinent "facts." These alleged facts, however, are often selectively perceived: new information uncongenial to dominant attitudes and beliefs may be rejected, and only information reinforcing prior attitudes and beliefs may be accepted. Moreover, individuals may not always be equipped to apply appropriate validity tests to these "facts," nor competency tests to "authorities" who purvey them.

3. Attitudes and beliefs vary in strength. These studies indicate some significant variables:

(a) Marple (1933) concludes that "there appears to be a decline of suggestibility with increasing age," that as we grow older and preserve our beliefs they tend to become stronger, and we are less likely to relinquish them.

(b) Marple's study also indicates a positive correlation between group opinion and personal belief: "Group opinion . . . is more powerful in affecting individual agreement than is expert opinion." Burtt and Falkenberg (1941) and Wheeler and Jordan (1929) support this judgment, although Kulp (1934) and Lorge (1936) found evidence to support the stronger prestige of the expert. We must conclude that group opinion is probably strongest in influencing individual attitudes and beliefs, but that the subject under discussion and the prestige of a particular expert may make for exceptions.

(c) Asch (1956) found that in situations where group members each announced publicly his conclusion on a question of judgment, only about one third of those in an extreme minority position (8 or 9 to 1) tended to distort their conclusions to conform with the majority. When the minority persons knew the judgments of others, but did not have to announce their own position, even fewer of them shifted toward the majority view. In a different type of situation, however, Sawyer (1955) found that audience members who were persuaded by a speaker's arguments judged that the majority of their fellow listeners were equally persuaded. Together these studies indicate that individuals have some concern for the congruity of their beliefs with what they feel to be the view of the majority, but that other resistant factors are also operative.

(d) Simpson (1938, p. 87) reported that in discussion situations, those who are the most influential with others are least likely to be influenced by others, indicating that belief-strength may be greater for those possessing attributes effective in influencing the beliefs of others.

(e) Schanck and Goodman (1939) found that existing beliefs and prejudices were intensified when listeners heard both sides of a fairly academic controversy, but that there was more open-mindedness, or a lessening of the intensity of belief, when the listeners felt the issue was closer to reality.

(f) Lund (1925) discovered a correlation of over +.80 in ranking between the order for "belief strength" and "desirability" of the belief.

Opinions

Any discussion of attitudes and beliefs inevitably leads to a consideration of opinions. While attitudes and beliefs tend to interact, sometimes making them difficult to distinguish from each other, opinions are clearly responses derived from a combination of attitudes and beliefs. In practice an opinion is an overtly verbalized attitude or belief, sometimes both. Like a belief, it is a statement of a proposition; like an attitude, it is favorable or unfavorable. Operationally, say Hovland, Janis, and Kelley (1953, p. 6), "opinions are viewed as verbal 'answers' that an individual gives in response to stimulus situations in which some general 'question' is raised." The communicator normally thinks about "influencing opinions" rather than attitudes or beliefs, since he assumes that opinions are indexes of probable action by his hearers. This is not always a safe assumption: sometimes various pressures may induce an individual to state an opinion that he feels will be socially acceptable, rather than one truly reflecting his attitudes or beliefs.

Measuring Attitudes and Opinions

Any communicator is naturally concerned with measuring his message's impact upon his listeners. We will briefly describe five measurement methods, each useful in determining the impact of communication on attitudes, beliefs, or opinions, but not the amount of information that may be conveyed to the respondent. The measurement of impact, of course, necessitates using the instruments both before and after the communicative act.

1. The simplest device for measuring attitudes is the *linear* scale, a line theoretically representing the possible range of attitude on a specific issue from complete endorsement to complete rejection. The respondent is asked to check a point representing his present attitude on, for example, "What is my attitude toward federal aid to education?" from "10-extremely favorable" to "0-extremely unfavorable."

2. A more sophisticated device, and more time-consuming both in preparation and application, is the *attitude test*. The standard procedure is to formulate a final test by (a) collecting as many relevant, simple, and unambiguous statements as possible about a specific issue, (b) having these statements sorted by a panel of experts into eleven categories, ranging from "extremely favorable" to "extremely unfavorable," in order to establish scale values, and (c) selecting for the final test perhaps

twenty or thirty statements, spread across the whole range of eleven scale values. In administering the test the respondent is instructed to check "agree" or "disagree" for each statement. A simple mathematical calculation of responses indicates the position of the respondent on the "extremely favorable" to "extremely unfavorable" continuum.

3. The *public opinion poll* is the most familiar measuring instrument, consisting of a series of "Do you favor . . . ?" or "What do you think about . . . ?" questions, designed to be asked in personal interviews. When the questions are properly phrased, presented in the right context, and to a representative sample of respondents, this is a satisfactory method.

4. The *shift-of-opinion ballot* has also frequently been used in measuring impact, especially where an effort has been made to present both sides of an issue, as in a public discussion or a debate. On the pre-test the respondent is presented with three choices: "I am in favor . . ." "I am undecided . . ." "I am opposed . . ." The post-test ballot carries the same three and two additional options, one at each extreme: "I am more strongly in favor . . ." and "I am more strongly opposed . . ." Thus the post-test form permits the respondent to reflect an intensification of his original opinion, a shift in varying degrees to the opposite opinion, or no change at all.

5. The most recently developed measuring instrument is the *semantic differential,* posited on the assumption that human judgments as reflected in verbal behavior may be reduced to a limited number of primary dimensions such as evaluation, activity, and potency. While studies in the field of speech are just developing applications of this method of analysis (Smith, 1959) they show great promise. The instrument itself usually consists of a set of ten to a dozen seven-step, bi-polar adjectival scales (such as "optimistic . . . pessimistic," "true . . . false," and "calm . . . excitable") designed to tap previously determined dimensions of meaning. The subject rates a concept (such as "emotional appeals" or "reasoning") by checking the appropriate cell of a linear scale. While the test is easy to administer, researchers are still working on a simple method of analyzing and interpreting its data.

FUNCTIONAL FACTORS

An understanding of the relation of psychology to communication requires familiarity with pertinent functional psychological factors. In the rest of this chapter we shall describe a number of these in general terms, saving until later chapters the specific applications of these factors to various patterns of communicative behavior.

Attention and Perception

Attention has always been a central concept in psychology, and it is also a key functional factor in communication. No matter how significant the communicator's message, and no matter how strongly he feels about it, it will be lost unless his hearers attend to it. As we indicated in Chapter 9, the psychology of listening is predicated upon the concepts of attention and perception. When we listen we attend: we organize a maximum concentration of our sensory receptors upon the communicative stimulus consisting of audible (spoken words) and visible (bodily action) symbols. Only after we attend can we perceive: we are aware of the stimulus symbols and of the objects, conditions, or relationships which they represent. When we both attend and perceive we respond: we manifest this response by some overt or covert muscular movement or glandular activity.

It is no mistake if this description of the attention-perception-response sequence suggests an inseparability of the elements. Attention is a preparatory process, leading into perception, and culminating with response, sequentially but almost simultaneously. In the following discussion of attention, therefore, we are inevitably also referring to perception.

Before examining the concept of attention in detail we should underscore its significance in the communicative situation: it is one of the two major psychological contributions to rhetorical theory. The psychologist William James (1892, pp. 448-449) stated the basic principle: "What holds attention determines action. . . . What checks our impulses is the mere thinking of reasons to the contrary—it is their bare presence to the mind which gives the veto." Psychologist James R. Angell (1908, p. 402) expanded the principle: "No idea can dominate our movements which does not catch and hold attention. When we keep our attention firmly fixed upon a line of conduct, to the exclusion of all competitors, our decision is already made." And rhetorician James A. Winans (1915, p. 194) incorporated the principle into his then-revolutionary definition: "Persuasion is the process of inducing others to give fair, favorable, or undivided attention to propositions."

1. *The duration and span of attention.* A listener cannot give continuous attention; even when he tries very hard to attend, he does not hear everything. Attention comes in spurts, like an irregular succession of waves breaking on a beach. While early experimenters estimated that the length of an attention unit is from five to eight seconds, psychologists now conclude simply that the duration of attention is brief, and that it is impossible to specify an absolute time value since that depends

upon the intensity of the stimulus. Even assuming that an individual's capacity for sustained stimulus selection is thirty seconds, however, it is obvious that when listening to a speech delivered at the rate of 150 words per minute, the listener would hear only about 75 words in one unit of attention. The duration of attention varies with individuals, and their powers of concentration are affected by such factors as interest in the communication, fatigue, and so on.

The span of an individual's attention also varies. Psychologists commonly refer to a *focus*, where perception is sharp, and a *margin*, where awareness is slight. As Chapman and Brown (1935) found, clarity of perception is greatest when the stimuli are clustered in focus. While individual differences and the type of stimuli involved will affect the span of attention, laboratory experiments suggest that four or five visual stimuli, and five to eight auditory ones, represent practical limits.

2. *Types of attention.* Thus far we have spoken of attention as though it always takes the same form. In fact, psychologists commonly recognize three varieties of attention: involuntary, voluntary, habitual.

(a) *Involuntary attention* is sometimes called passive, since it requires no effort on the part of the individual; instead, he attends because some stimulus is compellingly attractive compared with other stimuli. Operationally this may be illustrated by the "figure-ground" concept, in which unusual stimulus symbols stand out from the background of the familiar. Thus a printed word is a "figure" against the "ground" of a white page, a speaker's striking gesture is a "figure" against the "ground" of normal delivery. Everyday life is filled with fire sirens, neon signs, dramatic slogans, and even certain social forces, that compel our involuntary attention.

(b) *Voluntary attention* results from deliberate action on our part, sometimes requiring great effort. Studying for a final examination, performing an unpleasant task in the office, or listening to an uninspiring speaker, exemplifies attention of this sort. These examples also explain why voluntary attention is often referred to as active, demanding conscious, although perhaps reluctant, focus on the stimulus.

(c) *Habitual attention* is sometimes referred to as nonvoluntary, suggesting its roots in both of the other types. If it is caused by aroused interests, or opportunities to satisfy needs (such as a listless lecturer but one who presents vital pre-examination information), it will have some qualities of voluntary attention. If it comes from a psychological "set" for a repeated experience (it *is* customary to listen to classroom lecturers), it will have some characteristics of involuntary attention.

In many situations the listener may shift or be shifted, from one type of attention to another. For example, a communicator who lacks prestige, or whose message will not command voluntary attention, may begin with a device that compels involuntary attention, then try to develop sustained habitual attention.

3. *Unlearned attention values.* The communicator who wants the attention of audience members must recognize that his stimulus must not only be strong enough to energize their sensory organs, but compelling enough to compete successfully with other stimuli. Thus he must find what Murphy (1951, p. 140) calls "factors of advantage," stimulus attributes commanding priority. Psychologists are in general agreement on the nature of these attributes and in considering some of them to be unlearned, others learned. Here are five natural or unlearned values:

(a) *Change* is the most basic and significant attention value. When the attention-perception-response cycle has been completed for any one stimulus it tends to lose its potency, and a new stimulus is necessary to attract further attention. A changing stimulus is one that moves in some direction, from high to low, weak to strong, background to foreground, and so on. Thus the television director tries to maintain attention by alternating "long" and "closeup" camera shots. If the diversification of stimuli becomes too rhythmical, however, as in the "sing-song" recitation of a poem, then the movement becomes predictable and the value of change is lost. In using vocal and physical energy as attention devices, therefore, the stimuli need not only change, but must also incorporate a variety of change.

(b) *Intensity* as an attention value may be described this way: whenever there are competing stimuli the most intense one (strongest, loudest, brightest, largest, etc.) will command our attention. This principle operates with both visible and audible symbols, such as the full-page color advertisement against the quarter-page black and white one, or the strong and vibrant voice against the weak and flat one. As with the principle of change, however, variety is also an important concomitant of intensity. Actors, for example, learn to vary the vocal intensity of their playing in order to extract maximum value from its use in "building" a scene.

(c) *Striking quality,* sometimes simply in the form of novelty of stimulus, has obvious attention value. Some of its virtue may be drawn from the incorporation of the values of change or intensity. If we suddenly shout in a high pitch we probably use greater intensity, but even without increasing the intensity the high pitch alone would attract attention. Even a physically stronger stimulus may yield to a lesser one of striking quality, such as a smooth pressure on a large area to a light pinch in a localized area, pastels to saturated colors, or an open trumpet to a muted one.

(d) *Repetition,* within limits, has high attention value. Its advantages lie in the added strength given to the stimulus by repeating it and in the consequent increase in our sensitivity to the stimulus. This increased sensitivity develops from what is often described as a "summation of stimuli" and a consequent "neurological summation" of response. Plutarch reported that when Demosthenes was asked what were the three parts of oratory he replied, "Action, *action*, ACTION!" With this repetition we cannot fail to get the point. The possibility of monotony may be avoided and even greater potency often achieved if the repeated stimulus is varied slightly in form while retaining the central theme. This application of repetition is a hallmark of good design and composition, whether in music, architecture, stage scenery, or public relations campaigns.

(e) *Definiteness of form* has great natural attention value because perception is easier when stimulus objects are sharply outlined, or when multiple stimuli can be viewed as a patterned group. Thus we attend to the grouping of stars into the Big Dipper, the arrangement of musical notes into a melody, or the organization of arguments into a cumulative sequence. Our ability to perceive stimuli in patterns is so strong that we often fill in gaps, in effect "seeing" a whole even though some parts may be missing. We expect to find eleven men in a football lineup and so may not notice when the ball is snapped with one player still on the sideline. Our tendency to attend to, and to perceive, definiteness of form is strengthened when the stimulus objects are similar to each other, close enough together to be seen as a whole, arranged in an orderly or a symmetrical pattern, or forming some sort of continuity.

4. *Individualized attention values.* In addition to the natural and universal values influencing the direction of attention there is a complex of subjective or individualized "factors of advantage." Psychologists also agree generally on three types of learned values.

(a) *The organic condition* of the individual may determine the stimulus to which he is most apt to respond at any given moment. If we are fatigued, stimuli related to rest will have special potency; hunger renders us unusually receptive to stimuli related to food; and if we are perplexed about a problem we respond to stimuli offering resolution. Thus the individual selectively attends to whatever stimulus is most closely related to his paramount biological needs.

(b) *Social suggestion* is often a determinant of attention and perception. What is pointed out to us by others—or what we see others doing —often influences our own behavior. Especially is this true if the suggested action will gain social approval or special prestige. Opera halls and art galleries alike are populated not only by true connoisseurs, but also by those seeking status rather than culture. Even "sidewalk superintendents" may be attracted not so much by the construction project as by the fact that others have apparently been attracted.

(c) *Predispositions* of an individual also operate as selective factors in determining what he attends to. His interests, wants, experiences, or habits predispose him to attend to associated stimuli. A fire siren may not disturb a sleeping mother, but she will awaken with a start at the slightest outcry from her baby. An audience may be unaware of an actor's miscue, but a person familiar with the script will discern the mistake at once. Or, to put the matter another way, several individuals may attend to the same stimulus but be guided by their predispositions into "seeing" it quite differently. A mathematician may see a simple circle as a symbol for zero, a garage mechanic interpret it as a piston ring, and an artist view it as a design element.

Interest

In considering functional psychological factors in communicative behavior it is logical to move from attention to interest for they are not only associated but nearly inseparable. As William James (1892, p. 448) put it: "What-we-attend-to and what-interests-us are synonymous terms." The distinction between them, a thin one, is that attention is concerned with the initial organization of our sensory receptors toward a given stimulus and that interest is what maintains subsequent orientation. We have already noted that the only thing constant about attention is that it ebbs and flows; the effect of factors having inherent interest is to stabilize it as much as that is possible. We describe here the most common natural factors of interest.

1. *Animation* as an interest factor is analogous to the attention values of change and intensity. When the attention-perception-response cycle set off by one stimulus is completed, a change in the stimulus requires a readjustment and tends to evoke new interest. The stationary painted barber pole, the revolving pole, and the new one with neon lights, illustrate our point. So do the animated television commercials where few products are static but shaving cream lathers and beer foams, and the digestive tract is in a constant state of upset.

2. *Vitalness* in a stimulus almost guarantees interest, especially when its vital quality is related to self. Even the individual who prides himself on objectivity and intellectuality is seldom able to suppress interest in anything affecting his basic physiological needs. Those who sell medical nostrums rely on this fact, and so do those who promote safety on the highways. What affects our vital interests concerns us because they are *our* interests.

3. *Familiarity* in a situation sustains interest because it gives us a sense of security; we "feel at home" with what we already know. This is why politicians often apply accepted labels to new proposals: "The undistributed profits tax is merely an extension of the individual income tax."

Even what is not itself familiar, but similar to something previously experienced, may also hold interest; we have some confidence in likenesses and do much of our learning by association.

4. *Novelty* contrasts sharply with familiarity, but may be no less potent as an interest factor. If situations are too familiar, repeated exposure to them may become monotonous. Instead of feeling secure, we may become apathetic. "This is where I came in" is a common phrase indicating a loss of interest. A novel stimulus tends to counter this reaction; because it is new it excites curiosity and revives interest. Perhaps the most effective presentation combines familiarity and novelty: "Old wine in new bottles." In terms of communication this might mean familiar ideas and sentiments applied to new situations and in novel language.

5. *Conflict* interests almost everyone. Most of us regularly engage in some form of it, playing in team sports, working to earn promotions, trying to write better books, or just "keeping up with the Joneses." It is natural, therefore, that we also become interested observers of the presentation of conflict and may identify with and respond especially to one of the combatants. The modern mass audiences for professional sports illustrate the point, and so does the theatre-goer whose interest in a play is at least partially due to its resolving a conflict situation. Burke (1945) even views persuasive speaking from a dramatistic approach and sees its modes of action in the form of conflict.

6. *Suspense* is inextricably tied to conflict in the maintenance of interest; if we become involved in a conflict situation, even as observers, we want to know how it comes out. Psychologically, an unresolved conflict is an incomplete configuration; we are annoyed because part of the picture is missing, and we sustain our interest until the picture is filled in and we can react to the complete situation.

7. *Concreteness* commonly holds interest while abstractness loses it. The psychological principle is the simple one that any stimulus is a symbol which must be interpreted in terms of our experiences, and that our experiences seldom survive as abstractions but rather as memories of concrete things we have seen, sounds we have heard, and so on. Thus concrete stimuli are most effective in calling up concrete images. It is true, however, that the more intelligent and sophisticated individual usually finds it easier to translate abstractions, and may even enjoy doing it.

8. *Humor* is an ambivalent factor of interest unless it is clearly relevant to the total situation. A humorous anecdote, built on incongruity, becomes itself incongruous when unrelated to the central experience: "It's funny, but what's the point?" Both variety and relaxation of tension may be introduced into a situation, however, by an occasional and pertinent turn of phrase, an unexpected comparison, or a play on sound or sense.

Motivation

In an earlier chapter, we introduced the concept of emotion in our discussion of affective behavior and speech. Here we restate briefly some of what was said, as a prelude to our comments on motivation. We give this subject emphasis by repetition because it is so commonly believed that man is a completely rational being, that we always "make up our minds" by applying reason to problem situations and in choosing among alternative reactions. Our study of psychology compels us to disagree with this view. Man's fulfillment of his maximum potentialities does depend upon the controlling force of reason, but he seldom achieves this goal. "Reason," says Overstreet (1949, pp. 104-105), "is a *capacity* in man, not necessarily an achievement. In most men it lies largely dormant while something else, which is far from reason, takes over."

A major factor in that "something else" which takes over from pure reason is emotion. Psychologists do not always agree upon how to classify emotions; indeed, they prefer not to consider emotions as discrete entities, but to think of affective behavior as a single, basic, and confused pattern of response. This behavior they measure by such indicators of satisfaction, relaxation, irritation, or frustration as galvanic skin response, blood pressure and volume, muscular tension, heart rate, and respiration. In general it would be agreed that both bodily states and expressive actions reveal characteristics of affective behavior commonly elicited by three basic situations:

1. Those situations that are completely new or strange, that develop suddenly and unexpectedly, threatening an individual's physical or social security and creating anxiety, tend to arouse a *fear* response.

2. Those situations which restrain the individual in any way, frustrating his desires or preventing him from behaving in ways that will satisfy him, tend to arouse an *anger* response.

3. Those situations which remove threats to the individual's feeling of security, relieve his anxieties, or eliminate frustration, and thus permit the satisfaction of his desires and needs, tend to arouse a *pleasure* response.

From this application of what we have said earlier about affective behavior, we conclude that any physiological or environmental circumstance which annoys or satisfies the individual does so not solely because it brings him pleasure or pain, contentment or irritation, joy or depression, but primarily because it either satisfies or thwarts particular desires and wants. These desires and wants give an emotional impulse toward behavior which helps the individual adjust to the circumstance confronting him. In short, his behavior is motivated.

In 1938, one of the authors of this book introduced a discussion of motivation by declaring that: "The amount of organized human behavior that is not determined by an individual's wants, interests, and purposes is so small as to merit attention only because of its rarity." Despite the enormous amount of psychological research in the subsequent quarter of a century, there is no reason to modify this statement. The more we study human behavior the more sure we are that it is dynamic, characterized by great energy stemming from basic inner drives—wants, interests, and purposes.

These motives are so closely articulated with our behavior that we seldom identify them in isolation. Indeed, we may never recognize them unless we are caught in the vise of conflicting motives operating upon us simultaneously. After momentary frustration we normally resolve the conflict and shape our behavior to satisfy one drive or the other. In abnormal behavior, of course, the individual fails to make a choice and meets the conflict by various stratagems of avoidance or dissembling, such as rationalization, projection, repression, or sublimation.

Since we cannot observe motivational drives directly, we are obliged to identify them by observing the characteristics of motivated behavior. Stagner and Karwoski (1952, pp. 35-36) list three primary ones: energy, persistence, and variability. Motivation operates, they say, in proportion to the energy expended in a given situation, and thus they assume that if one student works more energetically than another, he is more strongly motivated. They also point out that a highly motivated person does not give up easily; if his initial behavior does not lead directly to his goal, he persists by trying other behaviors. The third characteristic of variability is thus a product of the second; the highly motivated person varies his techniques as he continues to seek satisfaction.

These observations suggest that motivation operates in a sequence of three steps. First, the individual feels a need, stemming from his wants, interests, or purposes. Second, this feeling of need leads him into some form of instrumental or problem-solving behavior. Third, if this behavior is efficient, it achieves a specific end that satisfies the original need. The omnibus term describing this complete sequence is motivated behavior.

Before we attempt a classification of basic drives that result in motivated behavior, note should be taken of the significance of motivation in the communicative situation. In discussing the concept of attention we observed that it was one of two major psychological contributions to rhetorical theory; the second is the concept of motivation. Winans (1915, p. xiii), building upon the concept set forth by James, was explicit: "The key word [in public speaking] is Attention." Concurrently he held that persuasion was a mental process. Brigance (1935) took cognizance of later psychological research on motivation: "the generally accepted view today, however, is that persuasion takes place, not on an intellectual, but rather on a motor level," and "the lines of modern research, to say nothing of common sense, converge to show that desires are the basic determinant of persuasion." Thus Brigance accepted the James-Winans notion that attention was the *channel* for the flow of persuasive communication, but argued that its *headspring* was desire. This view of the dominant function of motivation is standard today.

We now conclude this discussion of motivation by describing the fundamental drives affecting normal human behavior. While modern psychologists agree upon the existence and the significance of these wants, purposes, and interests, each tends to draw up his own list of exactly what they are. We shall follow that precedent and present our own list. These are the basic, unlearned drives, universally present in all human beings:

1. *Human beings direct their activities toward the satisfaction of physical wants and general well-being.* They avoid, whenever possible, situations that may bring about physical deprivation, including pain, hunger, thwarting of sex impulses, and a need for sleep. Much contemporary advertising promises these satisfactions, whether from headache remedies, fancy foods, or form-fitting mattresses. An individual can suffer any of these deprivations temporarily, however, and he may knowingly enter into situations which will deprive him for a time if he believes that there will be ultimate satisfaction. The willingness of astronauts to undergo periods of intense training is at least partially explainable in terms of the ultimate respite they know will come at the end of their missions.

2. *Human beings normally behave in ways that will lead them toward success, mastery, and achievement.* They try to avoid situations that may thwart, frustrate or disappoint them. Again, however, individuals may often knowingly accept temporary disappointment when there is promise of future success or achievement. Some students, for example, may withdraw from athletic competition if they fear that they cannot "make the team"; but others willingly engage in rigorous drills if they believe that "practice pays off." It is normal to want to "be the best of whatever you are."

3. *Human beings tend to behave in ways that will help them to gain recognition, admiration, respect, and approval.* They avoid action that may result in being ignored, looked down upon, or merely tolerated. Even temporary disdain may be accepted by an individual if he feels there is a possibility of gaining lasting respect; tomorrow's cheers will compensate for today's jeers. Those who study social influence on behavior often refer to "status needs," the drives to achieve favorable prominence in one's own social hierarchy. Some groups accord high status to great intellect or creative talent; in others these virtues count

for little, but material possessions—costly cars, lavish wardrobes, or un-limited expense accounts—are status symbols. So common is this drive for recognition that "status seeker" is now a widely used label.

4. *Human beings generally act in ways that will lead toward their being loved, and the realization of a feeling of being wanted.* They tend to avoid behavior that keeps them from "belonging," and to indulge in activities that are not intrinsically satisfying—such as going to concerts or attending cocktail parties—if participation will strengthen group ties. Human beings usually prefer the company of others rather than being alone, and prefer to be with familiar persons rather than strange ones. There are notable exceptions, however; explorers may visit isolated areas or strange people, and recluses may shun all human contacts. But such persons may well be motivated in their behavior by other drives which are for them, at least at the moment, more fundamental.

5. *Human beings usually act in ways that will bring about peace of mind, security, and a feeling of release from worry and anxiety.* They try to avoid involvement in situations that create fear, anxiety, or in-security. Students lacking confidence in their mathematical abilities may avoid science courses; others, feeling deficient in social qualities, may refuse opportunities for group memberships. In some circumstances, of course, individuals may be oppressed by more than one of these con-cerns, and be forced to accept a lesser, and perhaps temporary, worry in order to put off a more serious one. Thus "robbing Peter to pay Paul" or "choosing the lesser of two evils" are common behavioral guides.

6. *Finally, human beings indicate by their behavior that they seek some adventure, new experiences, and zestful living.* They tend to avoid boredom and monotony. How much adventure or how many new expe-riences a person seeks is a highly individual matter. The man who is responsible only to and for himself may often enter into situations that are not only new but dangerous, in his search for zestful living. But the less mobile man, such as the head of a family, tends to suppress his drive for new experiences in favor of mundane security. Generally, how-ever, individuals seek a condition of life with enough novelty to prevent monotony, but not so much novelty that living will be difficult because of the necessity of making continuous adjustments to too rapid change. The appeal of eating in exotic restaurants or of watching adventure programs on television may thus be compensation for otherwise humdrum living.

Learning and Remembering

The primary aim of the communicator, we have said, is so to transmit his message to his hearers that it will change their behavior. Another way to say this is that the communicator wants his hearers to "learn" his propositions and to "remember" them as bases for immediate or future action. In short, as Berlo (1960, pp. 99-100) has compared the two, a "model of the communication process encompasses the model of learning. . . . The two models represent only a difference in point of view. A learning model usually starts with the decoding function, a communication model usually starts with a discussion of purpose. That is the primary distinction between the two, and it is not important theoretically." What is important is that the concepts of learning and remembering are important functional factors in the psychology of communication.

In Chapter 6 we discussed in some detail the psychology of language learning; and earlier in this chapter we touched again on the concept of learning in our discussion of attention and perception. We now consider some implications of specific aspects of the learning and remembering process for the communication situation.

For our purposes we need review here only that type of learning called perceptual. Learning results from our discriminating understanding of concepts. Concepts are generalizations that remain constant as our guides to the meaning of objects, persons, qualities, or relationships. We learn literally thousands of concepts, usually in terms of word symbols but occasionally in terms of visual or other sensory images, such as "purple," "Easterner," "vitality," or "love." (By the process of abstraction our concepts may be extended, broadened, reduced in complexity.) Working from a base of acquired concepts we perceive a wide range of stimuli. This perception becomes discriminative learning as a consequence of what is called differential reinforcement. The reinforcement consists of providing an incentive for responding (perceiving) in a particular way to a specific stimulus. To be effective this incentive must be related to the satisfaction of a physiological need or one of the basic drives we have previously discussed. We refer to the reinforcement as differential because it rewards the response to one stimulus but not to another. Thus we identify perceptual learning as that involving the perception of new concepts (or the modification of old ones) about objects, persons, qualities, or relationships, and resulting from the presentation of reinforced stimuli.

With this limited review we now consider learning and remembering in a variety of communication situations. Specifically, communicators should appreciate the influence of the listener's selectivity upon what he will attend to, the utility of categorization and of suggestion in stimulating both learning and remembering, and specific techniques of impressiveness in assuring retention.

1. *Selectivity in attending and perceiving.* An understanding of psychological barriers to communication, and an appreciation of the elements

creating resistance to change, are both important in a complete assessment of learning in communicative situations. For our purposes, it is sufficient to generalize about the influence upon learning of selective perception. It is apparent that not all persons attend and perceive in the same way, to the same degree, or for the same reasons. In addition to such variations explainable by differences in personality, it should be recognized that individuals may be deliberately selective in exposing themselves to learning opportunities. This fact is underscored in the following conclusions about the relationships between opportunity for learning and actual learning. They were derived from a careful examination by Hyman and Sheatsley (1947) of surveys made by the National Opinion Research Center:

(a) There exists a hard core of chronic "know-nothings." "There is something about the uninformed which makes them harder to reach, no matter what the level or nature of the information."

(b) Interested people acquire the most information. "The widest possible dissemination of material may be ineffective if it is not geared to the public's interest."

(c) People seek information congenial to prior attitudes, and tend to ignore uncongenial information. "Merely 'increasing the flow' is not enough, if the information continues to 'flow' in the direction of those already on your side."

(d) People interpret the same information differently. It is "false to assume that exposure, once achieved, results in uniform interpretation and retention of the material." Memory and perception are distorted by wishes, motives, and attitudes.

(e) Information does not necessarily change attitudes. Informed people react differently from uninformed, "but it is naïve to suppose that information always affects attitudes, or that it affects all attitudes equally. . . . There is evidence . . . that individuals, once they are exposed to information, change their views *differentially*, each in the light of his own *prior* attitude."

2. *Learning and remembering by categorizing.* Outstanding in recent psychological research has been that in the Harvard University Cognition Project. Of particular interest here is its focus upon a process called categorizing, the way a person establishes equivalences or distinctive similarities among concepts, as he "sorts out and responds to the world around him." This process is related to learning and remembering in communicative situations, as we can see by summarizing from Bruner, Goodnow, and Austin (1956, p. 11-15) the utility for the individual of categorizing discriminably different objects, persons, qualities, relationships, or events:

(a) By categorizing, the individual reduces the complexity of his environment, abstracting and defining in terms of previously perceived groupings.

(b) Categorizing provides an individual the means for identifying the objects of the world about him and assigning each one to its established class.

(c) Because categorizing does reduce the complexity of the environment by establishing identification patterns, it also reduces the necessity for constant learning by the individual. He can capitalize upon his recollections of previous experiences.

(d) Categorizing provides the individual with direction for instrumental or problem-solving activity; it gives him a set of relatively reliable a priori judgments about how to behave with respect to recognized concepts.

(e) The individual is enabled by his categorizing to order and relate different classes of objects, events, and so on. Organized and related systems of categorized classes permit him to relate classes of objects and events rather than individual ones.

Closely related to the process of learning and remembering by categorization is the process of generalization in critical thinking, or developing universal conclusions from inductive analyses of particular instances. Categorizing and generalizing are both ways of learning about events, relationships, and other concepts.

3. *Suggestion in learning and remembering.* We observed that individuals exercise some selectivity about what they choose to learn, but we must turn the coin over and note that individuals may also be quite unselective in this respect *if the force of positive suggestion is strong enough* (Coffin, 1941). "I would like to suggest" says the professor, "that my lecture today will cover materials that are significant for the final examination." This unsubtle suggestion is a stimulus sure to evoke attention, interest, and learning from all but the most indolent student.

Any positive suggestion is a social stimulus designed to elicit an uncritical and more or less automatic response. That it can do so results from the fact that humans tend to prefer being in a passive rather than an active state. Acceptance of a suggestion is a normal response, requiring little or no discriminative activity. To doubt, on the other hand, is more difficult; it demands active and critical analysis. If the suggestion comes from a person with prestige or authority, it is even more likely to be accepted. In our illustration of the preceding paragraph, the psychological odds are all in favor of the professor.

We conclude these observations on the role of suggestion in learning with a series of generalizations about the nature of suggestion and its demonstrated effects upon behavior:

(a) Suggestion operates most effectively when it is directed toward an existent response-pattern.

(b) Suggestion operates most effectively when it encounters a receptive attitude; there must be no other suggestions that set off stronger or better established response patterns.

(c) Suggestion is increased when there is a lack of adequate knowledge concerning the subject at hand.

(d) Suggestion is increased when it is related to desire—a fundamental want, drive, or belief.

(e) Suggestion is increased by the prestige of the person making it.

(f) Suggestion is increased by excitement which is usually accompanied by a relaxation of reason.

(g) Suggestion is usually increased by group situations.

4. *Impressiveness in learning and remembering.* A final significant influence upon the learning and remembering process is the impressiveness of the stimulus employed to bring about the desired response. A general principle is that the stronger or the more potent the stimulus, the greater impress it will make upon the responding person. The best omnibus word to describe this principle in operation is *emphasis,* the special stress or weight given to particular stimuli. In the communicative situation this means the emphasis given to particular stimulus units (whole arguments, propositional sentences, important phrases, key words) by presenting them with special potency. To give emphasis of this sort implies, realistically, that in any total learning some parts are more critical to understanding than others. We apply this fact whenever we reduce a fifty-word message to a ten-word telegram, retaining only the essential information.

Some of the earliest investigations into the relative potency of stimuli in oral communication situations were reported by Jersild (1928) and Ehrensberger (1945), and many subsequent studies have been done by researchers in the field of speech. From these experimental inquiries into the impressiveness of stimuli we draw the following generalizations:

(a) The intensity of a stimulus increases its potency: loud sounds more than soft ones, vivid hues more than moderate ones, and so on.

(b) The potency of a stimulus is related to its duration. The prolonged wail of the fire siren has more impact than a short blast, and an argument fully explained makes more impress than one merely alluded to.

(c) Even though a stimulus may be intense and prolonged, its potency may further be increased by the specific reinforcement of an accompanying stimulus such as a vigorous gesture, or an orienting one such as an anticipatory pause.

(d) Stimuli repeated as many as three or four times tend to be more impressive than those presented only once. Beyond four, however, further repetitions do not appear to affect responses proportionately.

(e) Repetitions of stimuli appear to be most potent when they are spaced out in intervals of time. This may well be because distributed repetitions have a better chance of striking the listener during one or more of his spurts of attention than do successive ones.

(f) In any series of stimuli a specific one may be given greater potency by being placed first or last. While there seems to be greater experimental support for an anticlimax order of stimuli, whether primacy or recency is most effective is a matter still in doubt.

(g) Finally, the potency of a stimulus may also be increased when it is reinforced by the phenomenon of social facilitation. An individual who is aware of favorable responses to a specific stimulus by other viewers or listeners, tends to be more impressed by that same stimulus. The mere sight or sound of others responding makes it more comfortable and desirable for him to respond in the same way.

In subsequent chapters we will consider the applications of these basic psychological factors to various forms of communicative behavior.

REFERENCES

Allport, G. W. In Murchison, C. (Ed.), *Handbook of social psychology.* Worcester, Mass.: Clark University Press, 1937.

Angell, J. R. *Psychology.* New York: Holt, Rinehart, and Winston, 1908.

Asch, S. E. Studies of independence and conformity: I. a minority of one against a unanimous majority. *Psychol. Monogr.,* 1956, 70, 416, 70 pp.

Berlo, D. K. *The process of communication.* New York: Holt, Rinehart, and Winston, 1960.

Brigance, W. N. Can we redefine the James-Winans theory of persuasion? *Quart. J. Spch,* 1935, 21, 19-26.

Bruner, J. S., Goodnow, J. J., & Austin, G. A. *A study of thinking.* New York: Wiley, 1956.

Burke, K. *A grammar of motives.* Englewood Cliffs, N. J.: Prentice-Hall, 1945.

Burtt, H. E., & Falkenberg, D. R. The influence of majority and expert opinion on religious attitudes. *J. soc. Psychol.,* 1941, 14, 269-278.

Chapman, D. W., & Brown, H. E. The reciprocity between clearness and range of attention. *J. gen. Psychol.,* 1935, 13, 357-366.

Coffin, T. E. Some conditions of suggestibility: a study of certain attitudinal and situational factors influencing the process of suggestion. *Psychol. Monogr.,* 1941, 53, 241, 125 pp.

Ehrensberger, R. The relative effectiveness of certain forms of emphasis in public speaking. *Spch Monogr.,* 1945, 12, 94-111.

Hovland, C. I., Janis, I. L., & Kelley, H. H. *Communication and persuasion.* New Haven: Yale University Press, 1953.

Hyman, H. H., & Sheatsley, P. B. Some reasons why information campaigns fail. *Publ. Opin. Quart.*, 1947, 11, 412-423.

James, W. *Psychology, briefer course.* New York: Holt, Rinehart, and Winston, 1892.

Jebb, R. C. *The attic orators.* New York: Macmillan, 1876. 2 vols.

Jersild, A. T. Modes of emphasis in public speaking. *J. appl. Psychol.*, 1928, 12, 611-620.

Krech, D., & Crutchfield, R. S. *Theory and problems of social psychology.* New York: McGraw-Hill, 1948.

Kulp, D. H. Prestige, as measured by single-experience changes and their permanency. *J. educ. Res.*, 1934, 27, 663-672.

Lasswell, H. D. In Smith, B. L., Lasswell, H. D., & Casey, R. D. (Eds.), *Propaganda, communication and public opinion.* Princeton: Princeton University Press, 1946.

Lorge, I. Prestige, suggestion and attitudes. *J. soc. Psychol.*, 1936, 7, 386-402.

Lund, F. H. The psychology of belief. *J. abnorm. soc. Psychol.*, 1925, 20, 63-112, 174-224.

Marple, C. H. The comparative susceptibility of three age levels to the suggestion of group versus expert opinion. *J. soc. Psychol.*, 1933, 4, 176-186.

Murphy, G. *An introduction to psychology.* New York: Harper & Row, 1951.

Overstreet, H. A. *The mature mind.* New York: W. W. Norton, 1949.

Sawyer, T. M., Jr. Shift of attitude following persuasion as related to estimate of majority attitude. *Spch Monogr.*, 1955, 22, 68-78.

Schanck, R. L., & Goodman, C. Reactions to propaganda on both sides of a controversial issue. *Publ. Opin. Quart.*, 1939, 3, 107-112.

Scott, W. D. *The psychology of public speaking.* Philadelphia: Pearson Brothers, 1906.

Shannon, C., & Weaver, W. *The mathematical theory of communication.* Urbana, Ill.: University of Illinois Press, 1949.

Simpson, R. H. *A study of those who influence and of those who are influenced in discussion.* New York: Teachers College, Columbia University, 1938.

Skinner, B. F. *Verbal behavior.* New York: Appleton-Century-Crofts, 1957.

Smith, R. G. Development of a semantic differential for use with speech related concepts. *Spch Monogr.*, 1959, 26, 263-272.

Stagner, R., & Karwoski, T. F. *Psychology.* New York: McGraw-Hill, 1952.

Wallace, K. R. The field of speech, 1953: an overview. *Quart. J. Spch*, 1954, 40, 117-129.

Wheeler, D., & Jordan, H. Change of individual opinion to accord with group opinion. *J. abnorm. soc. Psychol.*, 1929, 24, 203-206.

Winans, J. A. *Public speaking.* New York: Appleton-Century-Crofts, 1915.

15

Psychology of
Group Discussion

IN THE PRECEDING CHAPTER we considered those psychological factors significantly related to all circumstances and forms of oral communication. Here we will make specific applications of these factors to communication by group discussion. Although groups have long been recognized as significant social units, relatively little was written about group behavior as related to oral communication until a decade or two ago. It was about 1945 that Kurt Lewin pioneered in research in this field. While legitimate questions were asked about the soundness of research procedures used by some early investigators, unquestionably valuable research has been done on group behavior by recent investigators in the fields of speech, social psychology, education, and sociology. This has led to an enrichment of the descriptive literature on the psychology of groups, group leadership, group membership, and the processes by which groups achieve their goals. It is upon this literature that we draw in summarizing concepts pertinent to the psychology of group discussion. (Standard and current bibliographies are listed in these references: Auer, 1953; Cleary, 1957ff.; Haberman, 1948-1956; Haiman, 1954; Strodtbeck and Hare, 1954.)

PRELIMINARY DEFINITIONS

First of all, a few definitions are in order. What do we mean by a group? And what is its social function? Social psychologists distinguish between primary and secondary groups. The latter term refers to large and artificial categories, created by the accident of circumstance or even

253

by the imagination: persons "belonging to" nations or local communities, ethnic or religious aggregates, socio-economic classes, or those
who have merely paid their dues to a single organization. Our concern
is not with these secondary groups, but with primary ones. Cooley (1909,
p. 23) was perhaps the first to describe them: "By primary groups I mean
those characterized by intimate face-to-face association and cooperation.
They are primary in several senses, but chiefly in that they are fundamental in forming the social nature and ideals of the individual. The
result of intimate association, psychologically, is a certain fusion of indi-
vidualities in a common whole, so that one's very self, for many purposes
at least, is the common life and purpose of the group. Perhaps the
simplest way of describing this wholeness is by saying that it is 'we';
it involves the sort of sympathy and mutual identification for which 'we'
is the natural expression."

Cooley's description still provides a standard frame of reference for
investigations of primary groups and their behavior. The possibility of
interaction through direct communication, of course, is a key element
of the primary group. Homans (1950, p. 1) makes it central in his definition: "a number of persons who communicate with one another over a
span of time, and who are few enough so that each person is able to
communicate with all others, not at secondhand, through other people,
but face-to-face."

A CONCEPT OF THE GROUP

Any concept of the group must account for the nature of membership
and common and differentiating group characteristics.

Individuals in Groups

The most important thing to remember about groups is that they are
made up of people. Thus, we first consider the relations of individuals
to groups.

1. *Each individual lives in a society that is built upon group organization.* Although humans consider themselves to be individualists, they
seldom act completely independently. Instead they enter into formal or
informal group relationships, not merely for social convenience, but because human beings are increasingly dependent upon structured groups
and collective action for their economic, political, and cultural sustenance.
In modern society the "survival of the fittest" theory applies as much
or more to groups than to individuals.

2. *Each individual belongs to overlapping groups.* "We are all bundles
of hyphens" is one way of generalizing about the multiple groups to

which each individual belongs in his various social roles as wage earner, churchgoer, citizen, voter, parent, etc. Intellectually, emotionally, and often financially, individuals contribute to these groups and, in turn, are influenced by them. Only a few fortunate persons find all of their group memberships compatible; more often they are "at war with themselves" in a battle of conflicting loyalties.

3. *Each individual is sometimes apart from all groups.* As he participates in any one group, he must react to its pressures in consonance with his other group relationships. To make this intricate adjustment of conflicting psychological forces, the individual must try to stand apart from all of his affiliations. The decisions he reaches in this state of temporary isolation may seem to him to be independently arrived at, but they are nonetheless achieved in the shadow of the groups to which he belongs.

Similarities Among Groups

Whether formal or informal, any group consists of persons who are at a particular time organized in a special way for a common purpose. In certain aspects, therefore, all groups are similar.

1. *Groups are usually built around common interests.* Though on many matters members of a group may disagree, even violently, their existence as a group requires that at least temporarily they must agree on the main purpose for which they are organized. This fact alone is usually responsible for developing cohesiveness among members and group loyalties. Both cohesion and loyalty may disappear, of course, if the common interest is lost.

2. *Groups commonly determine their own membership.* Persons who do not share a group's common interests are seldom knowingly invited to join; groups tend to think non-believers are nuisances. And persons who cannot "see the light" tend to agree. Thus a sense of unity is maintained, at least on the group's main interest or cause, and differences are limited to ways and means of achieving it.

3. *Groups tend to be dynamic rather than static.* Those that are literally static seldom survive in a competitive society. Instead, groups maintain their vitality by recruiting new converts, or by redefining or replacing old objectives. Even groups determined to maintain the status quo need to be dynamic in developing new methods for resisting change.

4. *Groups usually try to transmit their sense of values.* Social and cultural values, especially, are transmitted through group structures, rather than by individuals. Though not done intentionally, this still tends to give stability to a group, even across spatial and temporal divisions.

5. *Groups tend to influence an individual's "life's chances."* An individual's normal expectations for health, education, wealth, occupation,

and cultural values—what the sociologist calls "life's chances"—are often determined by the groups he is "born into" or succeeds in entering. Thus a person's group memberships may provide a basis for a fairly reliable prediction of what social or professional opportunities will be open to him, and how he will react to them.

Differential Characteristics of Groups

Although we have identified some features common to all groups, certain differentiating aspects must also be noted. It has often been said that an individual in a group tends to behave just as he would when alone, only more so. This observation assumes that formal and informal groups are composed of like-minded individuals, and that it is therefore possible to think of group behavior as the composite projection of the behaviors of the individuals composing it. This does not mean that a "group personality" or a "group mind" exists as an entity apart from individual members. It does mean, however, that certain behaviors may be identified as characteristic for members of particular groups. For convenience in distinguishing among groups, analyzing them, and sometimes for predicting their probable behavior, seven specific characteristics have been isolated in the research literature on groups.

1. *Group conformity.* Most individuals tend to behave, as we noted in our discussion of motivation in Chapter 14, in ways that will gain recognition, admiration, respect, or approval. This desire for acceptance and status is especially strong when it concerns groups to which we belong; through trial and error we learn that one way of gaining acceptance is by conforming to the standards and mores of the group. Thus it is that group opinion often influences belief and behavior more than does expert opinion, and that a tendency to conform is common enough to be called a characteristic of groups. The degree of conformity, in turn, determines how free members feel to express their own opinions, and how freely these expressions will be accepted by the group. In psychological literature it is common to call the group atmosphere "permissive" when little conformity is demanded, "autocratic" when independent judgment is discouraged.

2. *Group prejudices.* Though we often believe that other persons are prejudiced, few of us willingly admit to prejudices of our own which make us intolerant of the race, religion, social status, or nationality of others. In general we find prejudice most apparent among cohesive groups of like-minded people, and it is intensified when they are in the group environment.

3. *Group resistance to change.* New concepts seldom win complete and immediate acceptance, particularly when they lead to social changes.

True as this is for individuals, it is even truer for individuals in the company of their fellows. Thus, another important index to a group's behavior is the degree to which it resists change, either within the group or in its relations with other groups. Equally characteristic may be the group's strategy of resistance. On the other hand, groups may also follow particular patterns in accepting, or bringing about, change. In effecting change, for example, a group may follow the dictate of a leader, establish a consensus, and so on.

4. *Group structure.* One of the focal points of recent small group research has been the status of individuals within the group, and their relations with other members, both directly and through subgroups. In some large groups, of course, subgroups develop not only because of common interests, but because the work of the parent organization may be more efficiently performed by smaller task forces, or because it is more convenient to have a number of smaller meetings than one large one. Inevitably the activities of the subgroups and their relationships to the parent organization may profoundly affect the ways in which members (a) communicate with each other, (b) interact, and (c) control each other's and the group's behavior. When group processes break down, the first step in understanding why, and in restoring them, may be to make a careful analysis of the structure of the group.

5. *Group values.* Another characteristic differentiating groups is the set of values or ideals it endorses or maintains. An analysis of these values —and of the probable attitudes and beliefs giving rise to them—will aid in understanding a group's behavior. Such an analysis may also serve to explain one group's feelings of hostility or aggressive behavior toward another. Finally, an understanding of those values cherished by a group may provide a basis for predicting its behavior, especially in terms of the programs or propositions it will accept and support.

6. *Group patterns of decision.* By common practice a group may follow a more or less constant procedure in decision-making, and this will reflect another behavioral facet. Some groups are autocratically led by one individual and decisions are made by *authority*. More democratic groups conclude discussions by counting votes, determining majorities, and deciding by *enumeration*. In other groups the establishment of conflicting beliefs or alternate courses of action results in a yielding by each subgroup of some portion of its position, and a decision by the method of *compromise*. Under the most favorable conditions of all, a group establishes a true synthesis of the views of its whole membership and makes its decision by *consensus*. The climate requisite for reaching a consensus, or sometimes even for full discussion before compromise or enumeration, seldom exists when groups feel outside pressures, work in a state of tension, or are hurried by a deadline.

7. *Group patterns of discussion.* All of the preceding characteristics
of a group's behavior will be reflected in the nature and effectiveness of
its communication patterns. A given group, for example, may condone
or encourage noncomformity, be relatively free of prejudice, welcome
change, discourage the creation of subgroups, place a high value on individual feelings, and settle its differences by majority rule. In such an
extremely congenial combination of characteristics one might confidently
expect well-tempered, logical, and uninhibited discussion. With the
change of even a single factor in the group's characteristic behavior,
however—such as the development of a sudden desire for close conformity, or the establishment of cliques within the group—the group's
patterns of communication might be significantly altered.

THE GROUP AS A COMMUNICATION UNIT

We have defined the group as, among other things, a formal or informal organization which makes discussion possible. Discussion may be
defined as social interaction through face-to-face communication. Combining the elements of both of these definitions *we can define group discussion as a planned, but relatively informal, meeting in which those who
attend are invited to join in purposeful talk about a topic or problem of
common interest, under the guidance of a leader, chairman, or moderator.*
Several components of this definition should be singled out for comment.
They constitute elements that appear to be requisites for successful discussion. Because, as we shall note later, there are potentially disruptive
forces at work in many groups, we cannot say that communication will
necessarily be successful when these elements are present. We do believe
that *at least* these five elements must be present for effective communication in group situations. We came to this conclusion after a careful examination of the experimental and expositional literature on discussion.

1. *Planning* in advance, rather than relying upon spontaneous combus-
tion, seems essential for profitable discussion. Often a designated leader
takes the initiative for this planning, but it is best done when several
members of the group share in formulating goals and procedures.

2. *Informality* usually encourages greater participation than does a
rigid atmosphere, and the size of the group and the physical arrangements should be controlled to that end. The best description of this
element is organized informality.

3. *Participation* to the fullest extent of each member's capacity to
contribute is essential for good discussion. The basic assumptions of the
discussion method are that each member may have something valuable
to contribute, and that the best way to discover right solutions is through

cooperative pooling of all available information, evaluation, and judgment.

4. *Purpose* is a prerequisite for profitable talk of any kind, and especially for discussion. In some circumstances simple pleasantries or even socially useful talk may have a point, but group discussions are intended to be learning or problem-solving experiences.

5. *Leadership,* of some sort, is necessary for successful group discussion. This may be exercised by a prescribed individual such as the chairman of a committee or the senior member present, or it may be diffused among several members. In small groups whose members know each other, the functions of leadership may be shared by all participants.

We conclude these comments on the group as a communication unit by citing a few examples of discussion situations. Customarily we regard discussion as a method for learning and for problem-solving. Within each category there may be more specific purposes.

1. *Learning groups* may be concerned only with exchanging facts and opinions, as in typical classroom and study groups, workshops, and many professional conferences. Also basically learning situations, though designed so that members can form individual attitudes, are discussions centering on social and political problems, "Great Books" study groups, and so on. Another type of learning is involved when a discussion group's purpose is to release tensions and develop understandings, as in family councils, some labor-management grievance discussions, and group therapy sessions.

2. *Problem-solving groups* may engage in various types of work projects, but are most commonly concerned with reaching group decisions of some sort, as in legislative and business organization committees, international conferences, and the like. Occasionally a group goes beyond the task of finding a solution and also has administrative functions, including the determination of action steps to put the solution into operation, as with steering committees, executive councils, and boards of directors.

These examples do not exhaust the possible applications of the discussion method but are illustrative only. When we speak of communicating groups in this chapter we will mean any of the varieties of learning and problem-solving situations we have listed. The most distinguishing characteristic of all of them is that they involve face-to-face discussion, direct communication and interaction.

The three aspects of group discussion most thoroughly explored by experimentation are those involving the function of group leadership, the operation of psychological forces within groups, and the behavioral results of discussion. We now report on each of these topics.

A CONCEPT OF LEADERSHIP IN DISCUSSION GROUPS

Attempts to analyze the nature of leadership are at least as old as Moses, and have ranged from the glib assertion that "leaders are born, not made" to controlled studies of traits, methods, and effects of leaders. For those wishing to pursue this topic we have cited some of these studies in the comments that follow.

The Behavior of Leaders

Despite extensive research efforts to discover whether there are qualities common to all leaders, the facts are still elusive. (Beer, *et al.*, 1959; Browne and Cohn, 1958; Stodgill, 1948; Zeleny, 1939.) The precise nature of leadership—significant in all social and political structures— remains to be defined, though certain generalizations may be made. We know, for example, that those regarded as leaders are likely to be either very skilled in interpersonal relations or very adept in manipulating and controlling the behavior of others. We also know that many accepted leaders obtain their status through personal prestige, while others have it because they are feared. And we know that some persons exercise leadership because it is inherent in the positions they hold, while others become leaders without official sanction. Seldom, however, do we identify a complex of qualities making up what might be called a "leadership personality." We find instead that quite different sets of traits, skills, and techniques, exercised by different people, bring similar results; and that some leaders are effective in one situation but fail in another.

We conclude, therefore, that (a) leadership is not a stable quality, identifiable in all recognized leaders or in all situations, and (b) we need to study leaders and their functions in various situations to learn what they do, what groups expect of them, and how they influence behavior. Recent investigations of such questions suggest that these are significant theoretical considerations:

1. *A group's characteristics determine its concept of leadership.* We have suggested that a group profile may be drawn from an analysis of seven differential characteristics. The particular combination of these appears to determine whether a group conceives of its leaders as benevolent despots who make all decisions and initiate all actions, as mere presiding officers for discussions in which group members decide matters for themselves, or as something in between.

2. *A group's concept of leadership influences the techniques of its leaders.* If members of a group behave as though they want someone to tell them what to think or do, someone is likely to do just that. Even

the leader who attempts to create a permissive atmosphere and encourage free participation in decision-making may, if the members fail to respond promptly, succumb to the temptation to tell them what to do.

3. *A leader's personality and emotional needs determine his concept of leadership.* The personality of a leader may be as influential in determining the nature of his leadership behavior as the characteristics of the group. If, for example, he likes being a "boss," and likes the emotional satisfaction that autocratic behavior sometimes brings, he will find it convenient to mistrust the group's intelligence and intentions and conclude that he must dominate it—for its own good! On the other hand, if he draws emotional security from cooperative efforts, he will try to encourage the group and guide it toward reliance upon its own judgments.

4. *A leader's concept of leadership influences his choice of techniques.* Even unconsciously, a leader tends to determine first the kind of behavior he hopes for from his group; then he discovers and uses appropriate techniques of leadership. One leader may think his proper function is to "run things." He will then see that a rigid agenda is drawn up for every discussion, leaving nothing to chance; he will interpose his own opinions frequently, and use techniques of positive suggestion to win their acceptance. Another leader, democratically inclined, may think his proper function is to encourage and assist the group to run itself. He will then urge members to develop their own agenda, accepting even spontaneous changes; he will keep his own opinions in the background, try to remove any obstacles in the way of free member participation, and assist the group in synthesizing its own views.

Many persons in government, education, and business believe that the discussion method is important not only as a democratic method of solving problems, but also for improving interpersonal relations, and a large body of psychological research supports their view. It follows, therefore, that these persons are concerned with developing democratic rather than autocratic leadership. Despite some significant experimentation with training procedures there are still many questions to be explored. Here are a few of them.

1. How much advance planning and structuring of the group process is consistent with democratic leadership?

2. How far can a laissez-faire-inclined leader go in encouraging a group to determine its own procedures and make its own decisions—and mistakes—without actually creating conflict and frustration?

3. How much should the leader let himself be influenced by a desire for efficiency and economy of time and energy in achieving group goals?

4. How much attention can the leader focus on the process of problem-solving and upon interpersonal relations without jeopardizing adequate attention to the problem under discussion?

5. How can the leader discover and employ techniques that will give the group the benefit of his knowledge and ability and yet maintain a permissive climate for unrestricted member participation?

These questions may seem to imply a sharp distinction between leadership and membership, or followership. This is not our intention. Actually there should be no differences in the way all members, including the nominal leader, if any, view the purposes and goals of group discussion. Observations of groups in action suggest that they are most effective when everyone undertakes such responsibilities as these:

1. Help to develop and maintain group values and standards.
2. Contribute to the maintenance of group cohesiveness and morale.
3. Participate in setting general and specific group goals.
4. Try to make the enterprise truly a group one by building a permissive atmosphere for free discussion.
5. Understand and try to accommodate the emotional needs and tensions of other members.
6. Direct motivational drives of members into channels that will be productive in accomplishing group goals.
7. Employ appropriate skills and techniques for effective, intelligent, and responsible communication within the group.
8. Take part in an evaluation of the group's progress toward its goals and the effectiveness of its behavior.

The alert reader will note that this list of every-member responsibilities is similar to those commonly assigned to nominal leaders. This similarity is intentional. It underscores the notion that what may be called the leadership function in a group should be shared.

The Leadership Function

Our preference for the term "leadership function" rather than "functions of leaders" derives from our conviction that it is more important that the tasks of leadership be performed in a group than it is to designate who should do them. It may well be that the group leader, chairman, or moderator, is normally assumed to be responsible for all necessary leadership tasks. But it is likely that the experience of group discussion will be more satisfying psychologically when the leader shares this responsibility with qualified members, or when they exercise initiative in undertaking these tasks themselves. Indeed, one of the obligations of leadership is undoubtedly to train and encourage members to assume as many of the necessary leadership functions as they can.

Many of those who write about group discussion find it convenient to divide the leadership function into two types of activity: (a) those tasks related to *group functioning*, i.e., building, strengthening, and maintaining the group process by channeling interpersonal behavior into productive activity, and (b) those pertaining to *problem-solving*, i.e., locating, defining, investigating, analyzing, and solving the problem. In sharing the leadership function through the performance of these tasks individual members are often said to be undertaking task-related roles. A typical list of these member roles begins with those related to group functioning:

1. *The morale builder* encourages individual contributions to the discussion, creates a receptive atmosphere for new facts and opinions, and commends those who deserve it.

2. *The conciliator* recognizes differences of opinion, tries to anticipate conflicts and relieve tensions by focusing attention on common goals and emphasizing cohesiveness.

3. *The compromiser* tries to reconcile conflicting views, even if it means modifying his own opinions, and seeks to evolve a consensus, or at least a harmonious middle ground.

4. *The expediter* tries to facilitate the discussion process, assisting members in clarifying and communicating their ideas, rephrasing, repeating when necessary, and otherwise improving the level of communication.

5. *The standard-setter* helps maintain a high level of group achievement in the quality of reasoning that leads to solving the group's problem.

6. *The process observer* usually does not take an active part in the discussion but attempts to view it objectively, so that he may both make useful suggestions to the leader and help members evaluate their own contributions.

The second category of member roles includes those related to problem-solving:

1. *The inquirer* is concerned with discovering, disclosing, and analyzing the raw materials of reasoning, facts, and opinions.

2. *The contributor* tries to provide the raw materials of reasoning by submitting factual information or considered opinions about facts.

3. *The elaborator* attempts to translate generalizations into concrete examples, define ambiguities, and project the probable effects of proposed solutions upon future group behavior.

4. *The reviewer* tries to clarify relations among ideas presented, trace conceptual patterns, and reorient the group position in terms of agreed-upon objectives.

5. *The evaluator* weighs the group's thinking in terms of its own standards, raising questions about the evidence and argument presented in the discussion, or about practical applications of proposed solutions.

6. *The energizer* keeps the discussion moving toward its goal by redirecting the attention and arousing the interests of members, and channeling their motivational drives.

7. *The group recorder* performs a secretarial function, summarizing the discussion, noting agreements and open questions, and reporting decisions.

Sometimes these leadership functions must be directed toward modifying the behavior of members whose only contributions to the group are negative and disruptive of the communication process. Among such members are *dominators,* who assert real or alleged authority, demand attention, and behave aggressively in other ways; *blockers,* often frustrated dominators, who stubbornly resist all group efforts when their own authority is challenged; *cynics* who, when they fail to block the group's will, rationalize by denigrating the group process; *security-seekers* whose emotional needs for sympathy or recognition are stronger than their identification with the group's goals; and *lobbyists* whose concern for items on their own private—and sometimes hidden—agendas blinds them to the group's needs.

There is no magic, of course, in the labels we have given to these roles in which members share the leadership function. A different set might be equally useful in identifying and evaluating different functional contributions in group discussions.

PSYCHOLOGICAL FORCES IN DISCUSSION GROUPS

We are now ready to sum up the applications of what we have said in this chapter. For convenience we shall do this in terms of a series of psychological forces that research has shown to be significant in face-to-face discussion situations. As before, we will cite representative studies to serve as a point of departure for those who wish to pursue this topic further.

Cohesiveness

Our earlier comments on the concept of the group should have at least implied the importance of cohesiveness in discussion groups. Cartwright and Zander (1953) have distinguished three meanings for this term: "(a) attraction to the group, including resistance to leaving it; (b) morale, or the level of motivation of the members to attack their tasks with zeal; and (c) coordination of the efforts of members." Representative studies by Festinger (1951), Fouriezos, *et al.* (1950), Stotland (1959), and Torrance (1957) lend support to this description of cohesiveness and underscore its significance. They indicate that unless members have a psychological sense of identification with each other and are motivated to work enthusiastically together on a common task, group structure tends to disintegrate, resistance to change increases, values come into conflict, and patterns of discussion break down.

The leadership of a group, of course, can be a vital element in creating and maintaining cohesiveness. In terms of the four functional psychological factors we discussed in the last chapter, the leader should be concerned with keeping the *attention* of the group focused upon its task; creating a common ground of *interest* among members; channeling the strongest *motivation* for each member into a desire to achieve the group's goals and support its values; and guiding the discussion so that *learning* will be reinforced.

Goals

While we have referred first to cohesiveness among the special forces operating in discussion groups, we could almost as logically have started with the establishment of group goals, so closely are they associated. In practice, the discovery of common individual goals (learning about a subject, solving a problem, and so on) may be what attracts people to each other and causes them to form a group. It may also happen that the achievement of a group goal eliminates the chief reason for cohesiveness, and the group will break up unless further common interests are developed. Gerard (1957), Harnack (1955), and Keltner (1947) have shown experimentally the importance to the individual's role in the group process of clarifying goals and also of recognizing obstacles in the way of them. It is an obvious function of leadership to aid in this process of goal identification and then to turn the motivational drives of members toward achieving the goals.

Interaction

This term covers a variety of factors affecting the communicative behavior of a group of individuals. Kimball Young (1958, pp. 225-242) regards communication structure, power relationships, interpersonal relations, and size of a group as the most important ones. Much of our previous discussion can conveniently be summarized under these headings.

In the last chapter we noted that the communication structure of any group involves a speaker and his message, and his listeners and their responses. In a discussion group it is better to think of the messages and responses of speakers-listeners, since members take these roles alternately. Thus it is important that every participant understand and apply what is known about the functional psychological factors of attention and perception, interest, motivation, and learning and remembering.

Training for discussion speakers-listeners should also include appropriate applications of these factors in performing the various member roles related to group functioning and problem-solving.

On a more sophisticated level of training for participation in group discussion the studies of discrete classifications of member contributions should be consulted. In an early investigation Simpson (1938) identified various types of member contributions and, with more refined techniques for observing and recording, Bales (1950) evolved a classification of twelve categories of messages in discussion. In highly condensed form these classes are: A. *Positive Reactions:* 1. shows solidarity, 2. shows tension release, 3. agrees; B. *Attempted Answers:* 4. gives suggestions, 5. gives opinion, 6. gives orientation; C. *Questions:* 7. asks for orientation, 8. asks for opinion, 9. asks for suggestion; D. *Negative Reactions:* 10. disagrees, 11. shows tension, 12. shows antagonism. The use of the Bales categories for quantifying contributions, and of special techniques such as those suggested by Brandenburg and Neal (1953) for judging their quality, provide the basis for much of the experimental research on discussion.

When discussion theorists speak of power relationships, they have in mind the various factors that appear to give special potency to the contributions of individual members. In many respects their observations parallel our treatment in the last chapter of impressiveness as a functional factor in learning and remembering. One series of studies reported by Lippitt, *et al.*, (1952) established a number of indexes for measuring attributed power (reported about an individual by other members) and manifest power (observations of influential behavior by an individual). Subsequent investigations have focused sharply on the nature and operation of such power-producing factors as status, prestige, reinforcement, and different styles of leadership. (Gerard, 1957; Oakes, *et al.*, 1960; Torrance, 1957; Utterback, 1958; Wischmeier, 1955.)

In discussing the concepts of the group and of group leadership we have identified many interpersonal relationships which are fundamental to healthy interaction. Psychologists have given perhaps more attention to the question of how group members react to each other as persons than to any other aspect of communicative behavior in discussion. In addition to pertinent studies already cited, we suggest the scope of this topic by noting research exploring various significant continua such as certainty-uncertainty, agreement-disagreement (Simpson, 1960), cooperation-competition (Smith, *et al.*, 1957), and like-dislike (Moreno and Jennings, 1938).

The variable of group size also affects interpersonal relations in discussion. In terms of the differential characteristics we considered earlier, it can be generalized that as the size of a discussion group increases, conformity tends to lessen and resistance to change to increase, more conflicting subgroups are likely to emerge, consensus is harder to achieve, and the opportunity for individual contribution is limited. It is also apparent that increased size requires more complex, and perhaps more directive, leadership functions, and this in turn may result in less member satisfaction with the group process and product. The maximum size for informal group discussions has long been regarded as fifteen to twenty persons, and for effective committee work Slater (1958) supports the conclusion of Bales (1954) that five is probably the optimum number, with a range from three to seven. The relative efficiency of these numbers may, of course, be affected by other factors, such as the nature of the problem being discussed, the amount of experience members have had in working with each other, and various kinds of outside pressures.

BEHAVIORAL RESULTS OF DISCUSSION

Many of the studies reported in this chapter have utilized special methods for measuring the impact of discussion upon individual behavior by modifying attitudes and beliefs. We have already called particular attention to the quantifying procedures of Bales. Bass, *et al.* (1957) refined objective methods for studying group behavior, and have applied them to a number of variables, including the effect of motivation upon consistency of performance (Bass, 1959). Glanzer and Glaser (1959) reported special techniques for studying group structure as well as behavior, and Roby (1957) evolved a model for measuring complex variables in discussion. Dickens (1955) proposed statistical procedures for quantifying "spread-of-participation," and Matthews and Bendig (1955) for establishing an "index of agreement" on discussion outcomes. These reports should be among those consulted by persons interested in methods for measuring behavior in discussion groups.

Throughout this chapter we have dealt with the most significant psychological variables in the group discussion situation, and in most instances the research studies cited have measured the impact of discussion on behavior in terms of attitudes, beliefs, and opinions. It is beyond the purpose of this book to summarize all of the studies on the behavioral results of discussion, but from those cited, and supporting ones not reported here, we submit these general conclusions:

1. In many investigations it has been found that even relatively short discussions may significantly change the attitudes of as many as forty per cent of the participants. It has also been demonstrated that discussion can significantly change the overt behavior patterns of group members. The changes in attitudes may be in various directions if the problem discussed has several alternative solutions.

2. It has been found that members of discussion groups who have arrived at a consensus are more likely to feel personal involvement in the problem and greater responsibility for the decision than are members of a co-acting audience.

3. While the contributions of various group members obviously vary in both quantity and quality, experimental programs do establish that individuals may be trained to greater effectiveness in general participation and in leadership functions.

4. Even without discussion, it has been found that on matters involving judgment the group average is superior to the majority of individual judgments, although there will naturally always be some individuals who are superior to the average. Group conclusions reached after discussion are superior to individual conclusions whenever these factors are important: a variety of points of view on a problem, a large number of suggestions for its solution, or a large number of effective criticisms of alternate solutions.

5. In various experiments where it is possible to determine "right" answers by other means, it has been demonstrated that those who reach such conclusions through discussion tend to hold them more tenaciously than do individuals who have "wrong" answers. Research has also shown that discussion groups are more likely to accept sound suggestions than to reject them; more likely to reject bad ones than to accept them.

6. None of the available evidence suggests that the discussion method is a panacea. Discussion groups are made up of individuals who—even when in a permissive atmosphere and encouraged to proceed logically, efficiently, and responsibly—are still subject to limitations in attention and perception, fluctuations in interest, conflicts among motivational drives, and variations in the capacity for learning and remembering.

REFERENCES

Auer, J. J. Recent literature in discussion. *Quart. J. Spch*, 1953, 39, 95-98.

Bales, R. F. *Interaction process analysis.* Reading, Mass.: Addison-Wesley, 1950.

Bales, R. F. In conference. *Harvard Bus. Rev.*, 1954, 32, 44-50.

Barnlund, D. C. Consistency of emergent leadership in groups with changing tasks and members. *Spch Monogr.*, 1962, 29, 45-52.

Bass, B. M., Gaier, E. L., Farese, F. J., & Flint, A. W. An objective method for studying behavior in groups. *Psychol. Rep.*, 1957, 3, 265-280.

Bass, B. M. Effects of motivation on consistency of performance in groups. *Educ. psychol. Measmt*, 1959, 19, 247-252.

Beer, M., Buckhout, R., Horowitz, M. W., & Levy, S. Some perceived properties of the difference between leaders and non-leaders. *J. Psychol.*, 1959, 47, 49-56.

Brandenburg, E., & Neal, P. A. Graphic techniques for evaluating discussion and conference procedures. *Quart. J. Spch,* 1953, 39, 201-208.

Browne, C. G., & Cohn, T. S. (Eds.) *The study of leadership.* Danville, Ill.: Interstate Printers and Publishers, 1958.

Cartwright, D., & Zander, A. (Eds.) *Group dynamics: research and theory.* New York: Harper & Row, 1953. Pp. 73-85.

Cleary, J. W. A bibliography of rhetoric and public address. Annually in *Spch Monogr.,* 1957 ff., 25 ff.

Cooley, C. H. *Social organization.* New York: Scribner's, 1909.

Dickens, M. A statistical formula to quantify the "spread-of-participation" in group discussion. *Spch Monogr.,* 1955, 22, 28-30.

Festinger, L. Architecture and group membership. *J. soc. Issues,* 1951, 7, 152-163.

Fouriezos, N. T., Hutt, M. L., & Guetzkow, H. Measurement of self-oriented needs in discussion groups. *J. abnorm. soc. Psychol.,* 1950, 45, 682-690.

Gerard, H. B. Some effects of status, role clarity, and group goal clarity upon the individual's relations to group processes. *J. Pers.,* 1957, 25, 475-488.

Glanzer, M., & Glaser, R. Techniques for the study of group structure and behavior. *Psychol. Bull.,* 1959, 56, 317-332.

Haberman, F. W. A bibliography of rhetoric and public address. Annually, 1948-1956, in *Quart. J. Spch,* 34-36; in *Spch Monogr.,* 18-24.

Haiman, F. S. Materials in group dynamics. *Quart. J. Spch,* 1954, 40, 201-206.

Harnack, R. V. An experimental study of the effects of training in the recognition and formulation of goals upon intra-group cooperation. *Spch Monogr.,* 1955, 22, 31-38.

Homan, G. C. *The human group.* New York: Harcourt, Brace & World, 1950.

Keltner, J. W. Goals, obstacles, and problem formulation in group discussion. *Quart. J. Spch,* 1947, 33, 468-473.

Lippitt, R., Polansky, N., Redl, F., & Rosen, S. The dynamics of power. *Human Relat.,* 1952, 5, 37-64.

Matthews, J., & Bendig, A. W. The index of agreement: a possible criterion for measuring the outcome of group discussion. *Spch Monogr.,* 1955, 22, 39-42.

Moreno, J. L., & Jennings, H. H. Statistics of social configurations. *Sociometry,* 1934, 1, 342-374.

Oakes, W. F., Droge, A. E., & August, B. Reinforcement effects on participation in group discussion. *Psychol. Rep.,* 1960, 7, 503-514.

Roby, T. B. On the measurement and description of groups. *Behav. sci.,* 1957, 2, 119-127.

Simpson, R. H. *A study of those who influence and of those who are influenced in discussion.* New York: Teachers College, Columbia University, 1938.

Simpson, R. H. Attitudinal effects of small group discussions: shifts on certainty-uncertainty and agreement-disagreement continua. *Quart. J. Spch,* 1960, 46, 415-418.

Slater, P. E. Contrasting correlates of group size. *Sociometry,* 1958, 21, 129-139.

Smith, A. J., Madde, H. E., & Sobol, R. Productivity and recall in cooperative and competitive discussion groups. *J. Psychol.*, 1957, 43, 193-204.

Stodgill, R. M. Personal factors associated with leadership: a survey of the literature. *J. Psychol.*, 1948, 25, 35-71

Stotland, E. Determinants of attraction to groups. *J. soc. Psychol.*, 1959, 49, 71-80.

Strodtbeck, F. L., & Hare, A. P. Bibliography of small group research. *Sociometry*, 1954, 17, 107-178.

Torrance, E. P. Group decision-making and disagreement. *Social Forces*, 1957, 35, 314-318.

Utterback, W. E. The influence of style of moderation on the outcomes of discussion. *Quart. J. Spch*, 1958, 44, 149-152.

Wischmeier, R. R. Group-centered and leader-centered leadership: an experimental study. *Spch Monogr.*, 1955, 22, 43-48.

Young, K. *Social psychology.* (3rd ed.) New York: Appleton-Century-Crofts, 1958.

16

Psychology of
Public Address

In this chapter we will explore the special aspects of communication in the public address situation and suggest the applications to it of the basic psychological factors discussed in Chapter 14.

PRELIMINARY DEFINITIONS

In contrast to the face-to-face group discussion where participants play alternating roles as speakers-listeners, the public address situation is essentially one in which a single individual speaks directly to a number of auditors who maintain a relatively fixed focus of attention upon him. These listeners form a co-acting group, responding primarily to a common stimulus, rather than to each other. Typically this solo communicative performance is by a lecturer whose aim is to inform his hearers, or a public speaker whose purpose is to persuade them. Political campaign orators, ministers in their pulpits, lawyers before juries, or citizens in town meetings and voluntary associations may, of course, also inform their hearers by presenting new facts and opinions, but these are usually intended as bases for modifying attitudes and beliefs in some fashion and thus influencing the behavior of the hearers.

We also include under the heading of public address a number of special forms of speechmaking: the *symposium*, where three to five persons with special knowledge about a topic make speeches presenting different types of information or varying points of view; the *public hearing*, a meeting called by a committee or other formal agency in order to investigate problems or carry out governmental policy by giving representatives of various groups an opportunity to present their views on pending legislation; the *debate,* consisting of a series of speeches of equal length by relatively matched contestants, supporting and opposing a specific proposition; and the *legislative session,* providing for speeches for and against pending resolutions, and conducted under the rules of parliamentary procedure. In this chapter we will apply the term "public address" or "public speaking" to the communicative act in all of these special multiple-speaker situations, as well as to those where a single person addresses an audience.

Common to all public address communication is the use of two basic codes, audible and visible, or organized sound and light waves deliberately projected by the speaker. The bulk of this book has been concerned with audible or external verbal behavior. It is important to recognize, however, that "visible speech behavior" (the gesture, facial expression, or pantomime that accompanies spoken words) is also a significant element of communication. Indeed, the so-called "gesture theory" explanation of how man developed vocal speech (see pp. 14-18) assumes that visible gestures preceded audible words. And Skinner (1957, pp. 14, 465-466) regards gestures as verbal, though non-vocal, behavior. In recent years Birdwhistell (1952) and other linguists have made a study of kinesics, or meaningful bodily movements, and attempted to classify in terms of standardized symbols a variety of visible behaviors that convey specific meanings, such as pointing, headshaking, laughing, sneering, and eyebrow raising. Whether we label this behavior as kinesics or simply as bodily action, it must be identified as a form of communication, usually reinforcing spoken language, but sometimes substituting for it. We shall have more to say about the use of the audible and visible codes when we consider the specific tasks of the speaker as he faces an audience.

As with all other forms of communication, the speaker in the public address situation is concerned with response, the tangible evidence of his influence upon the behavior of his hearers. Some of this response may be visible, *immediate and overt:* listeners often applaud by clapping their hands, stamping their feet, or giving a rising ovation. Other immediate responses may be audible: shouts of "hear, hear!" or "amen!" are institutionalized forms of verbal applause. Some other verbal responses may also be regularized or even pre-arranged. Testimonials in religious meetings are often of this type. Most verbal responses, however, are *delayed and covert.* Only occasionally do speakers ask for immediate reactions that are initiated by sub-vocal but verbal responses, such as signing a petition or putting money into a collection plate. More commonly the speaker aims at the modification of attitudes and beliefs that will lead the listener, when the moment for action arrives, to respond as the speaker wants him to. In a political campaign speech, for example, the speaker's aim is to persuade the listeners to vote in a particular way when the time for voting arrives some weeks or even months later.

THE AUDIENCE

The psychological genesis of an audience is best understood if we think first of an unorganized group made up of individuals lacking any over-all orientation and having no common focus of attention. Unless some guiding pattern of orientation develops, these individuals will probably drift away from the group and it will cease to exist. If, on the other hand, the individuals do center their attention upon a common stimulus, even momentarily, what was a heterogeneous and unorganized group becomes homogeneous and organized, at least in terms of its response to that stimulus. The group becomes a collectivity, though a relatively unstable one, impermanent and with an anonymous membership. To such a group the social psychologist affixes the label of crowd. This general term he refines by classifying crowds as either mobs or audiences. Although there is still validity in certain elements of classic treatments of crowds by LeBon (1903), Martin (1920), McDougall (1920), and Freud (1922), our own concepts follow more closely the analyses of Roger W. Brown (1954) and Kimball Young (1958).

A mob, or action crowd, says Brown (1954, pp. 840-842) invariably has properties of mental homogeneity, emotionality, and irrationality, and can be classified as aggressive, escape, acquisitive, or expressive.

Of more concern to us, among the mass phenomena, is the audience. An audience may be (a) casual and informal, such as a group of "sidewalk superintendents" or a collection of persons whose attention is attracted by a sideshow barker; or (b) intentional and formal, such as the group that gathers for a Sunday morning sermon, an afternoon lecture, or an evening political rally. The formal audience, which is our subject here, Young (1958, p. 302) characterizes according to general purpose as: *information-seeking*, such as a classroom or popular lecture audience; *conversional*, such as a religious revival or political campaign audience; *recreational*, such as a movie or sports event audience.

As we have already at least implied, the formal or intentional audience is a form of "institutionalized crowd." It assembles with a definite purpose and is prepared to be affected and directed; it gathers at a predetermined time and place; and it displays fairly standard patterns of interaction. We will next consider these interaction phenomena, and then identify certain variants in audience structure and composition.

Interaction in the Audience Situation

Social psychologists have extracted three significant concepts from their observations of the behavior of audiences: polarization, social facilitation, and circular response.

Polarization is what makes a group of persons into an audience; it introduces structure into an unorganized group. Woolbert (1916) apparently first used the term to denote an "all-to-one" relation, expressed as a situation where a speaker occupies the audience's focus of attention. Young (1958, p. 303) describes polarization as a "shoulder-to-shoulder configuration" of a group, facilitating a single channel of communication in contrast to the face-to-face discussion group where many and varied channels are opened. When an audience is polarized it is established as one entity, separate from the entity of the speaker, but attending to him, and linked with him by communication in such a way that interaction is possible.

Many elements in the typical public address situation contribute to the polarization of the audience: the auditorium in which the audience gathers creates not only a physical closeness but also suggests a social and purposeful unity; the seating arrangement compels the audience to face the platform and the speaker as a unified group; the lighting may be arranged to attract attention to the platform or the speaker's lectern; and the platform itself, usually elevated above the level of the audience, provides a position of social command for the speaker. As we shall note later, certain elements of ritual, and the speech itself, may intensify audience polarization.

Social facilitation is a term frequently used to describe the reinforcement effect of the responses of one individual upon the behavior of others in the same audience. Allport (1924, pp. 261-262, 292) was perhaps the first to use the term to describe the interplay between members of an audience, tending to canalize and intensify their aims, feelings, and responses. The observable effect is "an increase in response merely from the sight or sound of others making the same movements [responses]." The phenomenon of social facilitation serves to release reactions for which the individual is in readiness, and to increase their quantity and intensity when once initiated. Imitation is one of the factors promoting social facilitation: exposure to similar stimuli tends to result in similar motor responses. If those around us are attending, we are likely to do the same. And even if we don't get the point of a joke, we are likely to laugh when those around us do. Another significant factor promoting social facilitation is suggestion. It will be recalled from our earlier discussion in Chapter 14 that suggestion's effectiveness is increased in group situations; the public speaker who employs it, especially with polarized and homogeneous audiences, encourages similar and intensified responses.

Parenthetically it might be noted that an ancient theatre and opera custom was to hire a claque, a group of paid applauders, to sit in strategic locations throughout an audience and stimulate general applause by their own simulated enthusiasm. A similar practice is not unknown in contemporary revival meetings and political rallies, where those already converted (or perhaps rewarded) facilitate the social responses of others by their own hearty cries of "Amen!" or "Give 'em hell, Harry!"

Circular response is a third phenomenon of interaction among audience members. In its operation on speaker-audience relationships it is analogous to social facilitation within the audience. It is a term used to describe the effect on the speaker of the responses of his hearers, the consequent reinforcement or modification of his own communicative behavior, and its subsequent effect upon the hearers. Sometimes this response by his hearers is called "feedback," to symbolize the flow of communication by overt physical response back to the speaker. Like the household thermostat, it is presumed that the speaker is self-regulating and will adapt to the implications of the feedback. As the listeners respond to a speaker they may frown their disapproval, smile or nod their moderate approval, or vigorously applaud or shout their enthusiastic approval. Miller (1951, p. 252) describes as "primary information" the original message that is being communicated, and as "secondary information" that "given to the talker by the recipients' responses." This information is reinforcement for the speaker's behavior: "the talker is rewarded by learning that he has communicated successfully." When the audience reinforces the speaker with visible or audible responses, he is stimulated to release new energy, and this in turn elicits new responses from the audience. As speaker and audience continue to play upon each other, all responses tend to be heightened.

The interactional mechanisms of identification and projection may also contribute to strengthening circular response. Young (1958, p. 282, 300) suggests that "the leader [speaker] is the symbolic projection of an ideal," and that "members of the crowd identify themselves with the leader's assumption of knowledge and power. In turn, he projects on them his own values and views which they quickly accept as their own."

In summary, we note that the three basic interaction phenomena that we have described strongly influence audience behavior by formalizing or institutionalizing certain relationships. Polarization crystallizes the relationships of a group to itself as an audience; social facilitation strengthens the relationships of audience members with each other; and circular response increases the relationships of audience members with the speaker. Through each of these relationships the social unity of the audience is intensified—it tends to become a "psychological crowd" and to manifest intense and predominantly affective behavior.

Some Variants in Audience Structure

Audiences, like individuals, are often unlike. There are at least three significant variations in the structure of audiences: physical setting, audience geography, and institutional ritual.

The *physical setting* for public address can have a significant effect upon audience behavior. As we have already noted, the typical elevated platform provides the speaker with a position of social command, at least figuratively. A semicircular arrangement of seats on a floor sloping toward the speaker's "well," on the other hand, may appear to place the audience in a superior position. In the manipulation of lighting and ventilation, or the display of symbolic banners, pictures, or slogans, the physical setting may be conducive to early and strong polarization. An interesting example of an effort to enhance the feeling of commonality in an audience occurred in England during the reconstruction of the House of Commons after it had been partially destroyed by bombs during the war. The architects felt that it would be sensible to take advantage of the occasion to expand the size of the house and provide enough seats for all 625 members. Winston Churchill, however, ruled that the building should be restored as it was, though it could accommodate only slightly more than two-thirds of the members. Psychologically, he argued, it was better to crowd in more than the chamber could comfortably hold than to run the occasional risk of some empty benches.

Audience geography refers to density, proximity, and distribution of listeners in the meeting place. An early modern comment on this topic was by Scott (1906, pp. 180-181) who submitted that in creating a psychological crowd "one of the most helpful methods is to get the audience to sit close together," that it is better to have a surplus of audience members than a surplus of seats, that if some seats must remain empty they should not be the ones immediately in front of the speaker, and that "touching elbows" help to propagate psychological unity. Indeed, Scott notes with apparent approval the whimsical argument that "it would be impossible to have a crowd of angels because they could not feel the bodily presence of others." Social psychologists, including Allport, Brown, and Young, perpetuate these notions and they are echoed in public speaking textbooks. As with many other axiomatic matters in rhetorical theory, the propositions about audience geography need extensive experimental study. We summarize here three relevant investigations.

Griffith (1921) analyzed more than 20,000 grades earned by university students and discovered that although alphabetical seating was a standard practice, there was an apparent relationship between grades earned and classroom seat locations: (a) seats in the middle of the room appeared to be worth 3-8 per cent higher grades than those in the front row or two; (b) seats in the middle of the room appeared to be worth 10 per cent higher grades than those in the last row or two; (c) seats anywhere in the main section of the room—when it was divided by aisles running in either direction—appeared to be worth 5-10 per cent higher grades than those in the peripheral sections. To our knowledge the literature contains no supporting studies. Without questioning the validity of these conclusions, however, two comments about them are appropriate. First, the findings relate only to the acquisition of information (some of which presumably came from sources other than the classroom lectures) and not to the modification of attitudes. Second, members of classroom audiences have an unusually strong predisposing set to attend to the speaker-stimulus and to accept his statements without question, in contrast to the audience in the persuasive speech situation where motivation to accept or reject statements is a major variable factor.

Thomas and Ralph (1959) conducted an experiment designed to test the effect upon listener attitudes of six variations of density, proximity, and distribution factors in audiences exposed to persuasive speaking. They concluded that although the speech did significantly change attitudes toward the communicator's message, there was no statistically significant effect of variation in the size of the audience or of the degree of proximity of audience members to each other or to the speaker. The findings about attitude shifts tended, however, to support Griffith's conclusions that less information is gained by those seated in the front and the back of the room than by those in the middle. In sum, this study did not confirm earlier judgments about the significance of audience geography. As Thomas and Ralph note, however, a different result might be obtained in a "crowd" situation where audience members are standing and in close bodily contact, rather than seated in formal rows of fixed chairs. And, we might add, different results might also be found if similar experiments were conducted in an atmosphere other than that of a university classroom. In a classroom the students' usual predisposing set may create a halo effect for any speaker, even if he is another student.

Furbay (1960) reported a descriptive study of listener responses to recorded speeches in both scattered and compact seating arrangements. He found that compactness of seating did not significantly affect listener liking for the speech, awareness of how other listeners were responding, judgment about the effectiveness of the speech, or the amount of recalled information. There was a significant difference of opinion change toward the propositions of the speeches: the compact audiences showed a lower ratio of change. Furbay speculated that if opinion shifts result from intellectual responses to factual information, then audience compactness may heighten crowd behavior, inhibit rational responses, and develop a "homogeneity of inaction." Our own speculation is that crowd behavior is not a form of inaction, though it may be conforming action, and that it cannot be assumed that opinion shifts result only or even primarily from intellectual responses. Beyond this, it would seem that using recorded rather than live speakers lessened the significance of the findings for application to co-acting audience behavior in typical public address situations.

Institutional rituals contribute to the atmosphere in which public address takes place, and it is recognized that manipulation of various atmosphere-creating factors may alter significantly the nature and degree of an audience's expectations and anticipatory responses. Young (1958, pp. 304-305) aptly refers to these as part of the "preliminary tuning" of an audience. This tuning may include appeals made in advance (promotional devices ranging from "word of mouth" advertising to formal newspaper, handbill, or broadcast announcements) and appeals introduced at the meeting place (such as flags, pictures, posters, symbolic figures and other decorational devices, musical fanfares and dimming of house lights, group singing, reciting of pledges or creeds, and other unifying behaviors).

To illustrate these institutional—and institutionalizing—rituals, contrast the typical religious service with the political rally. Advance announcements for the church gathering are formal and dignified; those for the rally are blatant and extravagant. The church itself, outside and in, creates a quiet, reverential setting, with stained glass windows, organ music, soft lights, and worship symbols; the political hall is designed and decorated to create excitement, with bright lights, blaring bands, gaudy posters, and party symbols. The minister speaks from his traditional pulpit, unheralded; the campaign orator talks from a colorful platform, enthusiastically introduced and clamorously received. From the emotional attitudes created by the ritualistic devices and behaviors there is created for each speaker an audience mood appropriate to his manner and message. The effect of this "transfer device," as propaganda analysts call it, is to predispose the listeners to respond to the speaker in the same way that they respond to the atmosphere created by the rituals.

Young (1958, p. 305) notes that these institutional rituals "may be more effective with younger, less intelligent, and more emotional audiences," but we would note that the use of the rituals also tends to lessen intellectual responses and to increase emotional ones in any audience. Nor do we think it completely appropriate to suggest that the utility of these rituals is largely limited to audiences to be persuaded rather than to those to be informed. "Preliminary tuning" may be at a minimum in the latter situation, but even a college classroom audience has a certain predisposing set of expectations and is subjected to certain ritualistic devices such as assigned seating, opening roll calls, and an occasional "grand entrance" by the lecturer.

Some Variants in Audience Composition

The reason that audiences are not all alike, even though they may have some similarities, is that the individuals composing them are not alike. Thus a discussion of variants in audience composition must identify those differentiating characteristics of individuals which are significant for the public speaker as he selects the substance, plans the structure, and determines the style of his communication. Essentially this is a task of audience analysis. We outline it here in a series of questions. Not all of these questions will be of equal importance in every speaking situation, and it will not always be possible to answer them all.

The first series of audience analysis questions relates to *the audience and the subject:*

1. *What is the significance of the subject for the audience?* Is its interest in the subject only casual, or is it motivated by real needs and wants? How far has its thinking about the problem progressed?

2. *What does the audience know about the subject?* Does it have essential factual information, or only opinions and sentiments? Are its sources of information sound ones, unbiased and complete?

3. *What beliefs or prejudices does the audience have about the subject?* In either case, what are the probable sources or influences in the formation of these existing notions?

4. *What is the attitude of the audience toward the subject?* Is it possible to estimate the percentage who are favorable, neutral, or unfavorable toward the problem or the speaker's proposition?

5. *What is the speaker's specific purpose in discussing the subject?* Can his general purpose be refined in terms of his audience analysis? Does the audience in any way affect his choice of purpose?

6. *What time is available for discussing the subject?* Is there enough for a complete treatment? If not, what meaningful aspect of the subject can be selected for adequate treatment?

A second series of questions useful in audience analysis relates to *the audience and the speaker:*

1. *What general social group does the audience represent?* Can it be generalized that it is drawn largely from housewives, small businessmen, skilled laborers, college students, and so on?

2. *What specific group or organization does the audience represent?* A service club, church group, labor organization, and so on? And what status does the group have in the community?

3. *What are the general characteristics of the audience?* Homogeneous or heterogeneous in terms of cultural and environmental backgrounds? General educational level? Common interests?

4. *What are the specific characteristics of the audience?* How is the audience distributed—when any of these are important—by sex, age, religion, political affiliation, and so on?

5. *What are the probable potent motivations of the audience?* Does it represent the satisfied or the dissident element of the community? Can its probable aspirations, expectations, and goals be identified?

6. *What is the attitude of the audience toward the speaker?* Does he have strong ethical appeal, a reputation for knowledge, character, sincerity? Have there been previous contacts with him?

Understanding the significance of questions such as these is comparatively easy; obtaining adequate answers is more difficult; and applying the information in preparing a speech is a real challenge. Most speakers will find it helpful, after analyzing an audience as thoroughly as possible, to relate what they have discovered to the basic functional factors in the psychology of communication, discussed in Chapter 14. What does the information gathered about the audience suggest concerning effective methods of getting and holding its *attention?* How can its known *interests* be capitalized upon? How can the substance and structure of the speech be connected with the audience's basic *motivations?* In what ways can the style and delivery of the speech make its substance *impressive?*

Audience analyses are often most helpful in determining style—the choice of appropriate language for the speaker's message. Ideal communication would require that a speaker's words have the same meanings for his listeners as they do for him. Since this ideal situation is rare, necessary adaptations of language usage must be made by the communicator; his hearers may have neither the ability nor the interest essential to translate his words into their idiom. Not only do persons of different cultural and educational backgrounds have different sized vocabularies, but persons of different regions, communities, trades, or professions have specialized vocabularies. Riesman (1960) has written a provocative and pertinent essay on this linguistic aspect of communication in the modern world, raising these questions: "(1) what are the differences between cultures that depend entirely upon the spoken word and those that depend on print? (2) what will be the significance of the written word now that newer mass media have developed? (3) what is likely to happen in those countries where the tradition of books is not fully established and where newer media are already having a decisive impact?" The significance of these queries for the linguistic choices of a public speaker, and their relevance to this discussion, are made clear when one tries to visualize the problems of a well educated and sophisticated diplomat in addressing audiences of Laotians, Pakistani—or even some Americans—who cannot read or write and whose culture is entirely dependent upon oral tradition.

In addition to ascertaining information about a specific audience, a speaker can generalize from available research about the significance of certain characteristics in the composition of all audiences. Consider the factor of age, for example. In Chapter 14 we cited the Marple (1933) study of suggestibility in different age groups; it indicates that an audience of older persons will be less suggestible, and hold its beliefs more tenaciously, than one composed of younger persons. In other studies (Brembeck, 1949; Howell, 1943) it appears that age is not a factor significantly correlated with critical thinking, as measured by the Watson-Glaser battery of tests designed to measure sound reasoning abilities.

On the factor of educational background (and using the level of terminal education as an index of general intelligence), a series of studies by Hovland, et al. (1949, pp. 147-175) suggests that persons of higher intelligence (graduation from high school) will tend to be more influenced than those with low intellectual ability by communications relying primarily upon logical arguments, and less influenced by communications relying primarily upon unsupported generalities or false, illogical, or irrelevant arguments.

As a final example of generalizing about the influence of a specific factor in audience composition, let us consider sex distribution. While there have been no experimental studies specifically concerned with the relative persuadability of the two sexes, a large body of studies of other variables (a sample of which we cite) has provided incidental conclusions about differential behavior of men and women in an audience. The evidence appears to indicate that women in a public address audience are more persuadable than men, as measured by shifts of opinion after hearing a speech. (Cherrington and Miller, 1933; Gilkinson, Paulson, and Sikkink, 1954; Knower, 1935; Paulson, 1954; Scheidel, 1959.) The evidence is not decisive on the comparative ability of men and women to retain what they have heard, as measured by information tests. In several experiments (Brandon, 1956; Mullin, 1957) women scored significantly higher on retention, but in each case the information was presented by television. In studies involving live speakers (Paulson, 1954; Sikkink, 1956) men made higher retention scores. There is also some evidence to show that women are slightly superior in identifying the logical or analytical arguments they hear (Brown, 1950), but that men score consistently higher on the Watson-Glaser tests of applied critical thinking ability (Brembeck, 1949; Howell, 1943). To date, the experimental evidence does not justify more categorical conclusions than these about the effect of sex differences on responses to persuasive public address.

LISTENERS IN AUDIENCES

From our consideration of audiences as collectivities we now turn to those who compose them and generalize about the behavior of individuals as listeners. Some of what we will say restates earlier comments for our present purpose; other observations are drawn from representative psychological literature.

1. *Listeners tend to believe what they want to believe.* Plato felt that men should always see things as they are, but the modern psychologist knows that "we see things not as they are but as we are." The thesis of our discussion in Chapter 5 of affective behavior and motivation was that man is driven by his wants, interests, and purposes. These drives shape his desires, and "desirability," in its turn, is the most significant force in determining his beliefs (Lund, 1925). Even in the face of contradictory evidence, observes Albig (1956, p. 87), "human reason and logical thinking are constantly diverted into nonlogical mental processes" and much so-called reasoning is actually rationalization, or the construction of "socially acceptable rather than real reasons for behavior."

2. *Listeners tend to believe and to do as they are told.* People are quite undiscriminating about what they can learn to believe, we said in Chapter 14, *if* the force of positive suggestion is strong enough. Modern advertising, in print and on the air, is an eloquent and expensive display of confidence in that proposition. Like the advertiser, the propagandist manipulates suggestion in ways that cause his hearers to relax their critical habits, and thus more readily believe or do whatever he proposes. As Young (1958, p. 461) says, "suggestion is the key to the operation of propaganda," and we add that the key to propaganda analysis is the study of the operation of suggestion.

3. *Listeners tend to act in accordance with their dominant attitudes.* Native desires and acquired beliefs create predispositions to behave in certain ways. When the resulting dominant attitudes are touched off by the persuader, and especially when he connects them through suggestion to basic motivational drives, the listener tends to respond favorably to the communicator's propositions. Thus it is that much of the research of advertisers and other propagandists is aimed at discovering what the consumer's dominant attitudes are (Packard, 1957); developing logical and emotional appeals directly keyed to these attitudes can then be done with economy.

4. *Listeners tend to make stereotyped responses to stereotyped stimuli.* Walter Lippmann (1922) introduced the term stereotype—to designate "the pictures in our heads"—into American psychological literature: "For the most part we do not first see, and then define, we define first and then see. . . . We imagine most things before we experience them. And these preconceptions, unless education has made us acutely aware, govern deeply the whole process of perception." Like many social psychologists, Albig (1956, pp. 80-86) has found the concept of stereotypes useful in explaining the mechanism of individual indulgence in "reification" (providing concrete illustrations of abstractions and conferring greater reality than is warranted by conceptions and perceptions), and in "simplification" (distorting reality by simple definitions, summarized conceptions, personified conceptions, and so on). Skillful persuaders realize that stereotyped responses are more likely to be uniform than accurate, and provide stimuli that will elicit them: the listener tends to laugh at the right times, applaud when it is expected of him, and make other standardized responses to appropriate audible and visible cues.

5. *Listeners tend to respond to the emotional connotations of words.* As we know, our experiences are accompanied by feelings of varying degrees of pleasantness and unpleasantness. We also know that by a process of conditioning, words and other symbols may acquire the power of arousing the same feelings that accompanied the original experiences. These words, carrying emotional connotations as well as logical denotations, belong to what De Quincey called the "literature of power" rather than the "literature of knowledge." In attempting to stir up appropriate emotional associations, therefore, speakers make generous use of connotative or "loaded" language. Although evidence about the effect of emotive language upon audience comprehension and recall is not conclusive (Matthews, 1947; Pence, 1954), Skinner (1957, pp. 154-159) emphasizes the effectiveness of connotative verbal stimuli in eliciting responses which can be reinforced by the listener's emotional behavior.

6. *Listeners tend to yield to the repetition of stimuli.* Although we have said that listeners tend to believe and to do as they are told, telling them only once may not be enough. Inattentiveness may mean that the listener fails to hear the stimulus words; simple inertia may keep him from taking them seriously; or he may receive them with skepticism or even hostility if they conflict with more potent habits of behavior, dominant attitudes, or strong beliefs. By employing the principle of summation of stimuli, however, succeeding repetitions of an idea normally encounter less resistance. We have previously noted that there appears to be a point of diminishing returns in repetition; there is also evidence that intermittent rather than continuous repetition is most effective. Our point about repetition would seem to need no repetition: as Albig (1956,

p. 334) reminds us, "recognition of the force of repetition existed among political leaders, tacticians, and philosophers long before the advertiser, under the tutelage of the psychologist, made himself almost insufferable to the sensitive."

7. *Listeners tend to accept ideas from those who have prestige.* Like many principles of behavior, this one cuts both ways: listeners also tend to reject equally good ideas from those who lack prestige. In its simplest sense, prestige is the attitude one person has toward another. Zander and Cohen (1955) illustrated one form of prestige by introducing two strangers to a classroom group, identifying one as a dean, the other as a freshman. What gained more attention and appreciation for the alleged dean was the prestige attached to his *ascribed status.* Henrikson (1940), in a similar setting, demonstrated that "likeability," or *earned status,* also brought prestige. In either case, speakers have prestige when listeners like them, accept them as authorities, defer to their judgment, or attach importance to what they say. And speakers having prestige significantly influence listeners more than those who do not (Gilkinson, *et al.,* 1954; Haiman, 1949; Paulson, 1954). In addition to reputation and character, Henrikson (1940) and Haiman (1949) also identified general speech competence as a significant factor in earning prestige. One curious aspect of prestige, as testimonial advertisements constantly remind us, is that a person who has gained it in one field of accomplishment (such as playing baseball) can apparently transfer it to another (such as judging breakfast foods).

8. *Listeners tend to conform to the beliefs and actions of fellow-listeners.* In Chapter 15 we reported the tendency to conform in their behavior as one of the characteristics of face-to-face groups, and in this chapter we have noted that the phenomenon of social facilitation operates to induce conformity of behavior in co-acting groups. Two additional observations are appropriate here. First, listeners in audiences generally prefer to avoid extreme behavior that will set them off from their fellows, though they might behave differently when alone. In this they are essentially conservative, Asch (1951) reported, even to the point of expressing judgments they know to be contrary to fact but conforming to apparent majority sentiments. They are fulfilling what psychologists call role expectations, behaving as they think other persons expect them to. Our second observation is that in most groups there are some few individuals who refuse to conform; Asch concludes that this independence may stem from confidence in their own perception and experience, "the necessity of being an individual" as a matter of principle, or simple dedication to making what they feel is a right decision. We would add that some persons are "negatively suggestible" out of sheer perversity, and others fail to conform only because they do not understand the role

behavior that is expected of them. An additional factor bearing upon the tendency to conform is the ability of an individual to estimate the majority attitude of his fellow-listeners. In a study by Sawyer (1955) a significant correlation was found between the extent to which the individual was influenced by a speech and his estimate of how other listeners were influenced.

9. *Listeners tend to respond in terms of overt action.* Anyone who has attended an exciting sports event or watched a suspenseful drama has undoubtedly responded overtly in that recreational audience situation. Our experiences in classroom or public lecture audiences, however, seldom include immediate overt responses, although we may acquire in such situations new ideas or attitudes that will influence later conduct. It is also true that responses in many conversional audience situations are limited to polarization and formalized overt action (such as appropriate laughter or polite applause). A speaker with especially vivid imagery, or unusually vigorous delivery, may also encourage overt empathic responses, though these usually take place below the level of the listener's consciousness. There are other occasions, however, when the limitations of conventionalized overt behavior are broken, notes Young (1958, p. 303), and "laughter, tears, applause, shouts of approval, and boos of disapproval are ideomotor evidences of the more active participation of the audience." Sometimes such behavior is accidental; the speaker may cause it by an egregious error in content or delivery, based upon faulty audience analysis. At other times a speaker may openly bid for overt responses by touching off elemental drives through appeals to prejudice, repetitions of provocative slogans, or signals to a hidden claque. Such extreme measures, tending to transform an audience into an action crowd or mob, are of course ethically unjustifiable. Ethical speakers should recognize, however, that it is normal for all listeners, when they are persuaded, to want to act overtly, and experienced persuaders provide something definite for their hearers to do. Signing petitions, making contributions, volunteering services, or even sustaining applause are overt actions that will reinforce the listener's acceptance of the speaker's propositions.

10. *Listeners tend to want to be rational.* "The masses have more in common at an emotional and primary-drive level than they do at an intellectual level," concludes Young (1958, p. 307), and audiences are often persuaded by "an apparently logical but basically emotional argument. This method meets our cultural expectation of logical reasons for our acts, an expectation to which we are conditioned in the home, in the school, and in other groups where we get our basic training." Nevertheless, the average listener *wants* to regard his responses as logical, and usually does. He is not flattered if told that his behavior is based upon

fear, self-interest, or a desire for status. Skillful persuaders recognize this desire for rationality in listener behavior and do what they can to encourage it. They structure their speeches for psychological effectiveness, but they also place their emphasis upon making the listener *want* to do what the evidence indicates he *ought* to do.

We conclude this discussion of behavioral tendencies of listeners in audience situations with a reminder that we have described tendencies, not absolutes. We are satisfied that substantial research in the psychology of speech supports each generalization. But we also know that any psychological proposition must allow for individual exceptions.

Since all of the tendencies we have described relate to the persuasibility of listeners, this is the place to say that no complete and satisfactory hypothesis about what makes a person susceptible to persuasion has yet been established. Who is influenced, how, under what circumstances, and with what effect, is an exceedingly complex question. Hovland and Janis (1959, p. 243), the editors of one extensive collection of studies on possible personality components of persuasibility, admit that their work is no exception to the rule that "research on a new set of problems typically generates more questions than it answers." We are not unsanguine when we recognize that there is still much to be learned about the psychology of persuasion.

THE SPEAKER AND HIS AUDIENCE

In this section we shall restructure in terms of its applications by a public speaker much that we have said about the psychology of communication. We have no intention of outlining a complete manual on rhetorical practice. Our limited purpose is to summarize, under eight headings, some of the contributions of modern psychological concepts to classical rhetorical theory. Our headings require two explanations: (a) each one begins with a transitive verb in order to emphasize that action of some kind is indispensable in every aspect of public address; (b) the four functional psychological factors discussed in Chapter 14 appear in the middle of the series in order to emphasize how they pervade the total process of communicating to an audience.

Analyzing Audience, Occasion, and Purpose

It is fashionable among modern rhetoricians—and psychologically sound —to describe public speaking as audience-centered rather than speaker-centered. The oratory of personal display is out of style, and never was in good taste. We agree today that no matter how important the speaker's message, or how strongly he feels about it, it is the complex of beliefs and attitudes of his listeners that he must deal with. The key to understanding this complex is a careful audience analysis, seeking answers to a series of questions such as we proposed earlier in this chapter. Though it may be impossible to study a prospective audience at first hand, an analysis of similar and familiar groups will be helpful: it is possible to make fairly safe generalizations, for example, about the attitudes of members of service clubs, labor unions, or college student-bodies, wherever they are. National or local public opinion polls can also provide useful information. The only alternative to advance analysis is to make impromptu adaptations when actually facing the audience, but this is a poor choice even for experienced speakers.

The occasion for the speech needs also to be understood. The concerned speaker will want to know what brings the audience together, what expectations it has both for his speech and the whole meeting. When on the scene the speaker should notice the apparent spirit of the audience as it assembles, organizational rituals, and other elements of "preliminary tuning" that may affect the tone of the occasion.

If the speech is to be audience-centered, then an analysis of the listeners and the occasion for their meeting will help the speaker in determining his specific purpose, as well as the means he uses to achieve it.

Acquiring Prestige

A speaker's prestige, referred to in traditional rhetoric as *ethos* or ethical appeal, determines his status with his audience. The first kind of status is ascribed, what the speaker is thought to be. This is determined by the business, professional, or social position he holds, and by his reputation, especially as an authority on his subject. Advance publicity for the meeting usually stresses this aspect of status and the chairman's introduction underscores it, sometimes "ad nauseam." As we reported (on p. 284), experiments using speakers otherwise unknown to their audiences consistently show that appropriate introductions ascribing high status "credentials" will significantly increase favorable attitudes resulting from the speech. In their investigation of the effect of an audience's prior judgments of a speaker's ethos upon its acceptance of his point of view, Berlo and Gulley (1957) submit that the significant correlations between these two factors are explained by the Osgood and Tannenbaum "congruity principle"—that attitude changes always go in directions that will increase their harmony with existing listener frames of reference or sets of expectations.

A second kind of status is earned—what the speaker proves himself to be. Since relatively few speakers can have high ascribed status, it is significant to report research on how speakers can earn status. Clark

(1951) found that general audiences, ranking fourteen qualities of speakers and speaking, listed "sincerity" and "poise" as the first and second most essential. This judgment endorses speaker behavior that appears to be honest, purposeful, confident, and considerate.

Credibility may also be earned by a speaker's manner: Bettinghaus (1961) found that effectiveness of delivery significantly correlated with credibility and thus with persuasiveness; and Harms (1961), using essentially "content-free" speech cues, found that high status speakers (well educated and in prestige occupations) not only could be distinguished from middle and low status speakers by "the way they talked" but that high status speakers were consistently rated as most credible. Credibility was greater for straightforward argumentative speeches, however, than for those using special techniques (such as deliberate attempts to manifest high integrity) in a series of political talks experimentally evaluated by Ludlum (1958). Part of the straightforward approach is using sound evidence to support a proposition rather than depending upon assertion and generalization. Cathcart (1955) found a significantly greater shift of opinion for speeches built on evidence, although enlarging upon it by citing or qualifying its sources did not necessarily make it more credible.

Two special facets of credibility are fairness and trustworthiness. When there was reason to be suspicious of a speaker's motives, Hovland and Mandell (1952) found that audiences concluded that the speaker did "a very poor job" of giving the facts and that they were "too one-sided," but the same speech was rated "a very good job" and "fair and honest" when the audience believed that the speaker had nothing to gain personally by having his proposition accepted. In another study by Hovland, et al. (1949, pp. 201-227) it was found that when the weight of the evidence supported the main thesis it was more persuasive to introduce the arguments of those who opposed it, rather than to present only materials supporting the thesis, "at least for the better educated men and for those who are already opposed to the stand." For less educated and initially favorably disposed listeners the reverse was true. It might be observed that when the speaker at least acknowledged the opposition arguments, he induced a feeling in his listeners that he was being fair. "Better educated" in this study meant graduation from high school and it covered about half of the subjects. In Paulson's (1954) similar study testing the same variable, all of the subjects were college students, and for them the introduction of opposing arguments was not more persuasive, though it improved retention. Paulson speculated that perhaps very sophisticated audiences felt that merely acknowledging, but not developing, opposing arguments was not as fair as it seemed to less critical audiences.

In sum, experimentation supports the conclusion that even the speaker who lacks ascribed status has it within his power to earn status with his hearers by giving evidence of his sincerity, poise, credibility, fairness, and trustworthiness.

Focusing Attention

We are willing to run the risk of redundancy to make an important point: William James said that "what holds attention determines action," and James Winans added that "the key word [in public speaking] is Attention." These two statements, repeated from Chapter 14, point up the inevitable first step in addressing any audience, whether information-seeking or conversional. Without gaining his hearers' attention, nothing that a speaker says will make any difference, unless he enjoys talking to himself.

If a speaker comes to an audience with high ascribed status, if he has already earned status with a specific audience, or if for other reasons his listeners are interested and friendly, he need make no special effort to gain attention. He can count on his prestige to work for him.

If, on the other hand, an audience is apathetic, uninterested, or skeptical about either the speaker or his subject, it must be roused or even jolted to attention. In his book on influencing human behavior, Overstreet (1925, pp. 110-124) described five of the available methods of "crossing the interest deadline," and we enumerate them here: "Start with situations. . . . Start with something that makes a difference. . . . Begin with an effect needing a cause. . . . or begin with a cause implying an effect. . . . [Begin with] the shock technique. . . . Present a conflict. . . ."

When a speaker faces a hostile or critical audience, he must utilize all possible resources for gaining attention. Observations of effective speakers reveal that in this predicament they most often work to find some common ground of agreement with the audience and then focus attention upon it. This platform of agreement with his hearers upon which the speaker hopes to stand may be built on common interests or associations: no matter how else they may be unlike, they all come from the same community, fought in the same war, belong to the same party, and so on. Common ground may also be sought in areas of belief or attitude: regardless of other differences, for example, the speaker and his audience believe in the same "way of life," worship the same God, revere the same flag, and share the same praiseworthy desire to solve their problems rationally and with justice for all. Like other persuasive methods, this one can be employed ethically and sincerely.

There is evidence that the common-ground technique, finding some basis for the speaker's identification with his hearers, is effective. Schachter (1951) concluded that a speaker cannot win a hearing from his audience if he deviates too far from the group norm; and Ewing (1942) found that a speaker's acceptance is increased when, at the beginning of his speech, he asserts that his views correspond with those held by his hearers, even if he really advocates a proposition contrary to their initial opinions. In a similar procedure Weiss (1957) demonstrated that a communicator can influence an audience more easily when, in discussing a controversial issue, he makes opportunities to express on another topic opinions which are in accord with those of his hearers. Should the speaker, by means of suggestion, persuade his hearers that the majority opinion is different than it really is, Marple (1933) reported, they will tend to shift their attitudes toward the alleged majority position.

We have previously described the concept of attention in some detail, and implied that all audiences are susceptible to the influence of five unlearned attention values: change, intensity, striking quality, repetition, and definiteness of form. We conclude this discussion by briefly suggesting some of the ways that speakers may apply these attention values in implementing four significant principles.

1. To hold attention the content of a speech must be impressive. What the speaker says should have *definiteness of form*, clearly presenting an easily grasped pattern of information or course of action; if it is also novel, has a *striking quality*, it will gain attention on that basis alone; and if it is presented with enough *repetition* to be sure that every listener understands it, the communication will have maximum potency.

2. To hold attention the organization of a speech must be clear. A well organized speech personifies *definiteness of form*, ordering information or arguments into a chronological, topical, logical, or some other pattern. Transitions between units of a speech are important, but the form in which they are stated should *change* from time to time. Not all parts of a speech carry the same load of significance; in itself this may provide for a variety of *intensity*, but intensification of a vital part may also be achieved by *repetition*.

3. To hold attention the style of a speech must be varied. A *change* in word stimuli will add variety, and speakers need to be wary, in any event, of overusing stock phrases to the point of redundancy. Putting ideas into words offers many opportunities for *striking quality*, creating graphic images, novel expressions, and so on. At the same time the value of *definiteness of form* may be required in order to achieve precision and clarity.

4. To hold attention, the delivery of a speech must be compelling. A monotonous voice and a static body seldom gain audience attention, but a *change* in stimulus, and especially a variety of change, invariably

will. There may be many distracting stimuli operating in a lecture hall, and unless the speaker uses *intensity* to strengthen his own, they may be lost. His action must be appropriate and coordinated, however, or it will lack *definiteness of form* and have reduced impact.

Maintaining Interest

"Thanks, anyway, but I'm just not interested," is a terminating statement that sends salesmen away from front doors frustrated. Just as effectively as these words, vacant stares on the faces of a classroom audience, or bored expressions from a church congregation, can fill a speaker with despair. He, too, is a salesman of sorts, peddling his wares of facts and opinions, arguments and propositions. Though they may give him their momentary attention, unless his prospective purchasers can be interested they will not buy.

Exactly what will command the interest of an individual at any specific moment is hard to determine, but there is little question about the importance of interest itself in public address. The very act of listening depends upon the listener's interest in what is being said. In a pioneer study Nichols (1948) identified fourteen factors significantly influencing listening comprehension. Three of these were: "real *interest* in the subject discussed," "ability to see *significance* in the subject discussed," and "*curiosity* about the subject discussed." If not synonyms, interest, significance, and curiosity are at least closely related terms.

Karraker's (1951) later study of the influence of interest on listening effectiveness led to the generalization that experience with a subject creates interest in it. Edwards (1941) found that experiences in accord with existing frames of reference ("desires, attitudes, wishes, values, etc.") tended to be learned and remembered better than those in conflict. While he did not use the term "interest" in his description, it was clearly implied as an omnibus factor. In a follow-up study Gilkinson, *et al.* (1953) found the same tendency. When Thompson (1953) studied the factors considered by students in evaluating public discussions he found that "interestingness contributes the most to the students' over-all evaluation," even more than organization and material. Finally, we report studies by Kretsinger (1952) and Lyle (1953) indicating that the degree of a listener's interest in a speech can be measured by electromagnetic movement meter recordings of gross bodily movements. When interest in the communication increased, as measured by subject rating scales, gross bodily movements decreased; as interest decreased, bodily movements increased. While these experiments leave certain applicational values unexplored, they establish that listener interest, like other response behaviors, involves overt muscular activity.

Earlier we described eight of the most common natural factors of interest. We conclude by referring to these factors again, as they might appear in public address.

1. *Animation* is, of course, important in speech delivery: modulations of pitch, variations in rate and loudness, and shifts in vocal quality, all adapted to the ideas presented, and vitality of gesture and physical expression, suiting the action to the word, will not only reinforce what the speaker says but provide a visible index of how he feels about what he says. When the speaker's speech itself is well paced, straight exposition is enlivened with narrative illustrations, supporting material is varied, and so on, then animation is aiding content as well as delivery.

2. *Vitalness* is not inherent in every speech topic, even though the speaker may be totally concerned with it. William James said we attend to what interests us, not that we attend to what interests the other fellow. The speaker, whether hoping to inform or persuade his hearers, must find in them the sources for giving vitalness to his topic: it is the relation of their desires and needs to his subject that the speaker must make clear if he is to maintain interest.

3. *Familiarity* is an interest factor employed by speakers to provide a common point of reference for their listeners. When Joseph Jastrow said that man is more analogical than logical, he pointed the way to an effective rhetorical principle: a new and strange idea is less forbidding if it is compared with a similar one within the common experience of the audience.

4. *Novelty* is familiarity's counterpart, and equally important in maintaining interest because too much reliance upon one stimulus may wear out its effectiveness. Listeners want enough novelty to offset monotony, just as they want enough familiarity to maintain stability. In supporting his arguments, for example, the speaker can employ unusual illustrations of familiar principles, and novel ways of phrasing traditional ideas.

5. *Conflict*, portrayed in narrative form or in straight exposition, tends to hold audience interest. It makes it easier for the listener to project himself, though vicariously, into the speaker's topic. The portrayal of conflicting forces—medical research against disease, tolerance against bigotry, democracy against totalitarianism—helps reduce complex problems to manageable proportions for the listener who is less well prepared to understand them than is the speaker. Speakers must use restraint in the portrayal of conflict, however, lest they oversimplify problems into sometimes unrealistic "either-or" patterns.

6. *Suspense*, when built by the speaker into long narrative explanations, or even short illustrations, is an adaptation to a public speech of the dramatic "chase technique" where the "good guys" pursue the "bad guys." Even when the listener knows who will win in the end, his interest

is maintained by the tantalizing notion that "this one may be different," or by curiosity about how the conquest will be achieved. Active verbs and figurative language are stylistic aids in building suspense.

7. *Concreteness* in presenting ideas to an audience is like reducing a complex equation to a simple one. It holds the listener's interest because it makes it easier for him to understand; and it applies the principle of "mental economy" by giving him understanding with less effort than would be required by abstractness. Conceptually, concreteness is achieved by reducing an expansive idea into several smaller ones; stylistically, by substituting "picture words" and examples for vague terms.

8. *Humor* best maintains interest in the speaker's ideas if it is articulated with them. Thus the witty comparison, the incongruous application, or the clever turn of phrase that seems to grow out of a substantive idea is more effective than the isolated and often extraneous joke (Grimes, 1955). Even when a funny story is intended to illustrate a speaker's idea, his audience too often remembers the joke but not its point.

Providing Motivation

George Washington once said "The people must feel before they will see." For that insight into human nature, he might be given a "first" in psychology as well as in war and peace. We tried to make the same point when discussing motivation in Chapter 14, though we fear not so succinctly. Modern psychologists are probably more in agreement on the dominant strength of affective behavior, and its origins in powerful motivations, than on any other point (Jones, 1953-1961). They agree that men are most likely to behave in response to their own motivations, not to others' reasons.

When this concept of motivation is applied to communication, it becomes the basis for persuasion. *Thus persuasion in public address is defined as the process of securing acceptance of an idea, or an action, by connecting it favorably with the listener's attitudes, beliefs, and desires.* This definition does not preclude the use of evidence and reasoning in the process, but it acknowledges that we must persuade those whom logic alone cannot command. In reference to our definition we would also point out that it is the listener who actually provides the motivations; the persuader's function is to channel them into support for his proposition.

As in treating other elements in the speaker-audience relationship, we will summarize a sample of recent research bearing upon motivation. Before doing this, however, we should make clear our understanding of how logic and reasoning are related to persuasion, for it is often assumed that the two are incompatible and that a speaker must depend upon either rational *or* emotional appeals. There are two ways of dealing with this erroneous assumption.

In the first place, one of the elemental desires of humans is to be rational. Indeed, some persons become quite emotional if they are publicly accused of being irrational. Because men want to be rational they seek to rationalize and find socially acceptable reasons for behavior that will satisfy their basic drives. As William Jennings Bryan observed, "it is a poor mind that can't fix up good reasons for doing what it wants to do!" We think it is a mark of the progress of civilization that men do prefer to believe, and to have their friends and associates assume, that they behave always on the basis of sound reasoning. Brigance (1931) constructed a theory about the genetic development of persuasion that puts the matter this way: primitive man relied first upon *authority*, then upon *experience*, as determinants of his behavior, and it is only the man of an advanced culture, alert and intellectually aggressive, whose behavior is shaped also by *reason*. Not only is this development apparent in the history of the race, it is also observable in the life of an individual: as a child he behaves in response to authority, later he incorporates experience, and still later he puts reason into his patterns of action. In sum, we believe that a persuader who includes rational arguments in his speech is tapping an important motivation in his listener.

In the second place, we do not believe that it is possible to construct and deliver a speech that depends solely upon logical or solely upon emotional appeals. This conclusion is buttressed by our examination of the very experiments designed to test the separate effects of the two. In many studies the speech variable described as logical appears to be a persuasive speech, but with a minimum of connotative language which would create visual images or carry emotional overtones. Yet even the remaining argumentative discourse of, say, the formal debater, still asks support for propositions on the grounds that they are practical, desirable, and beneficial. The mere addition to such a speech, on the other hand, of "loaded language" does not eliminate the partitioning and ordering of arguments that are part of the logical structure of any discourse.

In short, while we believe that decisions based upon the consideration of evidence and argument are likely to be better than those made under the spell of overwhelming emotion, we also believe that emotional appeals properly may be—and inevitably are—used to reinforce evidence and argument. This is the burden of pertinent research studies, as we read them. They only substantiate the axiomatic statement made years ago by Harry A. Overstreet (1925, p. 48) that "no appeal to a reason that is not also an appeal to a want is ever effective." Indeed, many of us have a great want for others to appeal to our reason.

We turn now to brief summaries of representative investigations of motivation. Collins (1924) reported on the interaction of logical and emotional appeals in four persuasive speeches. The most effective was the speech containing logical arguments, each followed by a short motive appeal. Less effective were speeches developed by an extended emotional appeal, an extended logical appeal, or an extended logical appeal followed by an extended emotional appeal. In an elaborate experiment comparing the effects of logical and emotional appeals, and their presentation orally and in writing, Knower (1935) found that "logical and persuasive speeches were equally effective," and that oral presentation consistently produced greater attitude shifts than did written.

In studies by Menefee and Grannenberg (1940) and Millson (1932), it was concluded that a predominantly emotional approach was more effective. Some questions are implicitly raised about these findings, however, by an experiment designed to discover whether listeners are able to distinguish between intellectual and emotional appeals in speeches they hear. Ruechelle (1958) reported that audiences could not dichotomize or classify persuasive materials as emotional or intellectual in content and, furthermore, that listener evaluations were based mainly on general impressions, less on content, and still less on delivery.

In terms of the effect of emotive materials on listener comprehension and recall, Matthews (1947) found that paired speeches containing "loaded" and "unloaded" language were equally effective in promoting retention. Pence (1954) discovered that emotionally loaded argument stimulated recall, but he did not compare its effects with that of non-emotional argument.

We have already reported research upon certain other matters related to motivation. In discussing interest, for example, we said that previous acquaintance with the subject of a speech apparently motivates greater interest in it; and we also described the apparent effects of the prestige and ethical appeal of a speaker upon his audience influence. In treating the stereotyped stimulus we noted the listener's tendency to respond to it. Here we cite one study of many demonstrating the operation of this essentially non-rational behavior. Hartmann (1936) found from an attitude test that his subjects were generally favorable to such collectivist policies as public ownership of industry and national resources. But when these same policies were presented with stereotyped labels indicating that they were socialistic or communistic, most of the subjects shifted to opposite positions.

A skillful persuader recognizes the potency of his listeners' motivations when they can be linked to his speech purpose. How does he tap these resources? *First*, he considers whether he can show that the adoption of his proposal (or the acquisition of the information he offers) will satisfy any fundamental wants, needs, or interests of his audience.

If he identifies any such relationships, he includes in his speech repeated references to them. *Second*, he appraises the general beliefs of his listeners and their probable attitudes toward his proposition. In planning his speech he attempts to integrate his thesis with the established beliefs of his listeners and devise ways to reinforce their favorable attitudes and break down hostile ones. *Third*, he inventories his stock of available evidence and argument. He selects from it for his speech content that material best suited to persuading the particular audience, and in terms of what his analysis has revealed about their basic motivations, beliefs, and attitudes. *Fourth*, he lists those emotionally loaded words and stereotypes to which his listeners are likely to respond favorably, and those to which they will respond negatively. In phrasing his speech he makes free use of the first list when referring to his proposal or those who already support it, and draws from the second list when talking about the opposition.

Perhaps only in a public speaking textbook should one expect to find a detailed statement about ethical practices in employing motivational appeals. But it is pertinent here to note that most discussions of the ethics of persuasion are essentially elaborations of Aristotle's view that "sophistical dialectic, or sophistical speaking, is made so, not by the faculty, but by the moral purpose." One psychologist, Robert E. Merton (1946, p. 186) makes this distinction: "Appeals to sentiments within the context of relevant information and knowledge are basically different from appeals to sentiment which blur and obscure this knowledge." Appeals of the first type he approves, but not those of the second.

Assuring Learning and Remembering

Those who carefully prepare and deliver speeches naturally hope that their listeners will comprehend and retain what they hear. Inexperienced speakers soon discover, however, that facts and opinions will not "speak for themselves." What they wish an audience to understand and recall must be presented in such a way as to make these processes as congenial as possible. Herbert Spencer (1907, p. 273) described the problem in terms of "mental economy" for the listener: "To so present ideas that they may be apprehended with the *least possible mental effort*, is the desideratum . . ." His assumption that the listener has a limited amount of perceptive capacity available at any given moment is supported by the observations of Hyman and Sheatsley (1947) on selectivity in learning, fully summarized in Chapter 14.

Thus far we have cited numerous studies reporting substantial shifts of audience opinion after hearing persuasive speeches; in each instance it is obvious that some degree of comprehension (learning) preceded the change. Remembering, when measured in these studies, continued for as much as nine weeks, but regression toward the original position was almost always discernible. In one study, however, Hovland, *et al.* (1949, pp. 182-200), it was found that "changes in opinion of a general rather than specific nature may show increasing effects [i.e., even greater strength] with the lapse of time."

After reviewing a number of studies on opinion change, Hovland, Janis, and Kelley (1953, p. 92) concluded that "attention, comprehension, and acceptance probably determine, to a very large extent, the degree of persistence of the opinion changes induced by a communication." We would expand that statement to say that each of the basic functional psychological factors in communication is important in learning and remembering: unless the listener's attention is focused he can not perceive, if his interest lags he will not be alert, and without being motivated he may not care. Beyond focusing attention, maintaining interest, and providing motivation, what can a speaker do to help his hearers comprehend and retain what he says?

To begin with, the speaker can study the conditions for optimum listening effectiveness. At least for the presentation of informational materials, as in a college lecture, Brown (1959) found the listener's anticipatory set closely correlated to his comprehension. In his investigation he prefaced the experimental speeches with brief remarks indicating the general nature and significance of their content, and thus shaped audience expectations. It is significant that these preliminary orientations aided good as well as poor listeners.

In a more comprehensive study of factors in listening, Nichols (1948) tested the comprehension of student subjects after hearing lectures in such fields as literature, economics, and biology. On the average they comprehended only 68 per cent of the material on which they were tested. After studying correlations of effectiveness in comprehending with thirty-three possibly influential factors, Nichols established fourteen significantly positive ones. Among them were some over which a speaker could have no control, such as the hearer's intelligence, vocabulary, and physical fatigue. Also significant, however, were five factors of which a speaker could take advantage by deliberately adapting, organizing, emphasizing, and delivering his materials: ability to make inferences, ability to structuralize a speech (that is, to see the organizational plan and the connection of the main points), listening for main ideas as opposed to specific facts, ability to see significance in the subject discussed, and audibility of the speaker.

Some specific techniques for making the adjustments called for by the Nichols findings could be inferred from our earlier discussion of learning. By categorizing discriminably different objects, persons, and qualities, for example, a speaker could assist his listeners in distinguishing main ideas. The formulation of generalizations would help the listener to cluster pertinent bits of evidence. The use of positive suggestion could guide the listener in drawing correct inferences and understanding their significance. Various means of gaining impressiveness might emphasize the total organizational plan of a speech, as well as units within it. Among these reinforcement techniques are repeating key ideas, giving significant material the advantage of primacy or recency influence by placement in the speech, and varying vocal and physical action in ways that reflect the speaker's judgment of the relative importance of what he is saying.

Constructing the Speech

Here we report on research studies relating to the speaker's three-fold task after he has selected the general subject and specific purpose of his communication: developing the substance, structure, and style of the speech.

The public speaker who turns to psychological research for advice on kinds and quantities of substantive material to use in addressing information-seeking or conversional audiences will be disappointed. This is a matter that must largely be determined by coordinating a knowledge of the general psychology of public address with an analysis of the specific audience. We have already commented, for example, on the studies of logical versus emotional speech content: assuming that the two can be discriminated, both seem to be of about equal value. During World War II government agencies found it desirable to obtain some form of quantitative measurement of enemy broadcasts, and methodologies for content analysis of many forms of communication have subsequently been developed (Berelson, 1954). These analyses, however, have been largely concerned with categorizing and determining the frequency of various themes or lines of argument as they appear in propaganda materials. While the same techniques have been applied to discover various rhetorical practices of individual speakers (Chester, 1949; Miller and Villarreal, 1945), the studies are descriptive only and do not suggest principles to be applied generally.

Other specialized quantitative measuring techniques, such as the type-token ratio analyses ("types" are different words and "tokens" are the total number of words in a given communication) also provide descriptive studies of language usage (Fairbanks, 1944; Lerea, 1956), but not of present value for public speakers. One of the few experimental studies dealing with varieties of proof materials was done by Grasham (1951). In speaking primarily to inform, he found, quotations or assertions were more effective means of support than specific instances. In speaking to persuade, supporting quotations were most effective; assertions were less so, and analogies were relatively ineffective. A study by Lull (1940) tested the effectiveness of humor in persuasive speeches; he found humorous and non-humorous speeches on the same topic about equal in interestingness and convincingness. Further research of this nature, and experimenting with a wide range of proof materials, could be fruitful in deriving principles applicable to the development of speech content.

The first question concerning the structure of a speech is whether a formal over-all organization is essential for retention or persuasion, and if so, what kind. Using relatively short speeches on current social and political topics, and varying the "normal" order by transposing introductions, conclusions, transitions, and the sequence of main arguments, Smith (1951), and Beighley (1952, 1954) found little difference in effects upon audiences. Gulley and Berlo (1956) organized similar speeches into climax, anticlimax, and pyramidal sequences of arguments according to their assertion-strength, both in the over-all structure and within separate units of the speech, and found no statistically significant advantage for any one pattern. Only in a study by Thistlethwaite, *et al.* (1955) was a well-organized speech found to be more effective than a poorly organized one. In this study, however, the speaker's explicit drawing or not drawing of a conclusion from the argument of the speech was also measured, to the substantial advantage of the former even in the case of the poorly organized speech, and thus it may be that the explicit statement of a speech goal is more significant than how it is reached.

One of the investigators, Raymond G. Smith (1958, pp. 106-107), makes this summary comment on studies experimenting with speech structure: "Evidence has been gradually accumulating to indicate that speech organization, so far as its effect on the audience is concerned, is unimportant for many if not all speeches, both for amount of information remembered and persuasive effect." He speculates, however, that the importance of organization undoubtedly varies with the length and difficulty of the speech: "Audiences will be unable to remember the main ideas of long speeches unless the organization and transitions are clear. Likewise, unless such relationships are clear, difficult material will not be grasped."

From these and other investigations of effective speechmaking, it is clear that distinctions can be made between well and poorly organized speeches. The over-all criteria are suggested by these questions: Does the introduction orient the listener toward the subject, both in terms of its general nature and its relationship to listener needs and desires? Does the body of the speech consist of identifiable separate but coherent arguments for the speaker's proposition, with clear topic sentences for each one, and transitions that show relationships among them? Does the conclusion summarize the arguments supporting the proposition and motivate listeners to want to accept it as a means of satisfying their needs and desires? Detailed criteria applicable to the organization of supporting arguments involve other factors such as primacy $v.$ recency and climax $v.$ anticlimax.

A so-called "Law of Primacy" in the placement of materials in persuasive communications was first stated by Lund (1925), and this position of importance was verified in a later study by Jersild (1928). Using a wider range of subject matter and more sophisticated techniques of control and measurement, however, subsequent investigators, Berlo and Gulley (1957), Ehrensberger (1945) and Tannenbaum (1954) would support a "Law of Recency" for the most effective placement of important materials. A fair comment is that the conclusion of a speech appears to be the position of greatest potency for retention, but that either the conclusion or the introduction is superior to the middle.

Rhetoricians have long classified major argumentative units of a speech as strong, average, or weak in inducing belief-strength, but have differed about whether arguments are most effectively presented in climax (from weakest to strongest) or anticlimax (from strongest to weakest) order. This aspect of speech structure has been studied both for its significance in retention and in attitude change. Sponberg (1946) found that an anticlimax order induced greater retention, but it should be noted that more time was progressively allotted in the speech for the presentation of weak, average, and strong arguments, thus introducing a variable of mass that may have been more influential than the variable of position. Later studies report no significant differences between climax and anticlimax order: Berlo and Gulley (1957), Gilkinson, et al. (1954), and Thistlethwaite, et al. (1956).

When considered in terms of effect upon attitude change, the accumulated evidence from the studies just cited, and from a study by Gulley and Berlo (1956), indicates that while climax order appears to shift more opinions than anticlimax, it is not significantly advantageous. As with the primacy-recency factor, it is presently possible only to conclude that either one has its merits, but that a decision on which one to use might best be made on other grounds, such as the familiarity or complexity of the materials presented. In those public address situations where two or more speakers present opposite points of view, as in a debate or a symposium, two studies by Cromwell (1950, 1954) demonstrated that climax order (i.e., weaker speeches, in argument strength and organization, first; stronger speeches second) had more effect upon initial attitude shift and upon persistence of that shift.

A substantially different aspect of structure was studied by Cohen (1957) who found that speech material is more effectively arranged when appeals to and arousal of audience needs are made first, and then followed by propositions alleged to satisfy those needs, rather than in the opposite sequence. When a single speaker has two sets of conclusions to present, one consonant with the desires and motives of his audience, and the other in conflict, McGuire (1957) concluded that greater opinion change was induced by presenting the more desirable propositions first. Both of these studies might be interpreted as supporting the significance of the primacy position and the anticlimax order, at least in the sense that in each case the most effective speeches presented first what would seem to be most necessary or desirable from the view of the audience.

The speaker's third task in constructing his communication is choosing the specific language forms for expressing the substance. While rhetoricians have stressed the importance of style in speechmaking for over two thousand years, only within the past few decades have there been any substantial objective studies of it, so that, as Cherry (1957, p. 108) notes, it is now "describable partly in statistical terms, by the comparative extent, richness, or poverty of vocabulary, by the syllabic length of words, the relative frequencies of sentences of different lengths, and by different grammatical structures." A good portion even of this research has been based upon analyses of written style in order to develop predictive formulas of "readability," such as those of Rudolf Flesch.

In developing approaches to the study of speech style, such as Ewbank's (1931), it has been assumed that there are differences between spoken and written styles and that the principles governing the effectiveness of one do not necessarily apply to the other; thus some studies, such as the early one by Borchers (1936), have concentrated on quantifying those differences. Studies of speech intelligibility received an impetus from the conditions of modern warfare, and the collection made under Army auspices and edited by Black (1946) has encouraged subsequent researchers. Primarily, however, these investigations have centered on such matters as the relation to intelligibility of loudness, pitch, articulation, and phonetic factors.

The single major study of the effect of specific word choice upon intelligibility in public address was made by Thomas (1956). Two speeches parallel in subject, substance, and structure were constructed for an experiment involving 2000 student subjects. One contained a maximum, the other a minimum, of those types of words, phrases, syntactical structures, and special language forms and usages characteristic of oral style. The major finding was that the use of certain elements of oral style definitely increased by about 10 per cent the amount of information imparted. This potency of oral over non-oral style was significant whether the listeners heard one or the other of two speakers involved, whether they heard a live speaker or a tape recording, and whether or not they were motivated to listen by being told they were participating in an experiment and would be tested after hearing the speech.

The eight specific types of oral style found in Thomas' study (1956) to contribute to intelligibility and listener comprehension were: specific words, colorful words, informality and simplicity of vocabulary, figurative language, personalization, informality of syntax, questions, and direct quotations. While these findings constitute specific direction for public speakers, additional research is needed, particularly to discover whether the same stylistic elements that appear to influence listener comprehension are equally efficient in changing listener attitudes.

Our previous discussions of functional psychological factors yield additional conclusions applicable to style. Recalling that listeners cannot give continuous attention, the speaker must, in style as in everything else, employ the attention values of change, intensity, striking quality, repetition, and definiteness of form. Indeed, when these values are compared with those oral stylistic devices recommended by Thomas, a reasonable causal relationship is apparent. Of these values it is likely that change is the most significant. Elsewhere in this book we have discussed aspects of language that suggest these further principles: (a) language requiring the least effort to comprehend is best understood, (b) a speaker's words are always interpreted in the light of the listener's own experiences, (c) meanings are attached more easily to concrete and specific word symbols than to general and abstract ones.

Delivering the Speech

The culmination of the speaker's behavior is the oral delivery of his speech to an audience. Quantitative studies of delivery appeared fairly early in the literature on speech behavior, perhaps because of the, now fortunately past, high emphasis upon the "elocutionary" aspects of speaking, but most probably because the laboratory equipment of the voice scientist permitted more precise measurement of various vocal attributes than was once possible for other factors in the total speech process. Here we select a small sample from that literature in order to illuminate significant topics.

There is substantial agreement among investigators that vocal skill (ability to be heard and understood) is positively related to the listener's comprehension, as is illustrated by Beighley's (1952) report. It is true, however, that most studies have measured gross impressions, rather than the specific effects of variation in pitch, force, rate, and quality. Of these four, the effect of variable rate has been most often investigated. Goldstein (1940) experimented with variations in reading aloud from 100 to 328 words per minute and found a consistent but not statistically conclusive decline in listener comprehension as the rate was increased, and Harwood (1955) reached a similar conclusion. The same results were found in a study by Nelson (1948) but he also discovered that when subjects reported their interest in the communications they heard, a rate between 175 and 200 words per minute was most satisfactory. In a study of modes of emphasis Jersild (1928) found a negative effect of slow speech on retention, but Ehrensberger (1945) discovered a positive one; both agreed that a pause before a word or phrase to be emphasized significantly aided retention. In a later investigation Diehl, et al. (1955) altered recorded speech by reducing pauses in such a way as to vary the rate between 126 and 172 words per minute. It was found that these alterations did not interfere with listener comprehension nor significantly change listener ratings of the quality of the speaker's delivery.

In considering delivery factors other than voice, such as gestures and facial expressions, it should first be noted that a substantial number of studies comparing identical communications by live speakers, recorded speakers, and in printed form, establish the superiority of the live speaker in changing listener attitudes (Knower, 1936; Utterback and Harding, 1955; Wilke, 1934). The chief difference between live and recorded speeches, of course, is that visible as well as audible cues are given to the listener.

Although in the investigations just cited the differences in affecting attitudes between the live speaker and the recorded speech ranged as high as 20 per cent in favor of the former, the only study of the specific influence of gestures upon listener comprehension, by Gauger (1952), showed higher mean scores for those who saw and heard the speaker, but not statistically significant ones. The same measured advantage for a speech delivered with gestures and an identical speech without gestures was found in this investigation. About the specific impact of facial expressions intended to express various emotional attitudes of the speaker, we know only that Dusenbury and Knower (1938) found listeners able to discriminate among as many as eleven different ones, but not whether the ability to make these identifications is correlated with their influence upon attitudes.

One investigation appears to contradict the conclusions concerning the significance of bodily action in public speaking. In his survey of general audiences, Clark (1951) found that only 27 per cent regarded "gesture," 46 per cent "co-ordinated bodily movement," and 54 per cent "animation" as essential to good speaking. While these findings seem to depreciate the positive effects of a speaker's action, they must be considered in the light of the conclusion by Monroe, et al. (1936) that listeners tend to respond and to evaluate speakers in terms of over-all impressions rather than upon discrete elements in the speaking process.

The judgments of Clark's audiences must also be tempered by the fact that they reported what they thought influenced them, not necessarily what did influence them. On this point such studies as Bettinghaus' (1961) are pertinent. In his investigation of listener shifts of attitudes toward congruous positions for various elements, including the speaker, his delivery, and his speech topic, he found that audiences do tend to balance their perceptions and, specifically, that hearers make their attitudes toward delivery congruous with their attitudes toward the speaker. The components of delivery rated in this study were: pitch, loudness, resonance, rate, pronunciation, articulation, and vocal variety. In these terms, Bettinghaus concluded, "effective" delivery produced a more favorable shift of attitude toward the speaker than "ineffective" delivery. Dietrich's (1946) study of two different types of vocal delivery compared attitude shifts resulting from "dynamic" (rapid, dramatic, enthusiastic, and formal) with "conversational" (relaxed, quiet, and informal) to the significant advantage of the latter, both in the immediate situation and on a post-test two weeks later.

Any conclusion about the role of delivery in public address must incorporate the findings of this sampling of a large number of studies indicating that even though listeners may not always be able to identify the separate elements of delivery, their reactions to effective use of voice and bodily action are measurable in terms of comprehension and attitude changes. These findings support the rhetorician's axiom that a good speech well delivered is more influential than the same speech poorly delivered.

A final comment should be made on listener reactions to one further variable in delivery: reading a speech from a manuscript versus speaking extemporaneously with no more than reference notes. The earliest objective study of this factor was by Moore (1919) who read and delivered extemporaneously the same materials to college classes and reported that the extempore method resulted in a 36 per cent greater retention. As Young (1958, p. 306) concludes from other studies, "audiences, except highly specialized ones, react more sympathetically and with more attention to papers read informally or to speeches delivered freely than to more formal presentations." When we recall that variety has an almost constantly positive effect upon listener reactions, it is easy to understand that the almost inherently more static quality of a speaker reading aloud from a manuscript will be less effective than lively, direct, and extemporaneous delivery. It is also true, of course, that the nature of the content of the speech is an important variable: the more highly technical it is, the less it lends itself to free extemporization. In any case, if a speaker recites long quotations or involved statistical data from memory, the listener may be less inclined to assume his accuracy than if he reads such material from a manuscript or a note card. Indeed, the speaker's ethos may be strengthened by this apparent concern for precision.

REFERENCES

Albig, W. *Modern public opinion.* New York: McGraw-Hill, 1956.

Allport, F. H. *Social psychology.* Boston: Houghton Mifflin, 1924.

Asch, S. E. Effects of group pressure upon the modification and distortion of judgments. In Guetzkow, E. (Ed.), *Groups, leadership and men.* Pittsburgh: Carnegie Press, 1951. Pp. 177-190.

Beighley, K. C. An experimental study of the effect of four speech variables on listener comprehension. *Spch Monogr.,* 1952, 19, 249-258.

Beighley, K. C. An experimental study of the effect of three speech variables on listener comprehension. *Spch Monogr.,* 1954, 21, 248-253.

Berelson, B. Content analysis. In Lindzey, G. (Ed.), *Handbook of social psychology.* Reading, Mass.: Addison-Wesley, 1954. Vol. I. Pp. 488-522.

Berlo, D. K., & Gulley, H. E. Some determinants of the effect of oral communication in producing attitude change and learning. *Spch Monogr.,* 1957, 24, 10-20.

Bettinghaus, E. P. The operation of congruity in an oral communication situation. *Spch Monogr.,* 1961, 28, 131-142.

Birdwhistell, R. L. *Introduction to kinesics.* Washington: Foreign Service Institute, 1952.

Black, J. W. Studies in speech intelligibility: a program of war-time research. *Spch Monogr.,* 1946, 12, 1-68.

Borchers, G. L. An approach to the problem of oral style. *Quart. J. Spch,* 1936, 22, 114-117.

Brandon, J. E. Presenting information by television. *Spch Monogr.,* 1956, 23, 272-284.

Brembeck, W. L. The effects of a course in argumentation on critical thinking ability. *Spch Monogr.,* 1949, 16, 177-189.

Brigance, W. N. A genetic approach to persuasion. *Quart. J. Spch,* 1931, 17, 329-339.

Brown, C. T. An experimental diagnosis of thinking on controversial issues. *Spch Monogr.,* 1950, 17, 370-377.

Brown, C. T. Studies in listening comprehension. *Spch Monogr.,* 1959, 26, 288-294.

Brown, R. L. Mass phenomena. In Lindzey, G., (Ed.), *Handbook of social psychology.* Reading, Mass.: Addison-Wesley, 1954. II, 833-876.

Cathcart, R. S. An experimental study of the relative effectiveness of four methods of presenting evidence. *Spch Monogr.,* 1955, 22, 227-233.

Cherrington, B., & Miller, L. W. Changes in attitude as the result of a lecture and reading similar materials. *J. soc. Psychol.,* 1933, 4, 479-484.

Cherry, C. *On human communication.* New York: Technology Press of Massachusetts Institute of Technology, Wiley, 1957.

Chester, G. What constitutes irresponsibility on the air?—a case study. *Publ. Opin. Quart.,* 1949, 13, 73-82.

Clark, W. K. A survey of certain audience attitudes toward commonly taught standards of public speaking. *Spch Monogr.*, 1951, 18, 62-69.

Cohen, A. R. Need for cognition and order of communication as determinants of opinion change. In Hovland, C. I. (Ed.), *The order of presentation in persuasion.* New Haven: Yale University Press, 1957. Pp. 79-97.

Collins, G. R. The relative effectiveness of the condensed and extended emotional appeal. *Quart. J. Spch*, 1924, 10, 221-230.

Cromwell, H. The relative effect on audience attitude of the first versus the second argumentative speech of a series. *Spch Monogr.*, 1950, 17, 105-122.

Cromwell, H. The persistency of the effect on audience attitude of the first versus the second argumentative speech of a series. *Spch Monogr.*, 1954, 21, 280-284.

Diehl, C. F., White, R. C., & Burk, K. W. Rate and communication. *Spch Monogr.*, 1959, 26, 229-232.

Dietrich, J. E. The relative effectiveness of two modes of radio delivery in influencing attitudes. *Spch Monogr.*, 1946, 13, 58-66.

Dusenbury, D., & Knower, F. H. Experimental studies of the symbolism of action and voice—I. a study of the specificity of meaning in facial expression. *Quart. J. Spch*, 1936, 24, 424-436.

Edwards, A. L. Political frames of reference as a factor influencing recognition. *J. abnorm. soc. Psychol.*, 1941, 36, 34-50.

Ehrensberger, R. The relative effectiveness of certain forms of emphasis in public speaking. *Spch Monogr.*, 1945, 12, 94-111.

Ewbank, H. L. Four approaches to the study of speech style. *Quart. J. Spch*, 1931, 17, 458-465.

Ewing, T. N. A study of certain factors involved in changes of opinion. *J. soc. Psychol.*, 1942, 16, 63-88.

Fairbanks, H. Studies on language behavior: II. the quantitative differentiation of samples of spoken language. *Psychol. Monogr.*, 1944, 56, 17-38.

Furbay, A. L. A descriptive study of the influence of physical arrangement of the audience upon response to a speech. *Spch Monogr.*, 1960, 27, 84. (Abstract)

Gauger, P. W. The effect of gesture and the presence or absence of the speaker on listening comprehension of eleventh and twelfth grade high school pupils. *Spch Monogr.*, 1952, 19, 116-117. (Abstract)

Gilkinson, H., Paulson, S. F., & Sikkink, D. E. Conditions affecting the communication of controversial statements in connected discourse: forms of presentation and the political frame of reference of the listener. *Spch Monogr.*, 1953, 20, 253-260.

Gilkinson, H., Paulson, S. F., & Sikkink, D. E. Effects of order and authority in an argumentative speech. *Quart. J. Spch*, 1954, 40, 183-192.

Goldstein, H. *Reading and listening comprehension at various controlled rates.* New York: Teachers College, Columbia University, 1940.

Grasham, J. A. An experimental study to determine the relative effectiveness of various "forms of support." *Spch Monogr.*, 1952, 18, 122-123. (Abstract)

Griffith, C. R. A comment upon the psychology of the audience. *Psychol. Monogr.*, 1921, 30, 36-47.

Grimes, W. H. The mirth experience in public address. *Spch Monogr.*, 1955, 22, 243-255.

Gulley, H. E., & Berlo, D. K. Effect of intercellular and intracellular speech structure on attitude change and learning. *Spch Monogr.*, 1956, 23, 288-297.

Haiman, F. S. An experimental study of the effects of ethos in public speaking. *Spch Monogr.*, 1949, 16, 190-202.

Harms, L. S. Listener judgments of status cues in speech. *Quart. J. Spch*, 1961, 48, 164-168.

Hartmann, G. W. The contradictions between the feeling-tone of political party names and public response to their platforms. *J. soc. Psychol.*, 1936, 7, 336-355.

Harwood, K. Listenability and rate of presentation. *Spch Monogr.*, 1955, 22, 57-59.

Henrikson, E. H. The relation among knowing a person, liking a person, and judging him as a speaker. *Spch Monogr.*, 1940, 7, 22-25.

Hovland, C. I., Lumsdaine, A. A., & Sheffield, F. D. *Experiments on mass communication.* Princeton: Princeton University Press, 1949.

Hovland, C. I., & Mandell, W. An experimental comparison of conclusion-drawing by the communicator and by the audience. *J. abnorm. soc. Psychol.*, 1952, 47, 581-588.

Hovland, C. I., Janis, I. L., & Kelley, H. H. *Communication and persuasion.* New Haven: Yale University Press, 1953.

Hovland, C. I., & Janis, I. L. *Personality and persuasability.* New Haven: Yale University Press, 1959.

Howell, W. S. The effects of high school debating on critical thinking. *Spch Monogr.*, 1943, 10, 96-103.

Hyman, H. H., & Sheatsley, P. B. Some reasons why information campaigns fail. *Publ. Opin. Quart.*, 1947, 11, 412-423.

Jersild, A. T. Modes of emphasis in public speaking. *J. appl. Psychol.*, 1928, 12, 611-620.

Jones, M. R. (Ed.) *Nebraska symposium on motivation.* Lincoln: University of Nebraska Press, 1953-1961.

Karraker, M. E. An evaluation of the influence of interest and "set" on listening effectiveness in the basic communication class. *Spch Monogr.*, 1952, 19, 117-118. (Abstract)

Knower, F. H. A study of the effect of oral argument on changes of attitude. *J. soc. Psychol.*, 1935, 6, 315-347.

Knower, F. H. A study of the effect of printed argument on change of attitude. *J. abnorm. soc. Psychol.*, 1936, 30, 522-532.

Kretsinger, E. A. An experimental study of gross bodily movement as an index to audience interest. *Spch Monogr.*, 1952, 19, 244-248.

Lerea, L. A preliminary study of the verbal behavior of speech fright. *Spch Monogr.*, 1956, 23, 229-233.

Lippmann, W. *Public opinion.* New York: Macmillan, 1922.

Ludlum, T. S. Effects of certain techniques of credibility upon audience attitude. *Spch Monogr.*, 1958, 25, 278-284.

Lull, P. E. The effectiveness of humor in persuasive speeches. *Spch Monogr.*, 1940, 7, 26-40.

Lund, F. H. The psychology of belief. *J. abnorm. soc. Psychol.*, 1925, 20, 63-112, 174-224.

Lyle, H. M. An experimental study of certain aspects of the electromagnetic movement meter as a criterion to audience attention. *Spch Monogr.*, 1953, 20, 126. (Abstract)

McGuire, W. J. Order of presentation in "conditioning" persuasiveness. In Hovland, C. I. (Ed.), *The order of presentation in persuasion*. New Haven: Yale University Press, 1957. Pp. 98-114.

Marple, C. H. The comparative suggestibility of three age levels to the suggestion of group versus expert opinion. *J. soc. Psychol.*, 1933, 4, 176-186.

Matthews, J. The effect of loaded language on audience comprehension of speeches. *Spch Monogr.*, 1947, 14, 176-186.

Menefee, S. C., & Granneberg, A. G. Propaganda and opinions on foreign policy. *J. soc. Psychol.*, 1940, 11, 393-404.

Merton, R. E. *Mass persuasion*. New York: Harper & Row, 1946.

Miller, G. A. *Language and communication*. New York: McGraw-Hill, 1951.

Miller, N. E., & Villarreal, J. J. The use of clichés by four contemporary speakers. *Quart. J. Spch*, 1945, 31, 151-155.

Millson, W. A. D. Problems in measuring audience reactions. *Quart. J. Spch*, 1932, 18, 621-637.

Monroe, A. H., Remmers, H. H., & Venemann-Lyle, E. *Measuring the effectiveness of public speech in a beginning course*. Lafayette, Ind.: Purdue University Studies in Higher Education, No. 29, 1936.

Moore, H. T. The attention value of lecturing without notes. *J. educ. Psychol.*, 1919, 10, 467-469.

Mullin, D. W. An experimental study of retention in educational television. *Spch Monogr.*, 1957, 24, 31-38.

Nelson, H. E. The effect of variation of rate on the recall by radio listeners of "straight" newscasts. *Spch Monogr.*, 1948, 15, 173-180.

Nichols, R. G. Factors in listening comprehension. *Spch Monogr.*, 1948, 15, 154-163.

Overstreet, H. A. *Influencing human behavior*. New York: W. W. Norton, 1925.

Packard, V. *The hidden persuaders*. New York: David McKay, 1957.

Paulson, S. F. The effects of the prestige of the speaker and acknowledgment of opposing arguments on audience retention and shift of opinion. *Spch Monogr.*, 1954, 21, 267-271.

Pence, O. L. Emotionally loaded argument: its effectiveness in stimulating recall. *Quart. J. Spch*, 1954, 40, 272-276.

Riesman, D. The oral and written traditions. In Carpenter, E., & McLuhan, M. (Eds.), *Explorations in communication*. Boston: Beacon Press, 1960.

Ruechelle, R. C. An experimental study of audience recognition of emotional and intellectual appeals in persuasion. *Spch Monogr.*, 1958, 25, 49-58.

Sawyer, T. M., Jr. Shift of attitude following persuasion as related to estimate of majority attitude. *Spch Monogr.*, 1955, 22, 68-78.

Schachter, S. Deviation, rejection and communication. *J. abnorm. soc. Psychol.*, 1951, 46, 190-207.

Scheidel, T. M. An exploratory study of the relationship between certain organismic variables and response to persuasive speech. *Dissertation Abstr.*, 1959, 19, 3415-3416.

Scott, W. D. *The psychology of public speaking.* Philadelphia: Pearson Brothers, 1906.

Sikkink, D. E. An experimental study of the effects on the listener of anticlimax order and authority in an argumentative speech. *Sth. Spch J.*, 1956, 22, 73-78.

Skinner, B. F. *Verbal behavior.* New York: Appleton-Century-Crofts, 1957.

Smith, R. G. An experimental study of the effect of speech organization upon attitudes of college students. *Spch Monogr.*, 1951, 18, 292-301.

Smith, R. G. *Principles of public speaking.* New York: Ronald Press, 1958.

Spencer, H. The philosophy of style. In Cooper, L. (Ed.), *Theories of style.* New York: Macmillan, 1907. Pp. 270-311.

Sponberg, H. The relative effectiveness of climax and anti-climax order in an argumentative speech. *Spch Monogr.*, 1946, 13, 35-44.

Tannenbaum, P. H. Effect of serial position on recall of radio news stories. *Journ. Quart.*, 1954, 31, 319-323.

Thistlethwaite, D. L., de Haan, H., & Kamenetzky, J. The effects of "directive" and "non-directive" communication procedures on attitudes. *J. abnorm. soc. Psychol.*, 1955, 51, 3-12.

Thistlethwaite, D. L., Kamenetzky, J., & Schmidt, H. Factors influencing attitude change through refutative communications. *Spch Monogr.*, 1956, 23, 14-25.

Thomas, G. L. Oral style and intelligibility. *Spch Monogr.*, 1956, 23, 46-54.

Thomas, G. L., & Ralph, D. C. A study of the effect of audience proximity on persuasion. *Spch Monogr.*, 1959, 26, 300-307.

Thompson, W. N. A study of the factors considered by students in evaluating public discussion. *Spch Monogr.*, 1953, 20, 268-272.

Utterback, W. E., & Harding, H. F. Some factors conditioning response to argument. *Spch Monogr.*, 1955, 22, 303-308.

Wickens, D. D., & Meyer, D. R. *Psychology.* New York: Holt, Rinehart, and Winston, 1961.

Weiss, W. Opinion congruence with a negative source on one issue as a factor influencing agreement on another issue. *J. abnorm. soc. Psychol.*, 1957, 54, 180-186.

Wilke, W. H. An experimental comparison of the speech, the radio, and the printed page as propaganda devices. *Arch. Psychol.*, 1934, 25, No. 169.

Woolbert, C. H. The audience. In Bentley, M. (Ed.), Studies in social and general psychology from the University of Illinois. *Psychol. Monogr.*, 1916, 21, 37-54.

Young, K. *Social psychology.* (3rd ed.) New York: Appleton-Century-Crofts, 1958.

Zander, A., & Cohen, A. R. Attributed social power and group acceptance: a classroom experimental demonstration. *J. abnorm. soc. Psychol.*, 1955, 51, 490-492.

17

Psychology of
Radio and Television

THE BROADCASTING MEDIA ARE primarily devoted to public entertainment, not enlightenment, and we leave to others an analysis of them as instruments of commerce and recreation. Approximately twenty per cent of network programming, however, consists of speeches, interviews, panel discussions, and commentaries, intended to inform or to persuade the radio and television listener. Essentially these programs are forms of public address. In this respect only, we are concerned in this book with the psychology of radio and television.

It should be emphasized at the outset that, as Ewbank and Lawton (1952, pp. xi-xii) put it, "while the mechanics of oral communication have changed with the discovery of the telephone and the microphone, the fundamentals of good communication have not changed." The main differences between customary public address and radio speaking are that "radio speakers generally talk to individuals rather than audiences, that they use the volume appropriate for a living room, and that speakers and listeners cannot see each other." The obvious difference of television is that listeners can see speakers as well as hear them, but still "the good television speaker . . . talks as he would to a few individuals in a relatively small room," though he cannot see them.

A review of the research literature on radio and television supports these observations. Commercial broadcasters have been concerned largely with market research—the size and composition of listening audiences, and the effects of various types of sales appeals—and educational broadcasters have experimented primarily with different program formats. In most of this research there has been an implicit acceptance of the premise that the operating psychological principles applicable to public address generally carry over to radio and television speaking. We present here, therefore, only a brief comment on the mass media, following the same topical outline established in the preceding chapter and stressing those characteristics of radio and television that differentiate it, in degree if not in kind, from traditional public address.

THE RADIO AND TELEVISION AUDIENCE

It is common to think of broadcast listeners as members of a mass audience, perhaps numbered in millions rather than in traditional dozens or hundreds for public addresses, but still homogeneous and institutionalized. This is true in only a limited sense.

The Audience Is a Microcosm

The broadcast audience, like other products of the electronic industry, is miniaturized, though retaining the essential elements of traditional audiences. The so-called mass audience is only a figurative collectivity, and actually consists of hundreds or thousands of small groups, usually of family members or friends. While each listening group may be extremely homogeneous, the total audience is quite heterogeneous, especially for national network programs. Consequently it is possible to say that in its size and makeup the broadcast audience in many ways resembles a small discussion group, but that its orientation is that of a co-acting group, uniformly attending to a single communicator.

The small group facing the television screen, for example, is focused on a common stimulus, but its polarization is less than in a public address audience, and listeners may stand up, stretch, or even wander out of the room, missing a few minutes of the broadcast before they return.

There is also some operation of the social facilitation phenomenon in the television audience, but usually of much less intensity than for the usual public address situation. In the semi-darkness of the television room there is a minimum of social interplay and mutual reinforcement of listener responses. As Fine (1952) notes, with some exaggeration, the television listening group has "unity without conversation."

The most marked contrast with the public address situation, of course, is the complete lack of circular response between speaker and listener in the radio or television audience. Except for the possibility of a selected and probably atypical studio audience, no one furnishes direct feedback to the communicator. His message is identical for all listeners, and his chief handicap is his inability to observe how they perceive it and to adapt to their responses (Head, 1956, p. 427). It might be argued that Knower's (1935) study suggests a compensation for the lack of circular response, since he found that hearing a speech as an individual listener is more effective than as a member of a large audience. While this may have been true in the face-to-face situation, it can hardly apply when the speaker and listener are connected only by a wave length.

Although we have referred here largely to the television audience, much of what we have said applies equally to radio. The radio listener, however, is increasingly one who listens alone, often irregularly and semi-attentively while doing something else, such as driving a car. Because of this changing pattern of radio listening, broadcasters are shifting away from "family circle" radio programs (Meyersohn, 1957).

The Audience Is Largely Unselected

The typical public address audience is always self-selecting in some critical respects: it is made up of members of a service club, citizens interested in a lecture on current economic problems, and so on. Thus speakers can assume certain common interests, identify and appeal to them, tap common motivations, encourage social facilitation, observe individual responses and adapt to them. But this commonality exists for broadcast audiences only in the small groups facing each screen or loudspeaker; all the groups together make an extremely heterogeneous audience. What the broadcaster calls a selected audience is usually any mass audience that can be attracted to listen.

Meyersohn (1957) borrowed a concept from Georg Simmel (1950) to explain how this unselected audience situation affects the broadcaster's behavior. Conversations between two people, said Simmel, may range over many different and intimate topics, but topic choices are compromised when a third person is added. When still more persons join the group more compromises are made and conversations are increasingly restricted to areas of common interest. When enough people are involved to make a mass audience, concludes Meyersohn, "it can be expected that absolutely nothing would be of common interest, or what is of common interest would never suit those who happen to have more than superficial concern with it." Thus the broadcaster, confronted with a largely unselected audience, often deliberately appeals to those persons at its lowest level of culture and intelligence. In general he avoids controversial public issues, except on an "equal time" basis for political speakers, and tries to offend no one.

The Audience Is Relatively Passive

If it is true that radio and television appeal to a largely unselected mass audience, it is not surprising that it is also a relatively passive one.

As Gunther Anders (1956) observed, "When the world comes to us, instead of our going to it, we are no longer 'in the world,' but only listless, passive consumers of the world." Cantril and Allport (1935) made a similar observation long ago about the radio listener's acceptance of a "plethora of platitudes," and Bogart (1956, p. 34) extended the judgment to television listeners. Bogart suggested that in part this passivity comes because it takes so little effort to "take in" the broadcast message. One of the basic principles of speaker-audience relationships, we noted in Chapter 14, is that individuals respond most readily when they are highly involved in the purpose of the communication; but to the extent that broadcast audiences have no active involvement in the listening-learning process, they easily become passive (Hovland, 1954). Indeed, observation leads us to suggest that much television viewing takes place not because of serious motivation, but just because the set is on.

Not all investigators, admittedly, are concerned about passivity. Klapper (1960, pp. 234-248) is unpersuaded that television viewing withers "the critical acumen and creative abilities" of listeners, and advances the theory that all media are used by both passive and active persons to reinforce their existing motivations. Although Maccoby (1951) found little interaction in viewing groups, more research is needed on this point, as on many others related to mass media listening. On the evidence to date we conclude that passive persons are attracted to the mass media more than to other communicative situations, and that the act of listening to the mass media appears to strengthen their passive tendencies.

The Audience Is Highly Suggestible

In Chapter 14 we posited that believing is often passive, doubting active, and that positive suggestion aims at passive acceptance. Within this framework of psychological assumptions we summarize here a few observations of mass media investigators upon the suggestibility of radio and television audiences.

Radio and television tend to confer a special status upon public issues, persons, organizations, and movements, through a kind of nonlogical circular belief described by Lazarsfeld and Merton (1948, pp. 461-462): "If you really matter, you will be at the focus of mass attention and, if you *are* at the focus of mass attention, then surely you must really matter." This high status and potential potency of radio and television suggestion was dramatized by a 1961 Elmo Roper public opinion study (Tebbel, 1962). If conflicting versions of the same news story came from four different media, the persons polled would be most inclined to believe each one in this order: television 39 per cent, newspapers 24 per cent, radio 12 per cent, and magazines 10 per cent. In rating these four media as *least* believable, only 7 per cent listed television and 9 per cent radio, but 25 per cent listed magazines and 28 per cent newspapers.

Radio and television tend to create only an illusion of reality. "Modern audiences . . . have become shrewder in their demands for perfection of technique and for reliability of information," says Adorno (1954), and while Albig (1956, pp. 482-483) believes that the distortion of information, which occurs in all media, is less evident in television, the alleged reality of presentation of opinions, moods, and facts may be satisfactory but still illusory. In particular this may happen because of a tendency to present simple back-and-white alternatives to the mass audience, rather than to deal with public issues in their true complexity.

Radio and television provide a flood of information for the listener, but some investigators feel that it may serve "to narcotize rather than to energize" him. Through vicarious contact with political reality, for example, the citizen "can congratulate himself on his lofty state of interest and information, and neglect to see that he has abstained from decision and action. . . . He comes to mistake *knowing* about problems of the day for *doing* something about them" (Lazarsfeld and Merton, 1948, pp. 464-465). In his study of the responses to broadcasts of the Kefauver Committee hearings on crime Wiebe (1952) found a kind of social impotence among listeners. Although their first responses expressed concern with the common problem of crime, creating "impulses compounded of undirected energy, power fantasies, dissociation, and some impulses toward problem-solving behavior," these were followed by "much talking at a lateral deference level [complaisant conversation on side issues], but little overt effort to solve the problem," and finally by a "strong tendency to reject even the problem-solving behavior as hopeless."

LISTENERS IN RADIO AND TELEVISION AUDIENCES

In characterizing the public address audience we submitted a series of ten generalizations about the behavior of individual listeners (see pp. 282-6). There is evidence to indicate that a number of these apply with equal force to listeners in radio and television audiences. Some of these behavioral tendencies are either more or less pronounced in the context of the mass media situation, however, and we single them out for brief comment.

Accentuated Characteristics

Listeners in public address audiences tend, we said earlier, to accept ideas from those who have prestige. In the case of radio and television it appears that the media as such can give prestige to speakers and the ideas and information they present (Klapper, 1960, pp. 104-106); the Roper survey revealed high credibility for radio and television newscasters in general, not for specific ones.

In our discussion of public address listeners, we noted that they tend to believe and to do as they are told. This influence of suggestion appears to be accentuated for radio and television audiences. The classic example was the Orson Welles radio adaptation of the H. G. Wells novel, *War of the Worlds*. Broadcast as a Halloween hoax in 1938, the program simulated an "eye-witness" account of an invasion by creatures from the planet Mars, complete with descriptions of military resistance, public hysteria, and property destruction. Listeners who missed the opening announcement on the program believed what they heard, and many panicked. In his detailed analysis of the event, Hadley Cantril (1940) underscored the high suggestibility of radio listeners which complemented their belief in the credibility of radio newscasts.

Public address audience members tend, we have already said, to make stereotyped responses to stereotyped stimuli, and also to respond to the emotional connotations of words. These tendencies become more marked in radio and television audiences, in part because they are relatively passive, less critical, and more suggestible. A pioneer study of the effects of repeated motive appeals, relying heavily upon stereotyped stimuli and connotative language, was Robert K. Merton's (1946) analysis of a Kate Smith eighteen-hour broadcast urging the purchase of war bonds. A classification of her appeals revealed a heavy emphasis upon such themes as sacrifice, competition, and participation. Their effectiveness was so marked that Merton felt obliged to question the moral aspects of such use of the broadcast medium even for socially desirable causes.

Less Apparent Characteristics

Listeners in public address audiences, we indicated earlier, tend to conform to the beliefs and actions of fellow-listeners. But we also noted the significance of social facilitation in prompting conforming behavior, and must mark here that relatively little opportunity exists for facilitation in broadcast audiences. Because these audiences are not congregated, except in small and already homogeneous groups before television screens, the tendency to conformity characteristic of public address audiences is less apparent. Young (1958, p. 419) also observed that there is little collective identification in mass media audiences.

In public address audiences we reported the tendency of listeners to respond in terms of overt action that may both reinforce and implement a speaker's propositions. Again because there is no real collectivity, and

316 Psychology of Communication

consequently less social pressure, the characteristic overt responses of public address audiences are less present in radio and television listening situations. Head (1956, pp. 429-430) adds that the "reference-group theory" of the dominant influence of the small primary social group to which an individual belongs in determining his overt behavior, as in voting, militates against the possible influence of the mass media. This conclusion gained support from the Lazarsfeld, et al. (1944) study of voting behavior in 1944, but may need to be revised in the light of certain investigations of the influence on voting of political broadcasts in 1960 (see Kraus, 1962).

THE SPEAKER AND HIS RADIO AND TELEVISION AUDIENCE

In our treatment of the contributions of modern psychological concepts to rhetorical theory for public speaking (see pp. 286-305), we said much that might be repeated here. Indeed, a great deal of research on all aspects of direct and purposive communication has universal application. In this discussion, therefore, we will limit ourselves to a brief comment on the special context for radio and television speaking, and suggest a few appropriate adaptations of normal public address techniques for each medium.

Radio Public Address

Two facts are especially pertinent: the radio speaker's stimuli are completely oral; and radio public address is usually oral reading rather than speaking.

Because listening is more of a social act than private reading, Young (1958, p. 420) notes that the radio speaker's voice "carries a wealth of social connotation which aids in the transmission of meaning. The human voice is tremendously effective, especially in its emotional appeal . . . [and] the voice alone is usually more effective than visual stimulation alone." In their study of the psychology of radio, for example, Cantril and Allport (1935) found that listeners made significantly accurate judgments of the personalities of radio speakers, although on the whole these judgments were less accurate than they were uniform. On the basis of this and other studies of radio speaking, Cantril and Allport concluded that the most effective radio speakers were especially well trained in vocal techniques and had more flexibility in rate, pitch, and quality than other speakers.

Because the radio speaker cannot be seen by his listeners, he usually reads from a manuscript instead of speaking extemporaneously. This means that in constructing his speech the radio speaker must master the uncommon art of committing good oral structure and style to paper. The general characteristics of this structure and style are not substantially different for radio than for other public speaking, but the mass media communicator must always remember that he has available none of the customary visual aids to understanding, such as transitional and emphatic gestures, bodily movements, and facial expressions. Consequently radio speech writers intensify both structure and style. They give greater than usual attention to precise statements of contentions, transitions, and summaries. And they provide more than the usual quota of specific details and illustrations, phrased in simple words and relatively short sentences.

Television Public Address

Television speaking is, in many respects, more similar than radio speaking to platform address. The sight of the speaker is restored to the listener, and the combination of visible and audible codes in communication is more effective than either one singly (Young, 1958, p. 420). Thus most of what we previously said about the psychology of public address is directly applicable to television speaking. To this general rule there are two exceptions.

First, the television speaker must remember that his audience actually consists of many small groups of persons, not a single large and massed body of listeners. His role is therefore that of an invited guest in a family living room, not that of a platform orator trying to project to the back row of seats. (This fact, of course, places speakers at a disadvantage when they face a large "live" audience and also a remote television one.) Effective television speakers consequently strive for intimate and conversational style in both content and manner.

The second variant in television speaking derives from the first: each listener sees the speaker with equal clarity. Expansive gestures, often necessary when addressing an audience in a large auditorium, seem exaggerated and unnatural on the intimate television screen. Through camera close-ups listeners get a microscopic and not a telescopic view of the speaker; facial expressions appropriate to platform address may appear as contortions. Thus the hallmark of television speaking is natural but restrained public speaking.

The use of a speech manuscript is standard for radio but it creates special problems on television. In the listener's living room he would hardly expect a guest to converse with his eyes glued to a prepared text. He is no more charmed by having his television guest read to him. Effective television speakers avoid manuscripts; though some use mechanical aids out of camera range, like cue cards or teleprompters, the best device, as in public speaking, is a set of note cards for idea sequences and an extemporaneous style.

In summary we restate our premise that communication by radio and television is a specialized form of public address, and that the psychological principles of effective public address are generally applicable to the mass media. At the same time we would note that significant research gaps exist in our understanding of both techniques and effects of communication by radio and television. In surveying what we now know about these matters both Hovland (1954) and Klapper (1960) have only emphasized what remains to be discovered by careful and intensive psychological research.

REFERENCES

Adorno, T. W. Television and the patterns of mass culture. *Quart. Film, Radio, and Television,* 1954, 8, 213-235.

Albig, W. *Modern public opinion.* New York: McGraw-Hill, 1956.

Anders, G. The phantom world of TV. *Dissent,* 1956, 3, 14-24.

Bogart, L. *The age of television.* New York: Frederick Ungar, 1956.

Cantril, H. *The invasion from Mars.* Princeton: Princeton University Press, 1940.

Cantril, H., & Allport, G. W. *The psychology of radio.* New York: Harper & Row, 1935.

Ewbank, H. L., & Lawton, S. P. *Broadcasting: radio and television.* New York: Harper & Row, 1952.

Fine, Bernard J. *Television and family life: a survey of two New England communities.* Boston: Boston School of Public Relations and Communication, 1952.

Head, S. W. *Broadcasting in America.* Boston: Houghton Mifflin, 1956.

Hovland, C. I. Effects of the mass media of communication. In Lindzey, G. (Ed.), *Handbook of social psychology.* Reading, Mass.: Addison-Wesley, 1954. II, 1062-1103.

Klapper, J. T. *The effects of mass communication.* New York: Macmillan, 1960.

Knower, F. H. Experimental studies of changes in attitude: I. a study of the effect of oral argument on changes of attitude. *J. soc. Psychol.,* 1935, 6, 315-347.

Kraus, S. (Ed.) *The great debates.* Bloomington, Ind.: Indiana University Press, 1962.

Lazarsfeld, P., Berelson, B., & Gaudet, H. *The people's choice.* New York: Duell, Sloan and Pearce, 1944.

Lazarsfeld, P. F., & Merton, R. K. Mass communication, popular taste and organized social action. In Bryson, L. (Ed.), *The communication of ideas.* New York: Harper & Row, 1948. Pp. 95-118.

Maccoby, E. E. Television: its impact on school children. *Publ. Opin. Quart.,* 1951, 15 (3), 421-444.

Merton, R. K. *Mass persuasion.* New York: Harper & Row, 1946.

Meyersohn, R. B. Social research in television. In Rosenberg, B., & White, D. M., (Eds.), *Mass culture.* New York: Macmillan, 1957. Pp. 345-357.

Tebbel, J. What news does the public believe. *Sat. Rev.,* March 10, 1962, 43-44.

Wiebe, G. D. Responses to the televised Kefauver hearings: some social psychological implications. *Publ. Opin. Quart.,* 1952, 16, 179-200.

Young, K. *Social psychology.* (3rd ed.) New York: Appleton-Century-Crofts, 1958.

18

Psychology of Stage Fright

IN THE PAST SEVERAL CHAPTERS we have been primarily concerned with how communicators adapt positively to speaking situations and influence the behavior of their listeners. In turning to the subject of stage fright we are concerned, instead, with a possible disintegrative effect of the speaking situation or of the audience upon the communicator. Conventionally the term stage fright is used to describe what happens to a speaker (actor, singer or other public performer) when he is both attracted to and repelled by the same stimulus (the audience), in an approach-avoidance conflict situation. Operationally we note that stage fright occurs most often in situations where the audience's response appears to the speaker to be unpredictable, and his consequent self-consciousness results in annoyance, frustration, or inhibition that is both observable and distracting. More formally, stage fright can be defined as speaker behavior that is disintegrated, poorly adjusted to the situation, and an interference with efficient and effective communication.

Internally the speaker with stage fright may feel nervous and confused, and even forget completely what to say next; or, as Winston Churchill once described it in physical terms, it may feel like a nine-inch square block of ice in the pit of the stomach. Externally the behavior of the speaker with stage fright may be marked by a quavering voice, muscle tension, random physical action, lack of poise, and general instability.

The phenomenon of stage fright has long been recognized by students of speech. "I turn pale at the outset of a speech," reported Cicero, "and quake in every limb and in all my soul." While such behavior is certainly not universal or inevitable, Knisely's (1951) survey of prominent contemporary public speakers revealed that even "the average experienced and successful speaker did have stage fright in at least a part of his speaking activity, but the reactions were mild and occurred infrequently." The investigator concluded that perhaps there were different types, rather than merely degrees, of the malady: "normal," or a customary response to any new and complex social situation, but one tending to decrease with repeated successful speaking experiences; and "abnormal," or an atypical response to the speaking situation, and one tending to continue even after repeated experiences.

EXPERIMENTAL RESEARCH

The amount of experimental research on stage fright is now substantial and much of it has been usefully synthesized by Clevenger (1959) and Robinson (1959). For our purpose we report on methods of measurement and then on some conclusions.

Measurement

Investigators have measured manifestations of stage fright in three ways: by means of observer rating scales for symptomatic speaker behavior, through introspective self-analyses by speakers, and through the use of various devices for recording physiological changes during the speaking act. Any of these three methods may have very high reliability, although instruments measuring differing dimensions of stage fright often seem to have comparatively poor intercorrelations.

Typical observational measures were reported by Dickens, et al. (1950), Holtzman (1951), and Clevenger and King (1961). In the latter study eighteen visible symptoms of stage fright were checked by observers, and these variables were correlated in a factor analysis that resulted in establishing three relatively independent dimensions of variation: Factor I, Fidgetiness, such as "shuffles feet" or "lacks eye contact"; Factor II, Inhibition, such as "knees tremble" or "tense face"; and Factor III, Autonomia, such as "moistens lips" or "breathes heavily." Perhaps the most significant conclusion from this study is that observable stage fright is not a simple or unitary variable.

Subjective reports by speakers on their own behavior have also added to our understanding of the nature of stage fright, in such studies as those by Chenoweth (1940), Gilkinson (1942), and Low and Sheets (1951). Various self-rating scales, questionnaires, and inventories have been developed to ascertain speaker reactions. Gilkinson, for example, employed a check list of 104 items reflecting feelings of confidence or fear in a "Personal Report of Confidence as a Speaker." Low and Sheets studied possible correlations between student evaluations of their own stage fright and their scores on various psychometric tests, such as the Minnesota Multiphasic Personality Inventory.

A third measure of stage fright has been provided by various physiological changes observed during public speech. Using a psychogalvanometer Redding (1936) measured galvanic skin response changes, and Dickens and Parker (1951) employed a sphygmomanometer and a stethoscope to measure blood pressure and pulse rate changes. In the latter experiment, for example, it was found that over 90 per cent of the subjects were measurably affected by the speaking situation in terms of its effect upon their normal pulse rates and blood pressure.

Analysis

From the accumulated research on stage fright, in studies we have cited here as well as in a number of unpublished ones reported by Clevenger (1959) and Robinson (1959) these generalized conclusions may be drawn:

1. Some degree of psychological and physiological arousal appears to be common for most speakers, whether experienced or inexperienced.

2. The disruption of communicative behavior caused by stage fright appears to be less apparent to observers than it is to the speakers. This suggests to Clevenger that observers tend to agree more on what constitutes the absence of stage fright than upon what constitutes its presence.

3. Stage fright affects both men and women. Men are more likely to have their stage fright observed; women are more likely to be aware of it themselves.

4. There is no apparent correlation between stage fright and intelligence, reasoning ability, or the more important phases of personality reflected in standard tests and inventories.

5. A reduction of stage fright appears to be correlated with increased self-confidence, and this seems to come with improved speaking ability, greater experience in speaking, and age.

These conclusions tell us a good deal about stage fright, although they do not lend specific support to any of the theoretical explanations usually advanced for it. While the construction of stage fright behavior indexes may be more important than the formulation of a general rationale, we would suggest that the concept of the communicative situation as one sometimes creating an *approach-avoidance conflict* is helpful in understanding the phenomenon of stage fright.

Modern psychologists, such as Wickens and Meyer (1961, pp. 201-225), interpret conflict situations as resulting from motive states that demand relief and consequently shape an individual's behavior. In general this behavior may take the form of *approaching* or *avoiding* an object, goal, or situation, depending upon whether or not it is desirable. It sometimes happens that a single object, goal, or situation attracts an individual, but also has characteristics that repel him; and it is this duality in its nature that creates a behavioral conflict for him. The speechmaking situation often has just these positive and negative elements. On the one hand an individual may be possessed of an idea that he feels impelled to communicate to an audience, but on the other hand he may also feel apprehensive about the very act of communicating. He may *fear* to do what he *wants* to do.

A common instance of this conflict, even for an experienced speaker, is his willingness to accept an invitation to speak upon a subject that is important to him if the request is made several months in advance. As the date draws nearer, however, he may feel timorous about fulfilling his obligation and even chide himself for having accepted it in the first place. Thus the reduction of what Miller (1959) calls the psychological distance from the stimulus has the effect of weakening his approach response and strengthening his avoidance one. Characteristic behavior in such circumstances is vacillation or inaction: an individual may be tempted to invent an excuse for escaping his commitment or he may postpone preparing for it.

The effect of this approach-avoidance conflict upon an individual is certainly not that of building up his self-confidence. Each urge to avoid the speaking situation reinforces his apprehension, and if he characteristically delays a firm resolution of his dilemma by preparing to meet it positively he has good reason for feeling less confident.

From this discussion it is evident that we believe a speaker's confidence in himself—in his ability to communicate his message clearly and persuasively, to obtain the desired response from his listeners—is an important ingredient in successful communication. Conversely, we also believe that a speaker's lack of confidence in himself may lead to that behavior we call stage fright. Note that we do not say that successful communication cannot occur without self-confidence on the part of the speaker, nor do we say that lack of self-confidence inevitably results in stage fright. What we do say is that conflicting approach-avoidance responses tend to reduce a speaker's confidence and that those responses also bear a marked resemblance to the three apparent dimensions of stage fright behavior isolated by Clevenger and King (1961): fidgetiness, inhibition, and autonomic activity.

Almost parenthetically we would note that what is sometimes called decision theory (Edwards, 1954), the effect of probabilities and incentive values on behavior, supports our view of the importance of a speaker's self-confidence. As Wickens and Meyer (1961, p. 224) phrase decision theory, and we add our own interpolations, the individual's feeling of confidence is a vital factor in this formula: *"Subject's estimate of probability* [of his own ability to persuade] × *Value to the subject of the gain or loss* [in succeeding or failing to persuade] = *Tendency to perform that particular act* [of making an effective speech]." In short, the speaker's self-confidence is in part derived from his assessment of risks *v.* rewards.

METHODS OF CONTROL

In resolving any conflict, such as an approach-avoidance situation, an individual can reinforce his tendency toward positive responses by altering his perception of his environment or by strengthening his motivation. As applied by a public speaker, this might mean trying to visualize the audience situation as potentially satisfying and to desire favorable responses from his listeners. Each of these measures will tend to create a confident attitude in approaching the act of communication. Beyond this, what more specifically can speakers do toward developing their self-confidence?

In a careful survey of thirty-five contemporary speech textbooks Edward R. Robinson (1955) found that 136 specific methods advocated for developing confidence could be grouped under three headings, and with these indicated frequencies: control of bodily activity, 71; emphasis on knowledge of the subject and preparation, 42; emphasis on the "message" of the speech, 23. Each of these categories of advice implied a separate approach to alleviating stage fright by building confidence. In an experiment using one of these approaches in teaching each experimental section of a course in public speaking, Robinson found that while there were no statistically significant differences in the effects of the three approaches, each of them did result in statistically significant gains in the self-confidence of the subjects. With this experimental support, therefore, we submit our own suggestions for developing speaker confidence.

Subject: Knowledge and Preparation

Speakers sometimes forget that they are subject to the same psychological principles that govern their audiences. If listeners attend best to what is made interesting to them, for example, the speaker will be most effective when his subject is interesting to him. If a speaker cannot generate his own enthusiasm about a topic he can hardly expect to arouse that of his hearers. Even with high interest in his subject, and in talking about it with an audience, the speaker should feel confident only when he is adequately prepared. Part of his ethos in speaking will stem from his apparent preparation to discuss his subject, the sureness of his knowledge of pertinent facts and opinions, and the expertness with which he adapts them to the information, attitudes, and beliefs of his listeners. Self-confidence is largely dependent upon a sense of personal adequacy to meet a situation; without that sense about his subject a speaker deserves to feel subject fright, if not stage fright.

Writers on the psychology of learning, such as Deese (1952), offer much sound advice that is applicable to preparation for speaking. One principle is that the rate of learning is accelerated when practice is spaced rather than massed. Another is that learning "by the whole" rather than "by the parts" is most efficient. A third principle is that a sense of meaningfulness about the learning will enhance it. For a public speaker these principles suggest that he can prepare and practice his speech most efficiently if he begins well in advance and works at frequent intervals, concentrates on the total pattern of the communication, and understands clearly his purpose and its significance.

In general it is thought that while precision of style is gained by memorization of a speech, this is offset by a consequent inability to adapt to observed audience reactions by extemporization. Many experienced speakers take a middle position in this matter by outlining their speeches on inconspicuous note cards, thus gaining in flexibility and spontaneity while at the same time feeling confident that their notes will remind them of what comes next if they need to know.

The Speaker's Focus

In an earlier discussion we characterized communication as behavior that should be subject-and-audience-centered rather than speaker-centered. This concept is closely related to the problem of avoiding stage fright. When the speaker focuses upon himself rather than upon his topic and the task of communicating about it with his hearers, he tends to become introspective, hypercritical, and even deprecatory. But being self-conscious is not the same thing as being self-confident. Effective speakers focus upon their communicative task of gaining desired responses from their listeners. They concentrate upon talking *with*, not *at* or merely *in front of*, their hearers. There is ample evidence to suggest that stage fright seldom attacks speakers who focus upon task rather than upon self.

Actual stage fright, of course, should not be confused with a degree of heightened feeling appropriate to any public performance. As reports from experienced public speakers show (Knisely, 1951), some physical tension is normal; until the speech is well under way, or perhaps even completed, the speaker naturally feels some concern about meeting his own and the audience's expectations. This concern will undoubtedly manifest itself in ways that are common to acute stage fright, such as a dry mouth or trembling hands. But the speaker who keeps his focus upon his task may find a source of energy in his tension; and he will not be disconcerted by modest autonomic responses if he recognizes them as normal.

Speech Delivery

Few persons are charmed by the unchanging expression of the face of a wooden Indian or by the unvaried ticking of a clock. They are no more inclined to attend to a speaker who lacks variety and vitality. The immobilized speaker may simply not understand the basic psychological factors involved in focusing attention and maintaining interest. More often his immobility is the result of his own physical tension, in turn resulting from his apprehensions about the speaking situation, or stage fright. Happily the same overt physical behavior that will capitalize upon the factors of attention and interest will also relieve his tension. Physiologically a state of psychological tension is reflected primarily in taut muscles, but also in respiratory and body chemistry changes. Any kind of bodily action will provide a release, and the draining off of built up energy will tend to reduce stage fright. But controlled and purposeful bodily action will have the same effect, and gain audience attention at the same time.

Thus the speaker's bodily action—and his vocalization as well, since tension is a total state—serves a significant and dual purpose. Vigorous and varied action that is keyed to what he is communicating, "suiting action to the word," should be a speaker's constant aim.

Absolute fear in the speaking situation is fortunately rare but, as we have seen, something less than absolute self-confidence is the norm, even for experienced speakers. The extinction of avoidance responses can be aided by following psychologically sound principles in preparing and practicing for speechmaking, and by focusing on the immediate task and employing purposeful bodily action while speaking.

REFERENCES

Chenoweth, E. C. The adjustment of college freshmen to the speaking situation. *Quart. J. Spch,* 1940, 26, 585-588.

Clevenger, T., Jr. A synthesis of experimental research in stage fright. *Quart. J. Spch,* 1959, 45, 134-145.

Clevenger, T., Jr., & King, T. R. A factor analysis of the visible symptoms of stage fright. *Spch Monogr.*, 1961, 28, 296-298.

Deese, J. *The psychology of learning.* New York: McGraw-Hill, 1952.

Dickens, M., Gibson, F., & Prall, C. An experimental study of the overt manifestations of stage fright. *Spch Monogr.*, 1950, 17, 37-47.

Dickens, M., & Parker, W. R. An experimental study of certain physiological, introspective and rating-scale techniques for the measurement of stage fright. *Spch Monogr.*, 1951, 18, 251-259.

Edwards, W. The theory of decision making. *Psychol. Bull.*, 1954, 51, 380-417.

Gilkinson, H. Social fears as reported by students in college speech classes. *Spch Monogr.*, 1942, 9, 141-160.

Holtzman, P. D. An experimental study of some relationships among several indices of stage fright and personality. *Spch Monogr.*, 1951, 18, 124. (Abstract)

Knisely, W. A. An investigation of the phenomenon of stage fright in certain prominent speakers. *Spch Monogr.*, 1951, 18, 124-125. (Abstract)

Lomas, C. W. The psychology of stage fright. *Quart. J. Spch*, 1937, 23, 35-44.

Low, G. M., & Sheets, B. V. The relation of psychometric factors to stage fright. *Spch Monogr.*, 1951, 18, 266-271.

Miller, N. E. Liberalization of basic S-R concepts: extensions to conflict behavior, motivation, and social learning. In Koch, S. (Ed.), *Psychology: a study of a science.* Vol. III. New York: McGraw-Hill, 1959.

Redding, C. W. The psychogalvanometer as a laboratory instrument in the basic course in speech, 1936. Reported in Clevenger, T., Jr., *op. cit.*

Robinson, E. R. An experimental investigation of certain commonly suggested teaching methods for the development of confidence in beginning students of public speaking. Unpublished doctoral dissertation, Indiana University, 1955.

Robinson, E. R. What can the speech teacher do about students' stagefright? *The Spch Teacher*, 1959, 8, 8-14.

Wickens, D. D., & Meyer, D. R. *Psychology.* (rev. ed.) New York: Holt, Rinehart, and Winston, 1961.

VI.

PERSONALITY AND SPEECH

19

Concepts of Personality

THE MEANING OF PERSONALITY

Perhaps nowhere in either the field of psychology or of speech is there greater evidence of man's ability to talk concretely about the abstract or abstractly about the concrete, or just talk, than in a discussion of personality. As long ago as 1937, G. W. Allport (1937) was able to find at least fifty definitions of the term personality, and almost as many meanings.

In our search for a definition of *personality* that would be more meaningful as well as more contemporary than the one we used in the first edition of this text, we investigated many sources. Psychologists—experimental, clinical, social, behavioral, and Gestalt—were investigated. So were anthropologists (mostly social), sociologists, linguists (psycho-, bio-, and plain), philosophers, semanticists (general and unmodified), and writers of books and articles that were directed at an audience of persons who wanted to improve themselves and sought to do so through alteration of their personalities. There was no lack of definitions, and Dr. Allport's fifty were only a beginning. By and large however, we found that the more advanced the book, the more mature the writer, and the more concerned the contents of the writing were with the subject of personality, the less the likelihood that the writing would include a specific definition.

In our study of definitions, characterizations, and concepts of personality, there were two underlying aspects that emerged. (1) A personality is as the person does. (2) A personality is in large measure what the individual thinks of himself. The first aspect emphasizes the acting out, the behavior that is apparent to the reactors other than the performer himself. The second aspect emphasizes the self-concept of the individual, the thoughts and evaluations that determine what an individual does and what he refrains from doing. Most theorists included both aspects in their concepts of personality. Emphasis, however, varied with the individual theorist and the "school" with which he identified. Behavioral psychologists tend, as we would expect, to emphasize the performance more than the beneath-the-skin reactions that preceded the given act of behavior. Gestaltists and social psychologists emphasized the pre-determining factors of behavior—the attitudes, inclinations, interests, etc. And almost all but the writers whose mission seemed to be to convince and provoke readers into improving themselves emphasized the complexity and the integrative forces that are dynamically involved in the production of that necessarily embodied entity referred to as *a personality*.

We might at this point indicate that the italicizing of the article in the last phrase of the last paragraph was not done without awareness and intention. The *a* is to emphasize the *unitary concept of personality* as well as the *uniqueness of individual* personality. In 1937, Allport (p. 48) presented a working definition that "personality is the dynamic organization within the individual of those psychophysical systems that determine his unique adjustments to his environment." The notion of uniqueness is expressed by White (1948, p. 107) when he refers to personality as ". . . an *integrated* pattern of *differential* tendencies." This, we surmise, is also what Donald Adams probably had in mind in his essay on *The Anatomy of Personality* (1954, p. 7) when he said: "By the term *personality* I shall mean an entity of the sort you are referring to when you use the first personal pronoun."

Before undertaking our own assessment of personality, we will present several additional definitions, characterizations, or evasions relative to the meaning of personality. According to Hall and Lindzey (1957, p. 9), "personality consists concretely of a set of values or descriptive terms which are used to describe the individual being studied according to the variables or dimensions which occupy a central position within the particular theory utilized." With this value judgment as a basis, we may evaluate the Kluckhohn and Murray (1948, p. 9) position that ". . . personality is the *organization* of all the integrative processes in the brain." This may be contrasted with the statistical approach of Cattell (1950, p. 2) who holds that "personality is that which permits a prediction of what a person will do in a given situation."

Guilford (1959, p. 2), acknowledging that the term personality has many meanings and many uses, gives his interpretation: "An individual personality, then, is his unique pattern of traits." Allport (1937, p. 6) says: "A trait is any distinguishable, relatively enduring way in which one individual differs from others." Along the same line, Eysenck (1953, p. 2) states: "Personality is the more or less stable and enduring organization of a person's character, temperament, intellect, and physique, which determines his unique adjustment to the environment."

With these relatively brief definitions and descriptive explanations, we are ready to consider the lengthier, omnibus statement of Krech and Crutchfield (1959, p. 609). These authors characterize or explain rather than define personality to include

. . . the individual's traits, abilities, beliefs, attitudes, values, motives, habitual modes of adjustment. It includes what we call *temperament*—the typical emotional reactions, mood states, and energetic attributes of the person—as well as what in older terminology was called *character*—the moral outlook and conduct of the person. And more than this, it includes the synthesis of all these—the particular manner in which traits, abilities, motives, and values are organized within the person. In short, it includes the *structure* of personality, that unique patterning of characteristics that constitutes an Emerson, a Beethoven, a Hitler, a Madame Curie, a corner grocer in Terre Haute, a sweeper in Calcutta, a Gaucho in the Argentine.

In the study of personality we are concerned with the *whole individual as our unit of analysis*. We seek to understand what characterizes the individual as a unified entity as he reacts to and copes with his environment. Our concern is not with the "disembodied" processes of perception, learning, thinking, emotion, motivation, but with the *person* who perceives, learns, thinks, feels, acts.

At this point the reader may say "Hold, enough, I think I have some notion of what we mean by personality." We will respect this wish by refraining from introducing still another definition of the multifaceted term. We will, however, summarize the impressions we would like to leave as a working basis for the remainder of this section.

1. Personality, as we will use the term, is an expression of many forces and influences, inherited and acquired, physical, environmental, and psychological. Because these forces are never precisely the same in two individuals, each somehow organizes and expresses his own personality.

2. Personality is the expression of the individual's values and attitudes that are modified if not initially shaped by interaction with a culture at large and a sub-culture in particular. Even more specifically, it is an expression of reaction to key persons and to established and so expected patterns of behavior in the more limited and special environment or environments in which the individual functions.

3. Personality, with all its variety of meanings, implies that there are two main kinds of reactions: a) those which determine what, in a given situation, an individual will do, and b) those which influence the reactions or effects on others of the personality-in-action with whom we are concerned.

4. The developing personality—the continuously organizing and reorganizing individual—anticipates certain reactions from his environment

and modifies his behavior-in-the-making in the light of these anticipations.

5. As a correlate of number 4 above, the individual's self-concept, his appraisal of his own personality, is determined by his anticipations and their realizations as he responds to the reactions he has evoked, or failed to evoke.

6. Although the personality is in essence the expression of relatively enduring traits organized in a relatively consistent manner so that a mode of behavior may be expected from the personality in action, there is room for "exceptional" behavior. A good natured man may occasionally be provoked to "fly off the handle" and in some way reveal hostility or resentment, and yet remain basically a good natured man. A Milquetoast does not become appreciably less timid if on only a single occasion he talks back to a store clerk.

There should be leeway for an individual who has to function in several markedly different settings to behave with relative consistency in one setting and yet in a manner apparently inconsistent in another setting. Thus, a mild mannered husband and father may be a harsh employer, or vice versa. A tight husband may, at his golf club, play the role of the big spender, big tipper. An irritable father may fairly regularly be a "hale fellow well met" among his business or professional associates. The apparent inconsistency or these differing modes of behavior may be explained on the grounds that the forces that made the "good" husband and father at home also impel him to release his built-up affect and to become a harsh employer. Conversely, the presumably insecure individual who behaves lavishly at his club has less to be lavish with at home. This, to be sure, is a relatively simple explanation of a complex of underlying causes that produce apparently inconsistent behavior. More complicated and perhaps more accurate explanations of underlying dynamisms can be supplied by representatives of the various psychoanalytic theories.

7. When one person responds to and places a value-judgment—such as "hostile" or "aggressive" or "withdrawn" or "timid" or, more severely, "paranoid" or "obsessed"—he does so as a result of interaction between his own personality and that of the individual on whom he is making a judgment. The judger is making inferences from the behavior of the judged. If he is able to make these inferences on a fair sample of behavior in a fair sampling of situations, his inferences and so his judgment may be correct. By "correct" we mean that they would be in essential agreement with the inferences of other persons who make judgments. It should be appreciated, however, that each inference and judgment and each name given to that judgment is also an expression of the individual making it. In an important sense, the individual who verbalizes a value-

judgment is revealing his own personality in the process and in the verbal product.

THE DEVELOPMENT OF PERSONALITY

A review of the many aspects and meanings of the term personality prohibits a consideration of the numerous specific factors that exercise influence in the formation of a given personality. Genetic factors such as body build, physical appearance, and native intelligence, are factors of obvious significance. Temperament, whether this is determined by our endocrine glands, or by environment, is also of obvious importance. But because no genetic factor exercises its influence except in an environment and in a culture, there would be little value in a consideration of any factor and its complexity of implications that would not exceed the space limitations and purposes of this book. Our emphasis therefore will be on the linguistic influences in a culture at large and in the more immediate environments of an individual that mold his personality and in large measure determine the formation of his self-concept.

Long before a child is born, his parents-to-be and grandparents-to-be have expectancies which have been verbalized about him (or her). Names have been tried out, and relatives put to the test as to how deserving they might be to have their names perpetuated. Feelings have been expressed in regard to possible names. Not infrequently, an old-fashioned name has to be modified to be up-dated and acceptable both to parents, deserving relatives, and the culture. Thus, even the choice of name is a function or expression of the attitude not only of a family but of a speech community, and the chosen name is determined only in part by family tradition and the sex of the newborn child.

From the very beginning of a child's conscious life, acts of behavior are accompanied by speech activity. Long before the child utters his first true words, he develops an inventory of sounds that, though pre-lingual, are nevertheless pre-determined for him. After the first two or three months, he is more and more likely to play with the sound of his environment than with the very early sounds of his reflex activity. So, not long after the birth cry and the undifferentiated crying, the child is making sounds that have cultural influences. By the time the child is seven or eight months of age, he may be imitating combinations of sounds that are frequently heard in the home. By the end of the first year, his sound inventory is selective and almost entirely that of his immediate environment. The nondescript (except to loving parents) infant begins to become a person, and a personality, as he becomes a sound imitator and a sound differentiator.

The first imitated words are accompanied by vocal tones, and these —words and tones— are expressions of attitudes prevalent in the home. The attitudes and connotations as well as the selected denotations of the words used, along with the manner in which they are used, are in an important measure a reflection of the larger environment and its cultural influences. Even before the child has uttered his first words and has begun to become a communicator, he has been influenced by verbal connotations, by human overtones that go beyond defined meanings. The communicative efforts he observes and responds to on a pre-verbal basis are potent determinants of whether, when, and how he will himself communicate. It is hardly possible to overestimate the importance of these influences which Hockett (1959, p. 359) sums up succinctly in the statement: "The emotional contexts of the child's earlier communicative participation—long before his earliest speech—establish a pattern of connotations that are germinal for the personality of the eventual adult."

PSYCHOANALYTIC CONTRIBUTIONS TO THE PARALLEL DEVELOPMENT OF SPEECH AND PERSONALITY

In his review of psychoanalytic viewpoints concerned with the interrelationships of speech and the emergence of the ego, Glauber (1958, pp. 76-78) makes a number of observations of importance for our discussion. According to Glauber, the transitional stages from babbling to communicative speech represent steps in development and change of direction from narcissistic to object-related [1] expression. When the child is able to relate to objects outside of himself, then the ego [2] has emerged as a separate mental structure. In layman's terms, the child has developed a personality, and has become a SELF whether he refers to that SELF as I or ME. "Thus speech becomes an ego function along with perception, thinking, reality testing. But because of its very nature, speech more than any other function is the symbol of the ego." (Glauber, 1958, p. 76)

Along with cultural anthropologists, psychoanalysts have observed that the ability to speak is experienced by the new speaker as a powerful achievement akin to magic. This new potency may come into conflict with speech as a tool for testing reality. On the one hand, the use of

---

[1] By *narcissistic* most psychoanalysts mean attraction or pleasure derived from concern and admiration of one's own body, normal in young children but not in older ones or in adults. By *object-relatedness* most psychoanalysts probably mean the ability to distinguish the body from its surroundings, to know where the physical and psychological self ends and matters external to it begin.

[2] The *ego* is defined as the organization of forces that "strives to integrate inner drive needs within itself and with requirements of reality and demands of conscience. The ego functions both consciously and unconsciously." (Glauber, 1958, p. 74)

words enables an individual to engage in more exact communication than is otherwise possible. The speaking child can name the object he wants, the activity that suits his mood, can say as well as do things that can be counted on to win praise and rewards. Anticipatory use of language evolves into thinking, and, according to psychoanalytic theory, consolidates consciousness. On the other hand, if mother jumps on hearing herself called "mama" and father does handsprings at hearing himself called "dada," and other key members in a child's environment can be manipulated through words, it may take some time for the child to know when this magic stops. Most children somehow learn that if words have magical power, they are not the only magicians. Some children regress when the potency of their words meets opposition from other more potent persons who also use words. Persons with psychopathologies are among those who often fail to make distinctions, for whom words continue to have magical power. They fail, at crucial times, to use words as instruments for testing reality, for projecting possible behavior, or for distinguishing between the word and the object or act. In the language of the general semanticist, they fail to distinguish between the map and the territory.

Early in the life of the child the ability to speak may have fearful consequences for both child and mother. The child who speaks and is physically separated from the mother has less excuse for direct contact with her than before words were achieved. This may traumatize both child and mother. The mother who wants her child to grow up may be torn between this wish and her need to be physically with her child; when the child calls she may answer in words rather than in her presence. If the words are not reassuring, if her tones betray anxiety rather than love, words may become an awesome barrier. The child may then regress to a prelingual stage to allay his anxiety and to recapture the warmth and reassurance of mother's physical presence.

SPEECH, CULTURE, AND PERSONALITY

In our discussion up to this point, we have frequently referred to cultural factors that influence the developing personality. We have indicated how much as well as how the key persons in the environment reflect the personalities of the key persons, their immediate environment, as well as the "filtered" influence of the larger culture. The intimate interrelationships among language, speech, culture, and personality may be appreciated from the following excerpt from the philologist Whatmough (1956, pp. 185-186).

The fact seems to be that a language is the expression of the attitude of a certain speech-community towards its culture, that is to say towards the sum total of conditions in which it lives, both natural and as transformed by human activity—a combination of external phenomena and of human responses to them, together with the unceasing interaction of the ones upon the other and all its products, including man's sensations. We say that language mirrors the psyche, and it is the culture, of a language-community.

PERSONALITY AND SELF-CONCEPT

In item 5 on page 334, we made a brief statement related to the development of self-concept, of how an individual comes to think of himself as a particular type of *I*. This point, because of its special importance for us, will now be given further consideration.

A person's self-concept is the product of the collective thoughts he entertains about himself. What does the person say about himself and how does he say it? Does he depreciate himself in the hope that his listener will refute his depreciations? How does he evaluate his assets and his liabilities? Does he have an ideal self, or an ideal of himself which is beyond his present balance of assets and liabilities? Is he doing anything to approximate his present self-concept to his ideal-self? How realistic is the ideal and to what degree is he aware of the difference and distance between his present self-concept and his ideal? Necessarily, one's self-concept is derived from interaction with others. Thus:

What we do, how we dress, what manner or mannerisms we affect, what tasks we undertake and what tasks we decline, what kind of society we seek, and so on, are determined not so much by our *actual* powers and limitations as by what we *believe to be* our powers and limitations—i.e., our "self-concepts." (Carl Rogers, unpublished paper, cited in Hayakawa, 1949, p. 299.)

If there is wide variance between one's self-concept and the concept other presumably-normal persons hold in regard to that self, then individual reassessment is in order. This does not imply, however, that the individual is invariably wrong and that 'others' are invariably correct in their evaluations. On the other hand, it is unlikely that the 'others,' whoever and how numerous they may be, are apt to be consistently and continuously wrong. On occasion it may be that "All the world is queer except maybe me and thee and sometimes I suspect thee," but this attitude also needs to stand the test of reality.

THE WELL ADJUSTING OR "NORMAL" PERSONALITY

Somehow, as a result of many interacting forces, the individual develops and incorporates dynamic forces which express his personality. Most personalities are reputed to be normal. Just what is a "normal" personality? How can we recognize it and its possessor? How does a normal personality express itself? How does an individual develop a concept of himself to feel and know that he is normal?

If we are to equate normality with mental health, or at least work on the assumption that most persons are able to distinguish between statistical normality and individual normality—or a striving for normality—we can arrive at a concept of the adjusted and mentally healthy individual and his objectives. According to the psychologist Fromm (1955), the mentally healthy individual possesses characteristics that include the following:

1. He is an unalienated and productive individual.

2. He relates to the world with love and employs his ability to reason in order to grasp reality objectively.

3. He is able to feel at one with his fellow men and yet he experiences himself as a unique individual entity.

4. He distinguishes between rational and irrational authority, and willingly accepts the rational authority of conscience and reason.

Hayakawa (1959, pp. 202-217) is, like Fromm, much concerned with the adjustment of the individual to his environment and stresses the need to distinguish between adjustment and conformity. Hayakawa uses the Rogerian term "fully functioning personality" to indicate his emphasis on the nature of good adjustment. The fully functioning personality is selective in his conformity to dominant persons and domineering influences in his environment. He does not do what everyone else (or most everyone else) in his environment does. Instead he relates to his environment as follows: ". . . he is *in* and *of* the society of which he is a member, but he is not a prisoner of that society."

The well adjusted, or perhaps better, the *well adjusting personality* is not necessarily a happy one, or one free of anxiety. His feelings are, however, determined by objectively real circumstances. His feelings are appropriate to the circumstances, and they change, though not necessarily immediately, as conditions change.

A sane person is not necessarily free of anxiety and fear and doubt and foreboding—if there are objective reasons for these feelings— . . . because such feelings can arise from non-neurotic sources in this troubled world—so that *externally he (or she) may* look just *as troubled and act just as troubled as a neurotic person* because there *are* troubles in the world which cause doubt, anxiety, and foreboding. *But his troubles would be real ones and not self contrived ones.* . . . Sanity does not mean the solution of all problems (cultural or psychological or economic, or whatever) but merely the abolition or avoidance of these problems which we create for ourselves through lack of self-insight. (Hayakawa, 1959, p. 216)

The reader may decide for himself how and when Hayakawa's characterization of the thinking and attitudes of the well adjusting person is to be reconciled with the ancient advice that "where ignorance is bliss 'tis folly to be wise."

It is of more than passing importance to appreciate that differences in intelligence and perceptiveness may give one individual cause for concern and foreboding where another may continue to be unconcerned and secure. On the other hand, some persons, despite intelligence, begin to worry about possible misfortune when the likelihood of misfortune is relatively remote. The fully functioning individual does not leave his home to camp out because most accidents that man is heir to occur in the home. He does not become anxious the moment his child is sent on an errand that requires crossing the street, or going down to a basement, or throwing on a light switch that is in good repair. On the other hand, he does not send a boy on an errand that should be performed by a man; he is careful that his light switches are in good repair, and that the steps leading to his cellar are clear of objects that might become hazards.

It may seem to the reader that the characteristics and goals of the well adjusting personality are beyond his reach. In measuring himself against them he falls short. Is he then to consider himself poorly adjusted or neurotic? By no means! If the individual is aware of his limitations, if he does whatever he can in the *direction of continuing his adjustments* and works without anxiety toward the *ideal* of the well adjusting or fully functioning personality, he is probably better adjusted than most. Within this concept there is even room for a little neuroticism.

SPEECH AND PERSONALITY

Stated and implied many times throughout this chapter and in earlier discussion is the observation that speech and personality parallel one another and that personality is directly expressed in speech. This generalization holds both for well adjusted individuals and for those whose problems of adjustment direct them to psychotherapists for help. Psychiatrists, aware of the personality-speech relationship, stress the importance of observing the patient's speech behavior. Ian Stevenson (1959, pp. 197 and 199), writing on the psychiatric interview, indicates that:

We now notice not only what the patient says but his manner of saying it as well, for this may show what his words conceal.

Emotions show themselves in many and sometimes unexpected ways. The patient's arrangement and manner of presenting his verbal statements reveal much. The psychiatrist should note what the patient says first (both at the beginning of an interview and subsequently in response to questions). What he talks about most, what he returns to many times, and what he omits or glides over quickly. . . . Unusual speed of speech, hesitations, blockings, amnesias, and confusions all deserve attention as signs of emotion, and hence, clues to the significance of events or topics. The order of the patient's remarks deserves attention, and especially the connections of thoughts associated in one sentence or adjoining ones. Verbal associations betray affective links.

Psychotherapists sensitive to verbal behavior are aware of the significance of quality and pitch changes in the client's voice, as well as the rate and the over-all fluency pattern. Neither do they overlook the significance of non-verbal behavior. Gestures, especially those which are autistic and tic-like, changes in skin color (referred to as skin talk), are important. Stevenson (1959, p. 199) advises ". . . the psychiatrist should watch for the play of emotion in the patient's face, in the posture of his body, and in the movements and gestures of his limbs."

Before leaving this point, words of caution are in order. It takes long and intensive training for a psychotherapist to know how to interpret affective reaction in his client. Unless the reader has had such training, he is not in a position to make firm judgments as to the state of mental health of his associates. We know, however, that we do assess persons by their speech behavior; we seek the company of some and avoid the company of others in part because of the way their speech behavior—voice, language, and gestures—influences our reactions. We project while listening and talking; if our empathic reactions make us uncomfortable, we are apt to avoid the cause of the discomfort. If our empathic reactions are comfortable, we are likely to seek the source in the future. Such inclinations are consonant with the normal drives to seek the pleasurable and to avoid the painful.

We have deviated somewhat from a direct answer to the questions relative to how a well adjusting personality expresses itself. These deviations were intended to highlight, by implication, what the trained psychotherapist looks for in his clients as indicators of poor adjustment, and the cause of poor adjusting. We will now return to more direct answers and more positive statements about the speech behavior of well adjusting personalities.

NORMAL SPEECH BEHAVIOR

Words

The person who is "of a culture but not its prisoner" speaks for himself and of himself, but unless he is talking *to* himself he is mindful of his listener. The words he selects initially, or reselects when he discovers that his intended meaning is not clear, are determined by what he anticipates his listener will understand. If he has listeners, and he has reason to believe at the outset that their backgrounds and understandings vary, he will choose those words that are likely to be understood by all or most of his listeners. If the reactions to his words indicate that his anticipatory assessment was wide of the objective, he makes necessary adjustments. If he truly wishes to communicate, he will not just speak his mind and let the words fall wherever and however they may.

The authors of this book, with many years of teaching experience in secondary schools and on the college and university levels, are aware that not a few of their colleagues engage in monologues before their students. These colleagues all too often speak aloud to themselves, and for themselves, without responding to student reaction or, if they do respond, they inhibit any impulse to do anything about it. The instructor who reads his thoughts from notes or from memory, or who extemporizes or improvises before an audience without modification that should result from listener reaction, is neither teaching nor communicating. If he does not ask himself what the students who are exposed to him are doing or thinking, he has an obligation to ask himself what, beyond his filling an academic period with word-like sounds, *he is doing before his students.*

Our criticism does not imply that all instruction should be carried out in the shortest possible words chosen from the thousand most frequently used in a linguistic system. It does imply that unusual words, or special words, require definition, explanation, or example so that the speaker's thoughts as well as the words are intelligible and provocative of immediate thought and continued thinking on the part of the listener.

Voice

The voice of the speaker—the variations in loudness, quality, initial pitch and range of pitch—should reflect the thinking, and feeling, of the speaker. The well adjusting speaker's voice is under control; variations are consonant with meaning and neither the speaker nor the listener need be surprised and wonder "Just what did that voice change mean?" The voice of the well adjusting person *reveals* rather than *betrays* his intentions about what he is saying.

Unless there is some organic anomaly, the well adjusting person's voice should leave no listener doubt as to the sex and relative maturity of the speaker. Again, in the absence of organic anomaly, the speaker's voice should be pleasant or at least produce no negative or wish-to-avoid listener response. It should be emphatic when emphasis is needed, and assertive when assertiveness is required, and yet it should not express confusion between an attitude of emphasis and one of chronic assertiveness. The voice should be easily heard, and yet not be overriding; it should be capable empathically of evoking a sympathetic response without suggesting a plaintive whine or chronic wish for sickliness.

Unless the speaker is intentionally employing innuendo, irony, or sarcasm—and these should not be chronic states—vocal changes should be consonant with the words used, and these in turn with any accompanying gestures.

Gestures

Gestures, as we indicated very early in this book, are used to emphasize meanings, to express feelings, and as (non-verbal) substitutes for words. The well adjusting speaker uses them for these purposes. Occasionally he may use gestures in the hope that the person he had thought would understand his words, but hadn't, might better be able to understand his more common if not completely international gestures. In any event, gestures should enhance rather than impair the meanings the speaker intends. When gestures distract, meaning is impaired.

The speaker's gestures, like his words, are derived from the speech community and should reflect this influence. Though the gestures conform to the culture, they, again like the specific selection of his words, also express individuality. The visible components of speech are produced and controlled by the individual speaker, and so they become his gestures.

The well adjusting person shows no concern about his gestures unless he finds that they are giving the listener-observer cause for concern. He does not inhibit gestures that will out, nor does he consciously and belatedly produce a gesture past its time to be out. The well adjusting speaker is aware, but without anxiety, that his movements have meaning, but he does not feel impelled to hasten to a psychotherapist to find out just what his last eye-twitch meant. On the other hand, the person who wishes to maintain himself as well adjusting, will seek counsel if he discovers that he has a recurrent tic-like movement that is produced in repeated situations, or with a given person or persons, or in a particular place.

THE SPEAKER-LISTENER RELATIONSHIP

Communication of thought and sharing of feelings are enhanced when well adjusting persons get together with insight into their speech behavior. Such insight should include occasional failure to understand the words, the voice, and the gesture of the speaker of and at the moment. Well adjusting persons, who are speaker-listeners or listener-speakers, appreciate that when in one role they should be ready to assume the other, and that both roles may be unified in the concept speaker (listener), about to be listener (speaker), and so on.

The listener, whether or not he is about to be a speaker, tries to determine a speaker's intention(s) so that he as listener can understand the meanings of the words he hears and sees. The well adjusting listener gives the speaker the benefit of the doubt, if he believes that there is some inconsistency between the speaker's intentions and the usual meaning of the words he has heard. The listener is careful, of course, first to ascertain whether in a given situation and context the speaker's meanings rather than his own are appropriate. The listener must be ever mindful that words have many meanings, and the more often the word is used, the more meanings it will have. The listener is aware that the connotations and affective reactions to words are more varied and even more individualized than the denotative meanings of words. If there is apparent inconsistency between meaning and intention, whether it be on the subjective or connotative sphere or the more objective denotative direction, the well adjusting listener assumes that the error is not necessarily the speaker's.

The well adjusting listener (speaker) as well as speaker (listener) appreciates the differences in the purposes and functions of speech which we discussed in Chapter 3. (Such appreciation does not necessitate that Chapter 3 should have been read.) He is sensitive to the non-communicative functions, the social gestures and expressive uses of speech that often replace direct activity. He is aware that "Good morning" is usually a way of indicating awareness of presence with a wish to be friendly and only rarely a commentary on the state of the weather. Hayakawa, who uses the term *presymbolic elements* where we use *non-communicative functions* of speech offers this advice to the literal-minded who do not intuitively sense the difference:

We cannot restrict our speech to the giving and asking of factual information; we cannot confine ourselves strictly to statements that are literally true, or we should often be unable to say even "pleased to meet you" when the occasion demanded. The intellectually persnickety often tell us that we ought to "say what we mean" and "mean what we say," and "talk only when we have something to talk about." These are, of course, impossible prescriptions. (Hayakawa, 1949, p. 78)

Well adjusting persons make no demands for the speaking of "literal truths." They interchange greetings to pass the time of day and do not feel impelled to utter or to listen to undying truths with each evocation. Literal mindedness has its penalties, and intuitive understanding of the many functions of speech has its rewards. The well adjusting young lady, of any age, knows intuitively what most men learn from experience. She knows, for example, that help is more likely to be offered for a stalled car standing hood open at the side of the road if the answer to an inquiring stranger's "Having trouble?" is "Yes, and I wish I knew what to do about it" rather than "Of course I'm having trouble, you oaf, or why would I be stalled here!" Literal minded drivers repair their own cars, and replace their own flattened tires or have them towed for repair. The listener who understands the speaker's intentions appreciates that "Having trouble?" may well mean "I know you're having difficulty and I think that I may be able to help you, but I don't want to be too forward. If you give me any encouragement, I'll do the friendly thing. If you don't, I'll be on my way." [3] The literal minded person who at parties is likely to be a flat tire, fixes his own flat tire on the roads. The well adjusting person is more likely to get some help!

In the next chapter, some of the implications of the not-so-well adjusted personality's linguistic habits will be given further consideration. We will also consider the deviant uses and the deviations of language and speech that reflect the severely neurotic and psychotic personalities.

REFERENCES

Adams, D. K. The anatomy of personality. *Doubleday papers in psychology.* New York: Doubleday, 1954.

Allport, G. W. *Personality.* New York: Holt, Rinehart, and Winston, 1937.

Cattell, R. C. *Personality.* New York: McGraw-Hill, 1950.

Eysenck, H. J. *The structure of human personality.* London: Methuen; New York: Wiley, 1953.

Fromm, E. *The sane society.* New York: Holt, Rinehart, and Winston, 1955. (See also Fromm, E. *Man for himself.* Holt, Rinehart, and Winston, 1947.)

Glauber, I. P. In Eisenson, J. (Ed.), *Stuttering: a symposium.* New York: Harper & Row, 1958. Pp. 171-220.

Guilford, J. P. *Personality.* New York: McGraw-Hill, 1959.

Hall, C. S., & Lindzey, G. *Theories of personality.* New York: Wiley, 1957.

Hayakawa, S. I. *Language in thought and action.* New York: Harcourt, Brace & World, 1949.

Hayakawa, S. I. The fully adjusted personality. In S. I. Hayakawa (Ed.), *Our language and our world.* New York: Harper & Row, 1959.

Hockett, C. P. *A course in modern linguistics.* New York: Macmillan, 1959.

Kluckhohn, C., & Murray, H. A. *Personality in nature, society, and culture.* New York: Knopf, 1948.

[3] Hayakawa (1949, p. 79) cites Dr. Karl Menninger's interpretation of the psychological meaning of "Got a flat tire?" as follows: The "question" means: "Hello—I see you're in trouble. I'm a stranger to you but I might be your friend now that I have a chance to be if I had any assurance that my friendship would be welcomed. Are you approachable? Are you a decent fellow? Would you appreciate it if I helped you? I would like to do so but I don't want to be rebuffed. This is what my voice sounds like. What does your voice sound like?" (Dr. Karl Menninger, in *Love Against Hate,* Harcourt, Brace & World, 1942).

Krech, D., & Crutchfield, R. S. *Elements of psychology*. New York: Knopf, 1959.

Menninger, K. *Love against hate*. New York: Harcourt, Brace & World, 1942.

Stevenson, I. The psychiatric interview. In S. Arieti (Ed.), *American handbook of psychiatry*. Vol. I. New York: Basic Books, 1959.

Whatmough, J. *Language*. New York: St. Martin's Press, 1956.

White, R. W. *The abnormal personality*. New York: Ronald Press, 1948.

20

Verbal Behavior of Not-So-Well Adjusted Personalities

IN THIS SECTION WE SHALL consider some aspects of the verbal behavior of persons who are not-so-well adjusted. In this population are included some persons who are chronically and "mildly" maladjusted and some whose difficulties appear only occasionally under conditions of special stress. For both groups the maladjustments tend to become evident in situations in which most persons are able to take in stride, with little or no evidence that any special adjustment or readjustment are necessary because of stress.

The subjects of our discussion are, by and large, working members of the community. They are likely to be hard-working, conscientious persons. Many, in fact, are obviously hard-working and almost obviously conscientious. A few may be unusually productive, but their productivity may be incidental to their expenditure of energy and not directed to anyone's interests except perhaps their own. Some members of the not-so-well adjusted group make open demands that if adjustments are to be made they are to be made by others to them. Some are hostile and reject adjustments in either direction. Still others may be querulous, or self-righteous, and insist that only their concept of what is right and proper become the standard of behavior for the community. A small number may be included with those who practice helplessness. This practice often results in placing the burden of adjustments and often the assumption of responsibilities on other members of the community.

THE NON-COMMUNICATIVE PERSON

The so-called non-communicative person is, in a strict sense, one who speaks *only* to communicate. For reasons related to his individual dynamics, his verbal efforts are usually limited to informing someone about what he specifically thinks, or wants to have done. He is not inclined to establish communion through his speaking, neither is he inclined to be verbally gentle or even verbally hostile. The so-called non-communicative person lets you know what he thinks, and then he is through with talking. If you fail to understand this speaker, he may repeat what he has said, working on the apparent assumption that you the listener must understand him and that his words, or his manner, require no modification. His words, of course, are logical, carefully ordered, and precisely articulated. His utterances mean, word for word, what the dictionary defines them to mean. Unfortunately, the words do not always convey a message to the listener because their speaker has failed to take the situation, the listener's readiness, his background, or his interests into consideration. Nor does this speaker fully understand his own intentions or appreciate either why he is talking or why he is deserving of a listener.

THE LOGICAL SPEAKER

This not-so-well adjusted person is a close cousin of the compulsively logical speaker. Ruesch [1] (1957, p. 127) characterizes the latter as one:

. . . who repeats the same statement or action without regard for the impact or the effect. . . . In daily life we meet this person as the overconscientious, meticulous, orderly individual who endeavors to classify experiences into categories. Such an individual is unaware that his statements convey little meaning to others and that they serve principally to alleviate his own anxiety.

The speech behavior of the compulsively logical person matches his over-all behavior. Gestures, words, and sentences have a remarkable nicety about them. His vocabulary is extensive, and features many critical terms. His verbal observations are timed so that the carefully chosen words can be precise as to moment and meaning. This speaker is less likely to initiate conversation, or to continue conversation on a social level than he is to make statements about other persons' statements. Often his verbalizations become conversation stoppers because they cre-

[1] This and other quotations from Ruesch in this chapter reprinted from *Disturbed Communication*, by Jurgen Ruesch, M.D. Copyright 1957 by W. W. Norton & Company, Inc., New York, N. Y. By permission of the publisher.

ate an "on guard" attitude in the original speaker who may have been talking to pass the time of day rather than to evaluate the specific qualities of the day. Small talk is not for the anxious and compulsively logical speaker. He has no appreciation for the importance of the trivial. Life is real, life is earnest, and he is grave about its goal.

The anxiously logical speaker does not seem to be concerned about the feelings of his listeners. As a speaker, this not-so-well adjusted person is more concerned with saying what he has to say than with determining the purpose or intent of the other speaker or listener. It may well be, of course, that the apparent obliviousness is a defense against the individual's finding out what the purpose of his own speaking might really be. It may, in short, be a defense against anxiety.

A conversation between two anxious, overly logical speakers is more likely to consist of synchronized monologues than of a free give and take. Neither speaker is likely to acknowledge the intent of the other; nor is either speaker likely to observe the expressed feelings or needs intended by the other's utterances. Because they are primarily concerned with their own verbalizations, true conversation is virtually precluded. If conversation does take place it is likely to take the form of a coldly logical repetition or restatement of the words of the last utterance. One may also hear such statements as "But ———— doesn't mean what you say it means. The dictionary says ————."

According to Ruesch (1957, pp. 129-130), the clinical history of the overly logical (compulsive) speaker includes a background of parental pressure *to do and say things properly* before the individual as a child is mature enough to appreciate the meaning of either the act or the words. Says Ruesch:

Because of the premature demands for mastery, the logical person learned early in life to ape the verbal statements of adults; the memorizing of words and sentences rather than the inquiry into what these words stood for on the part of the youngster satisfied the parents of precocious children. The time needed for developing analogic understanding was not granted them, nor were they shown how to react to other people in non-verbal terms. Pleasure thus was taken out of the process of communication, save for the critical biting, and sarcastic performances which usually took place in the family.

The non-communicative and compulsively logical speakers are likely to be persons who as children have been denied the pleasures that speech provides. Speech then serves limited purposes, or takes on or emphasizes other purposes. These may be for revealed or concealed hostility, for defense, and for the avoidance of social contact. These tend to become both the medium and the expression of the speaker's poor adjustment. Fundamentally, these speakers cannot engage in true communication with others because they are not in good communication with themselves. Having been denied the pleasures of speaking, they are insensitive to the needs and purposes of other speakers. Having become fearful of projecting feelings and attitudes, they are unable to listen with a wish to be understanding. Until they learn to listen and respond so that they are able *". . . to see the expressed idea and attitude from the other person's point of view, to sense how it feels to him, to achieve his frame of reference in regard to the thing he is talking about"* (Rogers, 1953, p. 55), they will continue to be among the not-so-well adjusted speakers. This ability to project and to see things for the moment from the point of view of the other speaker does not carry with it an obligation to agree with the other viewpoint. It does imply that often there can be disagreement without associated disagreeableness.

THE UNDER-TALKER

There are persons who achieve a reputation for being good conversationalists by virtue of knowing when to punctuate another speaker's remarks with "uh-huh's" or, by way of variety, lengthy "mm's." In some instances these speakers are merely maintaining contact by their sound signals. These sounds permit the more articulate speaker to believe that he has a listener, without need to pause for a more searching inquiry. Not a few elderly persons have assured us of how much they enjoy conversing with these monosyllabic, non-verbal respondents.

There is, of course, nothing wrong with saying "uh uh" or "You don't say" when it serves the purpose of continuing a conversation and does not interfere with the first speaker's intent. Something is wrong, however, when these same sounds are used in situations which call for more elaborate and more specific responses. Such limited sound signalling suggests a wish to avoid becoming involved in a true communicative interchange. It may suggest an unwillingness to attend to speech content closely enough to think through an appropriate response. One may suspect that underlying this type of undertalking there may be a feeling of inadequacy, a basic lack of self worth that engenders a fear of involvement. In some instances such feelings and such fears may go back to childhood and a home that featured one word leading to another and still another with accompanying release of hostility. Children from such homes learn to avoid linguistic involvements. This fear may continue into adult life and explain some undertalkers' speech behavior.

There are other undertalkers who use as few words as possible, who respond to verbal situations but seldom initiate conversation. They say what they must, often in a manner that suggests shyness and even a wish to escape from the possible consequences of their words. Among adolescents and adults who have brought this problem to psychotherapists a common familial history has been found. As children, these reluctant talkers failed to receive a satisfactory acknowledgement of their early communicative attempts. Some may have been told that children are to be seen and not heard; others may have been ridiculed or criticized for asking foolish questions, or knowing so little, or speaking so stupidly. A few may have had parents who overwhelmed the children with lengthy answers beyond the need of the situation or the capacity of the children. Occasionally we find that parents have distorted the child's question and have given him a sense of guilt which, in the first place, is probably a product of their (the parents') projection. Distorted answers, poorly timed answers, lengthy replies which exceed the need of the situation are all clinically associated with disturbances in the ability to engage in communication, and so in disturbances of personality.

THE OVER-TALKER

There are many speakers who make their point and who would succeed in their communicative efforts—if they only knew when or how to stop. Some of these speakers remind us of children who present a reasonable excuse for a bit of behavior and who would be convincing if only they were not so insistent and reiterative about their explanations. Many of these speakers are anxious individuals. Perhaps, like the children, they are afraid to conclude their talking because of their fear of the consequences. In their overtalking they betray their fears, and often their guilt-laden anxieties.

Most of us have been involved in social gatherings when, after considerable chatter, a sudden silence fell. Among hosts who measure the success of their parties by the length and loudness of the chatter, any measurable period of silence is the void to be avoided. We have known some hostesses who ran in panic from their kitchens to find out what was wrong because they became aware of a moment of disquieting silence. Occasionally we find guests who become as uncomfortable as their hosts when there is a period of silence. They twitch, they redden, they move in their chairs, and not infrequently they assume the responsibility of breaking the silence by uttering something, almost anything, to fill the void. We have known persons who admitted to memorizing "void fillers" so that they would not have to contend with silent periods at social gatherings. Our impression of some of these persons who seem unable to tolerate any period of silence is that they were apprehensive and inadequate. Somehow they were also burdened with a sense of fear which impelled them to keep away from silence.

There are some silence-breakers who might better be included among the "verbal pouncers." In conversations they listen not to what is being said but for an opportunity to break in and speak their piece. This piece may have little or no relationship with either the topic or the trend of the conversation. But this does not seem to matter. According to their "rules" any measurable silence entitles them to intrude their topic. We knew one middle-aged woman who went from group to group at a large gathering and spoke her same piece before each group. Occasionally she had something to say that was amusing, if heard but once. It ceased to be amusing if by chance you also changed groups and heard the apropos-of-nothing remarks two or three times.

We are not certain of what motivates the verbal pouncers. We conjecture that they must feel insecure and somehow need to say something rather than to play the role of listener. They are, in fact, poor listeners and so may be included among the anxious persons who fear that if they listen they may be expected to respond to the particular content and purpose of a speaker, and do not feel adequate for such demands. According to Ruesch (1957, p. 135), "an analysis of the communicative network in which *anxious people* participate reveals the existence of excitation which exceeds the capacity for reception, evaluation, or transmission of that particular person."

The persons we have described have worked out individual defenses against anxiety. They talk, or fail to talk, in different ways, but they share common dynamics and common backgrounds. They are unable to participate in a conversation as equal participants because they are not prepared to listen—to evaluate what they hear and to respond in terms of the what and the how, the content and the manner, of the other speakers. Nor are they able to speak in a manner which would invite continued conversation on another person's level of thinking. The over-all result often is a jamming of the normal networks of communication. The members of the network are poor receivers, poor transmitters, and in general inadequate to maintain a normal communicative process. Because they cannot completely avoid communication, or at least avoid becoming involved in networks of communication, their inadequacies and anxieties grow, often concealed from themselves but just as often revealed to perceptive listeners and observers.

We should not like to leave the impression that all talkative persons are to be included among the not-so-well adjusted. There are many talkative persons who are outgoing and who wish to give—or to share freely—of their thoughts and their feelings. Some specialize in telling amusing anecdotes, but do not limit themselves to this line of talk. If they do not feel the need to top another fellow's stories, or to intrude with "This isn't the way I heard it," there is no reason to equate over-talking with maladjustment. Above all, *if they are able to listen and then to respond in terms of what someone else has said,* we may assume that the verbosity is a form of giving rather than a form of creating a one way pseudo-communicative system.

THE TANGENTIAL SPEAKER

Among the most provoking of not-so-well adjusted persons are the tangential respondents. These persons specialize in replying to an incidental aspect of a statement in disregard of the intent but not of some of the words of the initial speaker. This type of verbal acknowledgement is referred to by Ruesch (1957, p. 54) as a *tangential reply.* Unfortunately, many parents unwittingly make such acknowledgements to the communicative efforts of their children. For example, an enthusiastic youngster may hold his first artistic effort up to his mother for acceptance if not admiration. If the mother's reply to "Look what I've done" is "Johnny (or more sternly, John) go wash your dirty hands and face," she has replied tangentially. The child's purpose in speaking has been ignored. But something the child did, and from the mother's point of view an undesirable something, was attended to critically.

The tangential respondent does not ignore the communicative effort of the initial speaker. What is ignored is the speaker's intention and the speech content. Few children are able to cope with such responses and to redirect their parents' attention to their speech purposes. Had the child been able to say "Why of course, Mother, I'll wash up soon—now look at what I've done," he might have been able to help his mother as well as himself toward better communication. Unfortunately, many children who are victims of tangential responses themselves become expert in this technique of speaking. As they grow up they respond to statements with side remarks that bear upon an incidental but not essential aspect of the first speaker's statement. Ruesch (p. 55), who has studied this form of *qualitatively deviant and damaging acknowledgements,* describes the results of the tangential response as follows:

By countering with a side remark, he confuses the sender, who does not understand the connection between statement and reply. The counterstatement of the receiver may bear upon any aspect of the initial statement; it may emphasize the type of language used, pick up one of the qualifications, comment on the emotions of the sender, or illuminate another facet of the same topic. In replying tangentially, the receiver deprives the sender of the pleasure of being understood; at the same time, he makes a bid for control by launching another statement which he expects to be acknowledged in turn.

In any sizeable gathering we are likely to find at least one tangential speaker. They are persons who must protect their sense of superiority either by devastating the initial speaker or by taking control of a conversation through the use of not quite relevant wit. There are no certain defenses against tangential speakers, but some of the following have been used with success. (In trying them it is important to remember that the tangential speaker is really not sure of himself or he would not protest and spar quite so loudly.) One might say: "You know, it is just barely possible that you may have something in what you just said. It may be worth a thought, but not just now." Or, one might say: "Why, I didn't know you were listening. How good of you." Or, perhaps better, the initial speaker might recounter with: "Say, now, that is an answer if ever I've heard one." All these, of course, are themselves types of tangential replies and are not really recommended either in the interest of social conversation or of a meaningful interchange of information. If these defensive techniques are to be used at all, they should be employed by persons with good verbal facility who are tough enough to accept possible consequences. As an additional precaution, we should like to point out that tangential conversations are frequently carried out by schizophrenic psychotics. These disturbed persons, however, are not apparently concerned with the effects of their remarks on one another.

Under some circumstances of stress, we are all capable of some of the misevaluations of meaning and intent that characterizes tangential speakers. Dorothy Parker, we think, has caught the spirit of this misadventure in meaning in her story "Here We Are." The misevaluators are two newlyweds in a compartment on a train about to take them off on their honeymoon.

"I guess I will take this darned old hat off," she said. "It kind of presses. Just put it up on the rack, will you, dear? Do you like it, sweetheart?"

"Looks good on you," he said.

"No, but I mean," she said, "do you really like it?"

"Well, I'll tell you," he said. "I know this is the new style and everything like that, and it's probably great. I don't know anything about things like that. Only I like the kind of a hat like that blue hat you had. Gee, I liked that hat."

"Oh, really?" she said. "Well, that's nice. That's lovely. The first thing you say to me, as soon as you get me off on a train away from my family and everything, is that you don't like my hat. The first thing you say to your wife is you think she has terrible taste in hats. That's nice, isn't it?"

"Now, honey," he said, "I never said anything like that. I only said—"

"What you don't seem to realize," she said, "is this hat cost twenty-two dollars. Twenty-two dollars. And that horrible old blue thing you think you're so crazy about, that cost three ninety-five."

"I don't give a darn what they cost," he said. "I only said—I said I liked that blue hat. I don't know anything about hats. I'll be crazy about this one as soon as I get used to it. Only it's kind of not like your other hats. I don't know about the new styles. What do I know about women's hats?"

"It's too bad," she said, "you didn't marry somebody that would get the kind of hats you'd like. Hats that cost three ninety-five. Why didn't you marry Louise? You always think she looks so beautiful. You'd love her taste in hats. Why didn't you marry her?"

"Ah, now, honey," he said. "For heaven's sakes!"

"Why didn't you marry her?" she said. "All you've done, ever since we got on this train, is talk about her. Here I've sat and sat, and just listened to you saying how wonderful Louise is. I suppose that's nice, getting me all off here alone with you, and then raving about Louise right in front of my face. Why didn't you ask her to marry you? I'm sure she would have jumped at the chance. There aren't so many people asking her to marry them. It's too bad you didn't marry her. I'm sure you'd have been much happier.[2]

THE "HELPLESS" SPEAKER

Among the chronically not-so-well adjusted are persons who are habitually helpless and yet who manage to have their way, sometimes from the ever available and habitually helpful. The "helpless" one sounds as if he is always sorry for and about himself. He is plaintive and utters words that sound as if they were self-accusatory and self-depreciating. The same remarks are likely to be repeated, depressing the listener with their recurring words, rhythms, and upward inflecting pitch patterns. Yet somehow these complaints also suggest accusation. In the complaints and assertions of helplessness there is an implication that the individual has been rendered helpless by circumstances beyond his control and that it is incumbent upon some listener to offer aid. Moses, in his *Voice of Neurosis* (1954, pp. 90-91) observes:

Complaining depresses the listener. It wants to elicit sympathy, companionship in suffering, and this means inflicting this suffering on others while asking for succor. The vocal dynamics of complaining bear witness to this ambivalence. Like self-accusation . . . complaint beats on the breast of the complainer with its insistent rhythm and at the same time it wants to beat on the ear and conscience of the listener. It combines the request for help and accusation.

It is often difficult to distinguish between the "helpless" and the dependent, infantile person. Perhaps such distinctions are not significant. Both of these poorly adjusted persons are much concerned with matters of health, with body functions, and with "body talk" in general. Illnesses, frequently those diagnosed by physicians as psychosomatic, are high on the list of topics for talk. Illness, or the threat of illness, is often used to control members of a family and to elicit special attention in social groups.

Infantile persons have narrow interests and, except for terms that

[2] From "Here We Are" by Dorothy Parker in *The Portable Dorothy Parker*. Copyright 1931, 1959 by Dorothy Parker. By permission of The Viking Press, Inc.

relate to their illnesses and disabilities, limited vocabularies. Many seem almost literally able to maintain contact only with what they can feel and taste. They have difficulty in projecting and cannot easily appreciate events which do not immediately touch upon their needs. In their talking they tend to be oblivious to possible events or, more generally, to think in terms of the future subjunctive. They tend to be ego-oriented and situation-bound. They can talk about what is and what was, but find difficulty in thinking and talking about what may be—except as their illnesses may be involved.

COMMON UNDERLYING CAUSES OF DISTURBED COMMUNICATION AND OF PERSONALITY

We have already indicated that there is a causal relationship between disturbances of communication and those of personality. Most of the not-so-well adjusted persons we have considered were probably victimized as children by failing to receive satisfactory acknowledgement of their speech efforts. Expressive speech may have been misinterpreted as true communicative (information-giving or -requesting) attempts. On the other hand, communicative attempts may have been ignored, or acknowledgements delayed so that a period of frustration intervened between the message sent and the response received. Selective and tangential responses may have characterized the parental acknowledgement of the speech attempts. Ruesch (1957, p. 79) emphasizes the influence of *selectivity in reply* as a possible cause of communicative disturbances and so of pathology. Although some familial selectivity is normal as an expression of its members' interests and values, under certain conditions maladjustments may arise. These conditions include:

1. Responses which are either too discriminating or insufficiently discriminating in relationship to the child's developmental state.

2. Selection of responses on the part of the adult, especially if he is a key member of the child's environment, which overstimulate one function and neglect another. This, according to Ruesch, ". . . is particularly harmful when functions which are about to be learned or which have not been fully mastered are neglected."

3. Selectivity which is so one-sided—so peculiar to the particular home—that what the child learns from members of his family does not prepare him for conditions and values he will meet outside of his home.

4. Selectivity that ignores the child's innate and developing abilities and directs him in ways inconsistent with them.

There are, of course, other ways in which adults can be selective in their responses to children. They may hear the child only when he whines, or when he howls. They may respond to him only after his fourth or fifth attempt at speaking. They may ignore the child until he has become angry, or frustrated, and then scold him for these affective displays. Any and all of these techniques may produce maladjusted personalities who in turn will produce other maladjusted personalities unless a corrective or therapeutic process modifies and interrupts the continuing cycle.

"NEUROTIC" GENERALIZATIONS

Although we have avoided labelling as neurotic most of the maladjusted persons whose verbal habits we have considered, they are likely to be so regarded by many clinical psychologists and psychiatrists. Neuroticism may take many forms and express, or disguise itself, in many ways. Man's ability to deal with symbols, to generalize and to asbtract, make the varied forms of expression and repression possible. Man's special ability to have things stand for one another, and for words to symbolize things and events makes for normal thinking, normal activity, and for superior thinking and superior creativity. But man under stress, man frustrated and yet compelled to make decisions, tends all too often to generalize on the basis of incidental similarities, and to engage in unsagacious behavior. The basis of this behavior, because it occurs under stress, may become unpleasant and painful, and so be repressed, and yet the behavior, or the attitude and inclination for a form of behavior, be maintained by no longer recognizable forces. Because they are no longer recognizable, and no longer conscious, they are resistant to testing and modification by reality situations. Instead, these forces unless brought to the surface, become rigid and fixed and make their possessors neurotic. Kubie (1951, p. 12), in a discussion of the neurotic potential in human beings, relates this potential to man's ability to deal with symbols.

Both normal activity and the neurotic potential arise out of man's ability *to create symbols*. Normal symbolic activity enables man to form abstractions, to communicate to others through words and written symbols, and to plan future activity. Symbolic processes may also be used neurotically to represent some inner experience of which the individual does not wish to become aware. The ability to abstract psychological processes, to represent these abstractions symbolically, and to render certain psychological processes inaccessible to conscious introspection, constitute the neurotic potential. The neurotic process gets under way when some psychological process becomes too painful to think about. The process is repressed, and all that shows to the world is some combination of thought and behavior and feeling which stands as a symbol for what is buried. This symbol will be simple at first, but with the passage of time and the gradual accretion of new buried problems which are more or less related to the first one, the initial symbol can come to represent many hidden states, and further symbols can come to represent the initial symbol. The neurotic state crystallizes out of the neurotic potential as soon as circumstances occur which make this necessary.

Fortunately, man's ability to deal in symbols and to express himself through speech provides a way for a reversal of the neurotic process and for readjustment. Man can think and talk himself out of as well as into maladjusted behavior, including his own verbal behavior.

REFERENCES

Kubie, L. S. The neurotic potential, the neurotic process, and the neurotic state. *Armed Forces Med. J.*, 1951, 2, 1-12.

Moses, P. J. *The voice of neurosis.* New York: Grune and Stratton, 1954.

Rogers, C. R. Communication: its blocking and its facilitation. In S. I. Hayakawa (Ed.), *Language, meaning, and maturity.* New York: Harper & Row, 1953.

Ruesch, J. *Disturbed communication.* New York: W. W. Norton, 1957.

21

Personality Disturbances
And Speech

THE AUTISTIC CHILD

Autistic children, though varying considerably in their behavior and in the type and amount of language they develop, include many whose early environmental influences are atypical and lacking in parental warmth and stimulation. One of the implications of the background factors that are associated with the development of personality in the young child is that an environment with limitations in regard to speaking, or an environment that does not have normal speakers, is not likely to produce normal children. In our earlier study of pre-lingual speech development, we discussed the effects of deprived environments—one that did not afford the infants warmth of human contact—on the early speech development of children. Evidence is also available that many preschool children brought up in residential nurseries show some retardation when they are compared with children of nursery school age who live at home. (Pringle and Tanner, 1958) The findings indicated that both quantitatively and qualitatively, there were differences between the residential and the "home" nursery school children when considered as groups. Individually, however, there was appreciable overlapping between the children in the two groups. The differences between the groups revealed generally better developed vocabularies for the "home" nursery school children. In regard to formal aspects of language development (grammar and ability to define words) there was little to distinguish the two groups. Pringle and Tanner note qualitative differences that suggest that the residential children lacked language used for making social contacts with their contemporaries. These children also lacked language for verbalizing their phantasies. The authors observe that "opinions may differ as to which should be regarded as the cause and which the effect. But there is little doubt that such language difficulties as we found are likely to have long-term consequences unless remedied."

Early infantile autism is a term used by the psychiatrist Kanner (1957, p. 739) to refer to children whose withdrawal tendencies were noted during the first year of life. Their characteristic inability to relate to persons in their environment and to the human sounds that surround but yet fail to touch or envelop them, often creates the impression of feeblemindedness and hearing impairment. According to Kanner: [1]

The common denominator in all these patients is a disability to relate themselves in the ordinary way to people and situations from the beginning of life. Their parents referred to them as always having been "self-sufficient," "like in a shell," "happiest when left alone," "acting as if people weren't there," "giving the impression of silent wisdom." The case histories indicate invariably the presence from the start of extreme autistic aloneness which, whenever possible, shuts out anything that comes to the child from the outside. Almost every mother recalled her astonishment at the child's failure to assume the usual anticipatory posture preparatory to being picked up. This kind of adjustment occurs universally at four months of age.

Kanner found a significant commcn denominator among the more than 150 children he studied. "In the whole group there are very few really warmhearted fathers and mothers. For the most part the antecedents and collaterals are persons strongly preoccupied with abstractions of a scientific, literary, or artistic nature and limited in genuine interest in people. Even some of the happiest marriages are rather cold and formal affairs." (Kanner, p. 742) There are several other related developmental factors in the background of these autistic children. The autistic child's behavior seems to be governed by a need—an anxiously obsessive desire —for the maintenance of sameness. This may be disrupted, but only occasionally, by the child himself. Physical changes in the environment such as the rearrangement of furniture evoke frantic reactions. Autistic children are better able to relate to objects than to persons: Kanner observes "He can be fond of them (objects), or get angry at them, if, for instance, he cannot fit them into a certain place. When with them he has a gratifying sense of undisputed power and control."

In regard to the autistic children's relation to persons, Kanner (1957, p. 742) says:

It would be wrong to say that they are not aware of the presence of persons. But the people, as long as they leave the child alone, figure in about the same

---

[1] This and other quotations from Kanner in this chapter from Kanner, L., *Child Psychiatry* 3rd ed., 1957. Courtesy of Charles C. Thomas, Publisher, Springfield, Illinois.

manner as does the desk, the bookshelf, or the filing cabinet. . . . If an adult forcibly intrudes himself by taking a block away or stepping on an object that the child needs, the child struggles and becomes angry with the hand or the foot, which is dealt with per se and not as a part of a person. He never addresses a word or a look to the owner of the hand or foot.

Speech Behavior of the Autistic Child

Most autistic children acquire the ability to speak, though few if any speak normally. Among the group studied by Kanner, two-thirds learned to use language, while the others remained mute. Language for the autistic child rarely serves the function of conveying meaning to the listener. Autistic children seem to have private individualized and personalized references, for the words they use. Conventional word forms may be used for idiosyncratic meanings. New words (neologisms) may also be used instead of conventional words for objects and situations. Community of meaning becomes possible only if the listener places himself at the disposal of the child, notes the "words" that are evoked by recurrent situations, or succeeds in recalling the situation in which a particular word was first used. The language of autistic children who do speak often suggests poetic analogy and metaphor. In this respect, too, the "figures of speech" are so highly individualized that they cannot call forth either the meaning or the feeling that could be evoked for words with shared referents.

Kanner (1957, p. 537) succeeded in tracing some apparently irrelevant utterances of autistic children and writes of one of them:

. . . At five years of age, Donald had been scribbling with crayons; all the while he kept saying seriously and with conviction: "Annette and Cecile make purple." It was learned that Donald had at home five bottles of paint. He named each after one of the Dionne quintuplets. Blue became "Annette," and red became "Cecile." After that, Annette was his word for blue, and Cecile for red. Purple, not being one of the five colors, remained "purple."

Occasionally the apparently bizarre responses of the child can be understood if the sequence of situations can be recalled. Many autistic children delay their responses for so long that the observer or individual who was trying to evoke a reaction may forget what situation was presented. Such was frequently the case with a child who came to the clinic directed by the first-named author of this book. His clinician presented him with a ball, which he ignored. The child was then in turn offered a doll, a crayon and paper, and a peg-board. All these objects seemed to be ignored. After a matter of minutes, the child picked up the ball and threw it at the clinician; scribbled on the paper with the crayon, and then threw both to the floor, and then pulled the pegs out of the peg-board. This done, he climbed to the top of the jungle-gym and looked impassively at what he had left below. A discerning clinician who could lip-read might also have noted that the child named each object he touched. The clinician might have lip-read the words "bouncer," "sister," "tear," and "pull-board." The articulatory pantomimes for these words were there, produced as if the child were rehearsing for a situation about to happen. The words were spoken by the child to himself and for himself. It was no concern of his if some onlooker understood his articulatory movements.

SCHIZOPHRENIA

The term schizophrenia, whether applied to the child, the adolescent, or the adult, is used with increasing incidence to refer to a group of disorders with some common factors and some wide behavioral differences rather than to a well defined and limited group of psychopathologies. Among the most frequent behavioral manifestations are the following:

1. Withdrawal from and retraction of interest in the environment.
2. Disturbances of thought expressed in blocking, symbolization, incoherence, perseveration, and condensation.
3. Increased daydreaming and autistic behavior in general.
4. Alteration of overt behavior with a tendency toward excess. This may be either in a marked increase of motor activity, or a marked decrease in the direction of immobility. Motor behavior tends to be characterized by perseveration and stereotypy.
5. Distortion or inappropriateness of affect, especially in regard to the underlying thinking of the individual and the meaning of the situation. The divergence between feeling and thinking is perhaps the most general characteristic of schizophrenic behavior.

The essence of schizophrenic behavior is summed up by Arieti (1959, p. 455):

Schizophrenic reaction [is] one of a group of psychotic reactions, often beginning after adolescence or in young adulthood, characterized by fundamental disturbances in reality relationships and concept formations, with associated affective, behavioral, and intellectual disturbances in varying degrees and mixtures. These reactions are marked by a tendency to withdraw from reality, inappropriate moods, unpredictable disturbances in stream of thought, regressive tendencies to a point of deterioration, and often hallucinations and delusions.

Although Arieti does not include young children in his characterization of schizophrenic behavior, other psychiatrists do. (See Kanner, 1957, Chap. 50) Many psychiatrists agree that though the frank expressions of schizophrenic behavior are not usually seen until the individual is chronologically an adolescent or a young adult, the origins can be traced to childhood. The genesis of schizophrenia is in a difficulty in establishing a warm and secure relationship between the child and the parents, especially between the child and the mother. Characteristically, according to Arieti (1959, p. 471), the parents are neither secure nor warm in their own relationship. Instead of a state of satisfaction and security we are likely to find a state of chronic anxiety.[2]

Whether or not schizophrenic persons have an organic basis for their personality disorders, or whether it is inherited or there is an inherited tendency for this group of disorders is presently much in dispute. There is no need for us to make any assumptions or to indicate a bias in this regard. There is fair agreement, however, that on the psychological side a number of observations may be considered as facts. These include the following:

1. Persons who become schizophrenic usually show early difficulty in establishing relationships with other people.

2. The acute expression of schizophrenic behavior is usually precipitated by psychological stress.

3. Social isolation, regardless of cause or course, is associated with the onset.

The factor of isolation has been used experimentally to induce reactions that are akin to those of the schizophrenic. Stevenson (1957) points out: "If you take an ordinary person and isolate him from all sensory stimuli by, for example, submerging him in a tub of warm water with a snorkel for breathing, you can within a few hours produce marked alterations in perceptions and thoughts. The delusions and hallucinations which he develops resemble closely those of dreams and of schizophrenia."

If the reader would like to appreciate the nature of schizophrenic reaction he needs but to recall one of his own terrifying dreams. Beyond this, he may recall his misperceptions and the associated fear that occurred when, only partly awake, he "saw" a hanging piece of clothing or a shadow as a menacing figure. The fearful individual may keep lights on, and sleep poorly, to avoid shadows and anxiety. He is not, however, always able to turn lights on in his fretful dreams. Much of schizophrenic behavior may be interpreted as a *turning away* from situations, and from their misperceptions, to avoid fearful waking states as well as fearful dreams.

We have italicized the *turning away* to emphasize that it is this reaction to the environment rather than the turning inward or so-called introverted behavior that characterizes the schizophrenic. The retiring,

[2] This position is by no means accepted by all students of schizophrenia. Some believe that hereditary factors predispose individuals to schizophrenic breakdown.

withdrawn person, who does not require as much social contact as most persons do and who has inner resources, needs to be clearly distinguished from the person who turns away from his environment because of his misperceptions and fears that are somehow a product of his initial anxiety. This anxiety state deprives the person of inner resources that might otherwise be present. His high state of emotionality with its accompanying state of mental disorganization is productive of severe distortions of perception and consequent impaired evaluations. This is the basis of the hallucinations (misperceptions) and delusions (faulty evaluations) of the schizophrenic.

Disorganization of Thought

In our discussion of affective behavior, we pointed out that states of heightened emotion are marked by a reorganization of behavioral patterns to help the individual to adapt to or meet the needs of the situation productive of the emotion. Reorganization of behavior is accompanied by a reduction in the intensity of emotionality. If there are no causes to make a state of emotionality chronic, there is only need for occasional marked reorganization of thought, to arrive at appropriately reorganized behavior. Most persons become "themselves again" after a period of fear, or ecstasy, or panic, or acute but object-related anxiety. If, however, there is constant anxiety, or fear, or a state of fear, there is chronic disorganization of thought. In the schizophrenic patient the disorganized state of thought occurs more frequently and for longer periods of time. Hallucinations and delusions which are a product of such mental disorganization also serve to maintain the state of disorganization. The cycle becomes self-reinforcing.

Stevenson (1957, p. 60) draws a parallel between the products of a prolonged state of anger and the state of schizophrenia:

. . . just as fever which combats infections may harm when it becomes excessive, so emotions, if too strong and too enduring, can bring disorder rather than adaptation. For all emotions influence the train of thoughts by tending to suck in other thoughts of the same quality. An angry person may suddenly find himself thinking of old injuries he had believed long since forgotten but which the present anger stirs into his awareness. . . . The thoughts run in a groove cut by the dominant emotion. They pre-empt the field of consciousness: if other thoughts gain ascendency for a moment, the more powerful emotional thoughts quickly obtrude again.

As these continue they become less and less representative of the external situation, and since they misrepresent the environment they no longer provide accurate guides to action. Behavior ceases to adapt the persons appropriately to the environment. Other persons become offended and act to protect their own interests, often aggressively. Their responses then augment the original fears.

Normal persons when angry do not stay angry too long before they become aware that their emotional states are excessive and not consonant with the situation and their thoughts. They are able to censor and check both their thoughts and their feelings as if to say: "So much for this matter. Now there are other situations that require attention for which I have more appropriate behavior. Anger is no longer needed." With such awareness, further behavior is likely to be characterized by consonance rather than divergence between thinking and feeling. The disorganized state of the schizophrenic does not permit of such awareness. Necessary and adaptive behavior fails to gain ascendency over non-adaptive behavior. In the schizophrenic state, thinking flows fleeting and unchecked. Thoughts are not accompanied by expected affect, perhaps because the thoughts are not entertained long enough to evoke appropriate affect. Feelings may lag behind "thinking" so that a tone of sorrow may be expressed which would have been appropriate for a thought that was verbalized a moment ago. The present "thought" may be one for which a neutral or even a gay affect might be expected. The term schizophrenia was first used by the Swiss psychiatrist Bleuler to highlight the "split mind" or divergence between thinking and feeling that is so characteristic of the disturbance.

A supplementary explanation of the divergence between thought and feeling, and between thought and action is offered by Ruesch, who emphasizes early childhood factors that produced a basic disturbance of communication. According to Ruesch [3] (1957, p. 133):

The parents' unresponsiveness in nonverbal terms prevents the child in the early years of life from learning how to relate through *movement and action*. The absence of early appropriate and gratifying communication through action, gesture, and object leaves traces. The movements of many schizophrenics are angular, jerky, and uncoordinated, and they are carried out with uneven acceleration or deceleration, at either too slow or too fast a tempo. . . . It is as if these patients were trying to relive the patterns of communication that were frustrating in early childhood, with the hope that this time there might be present another person who would reply satisfactorily in nonverbal terms. It is as if these patients knew that the basis for human relations is established in the nonverbal mode and that successful communication cannot be achieved before the step is mastered.

Ruesch further emphasizes that the withdrawn personality is found frequently in families in which verbal messages fail to coincide with the

[3] This and other quotations from Ruesch in this chapter reprinted from *Disturbed Communication,* by Jurgen Ruesch, M.D. Copyright 1957 by W. W. Norton & Company, Inc., New York, N. Y. By permission of the publisher.

meaning of the action. The child tries to resolve this contradiction or divergence by ignoring the words and paying close attention to the actions of others. As a result, the child is cut off from normal communicative interchange and becomes desperately lonely. Ruesch says (1957, p. 134):

It isn't that the schizophrenic did not in his childhood receive food or clothing, or shelter; it isn't that he was beaten or punished. No; on the contrary, all these things were usually attended to properly, but what was denied to him was the pleasure of acknowledgement. He was not appreciated as a person, and his *intentions* to communicate were *not acknowledged*. Most of the time he didn't even receive a tangential response; and if he received a response, it probably contained references to the anxiety of the other person. He learned to shut himself off from the anxious communication of others, and he felt that there was greater safety within himself.

We may note that Ruesch, in common with many other psychiatrists, shares the belief that *anxiety* is basic to the genesis of schizophrenia. He differs in emphasis from Stevenson in regarding the schizophrenic as one who withdraws into himself rather than turns away from his environment in order to achieve some sense of security. As we indicated earlier, many withdrawn persons maintain good or even superior organization of thought whereas the schizophrenic is disturbed and disorganized in his thinking and in the expression of thought.

Language of the Schizophrenic: Dynamics

Even our necessarily brief consideration of the nature of schizophrenic language modification would fall short of our objective if we did not first consider the purpose or dynamics of the speech behavior. The fascinating, often verging on the poetic, language of the schizophrenic is best appreciated as an *attempt to remove or avoid anxiety*. Arieti (1955, pp. 53-54) sums up this widely accepted assumption with the statement:

By rejecting the language of the society in which he lives, and by adopting his own individualistic modes of expression, the schizophrenic is motivated by one purpose: the removal of anxiety. If he disconnects himself from society—that society which causes him much suffering—he may be safe or less disturbed.

Arieti believes that the language of the schizophrenic serves an additional purpose beyond protecting him from anxiety. Through the highly individualized use of conventional word forms (through idiosyncratic word usage) and through "new" words (neologisms), the schizophrenic is able to express his individuality. Such expression was thwarted when the schizophrenic was a child. His unique use of language forms then serves the dual purpose of self expression and the rejection of the environment in general and his parents in particular. We assume that these dynamics are unconscious. According to Arieti, archaic ways of expressing thoughts and feelings emerge. These represent a regression to manners of expression long ago discarded in the course of evolution (1955, p. 54).

Although we accept Arieti's explanations as to the psychodynamics of schizophrenic language, we do not view the language that emerges as an archaic regression. The schizophrenic has enough developmental infantile states to which to regress without need to return to archaic man for his language behavior.

A flavor of the underlying dynamics—the wish somehow to express personality—as well as a token sample of individualistic word usage may be appreciated from some of the conversations between Alice and Humpty Dumpty. Lewis Carroll was, we recall, portraying a character so disorganized that "all the king's horses and all the king's men could not put him together again." It is no wonder, therefore, that Alice was puzzled during her wanderings in *Through the Looking Glass*.

"You're holding it upside down!" Alice interrupted.

"To be sure I was!" Humpty Dumpty said gayly, as she turned it round for him. "I thought it looked a little queer. As I was saying, that *seems* to be done right—though I haven't time to look it over thoroughly just now—and that shows that there are three hundred and sixty-four days when you might get un-birthday presents."

"Certainly," said Alice.

"And only *one* for birthday presents, you know. There's glory for you!"

"I don't know what you mean by 'glory,'" Alice said.

Humpty Dumpty smiled contemptuously. "Of course you don't—till I tell you. I meant, 'There's a nice knock-down argument for you!'"

"But 'glory' doesn't mean a 'nice knock-down argument,'" Alice objected.

"When I use a word," Humpty Dumpty said in a rather scornful tone, "it means just what I choose it to mean—neither more nor less."

"The question is," said Alice, "whether you *can* make words mean so many different things."

"The question is," said Humpty Dumpty, "which is to be master—that's all."

Alice was too much puzzled to say anything, so after a minute Humpty Dumpty began again. "They've a temper, some of them—particularly verbs, they're the proudest—adjectives you can do anything with, but not verbs—however. *I* can manage the whole lot of them! Impenetrability! That's what I say!"

"Would you tell me, please," said Alice, "what that means?"

"Now you talk like a reasonable child," said Humpty Dumpty, looking very much pleased. "I meant by 'impenetrability' that we've had enough of that subject, and it would be just as well if you'd mention what you mean to do next, as I suppose you don't mean to stop here all the rest of your life."

"That's a great deal to make one word mean," Alice said, in a thoughtful tone.

"When I make a word do a lot of work like that," said Humpty Dumpty, "I always pay it extra."

"Oh!" said Alice. She was too much puzzled to make any other remark.

Pathological Language

The pathological changes in schizophrenic language may be understood on the basis of three related intellectual and attitudinal impairments. These modifications, which also underlie other psychiatric disorders, are:

1. An impairment in the individual's ability or inclination to deal with the abstract.

2. An impairment of the individual's ability or inclination to engage in conventional symbol processes.

3. An impairment of the individual's ability or inclination to make normal social contacts and to integrate into the environment.

Modification of the Ability to Deal with the Abstract. We have emphasized the impairment of inclination because there is considerable question as to the precise nature of the disability. For example, in several writings, Kurt Goldstein (1943) argues that schizophrenic language is an expression of an impairment of abstract attitude. In this respect schizophrenia resembles the aphasic linguistic disturbances of persons who have incurred brain-damage after language was established (Goldstein, 1948). It is our clinical judgment that the impairment of abstraction is one in the nature and procedure, and so in the product, rather than an irreversible impairment in the ability per se. The question resolves itself to whether the schizophrenic is incapable of dealing with the abstract, or whether he abstracts "differently" in terms of his underlying psychodynamics. Ruesch (1957, p. 132) takes the position that "the schizophrenic is capable of symbolizing externally his internal events in an idiosyncratic manner. However, he does not wish to share with others his private system of symbolization." This position, which we accept, implies that the schizophrenic abstracts differently and in a manner which permits him to maintain his defense against anxiety. The schizophrenic may use concrete and highly ego-oriented terms for abstract concepts normally designated by more general terms. He may give his home address when normal persons would use the term *house*. In doing so, he may confuse the listener or the reader of his writing. His intention may be to maintain the least possible contact with his environment, and so to avoid anxiety that may arise from a more intimate contact that would take place if conventional and expected terms were used. An individual who is impaired in his ability to socialize can hardly be expected to use social language with referents that are shared and readily understood by speaker *and* listener. Perhaps the fundamental question is whether desocialization precedes and is the cause of the use of ego-oriented and apparently concrete symbol-words or whether the changes in language, and in thinking, produce the desocialization. It is quite likely, of course, that once the process begins, each aspect aggravates the other until possibly the patient reaches a point from which he cannot return without therapy. Such therapy necessarily requires an appreciation of the psychodynamics as well as of the linguistic products of the patient.

Another approach that may explain the schizophrenic's impairment in dealing with the abstract is based upon the principle or "law" of Von Domarus (1944). According to this principle ". . . whereas the normal person accepts identity only upon the basis of identical subjects, the schizophrenic accepts identity upon identical predicates." Thus, a normal person who knows that

> *Tom Jones is a man,* and that
> *All men are mortal* concludes logically that
> *Tom Jones is mortal.*

According to Von Domarus, the schizophrenic, illogically (or according to his type of logic) thinks:

> *Tom Jones is a man.*
> *I am a man,* and so
> *I am Tom Jones.*

In a similar manner, the patient may become Napoleon, or George Washington, or Peter the Great. If we accept this principle,[4] then we have a convenient explanation for some of the confused thinking of the schizophrenic. The principle seems to us, however, to be both over-simple and over-inclusive. Schizophrenics are not the only persons who come to erroneous conclusions because of their reactions and their misevaluations of *incidental similar elements in varying situations, verbal or otherwise.* An alternative observation is that neurotic persons, anxious persons, and persons in a state of stress tend to confuse different "wholes" because they happen to include incidental similar or even "identical" parts. Unobservant individuals might also come to erroneous conclusions if they

---

[4] A study by L. Gottesman and L. J. Chapman (1960) on "Syllogistic Reasoning Errors in Schizophrenia," (*Journal of Consulting Psychology,* 24, 3, 1960, pp. 250-255) in which adult schizophrenics were compared with normal controls failed to substantiate the "law of Von Domarus." Both the normal and schizophrenic subjects made similar errors. In individual instances, however, there were ". . . occasional schizophrenic deviancies which appear to be clear-cut manifestations of Von Domarus' principle of a sort that normal Ss would not commit."

permitted their perceptions, or misperceptions, to govern their thinking and acting, as some do. Most children in Western cultures are aware that men (most) wear trousers. They nevertheless soon recognize that mother does not become a man when she happens to be wearing trousers. There are other features of "mother" that earn her this continued designation as a woman. From our point of view the *the-whole-for-the-part* tendency of disturbed persons, schizophrenics included, is an acceptable alternate explanation for their apparent mental confusion. Perhaps it would be more accurate to observe that their mental confusion results in the errors that are a product of whole-for-part thinking.

Concretism

A strong feature of schizophrenic language is the use of general terms to designate concrete, specific, and often personal situations. This tendency may be regarded as another expression of the impairment of the abstract attitude. When a schizophrenic uses the term "eyes" he may be referring to his own rather than eyes in general. Thus "Eyes are brown" may be interpreted to mean "My eyes are brown" rather than "All eyes are brown." The patient, though dealing with the specific, continues to employ the language more commonly used for the general. This tendency may be explained by a limitation of meaning that accompanies the change from broad conceptualization to more restricted and individualized perceptualization. It is as if a word may have many meanings, but only one meaning at a time. "Bookness" as a concept is more difficult to entertain than "book" as a specific entity and designation of a particular (concrete) book in the experience of the patient. If the patient improvises a term such as "Bed-room-book" his designation is clear. If, however, he uses the term "books" and says "Books are on my sleeping" his meaning becomes abstruse.

Metonymic Distortion

Many terms used by schizophrenics represent what Cameron (1938) refers to as metonymic distortion, the tendency to substitute approximate but related terms for more precise ones. For example, a patient may talk about a "*menu*" when he means a *meal,* or about *smiling* when he means *laughing,* or about *reading* when he means *a library,* or use the word *sleeping* when he means either *bed* or *bedroom* or even an entire house. Some of the metonymic distortions may be appreciated as concrete substitutions or isolated functions for the more general term. (*sleeping* for *house*) They may also be understood as confusions of wholes for parts and parts for whole.

Loose Associations and Identifications

Metonymic distortion is closely related to the tendency for making *loose associations*. Menus quite appropriately recall meals, and smiling is certainly associated with laughing. Arieti (1955, p. 62) believes that though normal persons associate related terms, schizophrenics *identify* and treat as equivalents things and symbols which should only be associated. Thus, for the normal person, "George Washington, White House, and let us say Cherry Tree, Lincoln, Roosevelt, are all associated elements or, if we prefer, are all parts or elements of a certain context. For the schizophrenic they are all equivalent; one may replace the other. Each fragment of a context is equivalent to any other fragment or to the whole. What in a normal person is only an associative link, becomes in the schizophrenic an identifying link."

This explanation may be correct in many instances in which loose associations are employed. We think that there is also a possibility that the schizophrenic is not identifying associative words as equivalents but is not bothering or is unable to censor his associations. If he is not using language to communicate or to maintain a social relationship, he certainly does not need to monitor his words so that he may be understood.

Other Verbal Characteristics

Samples of schizophrenic speech recall other frequently common characteristics. These include clang association (rhymes and near rhymes) such as "buck, luck, tuck, tic tack toe tuck," repetition, alliteration, and stereotypy. Underlying this is probably a pervading tendency toward perseverative behavior. These characteristics, incidentally, are also found in the written efforts of schizophrenics.[5] Such characteristics may be studied in the samples of spoken and written language on pages 373 and 374.

We have gone into considerable detail to explain the possible basic dynamics that underlie schizophrenic language behavior. An appreciation of these dynamics, many of which pertain to the other serious disorders of personality, enables us to understand the relationship between disturbances in thinking and personality and their expression in the speech of the individual. Such an appreciation enables us also to understand the occasional lapses of normal persons under temporary conditions of stress.

[5] Despite the desocialization of schizophrenics, these patients often spend long hours in writing and leave their efforts to be found or deliver them to their physicians.

Gesture

The gestures of the schizophrenic, as we indicated earlier, are likely to be awkward, jerky, and repetitive. Grimaces, wry smiles, and tic-like expressions are frequently produced. Many patients posture and engage in elaborate ritualistic movements in their walking, their sitting (and preparing to sit), and in many of their routine activities. Stereotyped, repetitive movements suggest the existence of perseverative, automatic behavior and compulsive ritual. Much if not all of the gesture behavior of the schizophrenic is expressive rather than communicative. The patient's gestures are a product of his affective state. They resemble the movements of the preoccupied normal person who is thinking autistically, or who is hard at work solving a problem, and is not aware that he is being observed. The normal person's autistic gesture may be of help to him in release of feeling; some of the gestures may be remnants or tokens of full gestures that might be produced in a communicative situation. The schizophrenic who is desocialized has no more need to use conventional communicative gestures than he has for conventional oral symbols.

The Functions of Schizophrenic Speech

One may wonder why an individual who fears socialization and is disturbed in his thinking maintains speech—the tool of socialization—rather than becoming mute. Some schizophrenics do become mute and so negate both their environment and the medium for contact with it. But most schizophrenics continue to speak because other functions besides communication continue to be served. For one thing, the schizophrenic may still enjoy the pleasure of oral utterance, and the production of gesture activity. Beyond this, the expressive functions of speech, the release of affect, continues to be served. There is perhaps an additional function that is served. Although the schizophrenic is disturbed in his thinking, and confuses his listeners, he nevertheless succeeds in telling something about himself through his efforts. But he does not let his defenses down in the telling; his private world is protected from continued social penetration. Yet, if he does not regress to catatonic mutism, he leaves an avenue open for a possible return when his anxieties are reduced and his apprehensions subside.

Following are some samples of the speech of schizophrenic patients. These should permit an analysis of the characteristic language changes discussed earlier. The first is a specimen of schizophrenic speech by a girl eleven years old (from the author's files).

Q. Tell me a story.
A. Once there was a dog who had a dog bone. It was a big one. The dog liked it so he ate it up. He enjoyed the bone and then he slipped and ran away. He got sick and then he found himself in a crib and then he slipped and ran away.
Q. To whom did that really happen?
A. To a girl. To me.
Q. Where did you slip?
A. Before the slipping-and-running-away-door.
Q. What is a brain body?
A. A yellow thing with spikes. Runs around like a cow—in body [points to region of lower left rib]. Came to a hospital to have it taken out.

We observe in this specimen the repetition of a phrase "slipped and ran away" and the invention of the terms "yellow brain body" and "slipping and running away door." We may note also the preoccupation with bodily organs and body functions.

This example of schizophrenic speech is from an interview (in the author's files) with a 27-year-old male patient. We may note repetition of language, apparent incoherence, and strong suggestions of ideas of persecution. The patient is a high school graduate and had attended college for two years. His work history indicates that he worked at menial jobs inconsistent with his level of education.

(What is your problem?)
"I don't want to implicate any individual because of the legitimacy of the laws. I would like to approach it in a tactful and discreet manner by applying myself best and giving my best. In a sense I'm not looking to create any uncalled-for circumstances. I am more or less viewing the problem as it exists in relation to myself.
(What is the problem?)
"I can't state it definitely. I want to approach it more as one would in civil life. I want no complex in that sense. I would like to approach it in the sense that it pertains to the legitimacy of law."
(What do you mean by that?)
"I believe there is something on a law in my state pertaining to my problem. I would like to resort to law sources and see if I can apply myself by eliminating any grounds for any law interference."
(What is it all about?)
"I would like to apply myself more tactfully and discreetly. The law means I can appeal my problem and eliminate uncalled-for circumstances."
(Is someone attempting to do something to you?)
"There could be circumstances that create themselves. There are probably certain problems in life that would create themselves."
(Why were you in the hospital? Was it an injustice?)

"I couldn't say. I could not question the integrity of the gentlemen involved. For example, individuals came and told me I was to go with them. Naturally I went with them. I wouldn't even know if I belonged there."

The next is a "conversation" between a schizophrenic patient and his examiner in a problem-solving situation. (Cameron & Magaret, 1951, p. 510). The patient is a high school graduate who worked for eight years for a wholesale grocer. He is described as having been studious and fond of reading the classics. He is responding to the experimental board which is divided into sections.

"Each man has to have his way of walking on the earth. The earth is divided up like this; and these blocks—women have to be born and carry a baby up over the stars to put them out. I live up there. (*Where?*) Everything's got to live over the North Sea. The moon carries the water up. That's why nobody can eat watermelons until after I've eaten. Nobody can eat a watermelon that has green hate in it. If you eat a watermelon the next comes up with your name on it . . . I don't have any (name) through not being born yet . . . I'm not born through food. You people have eaten food and robbed me of my birth."

MANIC-DEPRESSIVE PSYCHOSIS

Manic Excitement

The cardinal symptoms of the manic stage of manic-depressive psychosis include exaltation or excitement, disorder of the thinking process characterized by an acceleration and flight of ideas, and increased motor activity.

The speech of the manic is symptomatic of his behavior in general and of his disordered thinking. He is likely to talk incessantly and rapidly, incorporating many marginal or tangential ideas into his stream of speech. The rapid tempo often results in slurring and in the production of word fragments. When these are run together they may suggest either neologisms or "word salads." The style of the manic's utterances tends to be telegraphic; many connecting words, participles, relative pronouns, and prepositions are likely to be omitted. Because the flow of ideas is not checked, the content of the patient's speech is highly diversified and is frequently far in excess of the listener's rate of absorption. The manic's speech is at first fascinating, but ultimately wearying. Little if any attention is paid to the auditor; the manic speaks to express his own emotional and mental state. The presence of an auditor serves as a stimulant for speaking rather than as a stimulant for communicative utterance.

The language behavior of the manic is not without purpose. Besides permitting a release of feeling it may, according to Arieti (1959, p. 427) have another goal, ". . . that of maintaining this superficial effervescent euphoria and of escaping from intruding thoughts which may bring about depression." With the manic, as with the schizophrenic, speech continues to serve expressive function as well as being a mechanism against anxiety and depression.

The following case study illustrates some of the over-all behavior as well as the speech of a manic patient. (Cameron & Magaret, 1951, p. 332)

A thirty-five-year-old biochemist was brought to the clinic by his frightened wife. To his psychiatrist the patient explained, "I discovered that I had been drifting, broke the bonds and suddenly found myself doing things and doing them by telegraph. I was dead tired, and decided to go on a vacation; but even there it wasn't long before I was sending more telegrams. I got into high gear and started to buzz. Then a gentle hint from a friend took effect and I decided to come here and see if the changes in my personality were real." He entered the ward in high spirits, went about greeting the patients, insisted that the place was "swell," and made quick puns on the names of doctors to whom he was introduced. Meanwhile his wife said she was "scared to death." "His friends used to call him 'Crazy Charley,'" she said, "but I haven't seen this streak in him for years."

When his wife had left, the patient soon demonstrated what he meant by "high gear." He bounded down the hall, threw his medication on the floor, leaped up on a window ledge and dared any one to get him down. When he was put in a room alone where he could be free, he promptly dismantled the bed, pounded on the walls, yelled and sang. He made a sudden sally into the hall and did a kind of hula-hula dance before he could be returned to his room. His shouting continued throughout the night, and betrayed in its content the ambivalent attitudes which the patient maintained toward his hospitalization: "What the hell kind of a place is this? A swell place? I'm not staying here. I'm having a hell of a good time. Oh, I'm so happy. I have to get going. My gray suit please, my gray coat please, my gray socks, all gray on their way, going to be gay. I'm going out as fast as I came in, only faster. I'm happier than I have ever been in my life. I'm 100 per cent better than normal."

Acute Depression

Not all depressed states are preceded by manic states, and depressed states may vary considerably in degree of severity. Acute depression as it occurs in many instances of manic-depressive disturbances is characterized by dejection, retarded flow of ideas, and markedly reduced motor activity. Occasionally the patient suffers from fixed ideas and obsessions, including the idea of committing suicide.

The speech of the depressed patient, like the manic's, is symptomatic of his disorder. The patient speaks slowly, often verbalizing the same thoughts over and over again. This is frequently a loss of insight or judgment as to the significance of the thoughts that are presented; the consequential and the inconsequential, from the listener's point of view, are offered as if they were of equal importance. Diversification of utterance is extremely low, so that the auditor becomes quickly bored and seeks an escape. His efforts to change the direction of discourse are generally futile. The depressive patient speaks to express himself, rather than to elicit responses from his auditor. The tired, sad Dormouse whom Alice met at a tea party during her adventures in Wonderland presents an example of depressive speech.

"They were learning to draw," the Dormouse went on, yawning and rubbing its eyes, for it was getting very sleepy; "and they drew all manner of things—everything that begins with an M—."
"Why with an M?" said Alice.
"Why not?" said the March Hare.
Alice was silent.
The Dormouse had closed its eyes by this time, and was going off into a doze, but, on being pinched by the Hatter, it woke up again with a little shriek, and went on: "—That begins with an M, such as mousetraps, and the moon, and memory, and muchness—you know you say things are 'much of a muchness' —did you ever see such a thing as a drawing of a muchness?"
"Really, now you ask me," said Alice, very much confused, "I don't think—"

Little purpose would be served by continued consideration of the other types of disturbed personalities. Mental illnesses may have their individual dynamics and may be expressed in different ways. But often the dynamics are much the same, and the modes of expression are more similar than they are different. Studies of verbal modifications in patients with mental illness often reveal strikingly similar features. By way of summary, we will abstract a study by Raven (1958) in England. Raven analyzed the vocabulary responses to 17 words selected from the Mill Hill Vocabulary Scale. On the basis of the answers of a mixed group of psychotic patients, Raven developed seventeen categories of deviant responses. Although some responses were characteristic of all the clinical groups, for the most part the deviations tended to be individual and more characteristic of particular patients. The more frequently occurring tendencies for the clinical groups included the following:

Disordered syntax occurred most often in organic psychosis and senile dementia. For example, the word "view" was explained as "What you can see on your own eyes as you look and regard everything you can see in the space of your own eyes."
Perseveration occurred most frequently in senile dementia, but was common to all forms of mental illness. It also occurred under any con-

dition of fatigue or exhaustion. The repetition of the phrase "see in your own eyes" in the sample above is an example of perseveration.

Bizarre content was typical of hebephrenic schizophrenia but also occurred in other groups. For example, "Mingle" was explained by "You could say mingle your eyebrows with mine."

Rigidity of expression—the maintenance of the same type of sentence construction—occurred frequently in manic-depressive patients in both the depressed and manic phases.

Poverty of expression—monosyllabic responses—occurred mostly in depressed psychotics.

Circumstantial talk—long, loosely structured responses which never quite got to the meaning of the word and frequent digressions to childhood anecdotes were found to occur in arteriosclerotic dementia.

Structurally vague responses were general to all clinical forms. For example, "Liberty" means "Having no difficulty about doing a thing. You can do what you like on a thing. Liberty is the thing I find very easy to do. It's very easy to manage."

Distraction due to intrusions of psychological or geographical origin were general to all clinical groups. The patient's thoughts or his surroundings appeared to distract him from giving a satisfactory explanation of the meaning of the word, or made it difficult for him to use the word as other persons do. Some examples follow: "Virile" meant "Manly, a person that's virile can frighten the thoughts, but they can't obey them always." The word "verify" was explained as "thinking of turning around what which was in his mind." As an example of intrusion of geographical origin "mingle" was explained as "A thing you could take—that's easy—the thing on the table."

Chain association, telescoped ideas, nonsense words, and echo responses occurred with relatively low frequency in several groups.

Stylized language and negativistic responses in low incidence occurred in some groups but not in all.

As a closing note, we should like to re-emphasize the intimate relationships between speech and personality. Normal persons when mildly disturbed may become aware of these changes, and may do something about their modified speech and the related causes. Severely disturbed persons lack such insight, and may in fact use their speech both as a defensive mechanism and as a barrier to prevent awareness and insight. Yet the most effective psychotherapeutic tool is speech—that of the patient and that of the psychotherapist. Even when he is disturbed, man remains distinctly man both because of his abilities and disabilities in using linguistic symbols. Man alone is able to learn to use symbols, to create them if necessary, and to employ them in modified ways for the various purposes which speech and speaking continue to serve.

REFERENCES

Arieti, S. Some aspects of language in schizophrenia. In H. Werner (Ed.), *On expressive language*. Worcester, Mass.: Clark University Press, 1955. Pp. 53-67.

Arieti, S. Schizophrenia. In S. Arieti (Ed.), *American handbook of psychiatry*. Vol. I. New York: Basic Books, 1959. Chap. 23.

Cameron, N. Reasoning, regression, and communication in schizophrenias. *Psychol. Monogr.*, 1938, 50, 1.

Cameron, N., & Magaret, A. *Behavior pathology*. Boston: Houghton Mifflin, 1951.

Goldstein, K. The significance of psychological research in schizophrenia. *J. nerv. ment. Dis.*, 1943, 97, 261.

Goldstein, K. *Language and language disturbances*. New York: Grune & Stratton, 1948.

Gottesman, L., & Chapman, L. J. Syllogistic reasoning errors in schizophrenia. *J. consult. Psychol.*, 1960, 24, 3, 250-255.

Kanner, L. *Child psychiatry*. (3rd ed.) Springfield, Ill.: Charles C. Thomas, 1957.

Pringle, M. L. K., & Tanner, M. The effects of early deprivation on speech development: a comparative study of 4-year-olds in a nursery school and in residential nurseries. *Lang. and Spch*, 1958, I, 4, 269-287.

Raven, J. C. Verbal dysfunctions in mental illness. *Lang. and Spch*, 1, 3, 218-225.

Ruesch, J. *Disturbed communication*. New York: Norton, 1957.

Stevenson, I. Schizophrenia. *Harper's*, 1957, 59-65.

Von Domarus, E. The specific laws of logic in schizophrenia. In Kasanin, J. S. (Ed.), *Language and thought in schizophrenia*. Berkeley, Calif.: University of California Press, 1944.

Index